Michael Moadella

FROM MERCENARIES TO MARKET

From Mercenaries to Market

The Rise and Regulation of Private Military Companies

Edited by
SIMON CHESTERMAN
and
CHIA LEHNARDT

A project of the Institute for International Law and Justice at
New York University School of Law

OXFORD
UNIVERSITY PRESS

OXFORD
UNIVERSITY PRESS

Great Clarendon Street, Oxford OX2 6DP

Oxford University Press is a department of the University of Oxford.
It furthers the University's objective of excellence in research, scholarship,
and education by publishing worldwide in

Oxford New York

Auckland Cape Town Dar es Salaam Hong Kong Karachi
Kuala Lumpur Madrid Melbourne Mexico City Nairobi
New Delhi Shanghai Taipei Toronto

With offices in

Argentina Austria Brazil Chile Czech Republic France Greece
Guatemala Hungary Italy Japan Poland Portugal Singapore
South Korea Switzerland Thailand Turkey Ukraine Vietnam

Oxford is a registered trade mark of Oxford University Press
in the UK and in certain other countries

Published in the United States
by Oxford University Press Inc., New York

British Library Cataloguing in Publication Data

Data available

Library of Congress Cataloging in Publication Data

From mercenaries to market: the rise and regulation of private military
companies / edited by Simon Chesterman and Chia Lehnardt.
    p. cm.
Includes bibliographical references and index.
ISBN-13: 978–0–19–922848–5
  1. Police, Private.   2. Private security services—Law and legislation.
3. Mercenary troops.   4. Security, International.   I. Chesterman,
Simon.   II. Lehnardt, Chia.
  K3465.F76 2007
  343'.015354—dc22   2007013102

Typeset by Newgen Imaging Systems (P) Ltd., Chennai, India
Printed in Great Britain
on acid-free paper by
Biddles Ltd., King's Lynn

ISBN 978–0–19–922848–5

1 3 5 7 9 10 8 6 4 2

Foreword

The publication of this book represents a breath of fresh air on a topic that hitherto has generated more heat than light. The emergence and proliferation of private military companies (PMCs) have been the result of three major developments: the end of the Cold War and the consequential dismantling of the Warsaw Pact; the end of the Apartheid system in South Africa; and the war against terrorism, particularly the war in Iraq. When the Warsaw Pact was disbanded some of its members were left with huge inventories of weapons systems. Most of the small arms used by PMCs in Africa in the 1990s came from these countries—weak arms export control systems made it easier to purchase arms to be used in civil conflicts. With the end of the Apartheid system in South Africa, it was necessary to downsize a military capability aimed at confronting opponents of the Apartheid system, particularly the threat of Cuban troops in Angola. One result was the ready availability of well-trained military personnel who were looking for new missions. The early PMCs benefited from this development. The war in Iraq presented a different opportunity for the expansion and growth of the PMCs: with the reluctance to deploy a large force in Iraq during and after the combat phase of the operation, out-sourcing of some military activities went to PMCs.

Although political scientists often announce the withering of the state and the prominent role of non-state actors, there is still a residue of belief that only sovereign states should possess a monopoly over the legitimate use of force. This may be one reason why the use of PMCs is so abhorrent to many. There has been a tendency to label most, if not all, PMCs 'mercenaries'. Even though some types of PMCs share some attributes with mercenary groups, they are not stereotypical mercenaries. More often than not, PMCs have contracts with legal governments and they are not collaborating with rebel forces to topple established governments. In one instance in Sierra Leone a PMC made a valuable contribution to the democratic process. Furthermore, not all PMCs have been engaged in combat operations. Many are engaged in training of police personnel and other forms of training, along with the provision of logistic support.

A different angle on the debate on PMCs gained strength in the United States in February 2007 when the US House of Representatives Government Oversight Committee held hearings on the role of PMCs and other private civilian contractors in Iraq. The first surprise was that the executive branch of the US Government could not determine how many of these contractors were operating in Iraq. This admission and other considerations led the Oversight Committee to arrange for a thorough investigation of all private contractors, such as Blackwater, USA, which is based in North Carolina.

Testimonies by families of Blackwater employees killed in Fallujah, Iraq in 2004 revealed woeful lack of supervision of PMCs in Iraq. For example, although the State Department has a contract with Blackwater, it was not known that a major contractor—Halliburton—was subcontracting to Blackwater, a fact judged by the Chairman of the Oversight Committee as illegal. Significantly, the senior military commanders that appeared before the Committee readily admitted that they could not carry out their heavy responsibilities without the assistance of PMCs like Blackwater. One commander even asserted that the new 'surge' of 21,500 troops being sent to Iraq could be ineffective without the utilization of PMCs.

Even though the use of PMCs goes back decades, it was the involvement of Executive Outcomes (EO) in Sierra Leone in the early 1990s that generated much debate. When, upon closer examination, the background of EO became clear and the fact that EO personnel were mainly recruited from the former South African military and police special forces, the criticism intensified. Many commentators at the time were too quick to consider EO as a group of hired killers. The fact that the government of the day invited EO to help defend the country against a group of mercenaries on the rebel side was ignored. The confusion over the nature and activities of PMCs became further embroiled in a major foreign policy debate in the British House of Commons when it was erroneously alleged that Sandline— another part of the hydra-headed EO—was primarily responsible for restoring to power the ousted, democratically elected President Kabbah of Sierra Leone in March 1998. Those who were uncomfortable with the declared 'ethical' foreign policy of the New Labour Government of Tony Blair made much about nothing of the Sandline Affair. The truth of the matter was that the Sandline weapons that had been purchased reached the Lungi airport in Sierra Leone after the armed Moni- toring Group of the Economic Community of West African States (ECOMOG)— mainly Nigerian troops—had defeated the rebel group. In any case, this type of PMC has been declared out of bounds.

The well-written and-argued presentations in this volume provide a comprehen- sive panorama of the whole array of positions regarding PMCs. They range from the argument that PMCs are morally indefensible, with no need to regulate them, to a forceful defence of the necessity of PMCs in the current environment. Even those who defend the use of PMCs do not always agree on the desirability of regu- lation. Many of the authors make persuasive presentations in favour of some form of regulation, although some are inclined to establish a threshold for regulation.

It would be foolhardy to deny that the international community has an obliga- tion to craft some form of regulation of PMCs. This is not to ignore the fact that some failed or weak states will seek assistance from PMCs if they believe that col- lective security measures under the Charter of the United Nations have failed. These were the circumstances faced by Sierra Leone when the National Provisional Ruling Council (NPRC) invited EO on the advice of a weapons merchant. There are other compelling reasons for some form of regulation when one takes into account that the democratic process in some industrialized countries is being circumvented by the employment of PMCs. The conduct of the war in Iraq would seem to be a clear example.

The pioneer editors of this book should be highly commended for undertaking this important venture of exploring all aspects of the debate about PMCs. Whatever viewpoint one may hold, PMCs are here to stay: governments find them useful and are prepared to pay for their services. This is a most informative book with exceedingly important analyses to enhance a better understanding of PMCs. A careful reading of these presentations should greatly benefit the general discourse on the subject.

James O C Jonah
Finance Minister of Sierra Leone, 1998–2001

February 2007

Acknowledgements

This book is the result of an ongoing research project at the Institute for International Law and Justice at New York University School of Law. Particular thanks are due to Benedict Kingsbury, Faculty Director of the Institute, and James Cockayne, who helped us to define and shape the research project. Further intellectual roots lie in the Institute's research project on Global Administrative Law, directed by Benedict Kingsbury and Richard B Stewart. For more information, visit <http://www.iilj.org>.

Many of the ideas presented in this book were shaped and discussed at a workshop at the Greentree Foundation Estate in December 2005 and a conference at New York University School of Law in March 2006. Thanks are due to Heather Lord of the Greentree Foundation, as well as Angela Ebanks and Ana Lara at NYU. The text benefited from close reading by, among others, James Cockayne and David A Jordan.

The project would not have been possible without the generous support of Carnegie Corporation of New York and the Canadian Department of Foreign Affairs. All views expressed in this volume, however, are solely those of the respective authors.

Contents

Table of Cases

Table of Treaties and Legislation

TREATIES

OTHER INTERNATIONAL DOCUMENTS

LEGISLATION

List of Contributors

Deborah Avant is Professor of Political Science and Director of the Institute for Global and International Studies at George Washington University's Elliott School of International Affairs. Her research (funded by the John D and Catherine T MacArthur Foundation, the Olin Foundation, and the Smith Richardson Foundation, among others) has focused on civil-military relations, military change, and the politics of controlling violence. Her recent work on the privatization of security has appeared in *The Market for Force: the Consequences of Privatizing Security* (Cambridge University Press, 2005) as well as articles in journals such as *Perspective on Politics, Review of International Studies, Foreign Policy*, and *International Studies Perspectives*. She is also the author of *Political Institutions and Military Change: Lessons from Peripheral Wars* (Cornell University Press, 1994) and articles on military change in *International Organization, International Studies Quarterly*, and *Armed Forces and Society*, among others.

Andrew Bearpark is the Director General of the British Association of Private Security Companies (BAPSC) and works as an adviser to governments, international organizations, and the commercial sector on post-conflict reconstruction. His previous posts include Director of Operations and Infrastructure, Coalition Provisional Authority (CPA), Iraq (2003–2004); UN Deputy Special Representative of the Secretary General and EU Representative with responsibility for economic development, Kosovo (2000–2003); Deputy High Representative, Reconstruction and Return Task Force, Sarajevo, Bosnia (1998–2000); Head of Information and Emergency Aid Departments, Overseas Development Administration (ODA), and Press Secretary to Minister Baroness Chalker (1991–1997); Private Secretary and later Chief of Staff to Prime Minister Margaret Thatcher (1986–1991).

Marina Caparini is Senior Fellow at the Geneva Centre for the Democratic Control of Armed Forces (DCAF), where she coordinates research working groups on civil society and internal security (policing, security intelligence, and border management). Her current projects focus on the privatization of security functions, civil society capacity building, and oversight and accountability mechanisms in security sector governance. Recent publications include *Private Actors and Security Governance*, A Bryden and M Caparini, eds (LIT Verlag, 2006); *Civil–Military Relations in Europe: Learning from Crisis and Institutional Change*, H Born, M Caparini, K Haltiner and J Kuhlmann, eds (Routledge, 2006); and *Civil Society and the Security Sector: Concepts and Practices in New Democracies*, M Caparini, ed (LIT Verlag, 2006).

Simon Chesterman is Global Professor and Director of the New York University School of Law Singapore Programme, and an Associate Professor of Law at the

National University of Singapore. Educated in Melbourne, Beijing, Amsterdam, and Oxford, his books include *Shared Secrets: Intelligence and Collective Security* (Lowy Institute for International Policy, 2006); *You, The People: The United Nations, Transitional Administration, and State-Building* (Oxford University Press, 2004); and *Just War or Just Peace? Humanitarian Intervention and International Law* (Oxford University Press, 2001).

James Cockayne is an Associate at the International Peace Academy. Before joining IPA, Cockayne was a Graduate Scholar at the Institute for International Law and Justice at New York University School of Law, and Principal Legal Officer in, consecutively, the Extradition and Transnational Crime Units at the Australian Attorney-General's Department. He is a member of the Editorial Committee of the *Journal of International Criminal Justice*, and has worked at the Special Court for Sierra Leone, the International Criminal Tribunal for Rwanda, and in commercial legal practice in Australia and France.

Laura A Dickinson is a Professor at the University of Connecticut School of Law. A graduate of Harvard College and Yale Law School, she subsequently served as a senior policy adviser to Harold Hongju Koh, Assistant Secretary of State for Democracy, Human Rights, and Labor at the US Department of State. She also served as a law clerk to Justices Harry A Blackmun and Stephen G Breyer on the US Supreme Court, and to Judge Dorothy Nelson of the Court of Appeals for the Ninth Circuit. Her work on transitional justice, legal responses to terror, foreign affairs privatization, and the interrelationship between international and domestic law has appeared in the *American Journal of International Law*, the *Southern California Law Review*, the *William & Mary Law Review*, the *Yale Journal of International Law*, and in books published by Harvard University Press, Stanford University Press, and Transnational Publishers. During the 2006–07 academic year, she was a Visiting Research Scholar and Visiting Professor at Princeton University. She is currently at work on a book that focuses on the increasing privatization of military functions, foreign aid, and diplomacy, the impact of such privatization on the efficacy of international human rights law, and the possibility that alternative mechanisms (such as contract, tort, and trust) could be used to help ensure accountability of private actors working abroad under government contracts.

Louise Doswald-Beck is a Professor of the Graduate Institute of International Studies and Director of the University Centre for International Humanitarian Law. She began her career as a lecturer at the Universities of Exeter and London. Between 1987 and February 2001, she was a legal adviser at the International Committee of the Red Cross (ICRC) and became Head of the Legal Division in March 1998. During her period at the ICRC, she played a major role in negotiations that led to various international instruments such as: the Statute of the International Criminal Court and its Elements of Crimes, Protocols II (amended) and IV of the Convention on Certain Conventional Weapons, the Ottawa Convention on Anti-Personnel Landmines, Protocol II to the Hague Convention on

Cultural Property, and the San Remo Manual on armed conflicts at sea. Between March 2001 and August 2003 she was Secretary-General of the International Commission of Jurists and then became a member of its Executive Committee. She has written extensively on subjects relating to the use of force, humanitarian law, and human rights law, and is the co-author of the ICRC's study on customary international humanitarian law.

David Isenberg is a senior research analyst with the British American Security Information Council (BASIC). He has been researching and writing on private military companies since the early 1990s. His 1997 monograph 'Soldiers of Fortune Ltd.: A Profile of Today's Private Sector Corporate Mercenary Firms' and 2004 study 'A Fistful of Contractors' are acknowledged staples in the field. He has written on the subject for numerous periodicals, lectured at US military schools and overseas on the subject, and been a frequent commentator on numerous radio and television shows on PMC activities.

Elke Krahmann is a Senior Lecturer in International Relations in the Department of Politics at the University of Bristol. She has published widely on international foreign and security policy, including *New Threats and New Actors in International Security* (Palgrave, 2005) and *Multilevel Networks in European Foreign Policy* (Ashgate, 2003). Her articles have appeared in *International Affairs, International Studies Review, Cambridge Review of International Affairs, Review of International Studies, Global Governance, Cooperation and Conflict, European Security, Contemporary Security Policy,* and *Conflict, Security and Development.* A forthcoming research monograph will examine the privatization of military services in Europe and North America, while her current ESRC-funded project analyses the theoretical implications of the commodification of security.

Anna Leander is Associate Professor of International Political Economy at the Copenhagen Business School. Her research focuses on the authority of non-state actors in international politics and particularly on the authority of private actors over the use of force. She has recently published articles on PMCs in *Millennium* and *Journal of Peace Research.* She has also published a book on the issue with the *Centro Militare di Studi Strategici.*

Chia Lehnardt is a doctoral student in Berlin. From 2005–2006 she was responsible for the research project on PMCs at the Institute for International Law and Justice (IILJ), New York University School of Law. Educated in Berlin, Oxford, Florence, and New York, she has previously worked as a consultant to the IILJ, at the German Federal Parliament, and with a law firm specializing in public law.

Angela McIntyre has worked in peacebuilding in Africa since 1993, conducting field research and implementing development projects in the areas of post-conflict disarmament, demobilization and reintegration (DDR), and humanitarian demining for both UN agencies and non-governmental organizations in Mozambique. She was a Senior Researcher at the Institute for Security Studies in Pretoria, researching children in armed conflict in Sierra Leone, Angola, and Mozambique and initiating a project on the regulation of the private military industry in Africa. She is currently writing a doctoral thesis (social history of the Angolan civil war) and working as an oral historian for the William Cullen Library at the University of the Witwatersrand in Johannesburg, South Africa.

Kevin A O'Brien serves as a public policy analyst and commentator on issues relating to the privatization of security, alongside other issues relating to public security and intelligence matters. He has served as Deputy Director of RAND Europe's Security Programme, as well as Visiting Fellow and Deputy Director of the International Centre for Security Analysis, Department of War Studies, King's College London, and Fellow in the Department of Politics at the University of Hull (Britain), from where he obtained his PhD in Security Studies. Dr O'Brien focuses his research on—amongst other topics—public security issues, with a strong interest in Africa. He has written extensively on the privatization of security, and has published more than sixty academic articles, chapters and reports. Dr O'Brien is currently completing a book on the history of South African intelligence.

Sarah Percy is a Research Associate in the Oxford Leverhulme Programme on the Changing Character of War and a non-stipendiary Research Fellow of Nuffield College, Oxford. She is the author of several pieces on mercenaries and PSCs, including a book, *Mercenaries* (Oxford University Press, 2007), and an Adelphi Paper entitled "Regulating the Private Security Industry" (IISS and Routledge, 2006).

Sabrina Schulz joined the British Association of Private Security Companies (BAPSC) as Director of Policy in 2006. Previously, she was a Fellow at the American Institute for Contemporary German Studies (AICGS) at Johns Hopkins University in Washington, DC. Dr Schulz studied at the Universities of Konstanz and Louvain and holds a Postgraduate degree in Public Policy and Management from the University of Potsdam. Furthermore, she holds a Masters degree in International Politics from the University of Wales at Aberystwyth where she also completed her PhD.

Taya Weiss has conducted extensive fieldwork studying the small arms trade and related peace and conflict issues in Sierra Leone and Kenya. As a research consultant to the Institute for Security Studies in Pretoria, South Africa, she focused on reducing the demand for small arms and on local peacebuilding efforts in several regions of Africa.

Introduction

Simon Chesterman and Chia Lehnardt

The claim to legitimate violence has long been understood to be the exclusive domain of states. Internally, the German sociologist Max Weber used this monopoly to define what a state is; externally, international law on the use of force seeks to regulate what a state does. Mercenaries and the modern phenomenon of private military companies (PMCs)—commercial firms offering military services ranging from military training and advice to combat—challenge this neat schema, a challenge that has achieved greater significance due to the rise in private military activity following the end of the Cold War.

The traditional response, driven in significant part by the post-colonial experience of mercenaries in Africa, has been abolitionist: prohibiting mercenarism or the use of mercenaries. That approach has failed, and in any case bears little relevance to the more recent experience of PMCs playing an increasingly accepted role in armed conflicts. Executive Outcomes turned around an orphaned conflict in Sierra Leone in the mid-1990s; Military Professional Resources Incorporated (MPRI) was instrumental in shifting the balance of power in the Balkans, clearing the way for the Dayton negotiations; following the 2003 war in Iraq, PMC employees supporting coalition forces and reconstruction efforts made up the second largest grouping of personnel after the United States military.

Whether or not this extensive use of PMCs is evolutionary or remains exceptional, the growth of the industry shows no signs of slowing down. The privatization of military functions reflects a general enthusiasm for the outsourcing of state capacities in the industrialized world, but is also a consequence of the growing reluctance on the part of key states to intervene in conflicts that are not of immediate strategic interest or where domestic support for intervention is lacking. In addition, non-state actors such as transnational corporations and humanitarian organizations operating in fragile states are increasingly targeted by non-state violence, prompting them to turn to the commercial sector for want of other security options.

Despite the growing attention paid to PMCs, however, there has been little sustained examination of the governance of such actors. The majority of the literature tends to focus on either descriptive accounts of incidents involving PMCs or normative arguments based on a relatively narrow human rights foundation. What has been absent is clarity about the phenomenon—in particular the distinction between modern PMCs and traditional mercenaries—and a realistic approach to regulation that addresses both the problems of unaccountable actors wielding potentially lethal force and the interests of the consumers and suppliers of an increasingly established industry.

This book seeks to fill these gaps. It does so by taking seriously arguments that the demand for such services will remain a persistent feature in international affairs and examining the governance issues that arise, particularly in the tension between efforts at regulation and market forces.

Acceptance of that market will largely depend on the reality and the perception of accountability mechanisms to guard against abuse. A useful starting point in the discussion on regulation is, therefore, to focus not on the identity of the actor but on the nature of the acts requiring regulation and accountability. Concerns relate primarily to the use of potentially lethal force by PMC personnel, but also to the impact these actors may have on the strategic balance of a conflict. Most of the existing regulation—notably international humanitarian law—is directed primarily towards the standing armies of states. As private actors take on more responsibilities a central question is whether the normative framework and accountability structures adequately address the new environment.

Most commentators agree that they do not. Instead, it is often implicitly or explicitly assumed that it is business interests—rather than international and national law—that govern the use and conduct of PMCs. There is, in this context, good reason to be concerned about leaving issues of peace and war, life and death, to purely market mechanisms. It would be naïve, of course, to assume that traditional armed forces are necessarily virtuous and private armies inherently harmful to public interests. But the fact that profit-driven interests play a role in conflict does complicate control, transparency, and accountability issues. Periodic outrage surrounding PMCs and the apparent impunity with which their personnel engage in misconduct supports this view, lending credence to the perception that PMCs fall through the cracks of both national and international law.

And yet this is only part of the story. The anecdotal manner in which discussion on regulation tends to be conducted, with parallel conversations of abolitionists on the one side against practitioners and proponents of a laissez-faire approach on the other, has hampered a serious analysis of the legal framework in which PMCs operate. The purpose of this book is to address the interaction between regulation and market forces in current and future operations of PMCs. It attempts to shed some light on the existing legal framework, to assess whether more regulation is needed, and in particular what role the market can and should play in regulation.

Contending that most firms provide only 'security services'—meaning that they engage only in defensive operations, as opposed to offensive manoeuvres—a distinction is often made between PMCs and private security companies (PSCs). The first category is sometimes said to include only those firms that actually fight wars alongside or in place of national forces, an exceptionally narrow definition that tends to confine the label to the wound-up companies Executive Outcomes and Sandline International. The term PMCs is used here more broadly: it denotes firms providing services outside their home states with the potential for use of lethal force, as well as training of and advice to militaries that substantially affects their war-fighting capacities. This definition includes firms engaging in those activities that are the focus of concern on the part of regulators and humanitarian agencies. It also takes into account the difficulty of distinguishing clearly between offensive and defensive operations in low-intensity conflicts where there is no clear front line. Semantically, the term 'military' better captures the nature of these services as it points to the qualitative difference between firms operating in conflict zones in a military environment and 'security firms' that primarily guard premises in a stable environment.

The book is organized around four sets of questions. First, what is the basis and nature of the concerns raised by the PMC phenomenon? Secondly, how have problems leading to a call for regulation manifested in different regions and contexts? Thirdly, what regulatory norms and institutions currently exist and how effective are they? And fourthly, what role does the nascent market for private security and military services play in regulation, and where is it going?

Part I sets the context for the subsequent discussion of regulation. A basic question is the relationship between traditional mercenaries and PMCs, and whether PMCs should be banned altogether. Proponents of abolition argue that PMCs are old-style mercenaries in a modern guise, suggesting that their very nature and their use are morally problematic. Sarah Percy examines these arguments in chapter one and shows how they continue to influence the discussion of PMCs and regulation, in particular the approach to the topic within the United Nations. She argues that a continuum traceable from mercenaries to PMCs does exist and that therefore the ethical objections against PMCs will be difficult, if not impossible to overcome—but that those concerns might usefully serve as an additional check on the use of PMCs alongside regulation. Both regulators and the industry, Percy notes, would be well advised in taking these ethical worries seriously.

A second prerequisite for meaningful discussion of regulation is clarity as to the subject to be regulated. Serious analysis in this area is often frustrated by the lack of agreement as to what it is that PMCs actually do. Kevin O'Brien surveys the industry in chapter two and creates a typology of private actors in the military environment. He then proposes a theoretical model of regulation, establishing the tightest oversight of military operations aimed at altering the strategic environment. A combination of licensing and registration regimes, O'Brien suggests, would provide the most adequate solution on the national level, though its effectiveness would depend on complementary action on the international level.

Chapter three, by Anna Leander, argues that, given the way PMCs shape security concerns and more generally political priorities, civil-military relations as a regulatory concern has been strangely ignored in the debate on regulation. She suggests that preoccupation with security professionals' role in shaping politics is as important when these professionals are privately organized in PMCs as it is when they are enrolled in public armed forces. Leander shows that existing regulation has not been adjusted to account for this fact and that the significance of regulating the role of PMCs in shaping politics is profoundly underestimated. She therefore argues that putting the issue of regulating 'civil-PMC relations' on the agenda is essential.

These ethical, definitional, and political problems are compounded by practical differences in the situations where PMCs have taken on significant roles. There is a difference, for example, between a state that retains the services of a PMC because it lacks effective control over its own territory, and a state that brings in private actors to reduce certain public and political costs of conducting hostilities. Part II of the volume looks at three different regional contexts in which mercenaries and PMCs have emerged as significant actors in conflict and post-conflict environments.

Although one of the main concerns with PMCs today is that they constitute a threat to the state's monopoly of violence, the involvement of the now defunct PMC Executive Outcomes in Sierra Leone and Angola in the mid-1990s tells a different story. The firm is credited with supporting governments challenged by powerful rebel groups and, unusually, reconfirming the state's control by temporarily questioning it. Angela McIntyre and Taya Weiss observe in chapter four that this use of PMCs points to a shift in the role of private military forces in Africa, though their support came at a hefty price. Contrary to the frequent assumption that the African experience of mercenaries and PMCs are aberrations of the past, the authors demonstrate that the problems arising out of private military involvement in African conflicts continue to have implications for the discussion of regulation. Analysing the convoluted relationships between PMCs, transnational corporations, and governments, McIntyre and Weiss conclude that shifts in political and commercial accountability, rather than legislative action, have been instrumental in the transition from mercenaries to PMCs in Africa.

The use and conduct of PMCs in Iraq, by contrast, have posed different problems and challenges to regulation. This is illustrated most starkly by the difference in treatment of individuals implicated in the Abu Ghraib torture incidents, depending on whether they were part of the US forces or PMC employees. In chapter five David Isenberg analyses how PMCs operating alongside the coalition forces—but outside the military chain of command—have complicated civil-military relations. He argues that this has created problems of coordination and created opportunities for the US government to evade public accountability for certain aspects of the Iraq conflict.

In chapter six, Elke Krahmann looks at the role of PMCs in security sector reform (SSR) and problems arising from their involvement for transitional states and donor governments respectively. While the work of PMCs in this sector has often been professional and efficient, the comparative disadvantages of PMCs in relation to a state's own armed or police forces lies in their private nature: the latter are in a position to establish military relations and have the authority and legitimacy to implement reform. As a consequence, Krahmann concludes that for a holistic approach to SSR, donor countries should reconsider what role their own uniformed personnel might play.

Part III turns squarely to the question of norms. In considering an adequate regulatory framework for the use and conduct of PMCs, it is important to take into account the transnational nature of the industry. When discussing the role of international law in governing the use and conduct of PMCs, many commentators have focused on the flawed mercenary conventions of the United Nations and the Organization of African Unity (OAU) and the ambiguous status of PMC personnel under the Geneva Conventions; many have concluded that international law is hopelessly incapable of dealing with these new actors. Chapter seven, by Louise Doswald-Beck, shows that this is at best a partial account of the position of PMC personnel under international humanitarian law. A crucial question in this context is the circumstances under which PMCs may be said to 'take direct part in the hostilities'.

One of the reasons why international law is repeatedly dismissed as irrelevant in the discussion of governance of PMCs is the fact that it largely focuses on states. As a result, despite the fact that governments constitute one of the major clients of PMCs or authorize their operations in foreign states, the question of under what circumstances the misconduct of PMCs engages the responsibility of states has received surprisingly little attention. Chia Lehnardt addresses this issue in chapter eight. She argues that the fear that PMCs might be used by Western governments to conduct 'foreign policy by proxy' is only partially warranted: from an international law perspective, states cannot evade responsibility merely by hiring a private actor to carry out certain functions. The conduct of PMCs is under certain circumstances attributed to the state, making that state responsible for any violation of international law committed by PMC personnel. Even where no such attribution exists, the state might still be responsible for lack of due diligence to adequately regulate and control PMC conduct. Like Doswald-Beck, Lehnardt concludes that claims of a 'vacuum' in international law are overstated, although factual power relationships between the PMC, the host state, and the exporting state remain unaddressed on the international level.

This points to the importance of regulation at the domestic level. It is primarily here that states have to take action in order to fulfil their international obligations. Moreover, domestic regulatory regimes are more likely to have an impact on the development of the industry, in particular by providing incentives for PMCs to establish best practices and positioning themselves as responsible actors in the sector. Given that PMCs operate mostly in weak states without the capacity or willingness to regulate and control their conduct, more emphasis falls on states exporting their goods and services. Such a regulatory system must walk the thin line between enabling the state to control and monitor PMC operations effectively on the one hand, while allowing PMCs to fill security gaps quickly and efficiently where needed. Of the key exporting states only three—the United States, South Africa, and Israel—operate licensing regimes controlling the export of commercial military services. In chapter nine, Marina Caparini examines two of these regimes with very different underlying principles. She shows that the regulatory system adopted in South Africa has proven ineffective due to its overly burdensome approach, causing firms either to circumvent it or to relocate altogether. By contrast, the US approach reflects the different perceptions of the industry as a potential tool for foreign policy. What both regimes have in common, however, is the power shift to the executive and the lack of sufficient resources to ensure enforcement.

Part IV turns on the role of market mechanisms in regulation. The commercial military sector falls short of being a fully developed market in several areas. Chapter ten, by Deborah Avant, examines the emergence of this market, focusing on the peculiarities of the industry—in particular the lack of competition and transparency, and the tendency of individuals to move easily between firms—and the limitations of market mechanisms when applied to extreme situations where the security of a state is threatened. The lack of other regulatory tools has increased the importance of the market, but this potential tool is too weak to maintain specific standards, since clients tend to disagree about the relevant benchmarks. The diversity of interests among PMC clients therefore significantly diminishes the importance of reputational costs of the industry.

The diversity of both the industry and its clients and the resulting variety of potential costs in the case of misconduct is taken up again by James Cockayne in chapter eleven. Drawing on insights from principal-agent theory in economics and political science, he examines the relations between PMCs and their clients and regulators, arguing that states use a variety of methods to try to make PMCs their 'agents', including employment, national regulation, and the promotion of soft norms. PMCs in turn respond, Cockayne suggests, by trying to maximize their own power through a variety of strategies, including playing off different principals against each other—for example by encouraging national executives to use PMCs to escape parliamentary, judicial, and electoral accountability—and in extreme cases asserting their own principality. These contending strategies intersect with industry consolidation, market incentives, and the shadow of litigation to produce a transnational hybrid state-market regulatory model, raising difficult questions about private regulatory power and its role in determining and providing public goods.

If such regulation is to have any effect at all, however, both states and interested NGOs will need to think more broadly about possible forms that regulation might take. Laura Dickinson in chapter twelve draws an analogy with existing domestic contract regimes and argues that the market, despite its underdeveloped state, can be significantly regulated by contract law. She argues that contracts, an archetypal private law tool, can be utilized to protect public interests and establish an ongoing oversight role of the hiring or host government.

Any attempt to regulate this rapidly developing sector will have to take into account what new fields of activity will become more important in the years ahead. In chapter thirteen Andrew Bearpark and Sabrina Schulz consider the future of the market. They acknowledge that a delicate balance must be struck between legitimate business interests and those of the public and turn to the regulatory tool favoured by the industry itself: self-regulation. They argue that this is both a realistic approach to current regulatory gaps and will be embraced as a competitive advantage for those firms accepting self-regulation, using the example of the British market as a case study.

The appropriate balance between private and public interests is a key question whenever the provision of a public service depends on private actors. Achieving this balance is imperative in situations where those private interests affect fundamental state functions such as national defence, warfare, and the claim to legitimate violence. Although the move of commercial military forces from mercenaries to market-driven, state-sanctioned PMCs tests traditional legal systems, which are premised on the assumption that states are the only legitimate actors in military affairs, a key insight of this volume is that an applicable legal framework does already exist. Although this framework is patchy, insufficient, and inadequately implemented, it provides a valuable starting point for progress. The conclusion, by the editors, seeks to map out the contours of this normative environment, as well as the incentives and disincentives that shape the manner in which PMCs operate. Moving forward, governance of the commercial military sector will depend on the interaction between these regulatory and market forces.

PART I
CONCERNS

1

Morality and regulation

Sarah Percy

The modern private military industry has, despite its best efforts, been dogged by accusations that its personnel are merely mercenaries in a modern guise, reviving long-standing debates that the use of private force is inherently morally problematic. On occasion these accusations have bordered on the hysterical;[1] others are more temperate, but still argue that private military companies (PMCs) are merely mercenaries dressed up in more respectable corporate clothes.[2] As a result, criticism of private security from a moral perspective has been dismissed as biased, inaccurate, and unfair. Today's PMCs assert that they are not mercenaries and that private force has a practical and potentially beneficial role to play in modern conflict. While it is true that PMCs bear little resemblance to the seedy mercenary celebrities of the 1960s and 1970s, no serious analysis of the moral case against private force has been made; it is accordingly impossible to assess whether or not moral criticisms apply to PMCs, and if they do, what role these concerns ought to have in regulating private force.

This chapter argues that understanding the main moral concerns about private force helps to illustrate why, despite the best efforts of the industry, all types of private force from mercenaries, to PMCs like Executive Outcomes (EO) and Sandline, to modern companies today that prefer to be called PSCs and PMCs, remain linked in the public eye. Moreover, understanding moral concerns provides a different foundation from which to examine regulation of the private security industry, by explaining why hostile reactions to PMCs persist, demonstrating that moral concerns are central to explaining the arguments for the abolition of private force, and outlining what regulation can and cannot do to overcome moral objections.

The chapter first defines the three main variants of private force in the international system. It then outlines the main moral objections to mercenaries and

---

[1] For example, Guy Arnold, *Mercenaries: The Scourge of the Third World* (London: Macmillan, 1999). Arnold argues that most mercenaries are 'little better than killer psychopaths'.

[2] Among many others, see Abdel Fatau Musah and J 'Kayode Fayemi, 'Africa in Search of Security: Mercenaries and Conflicts—an Overview', in Abdel Fatau Musah and J 'Kayode Fayemi (eds), *Mercenaries: An African Security Dilemma* (London and Stirling, VA: Pluto Press, 2000); Ken Silverstein, *Private Warriors* (London and New York: Verso, 2000) 187.

explains how they can help differentiate between the various types of private
actors who use force while revealing a core concern that applies to them all. The
latter half of the chapter examines how moral objections to private force have an
impact upon today's regulatory environment: most prominently, moral objections
to private force have led to calls for its abolition, especially within the United
Nations (UN). Such moral concerns will also affect efforts to create a regulatory
framework to govern the use of private force.

Definitions

There are three main variants of private force in the international system: mercenaries; combat PMCs; and security or non-combat PMCs. A mercenary can be defined
as an individual soldier who fights for a state other than his own, or for a non-state
entity to which he has no direct tie, in exchange for financial gain. The two main
instruments of international law dealing with mercenaries, Article 47 of Protocol I
Additional to the Geneva Conventions[3] and the International Convention Against
the Recruitment, Use, Financing, and Training of Mercenaries,[4] both highlight the
idea that mercenaries are defined by profit-seeking motivations and the fact that
they are foreign. Mercenaries will sell their services to the highest bidder and are usually unconcerned about the nature of their clientele.

Mercenaries were once common actors on the international stage. Until the
sixteenth century, the practice of individual mercenaries organizing bands and
selling their services to the highest bidder was widespread; by the seventeenth
century, it had largely disappeared. The mercenary trade continued in the sale of
entire regiments by one state to another, and by states selling licenses to other
states that would allow the recruitment of private citizens.[5] The state-to-state
trade in mercenaries ended by the mid-nineteenth century. Mercenaries, again in
the form of individual contractors, reappeared on the international stage in the
1960s, 1970s, and 1980s, fighting in the wars of decolonization in Africa.

Combat PMCs are tightly organized companies with a clear corporate structure
that provide military services, including offensive combat, in exchange for payment, for states or other actors. Examples include the now-defunct companies
Executive Outcomes (EO) and Sandline. Both of these companies insisted that
they would only fight for sovereign states and would be selective about their clients.

---

   [3] 1977. Hereinafter referred to as Article 47 of Protocol I.
   [4] 1989, entered into force 2001. This Convention was created by the UN. I will refer to this particular Convention as the UN Convention or the Convention, and specify when I am referring to another
UN Convention. This chapter will focus on these two documents, as they are the most universal and the
most often criticized. There is also an Organization of African Unity Convention for the Elimination of
Mercenaries in Africa (OAU Convention), created in 1977, which came into force in 1985.
   [5] For discussions of pre-nineteenth century mercenary action, see Anthony Mockler, *The New
Mercenaries* (London: Sidgwick and Jackson, 1985); Sarah V Percy, *Mercenaries* (Oxford: Oxford
University Press, 2007).

There are currently no companies of this type operating openly in the international system.

Non-combat PMCs are similarly organized companies that exchange military services stopping short of combat for payment. These services include translation, close protection, interrogation, logistics, and training, as well as security services for states, NGOs, and corporations. These companies may claim to use force only in self-defence; however, the majority of these services are provided in a military context, and the line between self-defence and combat might be blurred. Nonetheless, it is important to differentiate between the kinds of services provided by EO and Sandline and the type of services offered today. PMCs are no longer in the business of replacing the combat functions of state militaries.[6] PMCs seeking to maintain a legitimate market presence today must be selective about those to whom they offer their services. They are similar to combat companies in that they will work for a variety of states, including, in some cases, the state in which they are based.[7] PMCs also differ in the degree to which they are tied to their home states. American PMCs maintain closer ties with the US government, and do not undertake projects without the government's explicit approval of that state, granted through the Arms Export Control Act (ACEA). In other states, such as Britain, PMCs are free to choose their own clients, although the state often grants implicit or informal consent.

Private actors who sell military and security services in the international system can thus be differentiated in several different ways, summarized in Table 1.1 below.

An examination of Table 1.1 reveals that there is only one core similarity between these different types of private actor: they all exchange military and security services for payment. It is difficult to see, based purely on these definitions, that mercenaries have anything in common with PMCs, other than the military nature of the services they provide. However, mercenaries offer the broadest range of military services possible, including combat and illegal activities such as coups. The differentiation between combat PMCs and non-combat PMCs is not quite as sharp, although, again, these companies provide very different services. PMCs also differ in the relationship with their home states, with non-combat PMCs having both formal and informal ties with home governments. EO, a combat PMC, had no such ties with its home state government; indeed, South Africa passed quite stringent legislation to make it difficult for these companies to operate from South Africa.

A final difference, not visible in Table 1.1, is worth pointing out. There are only two examples of combat PMCs, and both are defunct; between the two of them, they

---

[6] The American company Blackwater, which recently offered to provide peacekeeping services, is a notable exception; presumably peacekeeping would involve actions resembling combat.

[7] This discussion of definitions is drawn from Sarah V Percy, 'The United Nations Security Council and the Use of Private Force' in Vaughan Lowe, et al (eds), *The United Nations Security Council and War* (Oxford: Oxford University Press, 2007). For an expanded discussion of the problems in defining private force, see Sarah V Percy, 'This Gun's for Hire: A New Look at an Old Issue,' *International Journal*, vol 58, no 4 (2003) 721.

Table 1.1. Private actors offering military and security services in the international system

	PMCs closely tied to their home states	Combat PMCs	Mercenaries
Engage in combat	No	Yes	Yes
Sell military or security services for money	Yes	Yes	Yes
Have approval of home state	Sometimes	No	No
Officially selective about clients	Yes	Yes	No
Corporate organization	Yes	Yes	No

only have three notable clients: the governments of Angola, Sierra Leone, and Papua New Guinea.[8] The lack of combat-PMC action, and the disappearance of these PMCs, suggests that these companies were only marginally legitimate and were far from accepted actors on the international stage. Conversely, there are dozens of non-combat PMCs working for a wide range of clients, from state governments to NGOs to international organizations. It appears that combat and non-combat PMCs also differ in the degree to which they are accepted by the international community.[9]

All these differences between private fighters might seem to suggest labelling today's private security industry as 'mercenary' is unfair. It is only through the examination of moral objections to private force that it is possible to see why these variants of private force are connected, and accordingly, what role moral concerns might play in regulation.

Moral objections and the continuum of private force

There are two main types of moral objection to the use of private force. This section will define each objection and discuss its origins in turn.

The first moral objection: killing without attachment to a cause

The private military industry has been criticized because of the idea that fighting for financial gain is morally problematic. More specifically, killing in warfare is usually justified by some sort of attachment to an appropriate cause, which has differed throughout history. Causes that have been deemed by society to justify war have varied over time; they include the pursuit or defence of religious or national interests, or the pursuit or defence of the interests of the sovereign state.

Mercenaries have been defined as actors who do not share this cause. This objection is not necessarily fair, in that it is not inconceivable that some mercenaries or

---

[8] See chapter two in this volume by Kevin O'Brien and chapter four by Angela McIntyre and Taya Weiss for further discussions of EO and Sandline.

[9] Some reasons for this difference will be suggested below.

PMCs might adopt the cause of those for whom they fight. Soldiers might also be financially motivated, and not motivated by attachment to a cause. However, as we will see, there have been persistent objections to mercenaries, private military, and private security companies on the grounds that fighting for financial gain rather than for a cause is problematic. Indeed, international law relating to mercenaries makes specific reference to financial gain. In the Diplomatic Conference that led to the creation of the Geneva Conventions, state negotiators defined a mercenary as a 'person who is motivated to fight essentially or primarily by the desire for ... "hard cash" '.[10] Article 47(2)(c) of Protocol I states that a mercenary 'is motivated to take part in the hostilities essentially by the desire for private gain' and this language was adopted wholesale in the UN Convention.[11]

During the late eighteenth and early nineteenth centuries, nationalism was increasingly used to justify war. Mercenaries were condemned for not sharing the cause of their employers and fighting only for money rather than national ideals. The French Revolution and its philosophy made the use of mercenaries untenable on moral grounds and associated them with the hated foreign soldiers of the *ancien régime*.[12] The 'new ideology looked down on men who served for money, calling them hirelings and mercenaries. Soldiering was only respectable when it was done voluntarily by citizens from love of their country, under which circumstances it became morally admirable'.[13] Some critics also point out that the new way of fighting, particularly the use of skirmishing troops required to operate independently and at a great distance from their commanders, privileged troops that were motivated by more than financial gain. National troops were deemed to be more capable of this sort of fighting than were mercenaries.[14]

During the British debates on the decision to send mercenaries to the Crimea,[15] Richard Cobden summed up the prevailing belief that a mercenary cannot be moral because of his motivation in the House of Commons:

[I]t is assumed that men fight for a cause, that they are actuated by a love of home, devotion to the country, or attachment to a Sovereign; these are the sentiments that are considered to

---

[10] CDDH/236/Rev.1 at para 99.

[11] See art 1, para b of the United Nations International Convention against the Recruitment, Use, Financing and Training of Mercenaries, available at <http://www.icrc.org/ihl.nsf/FULL/530?OpenDocument>

[12] Allan Forrest, 'La Patrie En Danger: The French Revolution and the First *Levée En Masse*,' in Daniel Moran and Arthur Waldron (eds), *The People in Arms: Military Myth and National Mobilization since the French Revolution* (Cambridge: Cambridge University Press, 2003) 9. There were 23 regiments of foreigners in the French army in 1789. Peter Paret, *Understanding War: Essays on Clausewitz and the History of Military Power* (Princeton: Princeton University Press, 1992) 54.

[13] Geoffrey Best, *War and Society in Revolutionary Europe* (Leicester: Leicester University Press, 1982) 77.

[14] Gunther E Rothenberg, *The Art of Warfare in the Age of Napoleon* (London: BT Batsford, 1977) 14.; Barry R Posen, 'Nationalism, the Mass Army, and Military Power,' *International Security*, vol 18, no 2 (1993) 93.

[15] The mercenaries were ultimately recruited but the war ended before they were sent to the Crimea. CC Bayley, *Mercenaries for the Crimea: The German, Swiss and Italian Legions in British Service, 1854–1856* (London: McGill-Queen's University Press, 1977).

hallow the pursuit of arms. But what motives have these men whom you endeavour to hire out of the back slums of the towns of Germany? They can have no pretensions to fighting from any moral motive whatever; *they are deprived of every ground upon which you can justify war*, and, as they want the motives which I have described, there is just the difference between them and an ordinary soldier fighting for his country that there is between a hero and a cut-throat.[16]

By the 1970s and through until today, states seeking to control mercenaries did so on the basis that what made them problematic was the fact that they were motivated to fight by 'hard cash'.[17] The British government Green Paper, drawn up in response to the actions of the PMC Sandline in Sierra Leone, remained concerned that an inappropriate motivation made mercenaries morally problematic and unable to support the state in the same way as a citizen army. The Green Paper argues that in modern society 'there is a natural repugnance towards those who kill (or help kill) for money'.[18] Enrique Bernales Ballesteros, the former UN Special Rapporteur on mercenaries, has stated that modern PMCs are not really different from their mercenary predecessors. He argues that although 'the manner and the nature of the activity in which mercenaries participate may change, that does not change the mercenary status of those who take part in illicit acts, offering and selling their professional skills for pay, well knowing that it is not for a noble cause, but to kill and destroy outside any licit or ethically permissible context'.[19] His successor, the final Special Rapporteur Shaista Shameem, pointed out that states might be ceding their traditional control over the use of force unconsciously, 'to private actors, whose motive is by definition profit as opposed to national interest or the protection of nationals'.[20] There is a very clear distaste for mercenaries on the basis of their profit motivation in the modern context.

Disapproval of mercenaries on the basis that they do not fight for an appropriate cause also stems from evidence that PMCs might not be acting in the common interests of the people who reside in the states that hire them. If, as many allege, EO and Sandline in Africa were paid in long-term mineral extraction concessions,[21] then the countries that hired them were effectively mortgaging their futures for ephemeral benefits.[22] Because they could not rely on their own citizens to fight for them, governments in Sierra Leone and Angola were forced to hire mercenaries, at a price that might weaken the state in the future. Even if the state itself was in grave danger, as was the case in Sierra Leone, the benefits provided by EO were only

[16] Hansard, *Parliamentary Debates*, 3rd Series ed, vol CXXXVI (London and Basingstoke: Cornelius Buck, 1854–1857), col 668. Emphasis added.   [17] CDDH/236/Rev.1 at para 99

[18] House of Commons Foreign Affairs Committee, 'Private Military Companies: Options for Regulation,' (London: The Stationery Office Ltd, 2002) 18.

[19] UN Doc E/CN.4/2002/20, 16.   [20] UN Doc E/CN.4/2005/14, 13.

[21] Alex Vines, 'Mercenaries and the Privatization of Force in Africa,' in Greg Mills and John Stremlau (eds), *The Privatization of Security in Africa* (Johannesburg: South African Institute of International Affairs, 1999) 53.

[22] David J Francis, 'Mercenary Intervention in Sierra Leone: Providing National Security or International Exploitation?,' *Third World Quarterly*, vol 20, no 2 (1999) 332.

temporary and the country plunged back into civil war as soon as EO left. The cost of not hiring EO might have meant that the Rebel United Front seized control of Sierra Leone, killing many people in the process; however, the cost of hiring them was significant long-term mineral concessions exchanged for the benefit of only a few snatched months of peace.[23]

A variation on this argument is that private actors, who are interested only in profit rather than the good of the state, will fight only in areas where there are profits, bringing security only to some states and only to some parts of those states. In Sierra Leone, 'wherever they [EO] went, civilians stopped dying. The trouble was that they only went where the payoff was high'.[24] David Shearer alleges that EO's strategy in Sierra Leone was financial; because it was partially paid in diamond concessions, Sierra Leone's diamond areas were opened first.[25] According to these arguments, security in Sierra Leone was geographically specific; it was not supplied as a public good. Because EO was not motivated by the common good, it behaved in a way that did not ensure the common good. The power of the moral objection in this case is fascinating, because it was made even in a situation where it could be argued that the state was no more motivated by notions of the common good than were PMCs. In Sierra Leone, where financial and military collusion between rebels and state soldiers was so rife that soldiers became known as 'sobels', or soldier-rebels, it seems certain that security was not provided as a public good. Moral objections can prevent clear-headed analysis of a situation.

There is a clear line of thought that to kill without an appropriate cause is unjustified and immoral, a line of thought that runs from the middle ages until today. Again, it is important to emphasize that even though these objections to mercenaries might be unfair, in that it is very difficult to prove the degree to which private actors are motivated by money, or that a financial motivation leads to bad behaviour, or indeed that the state or its forces are motivated by the common good in a way that private fighters are not, they cannot be dismissed. This is in part because of the prevailing belief, outlined above, that killing in warfare must be justified by, to use Cobden's words, a sentiment to hallow the use of arms. There are social rules about when killing is justified. When individuals kill, we require a reason, such as self-defence. When states go to war, they too have been required to supply reasons before they fight, in order to justify the lives lost. The problem with mercenaries is that many people simply cannot accept their justification for fighting and killing. Of course, one of the simplest solutions to the moral problems posed by fighting for money is to avoid actually fighting. Today's PMCs, which avoid combat, accordingly also avoid one of the main criticisms that can be levelled at the private

---

[23] Taya Weiss and Angela McIntyre discuss the ongoing ramifications of the EO contract in Sierra Leone in chapter four of this volume.

[24] Jeremy Harding, 'The Mercenary Business: "Executive Outcomes",' *Review of African Political Economy*, vol 71 (1997) 93.

[25] David Shearer, 'Exploring the Limits of Consent: Conflict Resolution in Sierra Leone,' *Millennium*, vol 26, no 3 (1997) 853.

security industry. Even if a PMC were directly ordered by a state government to engage in combat and fight and kill, it is likely that moral disapproval over the financial motivation of that fighting would continue.

The second moral objection: threatening democratic control over force

The second ethical objection to the use of private force centres around the idea that there is something morally important about the citizen's military contribution to the state. The military relationship between the citizen and the state, according to this argument, results in restraint over the use of force and the reach of the state. A citizen army restrains the state by making it more difficult for the state to engage in war, and specifically more difficult for the state to use the armed forces to quash rebellion among its citizens. Hiring mercenaries disrupts this relationship, because the state will be far less restrained by public opinion in the decision to fight wars if the soldiers are foreign, and in case of rebellion will not need to worry about sympathy preventing soldiers from crushing citizens from the same community. Moreover, the citizen's military duty to the state is a moral one, and mercenaries weaken the community's moral fibre by performing the citizen's duty.

The origins of this objection can be traced at least as far back as Machiavelli and his contemporaries. Niccolò Machiavelli argued that the citizen owed a special, and irreplaceable, duty to the state. He writes that 'the republic is the common good; the citizen, directing all his actions toward that good, may be said to dedicate his life to the republic; the patriot warrior dedicates his death.'[26] Machiavelli's concerns about mercenary use revolve around a deep-seated feeling that native sons *should* fight for the republic, to ensure its health and success at war. The republic drew strength from the military service of its citizens. Hiring foreigners to fight thus diminished the strength of the republic.[27]

Humanists during the Italian renaissance argued that hiring mercenaries would undermine the moral safety of the republic. The decision to hire mercenaries instead of relying on citizens would mean that:

> The citizens would be corrupted because they permitted inferiors to do for them what should be done for the public good; the mercenaries would be agents of that corruption because they performed a public function without regard for the public good; and any ambitious individual could set himself above the republic and destroy it, by bringing the unthinking mercenaries to do for him what should only be done for the republic.[28]

In other words, citizens would be morally weaker because of the decision to hire mercenaries, because mercenaries could not care for the republic in the same way

---

[26] JGA Pocock, *The Machiavellian Moment: Florentine Thought and the Atlantic Republican Tradition* (Princeton: Princeton University Press, 1975) 201.

[27] Michael Edward Mallett, *Mercenaries and Their Masters: Warfare in Renaissance Italy* (London: The Bodley Head, 1974) 97, 133.   [28] Pocock, *Machiavellian Moment* (n 26 above) 204.

as citizens. The republic would also run the risk of becoming dominated by a tyrant, because foreign mercenaries would be more willing to serve the interests of the tyrant rather than serve the public good.

Concerns that the use of foreign troops would lead to tyranny were shared during the French Enlightenment. Jean-Jacques Rousseau argued that the relationship between the citizen and the republic was especially virtuous, and that citizens would take the greatest care to look after the interests of the common good. A polity relying upon mercenaries is a polity in danger. Its citizens, 'no longer considering themselves interested in the common cause, would cease to be the defenders of the homeland'. Leaders will prefer mercenaries to free men 'if only to use the former at a suitable time and place to subjugate the latter more effectively'.[29] Mercenaries pose a grave threat to the liberty of the people, because they do not care for the common good; they submit to the orders of the leadership of the republic, rather than thinking of the needs of the polity itself. Mercenaries in Rome,

whose value could be determined on the basis of the price at which they sold themselves, were proud of their debasement, held in contempt the laws by which they were protected, as well as their comrades whose bread they ate, and believed it an honour to be Caesar's satellites rather than Rome's defenders. And given as they were to blind obedience, their task was to have their swords raised against their fellow citizens, ready to slaughter them all at the first signal. It would not be difficult to show that this was one of the principal causes of the ruin of the Roman Empire.[30]

The ideal army, recruited from and at one with the people, would prevent tyranny. Mercenaries, because they fight only for their employers rather than for the community at large, will find it easy to subjugate citizens. Citizen soldiers, on the other hand, with a strong conception of the public good, would be less prone to 'blind obedience' and more likely to disobey if the public good were threatened. Louis de Jaucourt, one of the contributors to the *Encyclopédie*,[31] also worried that mercenaries would lead to despotism.

Americans during the Revolution also took the position that the use of mercenaries led to tyranny. Indeed, the revolutionaries believed that England's use of German mercenaries known as Hessians indicated its decline into despotism, and demonstrated the moral bankruptcy of the English cause. The Declaration of Independence highlighted King George III's use of mercenaries as one of the prime grievances of the newly declared republic against its monarchical progenitor:

He is, at this time, transporting large armies of foreign Mercenaries, to compleat the works of death, desolation and tyranny, already begun with circumstances of cruelty and perfidy

---

[29] Jean-Jacques Rousseau, 'A Discourse on Political Economy,' in Denis Diderot (ed), *Jean-Jacques Rousseau: The Basic Political Writings* (Indianapolis and Cambridge: Hackett Publishing Company, [1755] 1987) 131. [30] Ibid.

[31] See Jaucourt's entry *Deserteur* in the *Encyclopédie*, Vol 4:881, available at <http://portail.atilf.fr/encyclopedie/>.

scarcely paralleled in the most barbarous ages and totally unworthy the Head [*sic*] of a civilized nation.[32]

In nineteenth-century Britain, an intense debate on the British decision to send mercenaries to fight in the Crimean war drew the same links between the use of mercenaries and tyranny. One member of parliament argued that 'the fact was, that wherever mercenaries were introduced there were found to be corrupt governments—there civil and religious liberty were crushed, and universal national demonization prevailed.'[33] Using mercenaries in the Crimea would put Britain in similar danger.

We can see two different echoes of the concerns voiced in the Italian renaissance and French enlightenment in relation to today's private military industry. There are concerns that both the states that host PMCs and states that hire foreign PMCs will be more likely to go to war and more prone to tyranny. Weak states like Sierra Leone, Angola, and Papua New Guinea have hired PMCs to assist them in fighting civil wars. One of the major concerns in these cases is that the PMC did not share the same conception of the common good as the hiring state, and that its interest in profit might lead to long-term problems for the state, undermining the common good.[34] This argument differs from its historical predecessors, largely because in some of these states the state's own armed forces also had no interest in the common good.[35] Critics have pointed out that attacks on the Sierra Leonean decision to hire a PMC seem odd indeed, and that the problems of the national military were such that a private company could only improve the situation. Understanding the moral argument that a citizen army provides a useful constraint on the state helps understand why these criticisms have persisted. Hiring a private company, even in a weak state where the national army is unwilling or unable to provide effective protection, denies that state the opportunity to develop the healthy relationship between the citizen and the state that constrains the state from going to war.

A second type of objection to the private military industry is that, just as mercenaries made it easier for the state to go to war and to repress its people in the past, private military and PMCs might make it easier for modern states to fight war and also reduce democratic control over war.[36] This argument finds echoes in theories

---

[32] The Declaration of Independence of the Thirteen Colonies, 4 July 1776, available at <http://www.law.indiana.edu/uslawdocs/declaration.html>.

[33] (1854–1857) Hansard: Parliamentary Debates (London and Basingstoke: Cornelius Buck), col 853.

[34] Isenberg notes this argument, David Isenberg, *Soldiers of Fortune Ltd: A Profile of Today's Private Sector Corporate Mercenary Firms* (2000 [cited]); available at <http://www.ciaonet.org/wps/isd03/>.

[35] In Sierra Leone, the state military was notoriously corrupt and prolonged the civil war. Herbert M Howe, 'Self-Help, African-Style: Nigerian Intervention in Sierra Leone Highlights New Trends in African Security,' *Armed Forces Journal*, June 1998, 44; Jimmy D Kandeh, 'Ransoming the State: Elite Origins of Subaltern Terror in Sierra Leone,' *Journal of African Political Economy*, vol 81 (1998) 349.

[36] A similar argument can be found in Deborah Avant, *The Market for Force: The Consequences of Privatizing Security* (Cambridge: Cambridge University Press, 2005), 155–6.

of the democratic peace, which argue that public opinion can exert a strong effect on making a state more reluctant to go to war, particularly if too many soldiers are killed or if soldiers' lives are placed in harm's way. As Kant argues, 'if the consent of the citizens is required in order to decide that war should be declared ... nothing is more natural than that they would be very cautious in commencing such a poor game, decreeing for themselves all the calamities of war.'[37] One objection to the private military industry is that it removes or lessens the restraints of public opinion, because the public will not notice or will be less worried about the deaths of private fighters than they would be about the killings of soldiers.[38] The use of PMCs might lead to a reduction of democracy in states which hire these companies by diminishing democratic oversight of decisions to go to war.

Many commentators have noted that PMCs are problematic because they might encourage covert wars,[39] or act as proxies in conflicts in which the state finds it politically inexpedient to get involved.[40] Both covert wars and the use of proxies allow states to enter into conflict without the usual range of democratic oversight. Even in open conflicts, the use of private military personnel instead of regular soldiers not only loosens the aforementioned constraint of public opinion but significantly reduces the number of obstacles to continuing a prolonged conflict. The current war in Iraq demonstrates the significant political obstacles to mobilizing larger numbers of troops. Because PMCs can perform a variety of military tasks, they can free up regular soldiers. The obstacles to increasing the number of PSC personnel on the ground are also far less significant than those in the way of mobilizing larger numbers of regular troops. The state might also find it easier to sustain wars that go against public opinion because of the presence of PMCs.

Another way of looking at the same problem is to argue that PMCs simply erode the citizen's duty to the state, which is important for a democracy. The fact that PMCs might not display loyalty to the community left the writers of a Green Paper, ordered by the British government to examine PMCs, 'uneasy':

To encourage such activity seems contrary both to our values and to the way in which we order society. In a democracy it seems natural that the state should be defended by its own

---

[37] Immanuel Kant, *Perpetual Peace and Other Essays*, trans Ted Humphrey (Indianapolis: Hackett Publishing Company, [1795] 1983) 113.

[38] This restraint is of course merely a restraint and cannot end war. Michael Doyle, 'Kant, Liberal Legacies and Foreign Affairs,' *Philosophy and Public Affairs*, vol 2, 3, and 4 (1983) 230.

[39] CH Enloe, 'Mercenerizaton,' in Western Massachusetts Association of Concerned African Scholars (ed), *US Military Involvement in Southern Africa*, (1978) 111; Francis, 'Mercenary Intervention' (n 22 above) 323; PW Singer, *Corporate Warriors: The Rise of the Privatized Military Industry* (Ithaca: Cornell University Press, 2003) 48; Peter Tickler, *The Modern Mercenary: Dog of War or Soldier of Honour?* (Wellingborough, Northamptonshire: Patrick Stephens, 1987) 134; Juan Carlos Zarate, 'The Emergence of a New Dog of War: Private International Security Companies, International Law, and the New World Disorder,' Stanford Journal of International Law, vol 34 (winter 1998) 148.

[40] Francis, 'Mercenary Intervention' (n 22 above) 333–4; Kevin A O'Brien, 'Military Advisory Groups and African Security: Privatised Peacekeeping?,' *International Peacekeeping*, vol 5, no 3 (1998) 78; William Reno, 'Internal Wars, Private Enterprise and the Shift in Strong State-Weak State Relations,'

citizens since it is their state. And it is not an accident that the business of fighting for money often brings in unattractive characters.[41]

It is important to note that these objections might not always tie to reality. In the United States, there are congressional oversight mechanisms on contracts with the private military industry, but these only apply when contracts involve more than $50 million and the same degree of public debate involved in sending the US military on an operation does not occur over specific contractual arrangements.[42] Furthermore, in weak states, where often no one, including the state's leadership, is much interested in protecting the common good, a well-intentioned PMC might do a great deal of good for the state, even if it is also focused on profit. Finally, the argument, as evidenced by the Green Paper, that a citizen's defence of his country is natural, and therefore that fighting for money is unnatural and will attract unsavoury individuals, ignores the fact that of course there could be citizen soldiers attracted to war for all the wrong reasons. However, these objections are all very real, and whether or not they tally with reality, they have had a significant influence on states which makes them difficult to dismiss.

The continuum of private force

Examining moral objections to private force reveals that there is perhaps more similarity between different types of private force than it first appears. Table 1.2 below summarizes the different moral objections to private force and their applicability to PMCs and mercenaries.

Discussing moral objections to the use of private force reveals that while private actors that use force might do very different jobs, and at first appear dissimilar, some moral objections apply to all types of private fighter. All the variants of private force outlined in this chapter have the potential to upset the relationship between the state and the citizen, and could make it easier for the state to use force, become tyrannical, or sustain an unpopular war. It is important to note here that this criticism relates to the state as much as it does to the private fighter. The state that decides to privatize aspects of the use of force is more morally responsible for the disruption of democratic control over the use of force than the private actor it hires. PMCs would not exist unless there was a demand for their services, and responsibility thus lies with the state. That said, the persistence of this objection to private force and its applicability to all types of private force helps explain why the mercenary label has been hard for the industry to shake off. Private fighters of all kinds are linked because they are subject to the same criticism: that they disrupt the military relationship between the citizen and the state.

International Politics, vol 37 (2000) 65; David Shearer, 'Private Military Forces and the Challenges for the Future,' *Cambridge Review of International Affairs* XIII, no 1 (1999) 82.

[41] House of Commons Foreign Affairs Committee, 'Options for Regulation' (n 18 above) 18.
[42] Avant, *Market for Force* (n 36 above) 156.

Table 1.2. Applicability of moral objections to the private military industry

	PMCs closely tied to home state	PMCs free to choose own clients	Combat PMCs	Mercenaries
Killing without an appropriate cause	No	No	Yes	Yes
Undermines the appropriate relationship between citizen and state	Yes	Yes	Yes	Yes

However, the link provided by shared criticism is the only link between these different types of private force. Objections that centre around the idea that it is morally problematic to kill for money rather than cause do not apply as obviously to non-combat PMCs, because these companies make a point of avoiding active combat where killing is likely, and indeed supply some services where the potential to use force is not part of the contract, such as translation. One of the reasons that PMCs have become more internationally acceptable is that they can avoid one of the primary criticisms levelled at mercenaries.

All the moral objections (and, indeed, some of the practical objections not outlined here) to private force can be further divided into objections about the *status* of private actors that use force and the *activities* of these actors. Objections that focus on the actions of the private military industry, like the objection that a private actor might be more likely to commit human rights abuses or lacks accountability, might be met or at least diminished with regulation that is designed to control actions. On the other hand, objections that stem from the *status* of the private military industry, based around the idea that the private use of force is morally inappropriate, cannot be met by regulation as easily. These objections are fundamental; they are not objections to what private fighters do, but an objection to what private fighters *are*: individuals or groups that exchange military services for financial gain.

Analyzing moral objections is thus crucially important in understanding the potential for regulation of the private military industry. Objections about activities might be met through regulation; the objection that private fighters do not kill for an appropriate cause can be met by changes in practice; but the objection that private force undermines the appropriate relationship between citizen and state is not so easily overcome.

Moral objections and calls for abolition of private force

Analyzing moral objections to private force also helps explain one of the dominant reactions to the increased use of private force on the international stage. While players within the industry, and indeed a number of states, have been calling for the regulation of the private military industry, an equally large number of critics, states, and organizations have called for its abolition. Abolitionist approaches to the private military industry stem directly from the fact that moral objections to private force are objections about its status rather than its activities. One way to resolve the idea that the use of private force is, in and of itself, morally problematic is to ban the use of private force entirely. The main source of abolitionism has come from the United Nations, particularly the UN Commission on Human Rights (now the Human Rights Council) and some voices in the General Assembly. Abolitionism perhaps reached its peak in the 1970s and 1980s, when the international law-making process dealing with mercenaries was at its most active and took a very hard line against mercenary activity.[43] However, the most important contemporary source of abolitionism remains the UN.

Abolitionism within the United Nations

Understanding moral objections to private force, and how they lead to abolitionism, helps explain (even if it cannot necessarily justify) the position taken by various actors within the UN system.[44] Abolitionism, based on moral objections to private force, has been strongly institutionalized within the UN and is still actively advocated by some players within it.

There are two main sources of opinion on private forces within the UN system. First, the Commission on Human Rights has been examining the question of private force since the early 1980s, and housed the Special Rapporteur on Mercenaries. Until 2004, the Special Rapporteur was Enrique Bernales Ballesteros; he was replaced by Shaista Shameem, who took a somewhat softer line on private force. In 2005 the position was abolished and replaced by a UN Working Group on Mercenaries, whose work will be discussed below.

Secondly, the General Assembly itself has been an active voice against the use of private force since the 1970s. The General Assembly has adopted over one hundred resolutions making specific reference to mercenaries and indeed, has repeated a strongly-worded resolution that calls mercenaries criminals annually since the mid-1970s.[45] General Assembly radicalism, of course, partially results from a vocal majority of states that have had experience with mercenaries (the African states) or states that use the term 'mercenary' to describe and condemn unwanted foreign actions in order to galvanize international opinion against a particular situation (Colombia, Nicaragua, and Cuba).

---

[43] For discussion of the process of law-making, see Percy, *Mercenaries* (n 5 above). The UN process is examined in depth in Percy, 'UN Security Council' (n 7 above).

[44] It is important to note here that the UN is a large body that includes a diverse range of institutional opinion. There are supporters of privatizing force within the UN, and indeed, the UN itself has used private security firms in non-combat roles. It is, however, extraordinarily difficult to get on-the-record comment about the UN's use of private security, suggesting that institutional discomfort with the idea remains.   [45] GA Resolution A/Res/31/34 (1976). Repeated annually.

The work of these two UN groups, in addition to the development of international law in the 1970s and 1980s, strongly institutionalized dislike of mercenaries on moral grounds within some bodies of the UN, particularly the General Assembly and what is now the Human Rights Council. The creation of international laws dealing with mercenaries early in their appearance on the world stage left many with a sense that mercenaries and PMCs are banned by international law, even though in reality no such explicit ban exists.[46] In addition, the mention of mercenaries in other international legal instruments, including the General Assembly's Definition of Aggression[47] and the Draft Code of Crimes against the Peace and Security of Mankind[48] meant that the idea of mercenarism as a criminal act was kept alive in other instruments. Indeed, the mere fact that mercenarism was *included* in the Draft Code alongside crimes like genocide and slavery demonstrates the degree to which international law-makers disliked the idea of private force.[49]

The repeated mention of anti-mercenarism in UN documents and in documents of international law, including the Draft Code, had a further institutionalizing effect. Those working *within* international institutions, in particular the International Law Commission and various organs of the United Nations, were left with a constant impression that mercenaries were illegal actors needing control. Thus, it is not surprising that when PMCs emerged in the 1990s they were dealt with within the parameters of existing international law and the traditional approach of the UN, regardless of whether or not PMC action was potentially good. The blind application of an existing institutional mechanism, even if it was unwitting, further reinforced the abolitionist tendency within the UN.

Neither the UN Human Rights Council nor the General Assembly distinguishes between mercenaries, PMCs, and PSCs. Ballesteros strongly argued that there was no effective difference between the three;[50] Shameem acknowledged that there might be a difference, but also indicated that companies that engage in combat ought to be included in any new international law created to regulate mercenaries.[51] The continued association between the three variants of private force is reflected in the fact that the UN Working Group on Mercenaries is the actor tasked with dealing

[46] PW Singer, 'War, Profits and the Vacuum of Law: Privatized Military Firms and International Law,' Colombia Journal of Transnational Law, vol 42, no 2 (2004) 531.
[47] GA Resolution 3314 (XXIX) 1974. Art 3(g) of the definition states that the sending of armed bands, groups, irregulars or mercenaries to carry out acts of armed force against states may constitute acts of aggression.
[48] A draft of the code is included in Timothy LH McCormack and Gerry J Simpson, 'The International Law Commission's Draft Code of Crimes against the Peace and Security of Mankind: An Appraisal of the Substantive Provisions,' *Criminal Law Forum* vol 5, no 1 (1994). It is worth noting that mercenaries and mercenarism are not included in the statute of the International Criminal Court.
[49] Mercenaries have since been removed, but the importance of their initial inclusion still stands.
[50] UN Doc A/53/338, 8. Ballesteros also argues that mercenaries and private companies are the same in UN Doc E/CN.4.2004/15, 10–11. Ballesteros was replaced in July 2004 by Shaesta Shameem, who acknowledges that there may be a difference between mercenaries and PMCs but also indicates that companies which engage in combat ought to be included in any new international law created to regulate mercenaries.   [51] UN Doc A/60/263 (2005) 17.

with the private security industry. A statement from PMCs[52] is appended to the final (2005) Special Rapporteur's report:

[I]n light of the fact that PMCs are frequently employed by UN member states and the UN own [*sic*] entities, we strongly recommend that the UN re-examine the relevance of the term "mercenary." This derogatory term is completely unacceptable and is too often used to describe fully and legal and legitimate companies engaged in vital support operations for humanitarian peace and stability operations.[53]

The continued application of the term 'mercenary' to PMCs can be explained by the shared moral objections to their use. Abolitionism, combined with a tendency to lump all private actors together, makes working through the UN to create regulation less likely. Not everyone associated with the UN thinks regulation is the best way to deal with actors who should be abolished, and the industry itself is unlikely to cooperate if it continues to be labelled 'mercenary'.

The Working Group demonstrates the influence of moral objections to private force in another way. The Group has stated that one of its main priorities is examining 'the role of the State as the primary holder of the monopoly of the use of force, and related issues such as sovereignty and State responsibility to protect and ensure respect for human rights by all actors'.[54] This focus, rather than a focus on the activities of the private military industry itself, underlines the fact that moral objections to private force are objections based on status. The Working Group is interested in private force because of *what it is*; by its nature, private force upsets conventional understandings of the monopoly on force. The notion that the state has (and ought to have) not only monopoly on the use of force but also must protect its citizens is related to the objections about tyranny outlined above.

Moral objections and a regulatory framework for private force

Moral objections and the tendency towards abolitionism suggest six sets of implications for the current regulatory debate and the shape of future regulation. First, it is important to emphasize that abolitionist concerns—based on the status of private actors, rather than their actions—are unlikely to go away; improving the behaviour of private actors and ensuring that it stays improved does not address the concerns of those who believe that it is simply wrong to privatize force.

---

[52] American Equipment Company (AMECO); Blackwater USA; Demining Enterprises International; EarthWind Holding Corporation (Groupe EHC); Hart; International Charters Incorporated (ICI) of Oregon; International Peace Operations Association (IPOA); J-3 Global Solutions; Medical Support Solutions (MSS); MPRI; Pacific Architects and Engineers (PAE); Security Support Solutions (3S); Special Operations Consulting-Security Management Group (SOC-SMG); Triple Canopy; and AEGIS signed the statement. See UN Doc A/60/263, 17 August 2005.
[53] UN Doc A/60/263, 21.
[54] UN Doc E/CN.4/2006/11, 5, 11. At the time of writing the Group planned to convene a roundtable on the subject.

Although it is difficult to overcome moral objections based on status with regulation, it is not impossible to devise regulation that takes moral concerns seriously. The second implication of moral concerns for regulation is that regulation should strictly hold PMCs to their promise of avoiding combat and try to shrink the 'grey area' between combat and non-combat operations as much as possible. Such regulation would go an extremely long way to eliminating the objection that private force is problematic because private fighters kill for money. This objection, as noted above, is already difficult to apply to today's PMCs; making it more difficult still would be a worthwhile goal of regulation.

Thirdly, regulation that forges clear links between home states and PMCs will help eliminate some of the objections about activities alluded to above. In particular regulation could reduce fears about accountability and human rights abuses. It is hard to argue that a PMC that only works for the state in which it is based undermines the sovereignty of that state. However, creating tight links between the state and PMCs will not address the concern that using private force undermines control over force, and in fact, might heighten these concerns. Unless a regulatory framework places home state PMCs under the same level of scrutiny—both in the public eye and in government—as national soldiers, then these companies can still be criticized for threatening citizens' control over the use of force. The state bears the lion's share of responsibility for ensuring that regulation, if it exists, is improved so that oversight mechanisms are enhanced, and for creating regulation where it does not exist. PMCs themselves cannot be accused of immorality on their own; they exist because of demand from states. Regulatory mechanisms are also only as weak as states wish them to be, and it remains to be seen whether or not states choose to make the use of private force more difficult.

Fourthly, although moral concerns about private force revolve mainly around what the private military industry *is* rather than what it *does*, it is important to note that a regulatory regime (rather than a ban on private force) must take the actions of companies seriously. Tables 1.1 and 1.2 demonstrate that while there is some continuity between different types of private force, there are also significant differences. A one-size-fits-all approach to private force might fail to control some of its more dangerous manifestations. This is not least because the continued activities of mercenaries should give us serious pause about the morality of external intervention in the affairs of other states, and because mercenaries continue to pose a serious practical threat to weak states.

Fifthly, a different way to deal with the role of moral objections in creating a regulatory regime is to let the objections persist. Moral objections, especially as expressed by individuals in blogs, by the press, and by human rights organizations, are in a sense the reassertion of democratic controls over the use of force. A lively public debate about the morality of PMCs can serve an informal but effective oversight role. The industry can be 'regulated' through criticism designed to hold the private military industry to high moral standards, even in the absence of formal legal standards. Making sure ethical questions continue will also ensure that regulation does not become simply a way to facilitate the profitability of companies without considering the broader impact of privatizing security.[55] While this informal role could not and should not replace more concrete regulation, it might be important not to quash moral concerns.

Finally, regulation must be more than cosmetic to deal with moral objections. Loose rules that serve to meet worries about accountability, or regulations that seek to make sure that employees of private companies are thoroughly vetted and thoroughly monitored, will do very little to address some of the deeper moral concerns about private force. Regulation might have to be more elaborate to address moral concerns, and even so, it is unlikely to make moral concerns disappear entirely.

Conclusion

Moral objections to the use of private force are far more than the self-righteous and unfounded criticisms of people who do not understand the complexities of today's private military industry. It might well be unfair to condemn mercenaries and PMCs because they fight for money rather than for belief in a cause, and it might be unjust to assume that the use of private force leads to tyranny. However, the impact of moral objections to private force cannot be denied, and in attempting to dismiss them the private military industry and its supporters look rather as though they are burying their heads in the sand.

The industry works actively to demonstrate that it is not 'mercenary' and seeks to distance itself from its more unsavoury ancestors. The difficulty is that moral objections to private force reveal there are very clear lines of descent from mercenaries through the PMCs and to the private security companies of today. While PMCs can, and have, worked hard to avoid the ethical objections regarding killing for money, they run into the same objections about tyranny as their predecessors. The disruption of the military relationship between citizen and state, in particular the removal of structures traditionally used to limit the use of force and the reduced influence of public opinion, could be leading states which use PMCs down a path that Rousseau and Machiavelli would have recognized and criticized. The obstacles created by ethical objections to the use of private force may be the only real obstacles in the way of the industry's route to genuine public acceptance. It may not be possible to remove these obstacles, as it might require significant changes in both the industry and the way we regulate it; even so, latent ethical worries may not go away. This is as it should be. If moral concerns continue to serve as a check on the state's ability to use force, and the state must work harder to start and to sustain wars, then moral objections might serve an important purpose alongside regulation.

---

[55] Domestic regulation of private security services suffers from precisely this problem. Lucia Zedner, 'Liquid Security: Managing the Market for Crime Control,' *Criminology and Criminal Justice*, vol 6, no 3 (2006).

2

What should and what should not be regulated?

Kevin A O'Brien

Since the Pretoria-based private military company (PMC)[1] Executive Outcomes (EO) first emerged publicly in late 1992, considerable international attention has been focused on the role and influence of such companies in securing and stabilizing—or destabilizing—national and regional security throughout the world. The high profile of PMCs such as EO has led to an understandable focus on their more sensational activities; such a limited focus has, however, too often skewed policy responses towards the exceptional rather than the more general problems suggested by the PMC phenomenon. The disproportionate attention is also understandable because the actions of the highest profile PMCs such as EO and its peers raise legitimate concerns about their interests in regional security. Often perceived, incorrectly, to be operating outside the laws of warfare[2] and strictly for financial gain, the background of these professional soldiers led to questions concerning their motives for becoming involved in conflict. Indeed, while the focus of attention on PMCs grew initially from an interest in tracking the involvement of EO in African countries, if EO had not come from the background it did—its personnel were almost exclusively former military and police special forces who served in the South African security forces during the apartheid era—such attention and reproach might not have been focused on the PMC sector as a whole. Too much of the international debate around regulating PMCs has focused on atypical, but high-profile companies, such as EO, Britain's Sandline International, and more recently US companies Blackwater and DynCorp, rather than on the broader spectrum of privatized military and security activities. The latter is more commonly predicated on protective security, training, or the very broad range of strategic

---

[1] This chapter will use the term 'PMC' to refer generically to any corporate entity which provides its clients with military or security services involving armed activities, and to specific corporate entities providing combat services to its clients. A distinction between these armed services and unarmed services—in the form of 'private security companies'—will be made further in this chapter, alongside distinctions between corporate and individual actors, etc. The introduction to this volume provides further delineation of these roles. [2] See chapter seven in this volume by Louise Doswald-Beck.

support activities that such companies undertake currently for Western governments as much as for developing states.

A second reason for the increased attention being paid to PMCs is the failure of
the international community to intervene successfully in regional conflicts. In the
face of an international outcry to 'do something' to halt the suffering perceived
each time on television, a blasé attitude has developed around many of these conflicts alongside a paradoxical unwillingness by the international community to
pledge the resources (military, humanitarian, or financial) to address these crises.
When PMCs become involved, they are criticized for being a 'band-aid solution'
to the crisis of the day without a long-term stabilization and peace plan being
implemented—although this is a failure of the international community and not
the PMCs themselves.

A third influence on the debate concerning regulation of PMCs is the fact that
(as clearly demonstrated in Britain's so-called 'Sandline Affair' in the spring of
1998) many of these firms operate with at least the acquiescence of major Western
governments and their security services. This brings into question just what policy
exists in Western government circles vis-à-vis such companies. In addition, the
perception—not always correct—that many of these companies operate on behalf
of Western mining and oil firms with little interest in the national wellbeing and
standard of living in the countries in which they operate has further tarnished the
image of these firms, painting them as neo-colonial exploiters of Africa.

When taken altogether, these perceptions present an extremely negative image
of the PMCs and their activities. Is this the reality, however? Why did PMCs
emerge so strongly when they did and who has supported their operations? Is there
any difference between the more 'traditional' mercenary-type operations of yester-
year which still raise their head every few years (witness the Zimbabwe-Equatorial
Guinea imbroglio of 2004) and the commercial military ventures in which modern
PMCs engage?

The perceptions internationally of PMCs as set out above may not ring true
when examining the rise and rise of the PMCs over the 1990s—and certainly
should be called into question even further when examining the role of PMCs in
the Iraq conflict. Indeed, it may be seen that, in many cases but not all, these
PMCs were much more effective in resolving conflicts in many African countries
than the international community, and that they take a much more direct interest
in the wellbeing of the populations in the countries in which they are bringing
a halt to these conflicts than the international community. Furthermore, in the
largest number of cases it has not been the fault of the PMCs that long-lasting stability and peace did not come to the countries in which they have operated, but
that of either the international community which failed to step in to secure that
peace, or of the participants in the conflict themselves who were unable to agree
to a post-conflict peace settlement following the withdrawal of the PMC peacebrokers. The situations in both Sierra Leone in 1997 and in Angola in 1996 provide respective examples of this problem.

PMCs do require regulation, given the inherent tension between a state-based international system in which the 'monopoly of violence' is (at least theoretically and originally) intended to reside in the hands of (ideally) publicly-accountable officials, and the corporate nature of private security and military companies. Determining the best approach to such regulation is essential for ensuring that public accountability and transparency is as strong as possible around PMCs' activities. If PMCs wish to develop—and be perceived to retain—the same degree of public trust and legitimate use of public violence that citizenry bestowed on the state a number of centuries ago (as Sarah Percy has noted in chapter one), then they must accept the same degree of public accountability as state institutions have. This will also go a long way towards legitimizing their activities as distinct from a more 'traditional' mercenary, and all the negative issues attached to that label.

This chapter will outline the key issues which—when examined from a broad perspective across the ever-evolving nature of the private military and security sector—must be confronted in any debate surrounding the regulation of such companies' activities. It will delineate the different types of activities which such companies undertake, as a basis for understanding why some should be considered acceptable generally while others should be considered for stronger regulation, and others restricted or prohibited. Finally, it will propose how such a classification of activities could support a regulatory regime—at either the national or international level.

Mercenaries vs PMCs and the state

The options outlined in this chapter are solely for the purposes of regulating the activities of fully-constituted companies, and not individuals involved in selling their military services and skills on an ad hoc basis. Legitimate PMCs do not constitute 'mercenaries' under any of the existing legal (national or international) or otherwise established definitions today—themselves deeply problematic. They do, however, require a degree of oversight and transparency much greater than, for example, any multi-national corporation due to the nature of their service-offerings.

While Africa was originally the focus of the popular interest in these firms (largely due to the fact that—as Angela McIntyre and Taya Weiss discuss in chapter four—the overwhelming majority of PMC operations were in Africa), outside of Africa a similar trend has emerged. In the former Soviet Union, the demobilization of hundreds of thousands of soldiers led to tens of thousands of them joining increasingly active private security firms, often involved in questionable dealings with the various elements of both organized crime and the security services of the former Soviet Union. Private 'security' companies (PSCs) have proliferated in Russia in particular since 1990, with—by 1999—well over 12,000 registered formally with the Russian government. This movement into the private sector has also been the case throughout Central Asia and the Pacific Rim, where demobilized combatants from guerrilla and low-intensity conflicts have sold their services to a variety of organized crime units involved in arms trafficking, prostitution, child slavery, and the drugs trade. Finally, in Latin America, the various drug cartels and families have, since the early 1980s, organized private armies composed of former soldiers, intelligence personnel, and mercenaries from throughout the Americas, in order not only to defend their interests against each other and the various governments, but also to take a proactive role against these same 'opponents' in order to maximize their portion of the narcotics trade. These latter cases are clearly examples of the extremely negative image of the mercenary.

Iraq presents a very different scenario—one not fully imagined by policy commentators on this topic in the 1990s: a situation where—during a full-blown conflict involving Western military forces—both national and multinational corporate actors required the services of highly-active PMCs to protect corporate assets in-country, in order to allow the country's services to be established and function. The national military forces involved in the conflict refused outright to provide this service, concentrating wholly on combating their enemies while attempting to establish and train a new national military in-country. Therefore, as noted in chapter five by David Isenberg, PMCs in Iraq operate in a parallel role to national statutory forces, where the PMCs' concerns are the infrastructure and corporate services (and service providers) in the country, costing an estimated $30 billion in 2003 alone; indeed, at the end of 2003, PMC personnel ranked second numerically— after the US contingent and before the British—in terms of armed personnel in Iraq.[3] This has resulted not only in a scenario never envisioned previously for PMCs, but also a renewed interest in the regulation of these activities—including amongst countries where no such interest was previously evident.

Given that war-fighting and security have traditionally been the domain of the state, the transfer of these capabilities to private corporations has launched a debate on the usefulness and involvement of these firms in security activities around the world, as well as on determining what steps should and can be taken to regulate such bodies, making them accountable to either national governments or some form of international authority. Under the current international system, national military forces are controlled through the civilian political leaders in their respective countries (within the democracies), who in turn regulate and control the activities of these forces in order to (ideally) make their usage always fall within national or international legal statutes and controls. The privatization of these activities cannot be controlled in the same manner, given that enterprises which enter into commercial agreements with other governments have not, traditionally, fallen under the rubric of military oversight or arms control.

But is this 'privatization of violence' a threat to regional or international security and stability? The nature of the organizations that are increasingly taking on the role of either (sometimes both) exploiter or peacemaker may lead one to believe this.

---

[3] Ian Traynor, 'The Privatization of War,' *The Guardian*, 10 December 2003.

These organizations are more business-like, motivated, funded, and governed—largely through a network of corporate fronts—than any other such entities have been since before the rise in dominance of the nation-state.

In discussing this 'privatization of war' (alternately known as the 'privatization of violence'), the environment in which they operate is key to appreciating their evolution. Within the relationship between sovereignty and security, the disintegration of Westphalian notions of state sovereignty—including their allied Weberian notion of the 'monopoly of violence' of the state—and the effects that this has on security and war cannot be underestimated when looking at conflict resolution and post-conflict reconstruction. Much of this 'monopoly' no longer resides with the state—especially in the developing world—but with agents which it has brought in. In numerous cases witnessed over the last two decades—EO in Sierra Leone, the plethora of PMCs in Iraq, and new initiatives in Liberia by DynCorp and MPRI—'public security' was being provided by a private, commercial actor where the state's instruments of such 'public security' were either insufficient, corrupt, or non-existent. Therefore, in a seemingly-paradoxical manner, private, commercial military, and security actors were reconstructing the state and its provision of public security to its citizenry while, at the same time, deconstructing the state's monopoly on armed force and public violence.

Coupled with the current general trend towards globalization and privatization, and the failures of the international community to respond to each and every massive humanitarian crisis effectively, it is little wonder that we are witnessing a substantial growth in private security today.

Thus, the question remains as to whether such corporations should be allowed to engage in the provision of security and other military-related capabilities without being placed more clearly under the national and international laws of warfare, or whether 'private enterprise'—as many pundits and critics see this—should be allowed to flourish in the same way that other industries are governed. The answer to this question is of increasing importance: while this privatization of warfare emerges as a force in regional security, it is demonstrating the capability and willingness to assume the role of peacekeeper or—more often—peacemaker in a variety of regional conflicts, either alongside or in place of the international bodies that have traditionally undertaken such missions. Given that such operations have generally been governed by international consensus as derived through a UN mandate, making it acceptable for commercial organizations to undertake such activities could be perceived to place them outside of such international consensus and therefore outside of such restrictions or controls that may exist through international law.

This is not to say that the role of private organizations in the world's trouble spots is anything new: increasingly, private humanitarian and relief organizations (such as Médecins Sans Frontières, the International Red Cross, CARE, and other groups) have been replacing UN agencies and funds in providing relief support in these trouble spots. Should the provision of security be any different in this regard?

Any long-term examination of the issues noted here will have to strike a balance
between idealized notions of the international security system and a more pragmatic utilitarianism. Ultimately, pragmatism must win the day: previously, many
commentators argued strongly against PMCs becoming the supplemental wings of
national armed forces—the negative example of the use of MPRI by the US State
and Defense Departments as 'surrogate training forces' in Croatia and Bosnia being
but one example of this caution. Indeed, Ken Silverstein warned against this when
he stated that 'the use of private military contractors allows the United State to pursue its geopolitical interests without deploying its own army, this being especially
useful in cases where training is provided to regimes with ghastly human rights
records'.[4] However, with over a decade's view on these issues, the frequent inability
or unwillingness of the international community to respond to complex emergencies in the developing world has led some to now consider options for such private
actors to operate in support of national interests and objectives.

Ultimately, though, the danger exists that, in such a situation, the impetus for
helping secure stability and peace for a people surrounded by war could become
lost, and the state's interests—whether national or mercantilist—become interventionist in another country, something prohibited under such norms of non-
intervention as Article 2(4) of the UN Charter, and only condoned under the
strictest of UN mandates. The deployment of private military forces as a tool of
state policy must, therefore, be avoided.

Surveying the landscape: differentiating companies, differentiating capabilities

What constitutes a 'company' for these purposes? 'Mercenaries' vs PSCs and PMCs

One of the greatest challenges for both policy and law enforcement lies in defining
the activities and actors in this area. The definition of 'mercenary' contained in
Article 47 of the First Additional Protocol of 1977 to the Geneva Conventions is
generally unworkable as a legal instrument: not only does it define the actor rather
than the activity, but to be construed as a 'mercenary' under its parameters, all six
elements of the definition must apply to an individual.

Such international definitions and conventions are either impractical for legal
purposes or (especially in the case of the OAU Convention for the Elimination of
Mercenarism in Africa, which was designed to stop neighbouring African rivals
from hiring mercenaries against each other) irrelevant to the most important issues.

---

[4] Ken Silverstein, 'Privatizing War: How Affairs of State Are Outsourced to Corporations Beyond
Public Control,' *The Nation* (28 July–4 August 1997) 4.

In many cases it has been the signatories of such conventions that have hired mercenary forces for their own interests—thus laying bare the hypocrisy inherent in much of the debate. For this reason, these conventions are quite rightly not supported by many countries—including Britain.

Rather than rely on such conventions, this chapter proposes that the activity and nature of the actor need to be taken into account; for these purposes, this study divides such 'private' actors into four categories: mercenaries, private armies, militias and warlords, private security companies, and private military companies. Previously, the latter—PMCs—had generally been defined[5] as any corporate entity which provided an armed service; however, Iraq has begun to change this distinction between PMCs and PSCs, especially as PSC staff are increasingly armed in such situations, thereby blurring the line between these two. Given the example of Iraq—alongside an understanding and assessment of which activities inform or are intended to influence or change the prevailing strategic landscape of any conflict— it is likely that PMCs will now be defined far more rigidly than before, with PSCs being seen as more 'the norm' and PMCs—and their associated activities—the exception.

Mercenaries

A *mercenary* is the traditional soldier, having only been replaced as an accepted combatant at the time of the French Revolution when national ideals were tied inextricably to military service. In modern times, the term 'mercenaries' has become a pejorative one, conjuring up an image of a hardened white soldier brutally intervening in a small, hitherto unknown African country for financial gain, or an 'international brigader' fighting through the streets of Srebrenica. Mercenaries, in this more traditional sense, continue to be active worldwide, as witnessed in the 1990s. The 'White Legion' during the 1996–1997 Zaïrian conflict is typical of the way mercenaries have been employed since the end of the Second World War. This unit of approximately 300 personnel was reportedly trained by former French Presidential Guard (GSPR) officer Colonel Alain Le Carro, former Gendarme Robert Montoya,

---

[5] See, eg, the extensive writings of this author on this topic: Kevin A O'Brien, 'Military Advisory Groups and African Security: Privatised Peacekeeping?' in *International Peacekeeping* vol 5, no 3 (autumn 1998) 78–105; 'Private Military Companies in Africa 1990–1998' in Kayode Fayemi & Musa al-Fateh (eds), *Mercenaries in Africa* (Pluto Books, 1999); 'Privatising Security, Privatising War? The New Warrior Class and Regional Security' in Paul Rich (ed), *Warlords in International Relations* (Palgrave Press, 1999); 'PMCs, Myths and Mercenaries: The Debate on Private Military Companies,' *RUSI Journal* (February 2000) 59–64; 'Freelance Forces: Exploiters of old or new-age peacebrokers?,' *Jane's Intelligence Review* vol 10, no 8 (August 1998) 42–6. See also Kim Richard Nossal, 'Roland Goes Corporate: Mercenaries and Transnational Security Corporations in the Post-Cold War Era,' *Civil Wars* vol 1, no 1 (spring 1998); J Cilliers and R Cornwell (eds), *Peace, Profit and Plunder: The Privatization of Security* (Pretoria: Institute for Security Studies, 1999); William Reno, 'African Weak States and Commercial Alliances,' *African Affairs*, no 96 (1997); Elizabeth Rubin, 'An Army of One's Own,' *Harper's Magazine*, vol 294, no 1761 (February 1997); Ken Silverstein, 'Privatising War: How Affairs of State are Outsourced to Corporations Beyond Public Control,' *The Nation* (28 July–4 August 1997).

and the Serbian commando, Lieutenant Milorad Palemis. The unit, composed of mercenaries from Serbia, Morocco, Angola, Mozambique, South Africa, Belgium, France, and Britain, was fighting for President Mobuto Sese Seko; following the defeat of Mobutu, they were reported to have moved south to Congo-Brazzaville, where they fought for the besieged Lissouba government in Brazzaville.[6] Other examples of modern mercenaries include dispossessed former combatants flooding out of conflicts in the former Soviet Union and Balkans; Ukrainians in Angola and Sierra Leone for both sides; specialist pilots in Zaïre, Congo-Brazzaville, Angola, Sierra Leone, Liberia, and Guinea-Bissau; Israeli, British, and American former special forces personnel in Mexico, Colombia, and the Iron Triangle training security forces of drug cartels; and former Spetznazsi and KGB personnel involved with the Russian mafia.

Mercenaries continue to exist across Africa and other parts of the world. More often than not, however, the role and presence of African mercenaries is overlooked by both national and international governments, as well as the media and international NGOs involved in these conflicts. It is the presence of African mercenaries (either individually, through tribal affiliations, or through the forcing of intervention by external national government actors with private interests and concerns in foreign conflicts throughout the continent) that far outweighs the presence of any Western (that is, 'white') foreign actors involved in Africa's conflicts.

While such activities have continued unabated, there has been a gradual change from the type of mercenary activity witnessed in the period following decolonization in Africa during the 1960s (for example, the interventions in the Belgian Congo by 'Black-Jacques' Schramme or 'Mad Mike' Hoare) to a situation where far more 'mercenaries' originate either domestically or in a neighbouring country, seeking the only lifestyle that they know. While today's mercenary may, therefore, be more 'reflective' than those of the past, it is also clear that the reasoning which pulls such people in is no longer a motivation based solely on monetary compensation, but also by a self-awareness that this is the only lifestyle which such an individual could have. This final point is a key problem in dealing with this 'new warrior' movement, as Ralph Peters refers to it.[7] The failure of re-education or training programmes to provide hope to former combatants has, no doubt, played a major role in making them continue life as warriors. Whether as guerrillas or members of statutory forces, for these men, who have spent the last two to three decades in combat, the realization that they do not fit into civil society has been a prime motivator in this tendency towards mercenary activity.

---

[6] French intelligence, according to the New York Times, allegedly used the company Geolink as a cover for the provision of these mercenary forces: 'French Covert Actions in Zaïre on behalf of Mobutu,' AFP, 2 May 1997; UNDHA Integrated Regional Information Network, IRIN Emergency Update No 74 on the Great Lakes, 8 January 1997; Robert Block, 'Mobutu Calls Up the Dogs of War,' *The Sunday Times*, 5 January 1997; John Swain, 'War-Hungry Serbs Join Mobutu's Army,' *The Sunday Times*, 9 March 1997; 'Fighting Intensifies; Militia Accuses Mercenaries of Joining,' SAPA-AP, 30 June 1997.   [7] Ralph Peters, 'The New Warrior Class,' *Parameters*, summer 1994, 16–26.

Private armies, militias, and warlords

Private armies, militias, and warlords continue to be dominant in many conflicts. These groupings of private forces represent the next rung up from mercenaries. Although such forces can include mercenaries in organized numbers (such as 5 Commando in the Belgian Congo during its wars of the 1960s), these groupings do not always have a national outlook to their conflict; indeed, these groups can often be transnational, supported by whatever country they can obtain funds and hardware from at any given time, and fight simply for control of a region or resource. Such diverse entities as transnational terrorist organizations, religiously-motivated combatant groups (such as those supported by the Islamic Brotherhood), and leaders such as John Garang in Sudan all fall into this category. They do, however, fight with more organization than mercenaries and their efforts are more directed over longer periods of time.

Private security companies

Private security companies (PSCs) first began to emerge on the world stage as long ago as the sixteenth century, when Italian mercantilism meant rival commerce families hired security elements against each other to control their businesses. This evolved, during the next few centuries, into the security elements of the great colonial exploration companies such as the Dutch Jan Compagnie and the British South Africa Company; even the British East India Company and the Dutch East Indies Company retained security elements partly seconded from their own national forces. PSCs evolved throughout the 1950s and 1960s, mostly in Africa, but also in Asia and Latin America. The most infamous of these were the operations by Sir Percy Stilltoe, a high-ranking British counter-espionage expert from the Second World War, who was hired in the 1950s by Harry Oppenheimer of DeBeers. Oppenheimer contracted Sir Percy to establish intelligence networks in Sierra Leone and use mercenaries to eliminate diamond-smuggling, forcing all to sell to DeBeers.[8] While most often they are accused of being 'mercenary forces' engaged in 'criminal activities and violations of human rights' (as was stated in the UN Commission on Human Right reports on the 'Use of Mercenaries as a Means of Violating Human Rights and Impeding the Exercise of the Right of Peoples to Self-Determination'),[9] there is a clear distinction between the more traditional mercenary forces and those engaged in high-profile, high-risk private security operations.

---

[8] Peter Klerks, 'South African Executive Outcomes or Diamonds Are a Grunt's Best Friend,' *Intelligence Newsletter* No 55 (10 March 1997); Pratap Chatterjee, 'Mercenary Armies and Mineral Wealth,' *Covert Action Quarterly* (fall 1997).

[9] Enrique Bernales Ballesteros, *The Right of Peoples to Self-Determination and its Application to Peoples under Colonial or Alien Domination or Foreign Occupation: Report on the question of the use of mercenaries as a means of violating human rights and impeding the exercise of the right of peoples to self-determination* (Geneva: UNCHR, 17 January 1996) sA22.

Where, ten years ago, such a category was composed of individuals primarily tasked with personal and installation protection, PSCs have grown to such a degree that today they are organized along corporate lines (including boards of directors, share-holdings, and corporate structures), their work has a clear contractual aim and obligation to their clients, and many of them now include capabilities in transport, intelligence, combat-firepower, and para-medical skills. While in an increasing number of cases—not just in Iraq but also in other parts of the world— PSC employees are armed in defence of their asset (an installation, an individual, a piece of land, a population, or an NGO), the security and military skills are tactical in nature and not aimed at shifting the strategic landscape in which they operate beyond the immediate situations at hand. Examples of such companies today include ArmorGroup/Defence Systems Ltd, Janusian Security, Olive Security, Erinys, Groupo-4, Aegis, The Corps of Commissionaires, and KMS.

PSCs can also include private intelligence or information brokers, which include competitive intelligence or risk analysis and information brokers (such as Control Risks, Oxford Analytica, the Economist Intelligence Unit), and 'hard-core' private intelligence firms (such as in Romania, where—by the end of the 1990s—there were believed to be more than 160 private intelligence agencies all run by former State Security or military intelligence personnel; or in Russia where by 1994 there were 6,605 'private security enterprises or security services companies', and 26,000 private investigation licences were issued by the Ministry of Interior).[10]

Private military companies

Private military companies are the ultimate evolution in capabilities and level-of-operation.[11] They engage in military operations—across the spectrum where necessary, something most PSCs traditionally have not undertaken—and operate under contracts in which their activities are designed to change the prevailing strategic environment in which they operate (such as defeating an insurgency, ending a war, undertaking peacekeeping or peace-enforcement operations, rescuing a besieged government), especially in zones of conflict in the developing world.

Lethality is not the only yardstick by which such companies need to be judged, however: other activities—such as military advisory services and advanced training—can also act to change the strategic landscape, as MPRI's alleged support for the Croatian military did in Operation Storm in 1995. However, this does not mean that all such services are to be judged the same: military training aimed at professionalizing or integrating developing world militaries will have a strategic impact but are not necessarily aimed at achieving the same outcome as a combat operation. Therefore, an appreciation of these differences must be had before deciding on the best course of regulation. In this category, therefore, one would find— at the sharp end—Executive Outcomes (South Africa), AirScan (United States),

---

[10] O'Brien, 'PMCs, Myths and Mercenaries' (n 5 above).   [11] Ibid.

Levdan (Israel), Gurkha Security Guards Limited (Britian), and Sandline International (Britain), and, at the softer end of the spectrum, companies such as ArmorGroup/Defence Systems Limited (Britain), MPRI (United States), KMS and its subsidiary Saladin Security, the Corps of Commissionaires (which has operated since the end of the nineteenth century), and BDM/Vinnell Corp (United States). Companies such as Aegis and DynCorp would include capabilities in both the sharp (for example, its operations in Colombia in support of Plan Colombia) and soft categories (for example, its protective services in Afghanistan, its monitoring activities in Kosovo, or its advisory and professionalization services in Liberia). Another well-known company—ArmorGroup/DSL—was hired throughout the 1980s and into the 1990s by international organizations such as the World Bank, the United Nations, and various humanitarian NGOs to protect their personnel and assets in regions of conflict; at the same time, DSL provided Military Assistance Training Teams (MATTs) to British government partners in the developing world, operating in Africa throughout the 1980s including Mozambique, Sudan, and Kenya, to name a few.[12] In this sense, companies such as ArmorGroup/DSL, DynCorp, Aegis and similar span the capabilities of both PSCs and PMCs—a reason for emphasizing the activity in any assessment of the private military and security realm, as opposed to focusing too narrowly on the companies.

There are differences in the composition of the PMC sector. While the strongest companies exist along established, corporate lines (such as EO, Sandline, DSL, and MPRI), there are many operating internationally that, while calling themselves 'companies', are little more than glorified mercenary operations, existing often for short periods of time only (such as South Africa's Stabilco, France's Secrets, and Britian's Security Advisory Services Ltd). There are also differences in the services that these firms provide. These can be divided between those PMCs that provide military services up to and including combat operations (the 'active') and those who provide training and support only (the 'passive'). Thus far, while EO and Sandline International were the principal firms to provide combat capabilities, many of the other firms could easily develop this capability (especially MPRI and DSL).

The importance of defining activities

The point of making these distinctions is that the line between mercenaries, PSCs, and PMCs is often blurred: individuals who previously engaged in what could be defined as 'mercenary' activity (that is, selling their skills on the open military market without a corporate affiliation) might be employed by either a PMC or PSC; PSCs involved in site protection might cross the line into offensive military operations. For this reason, defining the intended activity—based around the entity (rather than the other way around)—is crucial to approaching the issue of regulation.

---

12 Interview, ArmorGroup officer—London, June 1998.

In all of these senses, therefore, when considering regulation, two further points need to be noted. First, given that the regulatory focus should be on the individual actors and their activities (rather than attempting to categorize individuals and activities explicitly by labels such as mercenary, PSC, or PMC, given the problem with this categorization noted above), the distinction between individual actors and those working for companies is important for assigning responsibility. Individuals operating on their own—who generally will continue to constitute mercenaries due to the lack of possible or potential oversight and accountability present—must be considered differently from the individuals that sell their services to a company (PSC or PMC) who then on-sell those services as part of their overall corporate offering. In the latter case, the company is responsible for their employees in every sense: screening their backgrounds against acceptable criteria for hiring and employment (including both psycho-social issues, such as criminality, and professional issues, such as existing, proven skills and training), and being responsible for their activities both within the company and 'on mission'.

The second issue is the capabilities and credibility of the various entities in question. Too often, companies claim that they and their employees have professional, trained military skills to support a military mission, when they do not. Such 'cowboys' invite criticism of the industry but also endanger their clients and the operating environment in which they find themselves. Ensuring, therefore, that each PSC or PMC is actually qualified—through its personnel—in the areas that it offers services in and seeks contracts for is as essential as ensuring that the company is then responsible for those personnel during the lifetime of their employment. Both of these elements will enhance the legitimacy of the industry.

Distinctions in service offerings

Distinctions have to be made, therefore, between actors and their activities. But when considering regulatory activities, the most important distinction is between contracted operations that aim to alter the strategic landscape, and those involving local—in the narrowest sense—immediate impact only.[13] Under such a regulatory regime, the activities of PMCs (in the broad sense used in this volume) should be further distinguished. A first category of activities involves *military operations* by private actors intended to alter the strategic environment. These would include offensive and defensive operations, including operational combat support (logistics, air-support, intelligence, and so on); peacekeeping, peace-support or peace-enforcement operations (including as part of a national military contribution); military advisory services (including training) in support of national

---

[13] Immediate impact activities include transport, force professionalization training (both regular and irregular), para-medical services, physical (both personal and installation) guarding, humanitarian aid convoy protection, refugee protection, administration and logistics, and other non-front-line services—including potentially law enforcement and policing in countries in transition without the capability to provide this themselves.

military objectives;[14] and intelligence services in support of national security objectives (whether in support of another government, of a third-country government in a state of conflict; of commercial operations in a third country; or in support of national military objectives, whether war-fighting or humanitarian). A second category might include *military-support operations* by private actors—those operations not in themselves intended to alter the strategic environment of an ongoing conflict. These would include professionalization or integration training (both regular and irregular) and logistics (whether in support of another government, of a third-country government not in a state of conflict, or of commercial operations in a third country). A third category would include defensive or protective security operations by private actors—both large-scale installation and asset protection, or small-scale personnel protection. Finally, a fourth category would cover non-lethal security operations, basically those with local/immediate impact—including private (tactical, law enforcement or otherwise non-national security-related) intelligence support and law enforcement and policing in countries in transition without the capability to provide this themselves, as well as transport, paramedical services, humanitarian-aid convoy protection, refugee protection, administration and logistics, and other non-frontline services.

Such an appreciation lays the ground for introducing regulation of those activities—generally in the first category—which require strong oversight and accountability, and those activities—generally in the subsequent categories—over which there are lesser concerns.

Establishing a regulatory regime

Despite the concerns over 'costs', 'timeliness', and 'effectiveness' that are often raised in protest to government-imposed regulation of such activities, regulation should and must be undertaken by national governments; failure to do so would result in a potentially serious gap in existing legislation dealing with both the export of military services and corporate international responsibility.[15] It must, however, also be recognized fully that these companies (at the very least, since the late 1960s with companies such as WatchGuard International and KMS in Britain and Vinnell in the United States, as examples) have long assisted Western governments with operational interests overseas, supporting, or even supplanting military,

---

[14] The PMCs previously active in combat-support and combat operations (ie EO and Sandline International) have argued that there cannot be training without participation in front-line combat operations. This author would take a pragmatic approach to this *when dealing with a situation of armed conflict* (as opposed to a country at peace where personnel were engaged in force professionalization training for the sake of national stability—which falls under the second category): while personnel involved in training should not be prohibited from accompanying their trainees to the front line, they should generally provide support only and not actively engage in combat.

[15] See further chapter nine in this volume by Marina Caparini.

security, or intelligence forces in regions of the world where statutory forces could not officially be brought to bear. While Britain's practice in this regard has traditionally been much quieter than the more openly-declared operations of the US government in the same respect, this has been a long-standing practice for both governments and PMCs alike. The spotlight that has now been cast on this issue, however, means that this long-standing practice now demands regulation.

Any regulatory framework must—to be as holistic as possible—ensure both national and international regulation is introduced, as well as ensuring that it is clear on what it aims to regulate. Such an approach to regulatory options must include the distinction between the act and the actor, as well as offences and limitations (that is, allowable versus prohibited activities), including specifically support to national military operations in zones of conflict, combat services in zones of conflict, and so-called 'privatized peacekeeping' by PMCs in zones of conflict. The nature of the regulatory authority (such as any enforcement or oversight body, nationally and internationally) must also be considered, as enforcement will be the most difficult pillar of any such framework.

A model national regulatory regime

A national regulatory framework should include all of the following elements: first, a definition of allowable activity, controlling both the actor and activity; second, licensing provisions; third, certification and standardization by some licensing regime; fourth, the power to introduce recall, censure, and sanctions against companies that break the regulatory framework; and, fifth, the ability to prosecute those companies which engage in illegality.

In terms of allowable activity, outright bans on either military activity abroad or on recruitment for military activity abroad are neither practical nor enforceable. Any moves towards self-regulation, however, or company or industry codes of conduct, while laudable for the companies concerned, must take as a baseline respect for and governance by existing international and domestic laws of the sending and the host state. Compliance with such laws should be assumed of all such companies: it will be 'bad for business', in a number of respects, if they are known to be breaching the law in their operations.

A regulatory regime should also include a licensing regime for military services, some form of registration and notification of both companies and contracts, and a general licence for PMCs. The first step under such a regime would involve certifying and licensing the company: the government would first confirm that a company has the capabilities, administrative set-up, and sufficient powers and structure to conduct business in the manner in which it is proposing, and would then license individual companies for a range of activities possible in a specified list of countries. To operate in countries other than those listed on the licence, the company would have to obtain prior clearance based on ministerial decision. In so doing, the agreement could set out standards it expected the companies to meet, for example that they should not employ people with criminal records or ex-servicemen without an honourable discharge. In Britain the Security Industry Authority (SIA), which regulates the domestic security market, offers an 'Approved Contractor Scheme' that might serve as a basis for such certification and licensing. This step would serve to legitimize the company and its employees.

A second step, involving licensing the service capabilities of that company, would require companies to obtain a licence to undertake contracts for military and security services abroad. The activities for which licences are issued would be defined in the licence, and would be based upon an assessment that the company reaches a standard required for each of the services it offers. The services that the company could be authorized to undertake with this licence would include the second, third, and fourth category of activities defined earlier; activities under the first category—military operations aimed at changing the strategic environment—would require further certification on an individual basis. As long as the activity required in a contract matched the activities agreed in the company licence, the company would not require further authorization; should the contract require activities outside the scope of the company licence, then ministerial approval would be required—in addition to potential re-licensing of the company.

Such activities could be further divided between 'General Activities' (including a wide range of non-lethal activities), 'Operational Support Activities' (including services which provide active support to client requirements in an operational role, such as law enforcement or support to military operations), and 'Lethal Activities' (including the upper-end of support to military operations and combat services). 'General Activities' would be included as authorized under the basic licence; 'Operational Support Activities' would require notification to an industry authority—as long as the activity fell within the general confines of the company licence; finally, 'Lethal Activities' would require further authorizations or licensing—however, the circumstances under which a company could provide 'Lethal Activities' will be much restricted (see 'Prohibited or Constrained Activities').

The distinguishing characteristic between 'General Activities' and 'Lethal Activities' would be a determination as to whether such an activity would construe an 'act which would seek to change the prevailing political balance' in the country in which the activity was being carried out, and would consequently see the participants from a PMC become involved as combatants as understood by international humanitarian law. 'Operational Support Activities' would not go this far, but might include more direct involvement of the company in the internal activities of the country in which the contract is being fulfilled than would 'General Activities'. A schematic outline of these activities is included in Table 2.1 below.

The third step would require notification of individual contracts: companies would be required to notify the industry authority of each contract obtained; such information would be held in a central, controlled, and proprietary database. This would avoid any government claiming that it was not aware of what its corporations were up to, and would ensure a second level of oversight on such contracts.

Table 2.1. Classification of activities by PMCs

Lethal Activities	Combat Services
	Front-line/In-the-field Support to Military Operations
Operational Support Activities	Rear-Area/Training Support
	Force Professionalization Training
	Personal/Personnel Protection Services
	Physical (Installation) Guarding
	Military Advisory Services
	Intelligence Support
	Law Enforcement and Policing Services
General Activities	Procurement Advice
	Para medical Services
	Transport
	Administration and Logistics
	Humanitarian Aid Convoy Protection
	Refugee Protection

Finally, a fourth step would require all contracts for strategic military operations (the first category above) to be certified. For those activities under this category, individual ministerial approval would be required (in whichever country) to ensure that corporations operating from a given country were not conducting strategic operations in another country that were against the policies and wishes of their original country. As international humanitarian law and other international legal provisions remain primarily focused on states, the state has to retain responsibility for such activities.[16]

Such an 'ideal' licensing regime would ensure transparency of the company and the contract. It would also ensure that the companies are limited to the activities described, required to seek authorization for activities that fall outside of the initial licence. A sufficient and enforceable punishment and prosecution regime would have to be in place to ensure that breaches of these licensed parameters were met. Such a regime would also ensure client confidentiality between the contractor and contractee, and would avoid delays as the licensed activities would be spelled out clearly from the beginning.

Difficulties would continue to exist, the biggest one being the extraterritoriality of most of these activities. Since the activity which is licensed takes place abroad, it would be difficult to know (or prove) whether the terms of the licence were breached, though transparency conditions could be included in the licence: for example, licensees could be required to facilitate access to places where their activities were taking place. While companies not wishing to be subject to a licensing regime could move their operations offshore, this might mark them as being less

---

[16] See further chapter eight in this volume by Chia Lehnardt.

than wholly respectable; alternatively, the law could be extended to all citizens, both living in their country of nationality and abroad, thereby ensuring that even those operating offshore would be subject to the regime.

Prohibited or constrained activities

Activities that would be prohibited under such a regime would include operations by individuals rather than companies, which would be seen as 'mercenary' activity in the traditional sense and therefore prohibited.

A second category of excluded activities would be combat services in zones of conflict. Companies should be allowed to undertake physical security aspects of private security operations but these should always be defensive or protective in nature, and generally should not include offensive operations. This raises the very difficult issue of 'hot pursuit' or 'offensive defence', where attacks by opponent forces on areas, individuals, or installations protected by a PMC lead to the PMC pursuing the opponent forces away from the site of the attack—or, as happened in a number of cases (notably EO in Sierra Leone and Angola), engaging in pre-emptive offensive measures against opponent forces for defensive purposes. A pragmatic attitude should be taken towards this issue: the overwhelming majority of PMCs are composed of retired professional military officers and other ranks from (largely) Western forces, with a great deal of professionalism. The companies should be aware that they will have to justify any and all such activities to the home-country government after-the-fact, and therefore should be allowed—within the terms of the licence—to exercise best judgement in such a situation. This is not to say that blanket authorization should be granted for such operations; rather, that these operations should be construed as being wholly reactive to such threats. This will avoid breaches of the suggested ban on combat operations.

Such a prohibition should not include contracting by the home government to support either national stability operations in foreign zones of conflict in support of national armed forces, or supplementing or supplanting national armed forces in international peacekeeping operations in foreign zones of conflict. This so-called 'privatized peacekeeping' by PMCs in zones of conflict should be allowed for companies operating under direct contract to the home-country government. This should be allowed for a number of reasons. First, as noted in the opening to this chapter, due to the inabilities of the limited resources of many Western armed forces today to meet each and every crisis, humanitarian disaster, or so-called 'complex emergency', PMCs could be licensed to undertake these operations in support of national interests and objectives. In addition, it is clear that the United Nations is moving towards a situation (particularly through DPKO) where PMCs will be used in ever-greater capacities from their current existence as protectors and defenders of humanitarian aid operations in zones of conflict. In the not-too-distant future, the United Nations may be willing to accept (as the OSCE's Kosovo Verification

Mission did from the US firm DynCorp) the substitution by national governments of private-sector actors for national military forces—although whether this occurs for both monitoring missions and armed interventions remains to be seen. Finally, perhaps the greatest argument for such activities to be allowed is that many Western governments have traditionally done this for decades. Companies such as DSL (ArmorGroup) have long supplanted, under contract, the role of— for example—British Military Assistance Training Teams to numerous developing world countries in transition. The continuation of such activities should be encouraged.

Such a prohibition should not include support to national military operations in zones of conflict. As such support is either currently in place (in various forms) or being considered for the British Armed Forces, it would be impossible to ban it for British companies operating abroad. Such support could include any number of aspects (such as transport, intelligence, training, and para medical skills). In addition, arms brokering should be kept separate from licensing PMC activities and continue to be subject to the existing arms-export controls in Britain. Where crossovers occur, they should be noted on the PMC licence, but not authorized under this regulatory regime.

An industry authority

Existing international and national norms for regulation will be covered in other chapters in this volume. This brings us to the final question—alongside the above questions of 'what should be regulated?' and 'how should it be regulated?'—to 'who should regulate'? What body should govern any such licensing and regulatory regime? As Marina Caparini outlines in chapter nine, there are three clear models now in place. The first is South Africa, where the National Conventional Arms Control Committee (NCACC) of the South African Parliament is responsible for overseeing the Regulation of Foreign Military Assistance Act 1998 in all of its parameters. The second is the United States, where the US Arms Export Control Act 1968 regulates both arms brokering and the export of military services through the US Department of State Office of Export Controls, which oversees the International Transfer of Arms Regulations (ITAR)—granting licence to those companies which meet the requirements. The government maintains the right to take action to confirm that licensing provisions are being met. In addition to this licensing procedure, congressional notification is required before the US government approves exports of defence services worth in excess of $50 million. Even with the Iraq situation, this has not changed in its basic approach. Finally, in Britain, the Department of Trade and Industry is currently responsible—in consultation with the Home Office and the Foreign and Commonwealth Office—for overseeing the parameters of the existing strategic arms export controls in Britain. Such a similar approach—treating 'military services' as part of strategic arms exports—is another possible consideration.

International regulatory options: the importance of co-ordination

Even with an effective and comprehensive national regulatory regime for the activities and actors outlined here, any such regulation will only be partially effective; should a company not wish to be subject to the regulations put in place under such a regime in its home country, it can currently (and would still be able to once any regime is put in place subject to these recommendations) simply move offshore or to another country without such regulations and operate from there. Any national regulatory regime will be incomplete without complementary international regulations.

As indicated earlier, existing international legal instruments are either inadequate or impractical. It would, therefore, be desirable for governments to pursue at the international level the same approach advocated here for the national level, with a comparable international regime and separate authority. This approach might also be pursued through the European Union, as part of attempts to standardize a common approach to law enforcement, legislative, juridical, and security considerations across EU member states.

Finally, a 'level playing field' approach is required internationally between countries as well: it would be both unfair to, and commercially unproductive for, PMCs to have to deal with broadly different regulatory regimes in allied Western countries. Any standardized approach to national regulation in this sense should be encouraged strongly.

Conclusions and summary of recommendations

As a model of regulation, this chapter has suggested a four-fold system of licensing. First, certify and license the company: a government would license individual companies to exist as capable of performing a range of activities in a specified list of countries. Second, license the service capabilities: companies would be required to obtain a licence to undertake contracts for military and security services abroad. The activities for which licences were issued would be defined in the licence. Such activities would include those which were not generally aimed at changing the strategic environment in any contracted situation. Third, require notification of individual contracts: companies would be required to notify an industry authority of each contract obtained. Fourth, certify those 'strategic' contracts: for those activities that constitute activities aimed at changing the strategic environment, individual ministerial approval would be required (in whichever country) to ensure that corporations operating from that given country were not conducting strategic operations in another country that were against the policies and wishes of their original country.

Further, a prohibition of activities by individuals is recommended as well as serious constraints on both combat services in zones of conflict (with exceptions, the greatest being to support national objectives through international peacekeeping) and arms brokering. In addition, an industry regulatory authority should be established within a country's foreign ministry, as lead co-ordinator for the whole of government. Finally, governments must encourage—through all means available—the same approach at international and EU levels, perhaps through the rewriting of the existing Convention Against the Recruitment, Use, Financing, and Training of Mercenaries.

With such a strong focus today on the role of PMCs in the war in Iraq—as well as the historical regard for PMC activities in Africa and across the developing world—we remain at a unique point in time to influence the international approach to regulating the activities of such private actors; this must be done, leading with such a national regulatory initiative as outlined above, in support of a wider international regulatory regime. Without such an effective international regime in place, national regulation remains only part of the answer. As long as governments and commercial companies require armed protection or, indeed, armed military support against a rebel insurgency, PMCs will find a willing market for their skills and capabilities. The role that they play in these conflicts will remain of concern: as long as the international community is unable—or unwilling—to provide a regional security solution, this demand for support will continue to be met from the private sector. Given the current regional instability and disorder, this continued 'privatization of peacekeeping' may become the best option for a developed world unwilling or unable to intervene in the increasing chaos of regional conflict.

3

Regulating the role of private military companies in shaping security and politics

*Anna Leander**

Over the past decade the scale and scope of private military company (PMC) activity have both expanded to a degree few believed possible. Charles Moskos for example, writes that 'little did I realize when I first proposed a quarter century ago that the military was shifting from an institution to an occupation (the I/O thesis) that private profit making companies would one day actually do military jobs'.[1] This rise of PMCs has triggered considerable discussion about regulation. The problem is not that PMCs are 'unregulated': as the chapters in this volume testify, PMCs are 'regulated' by, among other things, export licensing systems and international humanitarian law.[2] PMCs and their employees can be held accountable individually. And the armed forces regulate their relations to contractors, as do states.[3] In fact, industry representatives present during a workshop organized for this volume talked about overregulation and considered themselves burdened by multiple, contradictory, and patchy rules that are often unclear about which administration is responsible when and for what.

One regulatory issue has nonetheless been strangely—and unacceptably—marginal, namely the regulation of the role PMCs play in shaping understandings of security and politics. Close to nothing has been said or done to adjust existing regulation to the rise of PMCs. Yet, as the first section of this chapter shows, this classical regulatory concern is as real when the 'specialists on violence'[4] shaping politics are 'private' and work for PMCs, as it is when they are 'public' and enrolled

* Thanks to Håkan Wiberg and the editors of this volume for constructively encouraging me to think about this topic.

¹ Moskos, Charles C Jr, 'Introduction,' in Jean M Callaghan and Franz Kernic (eds), *Armed Forces and International Security: Global Trends and Issues* (New Brunswick and London: Transaction Publishers, 2003) 6.

² See chapter seven by Louise Doswald-Beck and chapter nine by Marina Caparini in this volume.

³ See chapter five by David Isenberg and chapter eight by Chia Lehnardt in this volume.

⁴ This term is borrowed from Harold Laswell and used because it leaves open the status and organization of security professionals while focusing attention on their specific competence. See Harold Laswell, 'The Garrison State' in Jay Stanley (ed), *Essays on the Garrison State* (New Brunswick: Transaction Publishers, 1997) 55–76 (originally published in 1941 in the American Journal of Sociology).

in the armed forces. While elaborate institutional and sociological regulatory frameworks cover the public armed forces' role in shaping security and politics, or 'civil-military relations', nothing equivalent has been developed—or is even being contemplated—to cover the role of PMCs in shaping security and politics, or 'civil-PMCs relations'. As the second and third sections of this chapter show, the institutional regulatory frameworks covering public armed forces generally do not apply to PMCs and sociological regulation is largely dysfunctional. The aim here is to argue that the 'realistic' approach to regulation this volume strives to develop needs to encompass also this regulatory concern of classical realist thinkers such as Karl von Clausewitz.

The relevance of a classical realist concern for the regulation of PMCs

In von Clausewitz's formulation 'war is the continuation of politics by other means'. The police use force to impose laws agreed on through a political process. The military defends a national interest that is defined politically. In fact, thinking about the use of force as a prolongation of politics is so profoundly anchored that it is often turned into the defining characteristic of a 'legitimate' use of force. This is true not least in the Weberian definition (of the state as the institution with a 'monopoly on the legitimate use of force'), where the meaning of legitimate is left open and derives mainly and tautologically from the fact that force is exercised by the state.[5] There are of course many situations where force is used also by private actors pursuing private interests, rather than as 'politics by other means' and the legitimacy of the use of force by states is often strongly contested.[6] However, when states claim to use force legitimately they claim to do so as a 'continuation of politics' by other means.

In these situations the question that arises is: what politics? Whose interests and priorities are served and reflected? Who wins and loses? There is no uncontested national interest.[7] Different groups and individuals in society always have varying and incompatible priorities and some may have no preconceived political priorities at all but develop these through the process of deliberating with others. Moreover, there is no uncontested understanding of what kind of force (if any) should be used to pursue politics by other means. Also here a political process is at the origin of a common understanding. What politics a specific use of force is the prolongation of

[5] RBJ Walker, 'Violence, Modernity, Silence: from Max Weber to International Relations,' in David Campbell and Michael Dillon (eds), *The Political Subject of Violence* (Manchester and New York: Manchester University Press, 1993) 137–60.

[6] It has been pointed out that this relationship does not always hold—in complex emergencies and new wars the relationship is arguably inversed: politics is a prolongation of violence by other means. Similarly, force is sometimes used (including on a large scale for no well-defined reason).

[7] Jutta Weldes, 'Constructing National Interests,' *European Journal of International Relations*, vol 2, no 3 (1996) 275–318.

is, in other words, defined in a political process where different views are brought together and—in Arendtian fashion—a substantive understanding of the common good (or national interest) and how to best defend it is created. This process may encompass a smaller or larger number of voices depending on issues and contexts. There is no reason to suppose that everyone has an equal voice or even a voice at all in the process. Most US security policy, for example, is made in a political process involving a rather narrow set of individuals and institutions. However, it clearly matters whose voice can be heard and is allowed to shape this process.

When it comes to the use of force—internally or externally—a perennial question has been the extent to which the voice of specialists on violence should be heard. The answer is far from straightforward. On the one hand, specialists on violence are a necessary part of the discussion. The reason is their understanding of the technical aspects of the use of force. The specialists on violence know what can reasonably be obtained by what kind of strategy and at what cost. Moreover, in a long-term perspective, specialists on violence know what kind of capacities they need to develop to face a threat. These insights have to be taken into account when force is used as a continuation of politics. If they are not, decisions may be made to use force for political purposes where it has little or no possibility of being effective. This explains the fear that when specialists on violence are excluded from political processes, civilians may drift into 'military adventurism' or abuse security institutions to bolster their authoritarian and repressive regimes.[8] The necessary inclusion of specialists on violence in political processes means that they get a say over politics. They become part of making general decisions about how much to prioritize the use of force as opposed to other political means and goals. They also become part of specific decisions regarding what to do in any given security crisis as well as in defining what constitutes a security crisis.

The crux is how influential the specialists on violence should be in shaping politics. Even if, as just pointed out, their inclusion is essential, a consequence of including specialists on violence is the risk that their concerns may overshadow those of other actors. Precisely because they are specialists on violence, they may take matters into their own hands, using force in the way they consider just and imposing their views on the rest of society. From ancient Athens to contemporary Latin America the fear of military regimes has forced policymakers to find systems to control and limit the role of specialists on violence in politics. The current status of democracy as the only 'legitimate' political system internationally may have alleviated that fear of direct military rule. However, it has in no way answered the question of how to limit the role that specialists on violence play in politics.

---

8 Eliot Cohen, 'Are US Forces Overstreched? Civil-Military Relations,' *Orbis*, vol 41, no 2 (1997) 177–86; Kees Koonings and Dirk Kruijt, 'Military Politics and the Mission of Nation Building,' in Kees Koonings and Dirk Kruijt (eds), *Political Armies. The Military and Nation Building in the Age of Democracy* (London and New York: Zed Books, 2002) 9–35; Herbert M Howe, *Ambiguous Order: Military Forces in African States* (Boulder CO: Lynne Rienner, 2001).

This is a concern because the world view of specialists on violence is profoundly shaped by their professional experience (as is that of any professional category). Their outlook consequently privileges security more than would other groups in society, a point well illustrated by General Buck Turgidson in Stanley Kubrick's classic *Dr Strangelove*.[9] This is particularly true in a crisis situation where a professional outlook combines with heightened fear and need of vengeance. Hence, von Clausewitz insisted that the independent logic of war tends to become absolute and must be reined in and controlled not to undermine political aims.[10] Since specialists on violence retain their professional world views and crises abound, the issue of how to limit the impact of professionals of violence on politics is presing.

The consequence is that the regulation of the role of specialists on violence in the formulation of policies reflects two concerns: one with including and the other with limiting. On the one hand, security experts have an important role to play and therefore need to be included in the political process defining the common good and how to defend it. On the other hand, their presence may stifle or even kill that process and therefore has to be limited. This dual concern applies as much to PMCs as it does to other specialists on violence. PMCs are security experts. Professionalism is crucial to the industry. PMCs sell professional security services and they compete on the quality of the services they sell. Moreover, they are staffed by trained security professionals often with a background in public security establishments. PMCs constitute a category of specialists on violence in their own right.

As security professionals it is far from surprising that PMCs are involved in politics. PMCs are pulled into the process as they are consulted in all kinds of security related matters. Sometimes, this will concern how to best deal with a given political priority. But PMCs are also directly involved in establishing the priorities. They do so, for example, through their intelligence gathering and analysis as well as through their advisory and educational functions; both of which make PMCs part of the process of defining security concerns and political priorities. The role of CACI and Titan in the interrogations at Abu Ghraib has come to epitomize the role of PMCs in one form of intelligence gathering. But the firms also provide intelligence through more sophisticated channels. Moreover, military doctrine and strategy is increasingly developed by and spread through private firms. 'We make American military doctrine,' the head of MPRI boasted with some justification.[11] PMCs run military training, seminars, and educational programmes both in the

---

[9] In the film, a general (Jack the Ripper) decides to launch a nuclear war against the Soviets to find the definite solution to the threat posed by fluoride in the water. The bulk of the film focuses on the attempts of the US president to stop a nuclear war. General Turgidson is a military adviser whose obsession with security is caricatured by Kubrick.

[10] Carl von Clausewitz, *Geist und Tat. Das Vermächtnis des Soldaten und Denkers. Ein Auswahl aus seinen Werke, Briefe und Schriften von Dr Walther Malmsten Schering* (Stuttgart: Alfred Kröner Verlag, 1942) 89.   [11] Ed Soyster quoted in *Economist*, 8 July 1999.

US and abroad. Finally, PMCs and their lobby organizations are increasingly consulted on general policy issues. The industry has, for example, been invited to hearings in Congress on the development of peacekeeping and the development of the situation in Iraq.[12] PMCs are pulled into politics. They are invited, as specialists, to take part in a variety of discussions of policies. As private specialists on violence they are filling functions similar to those filled by their public counterparts.

PMCs may also on their own initiative and without invitation seek to influence politics. The reason PMCs do this is that their business depends on what happens to political priorities. How a problem is understood and what kind of solution is found for dealing with it, determines whether or not there will be a contract. PMCs therefore have to lobby both for an understanding of problems as security problems primarily and for the specific solution they have to offer. 'The leading defence company of the future will be primarily a manipulator of opinions ... Their key asset is the ability to influence the ways in which prospective buyers (governments and armed services) imagine the wars of the future.'[13] It is not surprising to find the International Peace Operations Association (IPOA) promoting a petition demanding military intervention in Darfur or publishing a special issue of its review on Sudan.[14] Both promoted a general understanding of political priorities in Darfur, rather than a well-defined role of PMCs. The need to shape broad political views explains the close links between political establishments and PMCs. Persons from the political and military establishment figure prominently on PMC boards. PMCs also figure prominently on the agenda of many policymakers, in some cases too prominently. This is true not only in the United States—where Vice President Dick Cheney's ties to the industry (Halliburton in particular) exemplify the controversy surrounding links—but also elsewhere, including Belgium, France, Germany, South Africa, and Sweden.[15]

[12] See, eg, Doug Brooks' 'Testimony to the House Committee on International Relations' regarding 'The Challenges of African Peace Keeping,' 2004, available at <http://www.internationalrelations. house.gov/archives/108/bro100804.htm> and Alan Chvotkin's 'Testimony to the House Committee on National Security, Emerging Threats and International Relations' regarding 'Private Security Firms: Standards, Coordination and Cooperation,' Statement of Alan Chvotkin, Senior Vice President and Counsel, Professional Services Council, to the Committee on House Government Reform Subcommittee on National Security, Emerging Threats and International Relations, 13 June 2006.

[13] John Lovering, 'Loose Cannons: Creating the Arms Industry of the Twenty-first Century,' in Mary Kaldor (ed), *Global Insecurity* (London: Pinter, 2000) 174.

[14] International Peace Operations Association is a lobby organization for PMCs. In 2006 it published a special issue on Sudan of its *Journal of International Peace Operations* vol 2, no 1. For a more detailed analysis see Anna Leander and Rens van Munster, 'Private Security Contractors in Darfur: Reflecting and Reinforcing Neo-Liberal Governmentality,' *International Relations*, (2007, vol 21, issue 2 201–16).

[15] In Belgium a series of scandals has linked high-ranking politicians including former NATO Secretary General Willy Claes to military contractors. See, eg, Craig R Whitney, 'Belgium Convicts 12 for Corruption on Military Contracts,' *New York Times*, 24 December 1998. In France, the 'Elf-Affaire', one of France's biggest corruption scandals ever, involved a range of military contractors (see Eva Joly with the contribution of Laurent Beccaria, *Est-ce dans ce monde-là que nous voulons vivre?* (Paris: Éditions des Arènes, 2003)). Two of Germany's biggest corruption scandals (the 'Flick Scandal' of the 1980s and the CDU party finance scandal of the late 1990s) both involved arms contractors and

　Anna Leander

Classical concerns that led to regulation of the role the 'public' military can play in politics pertain also to PMCs today. They are pulled into politics as experts and this in turn opens the question of how their influence can be limited. In chapter eleven, James Cockayne even asks whether PMCs do not at times cease to be agents of a principal and become agents in their own right. Since this is neither secret nor news, one might have expected the rise of PMCs to trigger a revisiting also of civil-military regulation or more appropriately of the regulation covering the role of 'specialists on violence' in shaping political priorities. However, as the two following sections will show, this has not happened. Whether regulation is narrowly thought of as an institutional set up or conceived in broad sociological terms as resting mainly on the manipulation of institutional culture, existing forms of regulation have little impact on PMCs and there is little sign of efforts directed at altering this state of affairs.

The underdeveloped institutional regulation of PMCs' role in politics

A first way of conceiving the regulation of the role of specialists on violence in politics is as an institutional regulatory framework set up for that purpose. There is a well-established tradition of regulating the role of specialists on violence in this way. However, existing regulation is largely inapplicable to PMCs because it assumes that the relevant specialists on violence are members of public armed forces. But even if that regulation were reformed to cover PMCs, it would fail to make a dent since—by and large—it misses its target. PMCs engage in politics by other channels than public armed forces and they increasingly do so in forums other than the classical Clausewitzean one.

An institutional regulatory framework is no doubt what most observers associate with the regulation of civil-military relations, in the sense of the role of specialists on violence in shaping politics. It certainly is the notion of regulation that is promoted by most international institutions concerned with the reform of military establishments and security sectors such as the Geneva Centre for the Democratic Control of Armed Forces (DCAF). The most common underlying rationale is that there are two partly contradictory 'imperatives' in society: a functional military one imposed by the needs of an efficient defence and a societal one imposed by the values, institutions, and ideologies of a society as Huntington formulated it.[16] Both

senior politicians; see Britta Bannenberg and Wolfgang J Schaupensteiner, *Korruption in Deutschland. Portrait einer Wachstumsbranche* (Munich: Beck, 2004). In South Africa, a string of scandals has tied ANC politicians to arms producers/exporters including the 2001 scandal involving the European Aeronautical Defense and Space Company (see, eg, <http://news.bbc.co.uk/2/hi/africa/1266950.stm>). In Sweden the links between Bofors and the Swedish government have often been contested and some speculate on links between these ties and Palme's assassination.

[16] Samuel P Huntington, *The Soldier and the State* (Cambridge: Harvard University Press, 1957).

imperatives are important but they are often incompatible. They therefore have to be protected and insulated from each other and their interaction controlled to reduce the risk of one sphere impinging on the other. The resulting regulation is one where strict norms, rules, and procedures serve to delimit the respective roles of military and civilian institutions and channel their interaction. The overall concern is to ensure that the military has primacy in ruling itself—that it enjoys professional autonomy and independent leadership—and inversely that civilians rule society and politics.[17]

There is substantial disagreement about how these institutions should look as well as strong contextual variation in the form regulatory institutions and practices actually take. However, some aspects of this regulatory set up recur. The first is an effort to channel and effectively delimit the context in which security professionals can take part in political debates. Most countries have well-defined institutional arenas where the armed forces can be consulted and asked to express their views. Characteristically, these are concentrated with the executive branch of government, which is also more often than not given primacy in deciding on the use of force. Contact between the military and the legislative bodies tends to be both less frequent and designed to allow one-way questioning (such as Congressional hearings) rather than to give security professionals the opportunity to participate in the formation of political priorities. The participation of specialists on violence in other words tends to be conceived in strictly and well-defined consultative terms.

Secondly, contributing to restricting the role of specialists on violence in politics are the formal and informal restraints imposed by the armed forces on the public conduct of their members. Most armed forces have their own formal rules for when and how any of their members may take a public stance and discuss political matters. Military hierarchy typically places strict limits on who within the armed forces can even imagine taking part in a public discussion, particularly if doing so entails questioning the positions of those higher in the hierarchy. But even more significant are the informal norms that regulate behaviour. Unwritten rules about acceptable behaviour place severe constraints even on those at the top. When, before becoming Secretary of State, General Colin Powell wrote opinion pieces in the *New York Times* and gave interviews on issues such as whether the West should intervene militarily in Bosnia, he was perceived as violating an unwritten code of conduct.[18]

A final recurring aspect of the regulation of the role on specialists on violence in politics is that it tends to be marked by a distance to broad (democratic) and political debates. The fact that the institutional regulation of security professionals' role in politics places them in a mainly consultative role, focused on the executive,

---

[17] Michael C Desch, *Civilian Control of the Military. The Changing Security Environment* (Baltimore and London: Johns Hopkins University Press, 1999).
[18] Desch, *Civilian Control* (n 17 above) 29.

also keeps them at arms length from general public debate. The term 'democratic deficit' is consequently one that appears with frequency in discussions about the political processes surrounding the use of force. Parliaments and publics have little insight and correspondingly limited possibilities to hold decision-makers and security professionals accountable for their decisions and acts. The rapid growth in multi lateral operations accentuates (or 'doubles')[19] the democratic deficit. By making international institutions, other governments, and military alliances central they move parliaments and publics even further away from the discussions of policies.

This institutional set up with its double democratic deficit is ill-suited to address the challenge of regulating the role of PMCs. Most of it is simply not applicable to PMCs at all. The basic assumption in the bulk of existing regulation is that the security professionals whose influence on politics requires regulation belong to the public armed forces or are indirectly controlled through the public armed forces. This assumption makes historical sense in view of the progressive nationalization of most functions in the armed forces in the twentieth century.[20] However, it is not adequate in a situation where PMCs have taken over many tasks conventionally defined as military, including tasks where the companies act independently of the armed forces.[21] Contracts for training, logistics, institutional reform, intelligence, and consultancies often directly involve the firms establishing policy priorities. Yet, guidelines regulating this role are non-existent because PMCs are not the public armed forces.

When it was decided that no less than half of the financial resources earmarked for post-conflict reconstruction in Liberia should go to DynCorp for training 2,000 soldiers, no institutional mechanism regulated the role of DynCorp in making this project a priority as compared with demobilization, judicial reform, education, healthcare, infrastructure repair, or civil society development.[22] There has been no clear institutional arena for the discussion between the public administration and DynCorp, there are no institutional restraints from outside the company limiting its participation in discussions and probably even fewer institutional restraints from within. One would expect the company to organize the promotion of this specific project and encourage employees to use the full variety of channels available to them to do so. On this issue, as on so many others, the rules establishing the form and

[19] Hans Born and Heiner Hänggi (eds), *The 'Double Democratic Deficit'* (Geneva: Ashgate/The Geneva Centre for Democratic Control of Armed Forces (DCAF), 2004).

[20] Anna Leander, *Eroding State Authority? Private Military Companies and the Legitimate Use of Force* (Rome: Centro Militare di Studi Strategici, 2006).

[21] For the discussion of this, see Major Michael E Guillory, 'Civilianizing the Force: Is the United States Crossing the Rubicon?', *The Air Force Law Review*, vol 51 (2001) 111–50. Major Lisa L Turner and Major Lynn G Norton, 'Civilians at the Tip of the Spear,' *The Air Force Law Review*, vol 51 (2001) 1–45; Lieutenant Junior Grade David A Melson, 'Military Jurisdiction over Civilian Contractors: A Historical Overview,' *Naval Law Review*, vol 52 (2005) 277–320.

[22] Francis W Nyepon, 'Liberia: Engaging US Foreign Policy for Development,' *All Africa*, 29 January 2006.

forums for consulting the specialists on violence are not applicable because the specialist is not a member of the public armed forces and hence is covered neither by the norms and rules pertaining inside the forces nor by those imposed on the armed forces from without.

Not only are existing rules mostly inapplicable. More seriously, even if they were reformed and extended to cover PMCs, they would miss their target and consequently be largely ineffective. One reason for this is that existing regulation is aimed at channels and forms of influence that are largely irrelevant to PMCs. Even if most of the staff of PMCs are trained in the public armed forces, even if the market for military services is profoundly shaped by public policies, and even if governments and public institutions remain key buyers of PMC services, PMCs are, as they adamantly insist, private companies. This alters their relationship to politics and to the formation of political priorities rather substantially. Like other private firms, PMCs treat lobbying and advertisement as a normal and accepted business strategy and naturally promote their views with administrators, policymakers, and the public at large. It is not surprising to find Chris Taylor of Blackwater giving speeches in various contexts arguing that Blackwater could offer a more efficient alternative to African Union (AU) or UN peacekeepers and therefore should be sent to Darfur.[23] The PMCs' private sector approach to politics makes most existing institutional regulation miss the key channels by which PMCs take part in policy-making. PMC influence on the process is more likely to be affected by general rules regarding lobbying and public debate than by the regulation of specialists on violence in the politics. The question is whether this is enough.

A further reason why the regulation of specialists on violence in politics is likely to remain ineffective (even if extended to PMCs) is that it addresses the wrong arena of politics. Much of the contemporary politics surrounding the use of armed force does not take place in the traditional Clausewitzean arena involving the home state, the people, and armed forces as the key actors. Rather, military operations are internationalized, involving other governments, military alliances, and international institutions. This development moves politics beyond conventional state boundaries and creates new regulatory challenges for public armed forces, including the 'double democratic deficit' mentioned earlier.

More than this, existing rules work on the assumption that specialists on violence work under the auspices of their home state. This does not hold for PMCs. They can and do work outside the control of their state and for non-state actors in ways that public armed forces rarely do. They work internationally for a variety of public actors on their own initiative and hence push for shifts in the political priorities both in the places where they work and at home in relation to these places. Public armed forces sometimes pursue politics of their own and shift

---

[23] Remarks by Chris Taylor, Vice President for Strategic Initiatives at Blackwater USA, at George Washington University, 28 January 2005, available at <http://www.blackwaterusa.com/btw2005/articles/042805taylor.html>.

national priorities. For example, during the Cold War part of the Swedish Armed Forces acted on their own initiative and outside of parliamentary control to consolidate collaboration with NATO and make defence against the threat from the Warsaw Pact a key political priority.[24] However, this kind of independent behaviour on behalf of public armed forces is a serious breach of norms and certainly not openly practised as a rule. With PMCs matters are different. PMCs sell their services on a market to a variety of buyers with whom their home state may or may not have a military alliance. This independence is sometimes a sham as governments use PMCs to circumvent policy restrictions and plausibly deny responsibility.[25] But often the industry is competing in international markets, and is treated as if it were, by its home government.[26]

Consequently firms may lobby for contracts within the frame of UN or the AU peacekeeping operations directly with these institutions and on their own initiative. They work for foreign governments independently of whether or not their home government has initiated this collaboration. Some PMCs, such as MPRI, underline that they will only engage in contracts acceptable to their home state, but then what is acceptable can be influenced by the firm.[27] Other firms, such as Blackwater, simply vow to work only for 'legitimate' clients, leaving the definition of legitimate conveniently open. The point is that the firms do work independently of their home governments. This shifts the location of the establishment of political priorities to places, channels, and issues not covered by existing institutional rules.

Finally, it is not only the location of politics that is changing but also the actors involved. Private contractors work not only for public actors—such as states, military alliances, and international organizations—but also for private actors, including NGOs, individuals, and private companies. These contracts mostly fall into the category of 'security' contracts and, since they are made with non-state actors, they are often assumed to have little relevance for politics and to be less contentious. But this assumption is not warranted. For example, guaranteeing the security of a firm or an NGO in a war zone often amounts to taking sides in the conflict. It secures resources for one side and stops the advance of the other. This explains the Darfur rebels' demand that all oil extraction should be halted in Sudan until the end of the conflict.[28] Moreover, when actors with opposing interests in a conflict hire security firms, the effect may be to prolong or aggravate the conflict.[29] This is the

---

[24] Ola Tunander, *Hårsfjärden—Det hemliga ubåtskriget mot Sverige* (Stockholm: Norstedts, 2001).
[25] See chapter six in this volume by Elke Krahman.
[26] Foreign and Commonwealth Office, 'Private Military Companies: Options for Regulation,' available at <http://www.fco.gov.uk/Files/kfile/mercenaries,0.pdf>, 2002.
[27] As eg when MPRI lobbied to be allowed to take on a contract upgrading Equatorial Guinea's coastal guard: PW Singer, *Corporate Warriors: The Rise of the Privatized Military Industry* (Ithaca: Cornell University Press, 2003) 196.
[28] Sylvain Besson, 'Malgré les tueries, une firme basée à Genève prospecte au Darfour,' *Le Temps*, 25 August 2005.
[29] UN, Report of the Panel of Experts on the Illegal Exploitation of Natural Resources and Other Forms of Wealth of the Democratic Republic of Congo (S/2001/357).

reason Abdel-Fatau Musah worries that 'the return of proxy wars could become a nightmarish reality where well-equipped foreign private forces are allowed to continue propping up opposing parties in today's conflicts'.[30] Lastly, security provision to non-state clients is sometimes intended to alter political conditions as illustrated by the ill-fated coup in Equatorial Guinea.[31] The blurred distinction between security and military services in many contemporary conflict situations[32] means that the institutional regulation covering the role of specialists in violence in public debate would have to be substantially revised. It would have to be adjusted to politics involving not only foreign governments and international institutions, but also private firms and NGOs. In fact, existing rules are all the more likely to miss their target as PMCs work with actors that (just like the firms themselves) are not covered by existing regulation.

The institutional framework covering the role of specialists on violence in security policies is, to say the least, underdeveloped when it comes to regulating the role of PMCs in shaping security and politics. The existing framework is designed to cover public actors exclusively. But more seriously it is ill-suited to cover the key forms of PMC participation in politics as well as the key arenas where this politics is taking place. Arguably, the problem is a long-standing one. In 1961 the US President Eisenhower focused his farewell speech on it. He pointed out that 'in the councils of government, we must guard against the acquisition of unwarranted influence, whether sought or unsought, by the military-industrial complex. The potential for the disastrous rise of misplaced power exists and will persist'.[33] However, that a problem is old does not mean that solutions are available. In this case finding solutions is not even on the agenda. Little effort has so far gone into updating the—mostly inapplicable but also outdated and therefore ineffective—rules covering the role of security specialists in politics to the emergence of PMCs.

A dysfunctional sociological regulation of PMCs' participation in politics

Institutional regulation is not the only way of shaping and controlling the presence of specialists on violence in politics. There is a sociological alternative. Instead of assuming that what is needed is a separation of spheres regulated by institutions, this alternative tradition argues for what Morris Janowitz termed a 'compatibility

[30] Adel-Fatau Musah, 'Privatization of Security: Arms Proliferation and the Process of State Collapse in Africa,' *Development and Change*, vol 33, no 5 (2002) 928.

[31] BBC, 'The Men Behind the "Guinean Plot",' *BBC Online News*, 13 March 2004.

[32] Often it matters more for the difference in connotations than for differences in substance. At the meeting preparing the publication of this book, a representative from a private firm argued that there were no private military companies (since the closing down of EO); only private security companies.

[33] President Dwight D Eisenhower, *Farewell Address*, available at <http://www.eisenhower.utexas.edu/farewell.htm>.

of values' between the military and society. A common political culture is the guarantee that security professionals will be present in politics without dominating it. As institutional regulation, this kind of 'regulation' exists in most countries. However, not only is it ineffective when it comes to dealing with PMCs, it is dysfunctional. The direction of regulation is reversed. PMCs seem to have more impact on public debates and values—including those in the public armed forces—than these have on the PMCs.

The sociological tradition departs from the view that, ultimately, formal regulation and institutional rules are less important than is the 'compatibility' of the culture in society at large and in the military. Formal regulation can never guarantee that the role of security professionals is positive. Only a basic shared world view can. The idea of a 'constabulary force' is a classical illustration of this line of thinking. The general idea is that the armed forces would be capable of evolving with society and adjusting to it: the 'military establishment is continuously prepared to act, committed to the minimum use of force, and seeks viable international relations, rather than victory, because it has incorporated a protective military purpose'.[34] This requires strong ties between the military and the civilian worlds. The sociological tradition does not suggest blurring the distinction between military and civilian society nor does it deny the Huntingtonian functional and societal imperatives.[35] However, instead of focusing on institutional rules of interaction, the sociological tradition highlights organizational structures, values, and identities in the military.[36] It focuses on *what* is said and done rather than the institutional channels and forums *where* it is said and done.

The sociological perspective on PMCs' role in politics, consequently, focuses on whether recruitment, training, advancement, hierarchies, and identities in the military produce values compatible with those in society or, alternatively, on how they could be reshaped to do so. As with institutional regulation, the aims, forms, and praxis of sociological regulation have varied considerably. Countries differ in their understanding of their armed forces and their role not only in public debate but also in society.[37] Integrating minorities, homosexuals, or women into the armed forces is both a way of ensuring that the armed forces reflect society and a road for these groups to claim full citizenship.[38] Moreover, armed forces also have varying

[34] Morris Janowitz, *The Professional Soldier: A Social and Political Portrait* (New York: Free Press, 1971) 148 and Morris Janowitz, 'Toward a Redefinition of Military Strategy in International Relations,' *World Politics*, vol 26, no 4 (1974) 473–508.

[35] On the contrary, Janowitz underlined that blurring the lines might undermine military functionality and lead to 'new forms of militarism' in society. See Morris Janowitz, 'Military Elites and the Study of War,' *Conflict Resolution*, vol 1, no 1 (1957) 18.

[36] Morris Janowitz, 'Changing Patterns of Organizational Authority: The Military Establishment,' *Administrative Science Quarterly*, vol 3, no 4 (1959) 473–93.

[37] Anna Leander and Pertti Joenniemi, 'In Conclusion: National Lexica of Conscription' in Pertti Joenniemi (ed), *The Changing Face of European Conscription* (London: Ashgate, 2006) 151–62.

[38] Ronald Krebs, *Fighting for Rights: Military Service and the Politics of Citizenship* (Ithaca: Cornell University Press, 2006).

institutional cultures and pasts. Consequently, the issues and forms of sociological regulation vary considerably. In Germany, the 1933–1945 legacy has created a military culture where individual responsibility and the limits of authority are essential which has no equivalent in France. Inversely, in France the focus on representation and on the integration of the '*beurs*' [French citizens of Maghrebi origin] has no equivalent in Germany. It is hence neither surprising that states regulate the links between armed forces and society sociologically, nor that they do so in highly diverging ways. The question is how this 'sociological regulation' works with regard to PMCs. Allowing for wide contextual variation, the answer is unsettling.

To some extent PMCs are affected by public attempts to socially regulate specialists on violence. States shape PMC culture and behaviour from the outside, for example, by establishing compulsory vetting procedures, by restricting acceptable activities, and by buying services only from firms that behave according to specified standards. In addition to this, public armed forces may influence PMCs through the close links between these institutions: PMCs may incorporate the organizational culture, values, and priorities of the public armed forces. These indirect processes may be reinforced by states treating PMCs as legitimate actors, inducing them to act as if they were. These mechanisms taken together could make existing sociological regulation (in a slightly updated and adjusted version) a good basis for regulating PMCs. In fact, PMCs could become a vehicle for socializing a variety of specialists on violence into a (publicly sanctioned) professional military culture. They could 'draw more actors into the prevailing system of social norms'.[39] However, there is little evidence that this is what is happening.

Rather, PMCs seem to be developing a variety of corporate cultures and value systems independently of each other but also largely outside the influence of public institutions (armed forces and states). Consider, for example, the impact public institutions may have on the values in PMCs through their influence on recruitment. The firms first and foremost recruit staff according to their own preferences and needs. Many PMCs recruit globally. As a consequence no government is likely to know the details of the staff recruited. Moreover, since many PMC employees have worked in a variety of countries and conflicts, it is difficult to imagine that blacklists held by any one actor would be helpful. Vetting procedures as well as self-regulatory blacklists aimed at controlling recruitment depend on the reporting of a wide range of actors.[40] Finally, only a limited numbers of firms would be likely to abide by procedures and report to blacklists in the first place. Even fewer would be likely to do so for all kinds of contracts. Vetting procedures, blacklists and the like are therefore likely to be of circumscribed effectiveness at best. The more realistic scenario is that PMCs continue recruiting according to patterns over which governments and armed forces have little say. The example of recruitment

[39] Deborah Avant, *The Market for Force: The Consequences of Privatizing Security* (Cambridge: Cambridge University Press, 2005) 49.
[40] Both kinds of measures are currently under discussion in different contexts.

illustrates a more general point: namely that there is little possibility for the public to shape the corporate culture developing in PMCs. Even if most established firms adhere to codes of conduct,[41] they do this if, when, and as they decide to.

More fundamentally, it is not clear that PMCs' organizational culture is converging with the professional culture of public armed forces, promoted by states. This observation concerns not only marginal firms, but also large respected ones as starkly illustrated by the Aegis 'trophy video' posted on the internet.[42] Obviously, similar videos could have been posted by members of the public armed forces. The difference is that in the public armed forces there is an institutional culture of sanctioning this kind of behaviour. There are mechanisms not only to reprimand such occurrences, but also for detecting them and preventing unacceptable subcultures from developing in the first place. It is far from clear that PMCs (including large ones such as Aegis) have anything equivalent to this nor is it clear that any attempts are made to impose it on the firms. It therefore seems far more likely that PMCs will continue to develop their own (diverse) subcultures than that they will draw a variety of security professionals into a publicly sanctioned professional culture.

This is all the more likely since, at present 'sociological regulation' seems to be working at least partly in 'reverse'. Rather than making values in the military compatible with the values in civil society, the rise of PMCs seems to have the effect of making values in civil society compatible with those of the military or more precise with those of the PMCs. PMCs work in competitive markets. They compete for contracts and market shares. This competition requires marketing products and creating demand. There is no need for conspiracies or immorality to explain PMCs' struggle to shape understandings of politics. The context in which they do so is one where private business and market solutions generally have a positive connotation.

There are indications that this is resulting in an increasing acceptance of PMCs and their worldviews in a variety of social spheres.[43] Members of the armed forces are expressing concern about the draining of their staff towards the private security business and about the consequences for coherence and norms in the services. More than this, in development thinking and development programmes, security holds an increasingly central position and PMCs services are valued. Public and private aid agencies hire PMCs for security. They also rely on PMCs and former PMC employees for tasks that are not directly security-related such as monitoring human rights or implementing non-security-related development projects.[44] Perhaps most surprisingly, PMCs seem to be fashionable, quite literally, as Paris

[41] See eg IPOA, 'Armorgroup: Standards and Code of Ethics. Q&A with Jim Schmitt,' *International Peace Operations Association Quarterly*, vol 1, no 4 (2005) 5–7.

[42] Aegis employees filmed their shooting at civilian cars while driving on an Iraqi highway, added music and began circulating it.

[43] Anna Leander, 'The Power to Construct International Security: On the Significance of Private Military Companies,' *Millennium Journal of International Studies*, vol 33, no 3 (2005) 803–26.

[44] For examples, see the special issue on Sudan of *Journal of International Peace Operations*, vol 2 no 2 (2006).

fashion stores carry Blackwater gear and the Internet is buzzing with sites, blogs, and lists relating to PMCs.[45]

It would be an exaggeration to claim that PMCs have gained general authority over security matters. However, the prospect that the values of PMCs permeate society raises Harold Laswell's concern that we may be 'moving toward a world of "garrison states"—a world in which the specialists on violence are the most powerful group in society'.[46] The worry in this world is not that specialists on violence take matters into their own hands. Rather, it is that their world view and understanding of problems becomes so dominant and so widely accepted that others take it for granted. The political cost of such developments is high. It limits the scope for thinking through options for international diplomacy and politics. But it also reflects inwards and limits national freedom and the scope for politics.[47] The costs are potentially so enormous that, at the height of the Cold War, Laswell found it 'inadequate to say that the dominant crisis of our time is socialism *versus* capitalism. More correctly, it is socialism *and* capitalism *versus* the garrison-prison state'.[48]

The 'sociological regulation' of PMCs' role in politics is, to sum up, ineffective at best but more probably dysfunctional. It is ineffective because PMC organizational culture largely escapes control and manipulation not only by civilian public authorities but also by public armed forces. Sociological regulation may even be working in reverse as PMCs increasingly shape worldviews in the 'public' and in society at large. PMCs may socialize actors into an existing system of norms, but there is little empirical or theoretical evidence that it would be the system of the professional public forces. It seems more likely to be the highly varying system of norms prevailing in the PMCs and the market for force which is a substantially different thing. More strongly, the section has made the point that the sociological regulation may be dysfunctional since the dynamics of the market for force tends to reverse sociological regulation: societal and political values are made compatible with those of specialists on violence; not the other way around.

Conclusion

In their introduction to this volume, the editors make the valid assessment that the 'abolitionist' stance on regulating PMCs is increasingly rare. They draw the pragmatic conclusion that what is needed is a 'realistic approach to regulation'.

[45] Elliot West, 'Paris Fashions Include Dior, Gucci and ... Blackwater,' *Raleigh Chronicle* 8 August 2006.

[46] Laswell, 'The Garrison State' (n 4 above) 56.

[47] For a classical statement, see Hannah Arendt, 'What is Freedom?', in Hannah Arendt (ed), *Between Past and Future. Six Exercises in Political Thought* (London: Faber and Faber, 1958) 143–72.

[48] Harold Laswell, 'The Universal Peril' in Jay Stanley (ed), *Essays on the Garrison State* (New Brunswick: Transaction Publishers, 1997) (originally published in 1950) 119.

This chapter shows that a central aspect of regulation in the 'realist' approach—namely the regulation of the role of specialists on violence in politics—has remained marginal in the discussions surrounding PMCs. This is not because it is unimportant or irrelevant. On the contrary, the political processes establishing for what purpose what kind of force is used are fundamental and PMCs do take part in them and do shape them. Yet, the present context is not only one where the abolitionist stance on regulation has disappeared. It is also one where PMCs are increasingly present as a new cast of efficient, competent, and apolitical security experts. In this context, the concern with regulating the way PMCs (as specialists on violence) shape politics is readily swept aside and forgotten.

This chapter has argued against this neglect but it has not proposed a blueprint for action for the simple reason that there can be no general blueprint. Views on the role of specialists on violence in politics differ as profoundly as do institutional contexts and histories of civil-military relations. Moreover, the multiplicity of arenas, actors, and issues defy simplistic blueprints. No blueprint could possibly inform regulation of the role PMCs play in political processes as diverse as those surrounding a UN intervention, Liberian reconstruction, the US presence in Iraq and the Chinese oil company Cliveden's operations in Sudan. Even if there can be no general response, however, including these concerns in the emerging regulatory frameworks remains vital.

PART II

CHALLENGES

4

Weak governments in search of strength

*Africa's experience of mercenaries and
private military companies*

Angela McIntyre and Taya Weiss

Modern private military companies go to some lengths to define themselves as professional and accountable entities and to distance themselves from the mercenaries of the past. In Africa, in particular, being a mercenary meant being an instrument of colonial resistance to self-determination, of support for secessionist movements, and general destabilization.[1] As the winds of change swept through Africa in the 1960s and power was handed to or taken by liberation movements, European business interests—proportionately more substantial then than they are today—had nonetheless to be protected. A series of mercenary interventions in decolonizing states to just such ends in Angola, Zaïre, Nigeria, and the Sudan, among others, would eventually prompt the Organization for African Unity (OAU) to adopt the Convention on the Elimination of Mercenarism in July of 1977.

The OAU Convention was an attempt to eliminate mercenaries insofar as they supported secessionists or resistant colonial enclaves whose main objective was to protect foreign business interests. The mercenary business moved into a niche created by volatile political transitions, economic upheaval, and uncertainty. In the three turbulent decades of liberation struggles and Cold War proxy interventions, the market for private force in Africa changed dramatically in response to broad economic adjustment programs and a sharp escalation in intrastate and small insurgent wars.

Some of the client base for private force today consists of sovereign states employing private companies largely for defence transformation and for multinational partners (in particular, oil and mining companies), who need protection of their commercial interests. The best known incidents of the employment of private force since the days of mercenary legends Bob Denard and Mike Hoare have involved not secessionist movements, but rather government elites safeguarding

---

[1] See Gerry S Thomas, *Mercenary Troops in Modern Africa* (London: Westview Press, 1985).

their partnerships in foreign business interests. In responding to this market shift, private forces have diversified their functions and adopted a cloak of corporate respectability. Since the transition from 'mercenaries' to 'private military companies', the new political/private-force/commerce relationships occurring in Africa have undergone relatively little scrutiny vis-à-vis their social, political, and economic impact or transparency.

This chapter seeks to illustrate change and continuity in the use of private force on the African continent. Although the clientele has changed and is now primarily composed of sovereign states and multinational corporations, motivations for the use of private force, in some cases, continue to revolve around the exploitation of natural resources. We suggest that there are potentially negative impacts arising from the use of private force by states with poor performance in the areas of human rights and governance. Where states struggle to maintain monopolies on violence in the face of civil unrest or rebellion, PMCs are sometimes used to safeguard the commercial interests that are the very source of discontent, thus becoming embroiled in and potentially exacerbating local political conflicts. In light of the role that PMCs may play in upholding less-than-democratic regimes and in ensuring that opaque state-corporate business partnerships thrive unhindered, regulation of the private military sector could face serious challenges in Africa.

The mercenary to PMC transition

To appreciate the transition between the historical African mercenary and the modern PMC, it is necessary to draw on a few cases of private military intervention in this period. In a historical example, Belgium and Belgian business interests attempted to retain control over the Zaïrian province of Katanga by supporting a secessionist movement led by Moise Tshombe backed by a multinational mercenary force. Members of this group later appeared on the scene of the Biafran war, a British-supported attempt to rescue the oil-producing portion of Nigeria from the horrifying spectre of French influence, which threatened to engulf the region if Nigeria's leaders were to entertain friendly relations with their neighbours. The mercenaries of this day proved culturally adaptable (a quality to which modern PMCs aspire) in their command of both the French guerrilla-style counterinsurgency operations involving the integration of local forces and the more regimented British leadership style, and also in heading settler revolts such as the one which occurred in Katanga referred to above.[2] The mercenaries of the day found opportunities in the power vacuums created by colonial transitions and were free to respond to the war-market in a way that today's private forces cannot, thanks to the end of colonialism, the fizzling-out of the Cold War, and new international

---

[2] Thomas, *Mercenary Troops* (n 1 above) 33–45.

norms that favour self-determination and state sovereignty. The market has changed, and so has the business.

The activities of modern private forces have been classified in a static way, as offered by PW Singer's 'Tip of the Spear' model.[3] There are several limitations to this classification, one being that companies engaged in the relatively benign facets of peacekeeping can also have activities that place them closer to the tip of the spear in other theatres (for example, a company could be engaged in supporting peacekeeping in Africa but undertaking different functions simultaneously in Iraq). This is understandable: a dynamic firm that is responsive to different markets will be successful, which means not necessarily adhering to a position on the continuum of non-lethal to lethal services. Discussions on the legitimacy and ethics of the use of private force have revolved around these issues, as well as around the questions of transparency and accountability, which are discussed elsewhere in this volume but in this case will focus not so much on the companies as their clients.

This chapter will discuss a different set of issues, very relevant in the African context but often overlooked in the larger debate over regulation. These concern consensus, oversight, and subjection to democratic control of force in the context of the profound governance problems that face Africa today. We will analyse this in terms of a spectrum—not of degrees of lethal force, but of legitimacy. At one extreme of the spectrum might be logistical support to peacekeeping operations overseen by the United Nations such as those currently ongoing in Sudan, the Democratic Republic of the Congo, and Liberia; at the other, coups d'état, accompanied by gradually diminishing accountability. While the extremes of this scale are occupied at one end by international consensus and rogue political pretenders, such as insurgent and opposition leaders inclined to take power by force, at the other, opposing positions are not so clearly occupied by sovereign states or non-state actors, as one might think. Although coups d'état are typically condemned, the ascension to power and quality of governance occurring in a number of African states lends their monopoly on the use of force only marginally more legitimacy than that of coup-plotters. In some cases, it is not only the purveyors of military force that bear scrutiny, but their sovereign-state clients. It may be that the conditions that attract coups d'état are similar to those that compel states to seek the services of PMCs, in that they result from poor governance. Thus the 'legitimacy' of the PMC derives from the nature of the functions it performs, and whether these add to, or mitigate existing problems.

The interventions of Executive Outcomes (EO) in Angola and Sierra Leone, for example, attracted significant criticism, but when attempts were made to understand the role they played in restoring temporary stability, the results were more nuanced. The leftovers from EO's more dramatic period in Sierra Leone were even put to good service shuttling military observers, mediators, and human

---

[3] PW Singer, *Corporate Warriors: The Rise of the Private Military Industry* (Ithaca: Cornell University Press, 2003).

rights investigators to the daunting hinterlands of Sierra Leone during the latter tenure of the UN Mission in Sierra Leone (UNAMSIL). It is unsurprising then that criticism has centred on the commercial interests of EO's affiliated companies and less so on their freewheeling success in driving insurgents from the capital city and on the sight of the mercenary-flown Russian Mi-24 helicopters that gave a sense of security even to the most pacifist humanitarians. Of greatest interest in Sierra Leone is the government-PMC-commerce relationship that was forged at the peak of crisis but left a legacy that will be discussed below.

At the 'bad' end of the spectrum, recent coup attempts on the Seychelles, Sao Tome and Principe, and Equatorial Guinea have been categorically condemned and considered criminal acts of freelance adventurism backed by shady corporate players and opposition leaders in exile or would-be military dictators. Equatorial Guinea, which will also be discussed later, provides a fascinating case study of a meeting place of both coup-plotters and corporate players, illustrating clearly the dilemma of client-legitimacy that must be contemplated seriously if the PMC industry is to avoid contributing to poor governance, instability, and human rights abuses in African states.

Executive Outcomes: a 'transitional' organization?

As well as having a history of private force intervention dating back to the 1960s, Angola played host to the grandmother of modern African PMC interventions, the Executive Outcomes operations. This is an episode in African history unlikely to be repeated, having gained momentum on the tails of Cold War politics, the end of the minority regime in South Africa, and the restructuring of its defence force. It bears mention as an example of how regime change creates recruitment pools for the private sector and how pre-existing command structures and *esprit de corps* make for quick recruitment and sometimes successful operations.

The disbandment of the counter-insurgency police unit Koevoet and of the Angolan-staffed 32 Battalion, as well as pre-emptive resignations among elite units of the South African Defence Force at the time of the change of government, marked the end of South African military hegemony in the region. It also marked the beginning of a continental shift in thinking about private force: it could work *for* post-independence governments rather than against them, on the side of state sovereignty and ostensibly for stability rather than against it. For the soldiers who had long experience in counterinsurgency warfare on the Namibia-Angolan border between 1975 and 1989, and who had supported UNITA's (National Union for the Total Independence of Angola) decades-long struggle for power against the MPLA (People's Movement for the Liberation of Angola) government, the EO operations were a natural next step.

The first of these was a small combat operation, involving at its peak only 28 men, mainly using small arms and light weapons and lasting less than two months.

It was successful in regaining control of UNITA-occupied, Ranger Oil West Africa-owned installations at Soyo. This was followed shortly afterwards by a much larger contract: an invitation to train and lead MPLA forces in combating UNITA in the diamond areas around Saurimo, which were one of UNITA's main sources of financing. Again, the services provided by EO had a commercial intent: their presence would not only regain territory for the government but enable the establishment of EO's sister company, Branch Energy, to pick up where UNITA had left off. Although the balance of power was shifted by this intervention, EO's tenure in Angola ended under pressure from the opposition during ceasefire and peace negotiations, followed by a fresh outbreak of war. It was only the death of Jonas Savimbi in 2002—rumoured to have been assassinated with the help of Angolan former SADF/EO operatives—that brought peace by default to Angola.[4]

The criticism of EO in Angola was muted given the political climate of the day. Savimbi was regarded as a paranoid megalomaniac whose movement was tainted by its association with Apartheid South Africa and the US Central Intelligence Agency. As a proxy force, UNITA had lost its political utility and external support once the 50,000-strong Cuban surrogate force withdrew from Angola, in parallel with the South African Defence Force, on the eve of Namibian independence. UNITA could not hope to compete against a government increasingly bolstered by a booming oil business and no longer perceived as an instrument of Soviet expansionism. Commercial interests overtook political ones as the Cold War and its accompanying political dogma fizzled out. In this context, EO was a fortuitous response to the shape-shifting of global politics and multinational business interests. A small, privatized piece of the South African Defence Force turned successfully on its former allies in defence of the commercial interests of its old enemy and erstwhile tool of Soviet imperialism. This remarkable scenario surely inspired entrepreneurial imagination in military circles and paved the way for business in Sierra Leone, another sovereign state client facing a prolonged insurgency.

Sierra Leone: the troubling legacy of private force

The African governments that most need the services of PMCs can often least afford to pay for them. Sierra Leone provides a case study for the complications inherent when PMCs are remunerated from the one 'account' such governments do have access to: concessions to extract natural resources from the client country. The widespread abuse of natural resources such as gold, diamonds, timber, and oil and the role of these resources in perpetuating conflict has been well documented

---

[4] The authors have addressed this question informally to veterans of the South African Defense Force and Executive Outcomes, who agree that there was likely South African involvement in the assassination, given the familiarity of veterans of the Angolan civil war with the *modus operandi* of UNITA.

in Africa, particularly Sierra Leone, Liberia, Sudan, Angola, and the Democratic Republic of Congo.[5] This literature, however, largely overlooks the mechanism by which PMCs, their executives, personnel, and affiliated companies become entangled in relationships with weak states and at-risk civilian populations even after the conflicts that brought them there have ended. Such relationships have certainly proven contentious and even violent in Sierra Leone; they also put PMCs and their affiliated companies at risk of often unwanted long-term responsibility for local governance.

As mentioned earlier, EO first made an appearance in Sierra Leone (after their debut in Angola) to drive the rebel RUF back from an assault on Freetown in 1995. PW Singer describes EO's arrival:

When the rebels approached within 20 kilometers of the capital city of Freetown, fears that the war would end in a general massacre grew. Most foreign nationals and embassies hurried to evacuate the country. The situation appeared hopeless. Almost immediately, though, the circumstances completely reversed. A modern strike force quickly deployed and hammered the rebel forces with precision air and artillery attacks.[6]

Late that same year, EO expanded their operations into rural Sierra Leone, re-taking the diamond mining areas. In early January 1996, EO re-took the Sierra Rutile mine, formerly a major source of revenue for the country. Both the diamond mine in Kono and the Sierra Rutile mine have become post-war flashpoints in the conflict between government and civilians over armed private security and local governance issues such as housing and development. The relationships between the PMCs and their staff and the companies that eventually invested and currently operate the mines is disputed, although it is agreed by all parties that the players involved in mercenary activity, private security, and mining are closely personally connected.

A United Nations report in 1996 noted that:

In Sierra Leone, mercenaries hired by Executive Outcomes are reported to be active in the Kono and Koidu districts and in Kangari Hills, and in Camp Charlie at Mile 91. According to the sources consulted, Executive Outcomes is receiving about US$30 million and mining concessions in the Koidu district for its mercenaries' operations ... all these activities are supervised by executives of the company.[7]

[5] Greg Campbell, *Blood Diamonds* (Westview Press, 2005). Global Witness, 'The Riddle of the Sphynx: Where Has Congo's Oil Money Gone?', December 2005, available at <http://www.globalwitness.org/media_library.detail.php/145/en/the_riddle_of_the_sphyx_where_has_congos_oil_money>; and 'An Architecture of Instability: How the Critical Link between Natural Resources and Conflict Remains Unbroken', December 2005, available at <http://www.globalwitness.org/media_library-detail.php/144/en/an_architecture_of_instability>.

[6] Singer, *Corporate Warriors* (n 3 above) 4.

[7] Report of Enrique Bernales Ballesteros, Special Rapporteur, Report on the Question of the Use of Mercenaries as a Means of Violating Human Rights and Impeding the Exercise of the Right of Peoples to Self Determination, 17 January 1996, UN Doc E/CN.4/1996/27, para 65.

In 1997, the *Globe and Mail* noted that 'many reports have suggested that there is a corporate link between the military group [Executive Outcomes] and Branch Energy, Ltd., the subsidiary of Vancouver-based DiamondWorks looking for gems in Africa'.[8] EO founder Eben Barlow responded in the same article that the two companies are 'often mentioned as being one and the same company [but] this is not correct ... The fact of the matter is, however, that I am personally on very friendly terms with the directors of Branch Energy and visa [*sic*] versa.' The technicalities become more blurred when two additional points are noted: first, the Financial Times reported separately in 1997 not only that 'employees of two Canadian diamond exploration companies ... were dramatically lifted to safety by a Russian-built helicopter operated by a company called Executive Outcomes',[9] but also that DiamondWorks, whose employee was one of those rescued, had Tony Buckingham as its biggest shareholder. The article confirms that, according to a DiamondWorks prospectus:

Buckingham provided introductions for Executive Outcomes to governments and advised governments on their commercial relations with that organization, either directly or through Branch Energy. The prospectus also showed that DiamondWorks had hired Lifeguard, an affiliate of Executive Outcomes, to guard its exploration properties in Sierra Leone for $60,000 a month ... Branch Energy was awarded diamond concessions after Executive Outcomes joined the fight against the rebels.[10]

Although Branch Energy planned to begin Kimberlite blasting at the Koidu mine in 1996 (a more expensive and technical process than alluvial mining), a coup in 1997 led to the evacuation of expatriates from the mine. A small security team of nearly a hundred armed men remained to protect the assets. This was legal under the 1995 lease, which had stipulated that the mine could have an armed security force. After eight months in RUF-controlled territory, the team escaped, leaving the RUF to destroy up to fifteen million dollars worth of investment, according to the company's representatives. Five years later, the Sierra Leone People's Party was re-elected and DiamondWorks, the parent company of Branch Energy, decided to re-invest in a joint venture with the Steinmetz Diamond Group; the joint venture became Koidu Holdings Limited in January 2004. Twenty-one million dollars of new investments had gone into the venture by 2004.[11] In addition to its two Kimberlite mines in Koidu, Koidu Holdings has four other exploration properties, including an 89 square kilometre property at Tongo Field.

Given Kono's recent history, Koidu Holdings has an obvious and defensible interest in protecting its current investments. The government also has a stake in

---

[8] Madelaine Drohan and Karen Howlett, 'Miner Linked to Mercenaries; Diamond Works' Shareholder Acts as Agent for Security Firm,' *The Globe and Mail*, 21 February 1997.

[9] Ken Gooding, 'Security Services: Diamond Dogs of War Prowl for Pusiness,' *Financial Times*, 15 September 1997.   [10] Ibid.

[11] Author interview with company representatives in Koidu, October 2004.

mine security, since high rates of taxation and fees levied on legal diamond exports makes it more like a major Koidu Holdings shareholder than an objective regulatory entity (up to 40 per cent of Koidu Holdings' profit is collected as corporation tax, surface rent, and royalties on diamond sales). The government, therefore, provided 23 armed Sierra Leone Police to guard mining interests, one contingent with an armed response vehicle on call from a nearby police station, and 24 officers from the Public Support Unit. The company's private security team (which is unarmed according to the law) nonetheless patrols with the police, making them almost indistinguishable from one another. Other mining companies are reportedly negotiating similar deals with the SLP in co-ordination with their own unarmed teams. The agreement extends to Freetown, where exporting takes place.

In part because of the security arrangements that seem to change the mission of the police from protecting citizens to protecting corporate interests, Koidu Holdings has come under protest from citizens dwelling in its immediate vicinity as well as from a national NGO, the Network Movement for Justice and Development (NMJD) and its Campaign for Just Mining. The World Bank Multilateral Investment Guarantee Agency (MIGA) refused to grant political risk insurance to the Koidu Kimberlite Project in 2004 due to the extremely inhospitable political climate. This prompted high-level government intervention to reverse the decision, setting off further fears that the government would continue to unquestioningly support the company's interests and ignore citizens' complaints. Complaints range from dangerous blasting in thickly settled areas to the company's slow pace of providing amenities such as a clinic for the community. Traditionally housing, medical care, and schooling fall into the realm of government responsibility, but with the company and government so closely aligned, local authorities are no longer clearly delineated. Residents of the area see Koidu Holdings as an extension or representation of local government: certainly, the most likely local entity to pay for or provide services. There is certainly an element of opportunism here, but that is part of the point. Whether founded or not, the claims against the company have put Koidu Holdings and its foreign executives in the unenviable position of trying to maintain an ethical image for its investors and insurers while facing constant negotiations with an impoverished, disgruntled, and war-traumatized local population.

At the Sierra Rutile mine, that other vestige of PMC involvement in the civil war, a heavily armed private security force has been accused by community groups of terrorizing the local population. It is privately acknowledged among those who worked for EO and Sandline and then stayed on in Sierra Leone that some of their number may be well suited for fighting guerrillas but not for living peacefully with a recently disarmed, peacetime population. One community activist in the Sierra Rutile area threatened that people would re-arm if the government did not intervene to rein in the mine's security force. The legacy of PMC involvement in the Sierra Leone civil war comes full circle in such a threat; by paying private companies to end the war in concessions requiring their continuing presence, the government may have created the environment that most threatens that expensive peace.

Today's PMCs, of course, distance themselves from such open adventuring as EO became famous for. However, the lessons learned from this episode in Sierra Leone's history are highly relevant to the way today's corporate providers of private force should weigh their involvement in weak states. It cannot be taken for granted that weak states will be legitimate clients, and even if they are that they must and will pay for the use of private force with natural resource concessions. Even if the international community and the community of states within Africa continues to leave gaps in development, governance, and military oversight that renders the need for such force 'necessary', the companies themselves must look at the ways in which in-kind payment binds them to long-term commitments that could end up approximating a local government role. Big oil companies are quite familiar with the challenges of this type of arrangement, and the wedge that mining operations and other extractive industries drive between a people and their (perhaps already distant) government can become volatile when combined with security staff and practices held over from armed conflict. Even if the methods of payment shift to more removed means, such as cash generated from multinational companies invested in the area, the provision of security after conflict constitutes a type of contract that will not go unnoticed by the local populations most affected by war, conflict, and the vagaries of such for-profit development.

Therefore, one question we should be asking is whether, when accounting for global human security (the implementation of which PMCs traffic in), we are willing to value the little-heard voices of African citizens in the debate. Almost all PMC executives emphasize their commitment to following strict rules of engagement, in part as a response to large client states like the US who demand 'clean' records of their contractors. However, with profit as motive, and not necessarily in any purposefully unethical way, some PMCs and multinationals will have interests in keeping private security unregulated and at a status quo in Africa, where there is little oversight of on-the-ground activities and where it is easier to get things done without it. With terrorist networks investing in places like Liberia,[12] however, it would be foolish not to see both the utilitarian and moral purposes in granting weight to governance, public relations, and ethics standards, even (especially) in countries that make regulation difficult.

Poor governance and economic predation: the new coups d'état?

Coups d'état are now generally condemned, to the point where the alleged attempt in 2004 to force a change of leadership (albeit still within the ruling clan) in Equatorial Guinea was considered something of an anachronism. What makes a country a feasible target for coup-plotters? Historically, the instability brought

---

12 Damien Lewis, 'Diamonds Are for Terror,' *Mail on Sunday (London)*, 25 June 2006.

about by decolonization processes was an invitation to pretenders. Without delving into the machinations of various plots over the decades, a fairly simple observation can be made: the temptation to forcibly snatch control of a state seems to be greatest where there is a concentration of wealth and power in the hands of a few elites and where there are weak armed forces of tenuous loyalty and poor governance. Few coups d'état have been motivated by the desire to wrest control of outstanding educational facilities, universal healthcare, independent judiciaries, and democratically controlled militaries. Like coup-plotters, insurgent movements such as UNITA in Angola and the RUF in Sierra Leone also capitalized on wavering popular support for negligent or oppressive governments, economic hardship, and resentment of flagrantly corrupt elites. Whether the spoils anticipated by insurgents and coup-plotters differ is immaterial here; the conditions that make states unstable attract both. It is this same instability that compels states to seek to bolster their monopoly on violence through external means, either to maintain a status quo that is an object of dissent (Equatorial Guinea), or to gain advantage in conflicts over access to and control of strategic resources (Sierra Leone, Angola, Nigeria). An intriguing illustration of the private force-state-corporate nexus exists in Equatorial Guinea where modern American and Israeli PMCs and a group of old-time mercenaries came dangerously close to meeting. As a major African oil producer, Equatorial Guinea was already attracting exploration in the 1970s, but it was only in the 1990s that the boom really began. Prior to this, subsistence agriculture, forestry, and cocoa farming were the mainstays of the economy. Although the country has become an important destination for foreign, and particularly US investment, Equatorial Guinea's paranoid and fratricidal regime has invested negligibly in anything but its own security and a highly personalized interest in the oil industry. President Teodoro Obiang Nguema took power in a coup in 1979, prompted by the arrest and eventual execution of his uncle, independent Equatorial Guinea's first president Francisco Macías Nguema. To say that the country is ruled by a small elite is an understatement, so much so that the term 'Nguemism' had to be coined to describe it.[13] Political parties not aligned with the government were all but banned and the country continues to fall under regular criticism from international human rights monitors for its excesses, which include political purging, trumped-up coup allegations followed by mass arrests, detention without trial, and the torture of prisoners.[14] Oppression in Equatorial Guinea seems to preclude any political opposition. The country's employment of private force seems to have been limited so far to the use of the American firm MPRI in training its coastguard (necessary to protect offshore oil installations) in 1997 and, more recently, the Israeli firm Aeronautical Defense Systems Limited, to train its Presidential Guard.

---

[13] Geoffrey Wood, 'Business and Politics in a Criminal State: the Case of Equatorial Guinea,' *African Affairs*, vol 103 (2004) 547–67.

[14] US Bureau of Democracy, Human Rights and Labor, 'Equatorial Guinea: Country Report on Human Rights Practices,' 20 September 2006, available at <http://www.state.gov/g/drl/rls/hrrpt/2005/61567.htm>.

A surrogate force of Moroccans served until recently as Obiang's Presidential Guard; a telling indication that the President cannot trust his own people with his life. The involvement of MPRI, although small in scale, is significant in that the company was initially denied a licence by the US State Department to respond to Obiang's request, due to Equatorial Guinea's abysmal human rights record. The company lobbied successfully to convince the authorities that the work would in fact be serving foreign policy interests and the licence was eventually granted. At best, this did not bode well for self-regulation in the industry; at worst, it indicated a willingness on the part of the US government to support a pariah state. The growing importance of African oil reserves to the United States is the only possible justification the US government could have used or accepted in reversing its original decision.

Although Equatorial Guinea may not yet have realized its full potential in terms of employing private force, the alleged 2004 coup attempt, backed by a collection of mainly British entrepreneurs and adventurers, may still prompt it to do so. A parody of the old days of African mercenaries, the coup attempt was foiled largely thanks to the information of a network of individual freelance intelligence merchants (another arm of the private security industry which, although distant from the tip of the spear, is perhaps more a vestige of old-time mercenarism than the modern PMC).[15]

In early 2004 the South African business partner of President Obiang's brother and Security Chief Armengol Ondo Nguema was arrested and sentenced without trial on charges of plotting a coup, along with 14 others. Simultaneously, a planeload of experienced security operators, including some EO veterans and its British co-founder, Simon Mann, was grounded in Zimbabwe. The bulk of its passengers were sentenced to 14 months imprisonment for immigration violations, while Mann remains on weapons charges related to an alleged attempt to buy arms from the para-statal Zimbabwean Defence Industries. Although the coup was initially attributed to the opposition leader in exile, Severo Moto, there are suspicions that the plan may have been to install another member of the Nguema clan in power, in the Equatoguinean political tradition of fratricide. The coup-plotters had corporate backing[16] from the very same industry from which the Equatoguinean regime derives the bulk of its income—the oil industry—and banked on weak and easily-swayed armed forces and minimal popular protest. The spoils, which in any case were of little benefit to the citizens, needed only to be wrested away from a small elite. With its current state of governance, lack of popular support for the government, and history of violent regime change, Equatorial Guinea is a coup waiting to happen. A sure way for the regime to maintain this status quo and secure its grip on power is through the use of PMCs. At the crux of the matter are

---

[15] See, eg, Adam Roberts' account of the Equatorial Guinea Plot, *The Wonga Coup* (London: Profile books, 2006). The major players in intelligence-gathering were freelancers who had personal connections to coup-plotters as well as multiple clients, including the South African, Equatoguinean, and British governments.   [16] See Adam Roberts, ibid.

the country's oil reserves, which will finance the regime's tenure at the expense of the welfare of the citizens and evidently with the blessing of the United States and multinational investors.

Patrons, clients, and private force

In the incidents of Angola and Sierra Leone, criticism of EO arose not from the fact that a private and not entirely accountable force had (if only briefly) vanquished the enemy, but from its links to oil and mining activities. Within the theatre of violent conflict, the exchange of concessions for military force, however roundabout, seemed unacceptable, but is this also the case in peacetime? In both cases, the use of private force assisted weak states in regaining their monopoly on violence (and, in the case of Angola, on the revenues that kept the laboured war machine running), placing the governments in stronger positions from which to negotiate peace. But what about the longer-term stability necessary for economic progress and reform?

Leading scholars on weak states in Africa[17] argue that the commercial alliances of weak states actually undermine the possibilities of reform and that reform could actually undermine the lucrative terms on which deals are made. In the face of dwindling support after the Cold War, argues Reno, African states were forced to re-work their relationships with external actors in order to balance power against domestic political rivals, with a resulting net gain in foreign influence in local politics and economy. Aid agencies and strong governments, he argues, are 'complicit in preserving the sovereign form of weak states and subsequently in supporting foreign firms and mercenaries that take over conventional state functions'.[18] Investing in good governance and legitimate power bases continues to be a risky, expensive, long-term strategy, and a strongman in the hand is worth two in the bush. As the demand and competition for oil concessions grow more voracious, so will the demand for the quick-fix of private force.

The use of free agents also presents dilemmas, unrelated to economic globalization, which have been pondered for centuries and that mainly centre around the social checks and balances within the state and society that keep armed forces, but not necessarily surrogates and privateers, loyal to the paymaster. Kenneth Grundy draws on Machiavelli's writing to illustrate problems that persist, half a millennium later, in Africa.

Success in warfare and ultimately control of the state are dependent on a military formed of one's own citizens, loyal to the state, with an interest in national

---

[17] See for example Patrick Chabal and Jean Pascal Daloz, *Africa Works: Disorder as a Political Instrument* (Oxford: James Currey, 1999); William Reno, 'The Politics of Insurgency in Collapsing States,' *Development and Change*, vol 33, no 4 (2002) 837; Jean-Fancois Bayart, Beatrice Hibou, and Stephen Ellis, *The Criminalization of the African State* (Indiana: Indiana University Press, 1999).

[18] Reno, 'The Politics of Insurgency in Collapsing States' (n 17 above) 184.

unity and in keeping the current government in power.[19] These fundamental conditions are lacking in weak African states and are the very reason they resort to private force to begin with. Sierra Leone's rebellion arose from a disgruntled junior officer class and gained momentum through the recruitment of economically deprived, politicized youth. Angola's civil war broke out after a failed political transition in which a minority seized power and immediately set about bolstering itself with external resources. The popular support was clearly not there, and scenarios of this nature continue to arise across the continent. The unrest in Nigeria's oil producing regions (discussed below), which were already a matter of contention in the Biafran war, carries on, while revenue from Angola's rich reserves continue to benefit only a small elite. Equatorial Guinea has managed to preserve a modicum of stability through sheer oppression; coup allegations, arrests and imprisonment without trial are a commonplace tool of governance in a regime that changes leadership only when the simmering cauldron of bad blood within the clan boils over. Different forms of private force will continue to play an important role in these places, so long as a substitute is needed for legitimate power and business with multinationals carries on as usual.

Although PMCs may no longer have the kinds of direct commercial interests that EO derivatives have had, for example in the form of mineral concessions and partnerships with petroleum companies, they are increasingly used to safeguard the corporate or state interests that foot the bill at the end of the day. Nigeria, arguably one of Africa's economic powerhouses and the world's seventh largest oil exporter provides a further example. The crisis of communities and multinationals that took hold of the oil-rich Niger Delta with the execution of activist Ken Saro-Wiwa in 1995 shows few signs of abating. Protests by community-based (and usually ethnically-identified) organizations have been met with harsh repression by government forces, subsidized by oil companies with equipment, food, and accommodation for troops. Since crude oil began to be commercially exploited by foreign companies, notably Shell, Chevron, Agip, and Elf, the indigenous inhabitants of the oil-bearing Niger Delta have pressured the government and the private sector to curb environmental damage and what they perceive as economic exploitation. Neither the multinationals nor the state seem able to resolve the bitter confrontation. Between 1998 and 1999, an escalation of violence in the region brought military occupation and culminated in the issuing of an ultimatum by civil society groups: withdraw the armed forces or face an escalation in violence. Protest movements, led in part by youth groups, have resorted to the sabotage of oil installations, kidnapping, and the assassination of local leaders thought to be in collusion with the government and the companies. Shell is at least one firm that has responded with the use of private security, in the form of Group4Securicor, which operates hand-in-hand with both police and armed forces, leading one

[19] Kenneth Grundy, 'On Machiavelli and the Mercenaries,' *Journal of Modern African Studies*, vol 6, no 3 (1968) 295–310.

commentator to remark that 'it is difficult to determine where public policing ends and private security begins'.[20] This situation, as with the Sierra Leone case, opens private forces up to allegations of being accessories to violence as the public does not always distinguish between private and public force, and places private industry directly in the throes of what is turning out to be a protracted political struggle.[21]

For the most part, though, given the past accusations of plunder by EO, remaining one step removed is *de rigeur* for staying above-the-board and respectable. Transactions like the ones between EO and the government of Sierra Leone are unlikely to be so direct in the future, with PMCs more likely to be paid with cash generated from multinationals invested in African resource extraction—rather than by the offer of a remote stretch of river rumoured to contain alluvial diamonds but inconveniently infested with Kalashnikov-wielding teenage guerrillas.

Conclusion

It could be exceedingly difficult to reach regional consensus on the modern use of private force in Africa, given the role of PMCs in protecting the interests of sovereign states and their corporate partners. The OAU Convention faced a much simpler problem: it addressed mercenarism as a threat to majority rule and self-determination in a context where these were being contested in political and ideological ways. Moreover, the involvement of PMCs in Africa in the area of peacekeeping support under international consensus, and in defence sector transformation (democratization and professionalization of armed forces) still outweighs their presence in corporate or state protection. This of course suggests the possibility of PMCs exacerbating governance problems only to be there to clean up after the resulting civil wars.

The conundrum of how 'legitimate' yet often weak African governments can reconcile long-term relationships with donors, aid agencies, PMCs, citizens, and civil society is one that deserves closer examination. As Singer points out, PMCs are now central to the development of the African state: 'To gain military power, regimes do not need to follow the old path of developing their economy or efficient state institutions to tax for military forces. Rather, they must simply find a short-term revenue source, such as granting a mining concession, to pay a private actor.'[22] Some difficult questions need to be asked. Can Nguemism, for example, really be considered majority rule? Does 'self-determined' really describe an economy and

---

[20] Rita Abrahamson and Michael C Williams, 'The Globalization of Private Security Nigeria Country Report,' 13, 20 September 2006, available at <http://users.aber.ac.uk/rbh/privatesecurity/country%20report-nigeria.pdf>.

[21] See also Andy Rowell, James Marriot, and Lorne Stockman, *The Next Gulf: Washington, London and Oil Conflict in Nigeria* (London: Constable and Robinson Publishers, 2005).

[22] Singer, *Corporate Warriors* (n 3 above) 56.

regime dominated by foreign corporate interests and debt repayments, where the revenues from resources give only marginal benefit to the citizens? Few modern PMCs want to be considered to be instruments for the meddling in the affairs of sovereign states as were their mercenary predecessors. But the role they play could have an even more profound influence, not only on national security, but on economies and governance.

It is comparatively easier, perhaps, to discuss regulation of PMCs in the context of functioning democracies such as the United States and Britain; but with the increasingly globalized nature of warfare, terrorism, and human security, the persistent instability of mineral-rich states in Africa is already becoming more and more 'relevant' to the conflicts that industrialized nations are deeply invested in, both financially and militarily. With African militaries generally on the decline, underpaid, and facing other crises of decimation such as the AIDS epidemic and the refusal of the United States to provide military funding to states that refuse to exempt American soldiers from the International Criminal Court, PMCs are the continent's most efficient and perhaps soon to become only effective accessible fighting force.

5

A government in search of cover

Private military companies in Iraq

David Isenberg

The standard explanation for the rise of private military companies (PMCs) is that the end of the Cold War gave states a reason to downsize their military forces, freeing up millions of former military personnel from a wide variety of countries, many of them Western. At the same time, the end of the Cold War lifted the lid on many long simmering conflicts held in check by the superpowers. Since markets, like nature, abhor a vacuum, PMCs emerged to fill the void, when conflicts emerged or wore on and no one from the West or the United Nations rode to the rescue.

In the United States, by contrast, one can trace the push for outsourcing of military activities back to the 1966 release of the revised Office of Management and Budget (OMB) Circular A-76.[1] Private contractors were prominent in the 'nation-building' effort in South Vietnam,[2] and grew significantly over the decades. One Department of Defense (DoD) guide listed several factors driving the expanding role for contractors and suggested some of the complications to which this has given rise:

Downsizing of the military following the Gulf War; Growing reliance on contractors to support the latest weapons and provide lifetime support for the systems; DoD-sponsored move to outsource or privatize functions to improve efficiency and free up funds for sustainment and modernization programs; and increased operating tempos. Today contractor logistics support is routinely imbedded in most major systems maintenance and support plans. Unfortunately, military operational planners have not been able to keep up with the growing involvement of contractors.[3]

---

[1] Defense Outsourcing: The OMB Circular A-76 Policy, Congressional Research Service, 2005, RL 30392, 21 April 2005.

[2] See James M Carter, 'The Vietnam Builders: Private Contractors, Military Construction and the "Americanization" of United States Involvement in Vietnam,' *Graduate Journal of Asia-Pacific Studies*, vol 2 (2004) 44–63.

[3] *Contractor Support in the Theater of Operations*, Deskbook Supplement, 28 March 2001, <http://www.dscp.dla.mil/contract/doc/contractor.doc>.

This chapter analyses PMC activities in Iraq as the extension of this trend and, perhaps, its azimuth. The sections that follow explore the underlying structural factors that led to the greatly expanded reliance on PMCs in Iraq, the challenges that this poses for oversight and accountability, and the impact it has had on civil-military relations and public control and accountability of the use of force.

The rise of the 'Third Wave'

The use of PMCs, especially in the United States, has increased dramatically over the past fifteen years. During the first Gulf War in 1991 for every contractor there were 50 military personnel involved. In the 2003 conflict the ratio was 1 to 10.[4] The US military had been planning to increase dramatically its long-term reliance on the private sector in 2003, independently of Iraq. The plan, overseen by Army Secretary Thomas E White, was known as the 'Third Wave' within the Pentagon and could have affected 214,000 military and civilian positions—about one in six army jobs around the world. It would also have provided a major boost to the Bush administration's effort to move large blocks of government work into the private sector.[5]

After the 11 September 2001 attacks on the World Trade Center and the Pentagon there was a notable increase in the formation of new PMCs.[6] But it is Iraq that focused world attention on the role of PMCs. Though much discussion focuses on the role of PMCs following the conclusion of major combat operations, PMCs played a prominent role during the war itself. The services relied, for example, on civilian contractors to run the computer systems that generated the tactical air picture for the Combined Air Operations Center for the war in Iraq. Other contract technicians supported Predator unmanned aerial vehicles (UAV) and the data links they used to transmit information.

This reliance on private contractors increased greatly after the initial major combat operations phase, due primarily to the fact that the US political leadership grossly underestimated the number of troops that would be required for stability and security operations. As part of its plan to bring democracy to the Middle East, Iraq was to be made into a new country: this would in turn require a massive reconstruction project to overcome the effects of more than two decades of war, against Iran and then the United States, and sanctions. But, once again, the

---

[4] Deborah Avant, 'The Privatization of Security and Change in the Control of Force,' *International Studies Perspectives*, vol 5 (2004) 153–7.

[5] For detail see Defense Outsourcing: The OMB Circular A-76 Policy, 17.

[6] 'The idea was to create a security consulting company that could work for entities like the Department of State and the Department of Defense to deal with the situations that were going to arise in a post- 9/11 world,' said Jamie Smith, a former Navy SEAL who founded SCG International Risk. Source: Kirsten Scharnberg and Mike Dorning, 'Iraq violence drives thriving business,' *Chicago Tribune*, 2 April 2004.

United States miscalculated and did not anticipate the emergence and growth of the insurgency. Since US forces were not available to protect those doing reconstruction, such firms had no choice, if they were going to continue to work in Iraq, but to turn to PMCs in order to protect their employees. At least ten to fifteen cents of every dollar spent on reconstruction is for security, according to the Inspector General for the Coalition Provisional Authority (CPA).[7]

PMCs provided three main categories of security services in Iraq: personal security details for senior civilian officials, non-military site security (buildings and infrastructure), and non-military convoy security. Rather than work directly for the US government or the CPA, most PMCs were subcontracted to provide protection for prime contractor employees, or were hired by other entities such as Iraqi companies or private foreign companies, seeking business opportunities in Iraq.

Concern over accountability and regulation of PMCs has long been a staple in academic discussion of the industry.[8] But the widespread use of PMCs in Iraq brought increased publicity to and discussion of the issue.[9] Given the frequent assertions that private military and security contractors suffer from a lack of control it should be pointed out that contractors also make many sacrifices that get little notice. In November 2005 Knight Ridder newspapers reported that 428 civilian contractors had been killed in Iraq and another 3,963 were injured, according to Department of Labor insurance-claims statistics. Those figures, however, were incomplete, and the true total is certainly higher.

Accountability of PMCs has, at least in a few countries, been a pressing concern for several years. The form of, and motivation for, regulation differs according to region. In South Africa, as discussed by Marina Caparini in chapter nine, attempts to regulate have been largely legislative, notably South Africa's 1998 Foreign Military Assistance Act (FMAA), and more recently, its Prohibition of Mercenary Activity and Prohibition and Regulation of Certain Activities in an Area of Armed Conflict Bill. The FMAA has been criticized for being too general in its definition of what constitutes 'foreign military assistance', and, despite its sweeping scope including extraterritorial application and progressive language, has not met with particular success. To date, only five convictions have resulted from the FMAA, each resulting in small fines being paid by South Africans who were found to be

[7] Seth Borenstein, 'Insurance, security prove costly for contractors in Iraq,' Knight Ridder/ Tribune News Service, 1 April 2004.

[8] See, eg, Paul Jackson, 'War Is Much Too Serious a Thing to be Left to Military Men: Private Military Companies, Combat and Regulation,' *Civil Wars*, vol 5 (2002) 30–55.

[9] Some illustrative articles from law journals are Devin R Desai, 'Have Your Cake and Eat It Too: A Proposal for a Layered Approach to Regulating Private Military Companies,' University of San Francisco Law Review, vol 39 (2005); James R Coleman, 'Constraining Modern Mercenarism,' *Hastings Law Journal*, vol 55 (2004); Mark W Bina, 'Private Military Contractor Liability and Accountability After Abu Ghraib,' The John Marshall Law Review, vol 38 (2005); Martha Minow, 'Outsourcing Power: How Privatizing Military Efforts Challenges Accountability, Professionalism, and Democracy,' Boston Law College Review, vol 46 (2005); and Laura A Dickinson, 'Government for Hire: Privatizing Foreign Affairs and The Problem of Accountability Under International Law,' William & Mary Law Review, vol 47 (2005).

involved in recruiting 'mercenaries' in Côte d'Ivoire and Equatorial Guinea.[10] The problem with South African legislation is that the government views PMC activity with suspicion, given that many South Africans working in this sector had their formative military experience back in the apartheid era, and thus, the government often views them as potential troublemakers, both in other countries as well as at home.

The United States, in sharp contrast, increasingly views PMCs as part of the total force. Its concerns, bolstered by its experience in Iraq to date, tend to be administrative: how to ensure co-ordination between theatre commanders and PMCs, how to prosecute PMC personnel if they commit a crime, how to ensure common standards for issuing and implementing contracts. During the period in which Iraq was administered by the CPA (21 April 2003–28 June 2004), the CPA provided a vehicle for establishing a legal framework for PMC activities. A CPA Public Notice issued on 26 June 2003 laid out the status of contractor personnel:

In accordance with international law, the CPA, Coalition Forces and the military and civilian personnel accompanying them, are not subject to local law or the jurisdiction of local courts. With regard to criminal, civil, administrative or other legal process, they will remain subject to the exclusive jurisdiction of the State contributing them to the Coalition.[11]

CPA Order No 17 specified that contractors were not subject to Iraqi laws or regulations in matters relating to the terms and conditions of their contracts and that they were immune from Iraqi legal process with respect to acts performed pursuant to the terms and conditions of a contract. CPA Memorandum 5, which implemented Weapons Control Order No 3, established a Weapons Authorization Program whereby individuals who could demonstrate a need to carry weapons could apply for temporary weapons authorization cards (TWCs) in order to do so.[12] CPA Memorandum No 17 established registration requirements for private security companies.[13]

It is clear that there have been numerous problems with accountability of private contractors of all kinds. According to a study released in February 2006 by the Special Inspector General for Iraq Reconstruction:

The US government also experienced shortcomings in accounting for personnel deployed to Iraq—especially civilians and contractors. There was, and still is, a lack of effective control procedures at many entry and exit points for Iraq, and there is no interagency personnel

[10] Henri Boshoff, 'Regulation of Private Military Companies (PMC) Private Security Companies (PSC): The South African Case Study,' Institute for Security Studies. Paper presented at the 'Guns 'n gates: The role of private security actors in armed violence' Cost Action 25 Working Group 3 roundtable, held in Bonn, Germany, 9–10 February 2006.

[11] Available at <http://www.cpa-iraq.org/regulations/20030626_20030626_CPANOTICE _Foreign_Mission_Cir.html.pdf>.

[12] Available at <http://www.cpa-iraq.org/regulations/20030822_CPAMEMO_5_Implementation _of_Weapons_Control_with_Annex_A.pdf>.

[13] Available at <http://www.cpa-iraq.org/regulations/20040626_CPAMEMO_17_Registration _Requirements_for_Private_Security_Companies_with_Annexes.pdf>.

tracking system. Official and contract personnel often arrived and departed with no system-atic tracking of their whereabouts or activities, or in some cases, with no knowledge of their presence in country. Shortly before its dissolution in June 2004, CPA was still unable to account for 10% of its staff in Iraq.[14]

Control and accountability of PMC personnel, however, is not just a matter of adherence to laws and regulations. It is also a quality control issue, in the sense of ensuring that qualified personnel are hired.

The most important factor is choosing and training the right people. PMCs generally subject potential employees to rigorous vetting.[15] PMCs usually have codes of conduct for their staff, but there is no uniform check of these by govern-ment agencies. In the United States contractors to the government are theoret-ically liable to prosecution but as yet this has happened just once thus far: David A Passaro, a former CIA contractor accused of beating an Afghan prisoner who later died in custody. Disciplining contractor personnel is the contractor's respon-sibility. Such problems were unavoidable, given the relative haste with which the reconstruction effort was mounted. But accountability was enough of a concern that members of Congress wrote to Defense Secretary Rumsfeld in April 2004 requesting proper screening of security companies in Iraq.

The CPA set some initial minimum standards for regulating PMCs and subse-quently new mandatory guidelines were adopted by the Iraqi Ministries of Interior and Trade to vet and register PMCs. A draft 30 June 2004 Interagency Policy Memorandum, 'Contractor Security in Iraq', prepared by then Deputy Secretary of State Richard Armitage and Deputy Secretary of Defense Paul Wolfowitz pro-posed guidance for all US government contractors working in Iraq and for govern-ment offices supporting and co-ordinating those contractors. It was intended to 'provide an initial blueprint for eventual adoption of common contractor coord-ination and security rules for all nations providing contractors for the reconstruc-tion of Iraq.'[16]

Some officials in the PMC industry greeted this new guidance with a cautious enthusiasm, though they thought the regulatory organizations involved lacked the necessary co-ordination ability required for a task of this importance. With the advantage of hindsight it appears they were right. The fact that the CPA sub-sequently issued a nearly $300 million contract to Aegis Defence, a British PMC, to co-ordinate activities between PMCs and allow the US military to track PMC security details shows that the US government did not have the capacity to do it on its own.

US government oversight of PMCs operating in Iraq was accomplished through contracting activities and various laws, regulations, and guidelines. These included

---

[14] 'Iraq Reconstruction: Lessons in Human Capital Management,' Special Inspector General for Iraq Reconstruction, January 2006.
[15] James Glanz, 'Modern Mercenaries on the Iraqi Frontier,' *New York Times*, 4 April 2004.
[16] David Isenberg, *A Fistful of Contractors: The Case for a Pragmatic Assessment of Private Military Companies in Iraq*, British American Security Information Council, September 2004, 41.

the Federal Acquisition Regulations, heads of federal agencies, heads of contracting activities, contracting officer, and contracting officer's representatives.

External oversight was provided by the Government Accountability Office (GAO),[17] the Special Inspector General for Iraq Reconstruction, DoD Office of the Inspector General, Defense Contract Management Agency, and the Defense Contract Audit Agency. The GAO focused both on co-ordination issues between PMCs and the US military as well as doing more traditional audits on PMCs doing logistical work, such as Halliburton. The Special Inspector General focused more on reconstruction work, so PMC activities were, at best, a secondary issue for it. The DoD Inspector General assessed DynCorp's work in training Iraqi police and also did numerous audits on various logistical contracts. The Defense Contract Audit Agency had overall responsibility for performing all contract audits for the Department of Defense; as such it had its hands full just keeping track of regular military forces in Iraq and had little ability to monitor PMC contracts, especially as most of their contracts, with the exception of Halliburton, were not directly with the Pentagon. And the Defense Contract Management Agency is the Pentagon component that works directly with military suppliers to help ensure that DoD supplies and services are delivered on time, at projected cost, and meet all performance requirements. As such it was not particularly relevant.

In hindsight this lack of official government agencies dedicated to the oversight of PMCs makes it easier to understand how atrocities like Abu Ghraib happened. The torture and abuse scandal at Abu Ghraib horrified people around the world and raised controversy over the role and activities of PMC personnel in the intelligence and interrogation process. The number of PMC personnel at Abu Ghraib is far from clear, but at least 37 interrogators from private contractors were operating in the prison. A whole series of mostly internal military investigations were conducted as a result of the revelations. At least two reports (the Taguba and Jones-Fay Reports) implicated contractor personnel in the scandal. A lack of proper vetting of PMC personnel was also uncovered.[18]

In the wake of the scandal a number of new laws and guidelines were proposed, including a new Contractor Accountability Bill in the United States, a new oversight mechanism involving the International Committee of the Red Cross (ICRC) and new Pentagon rules regulating contractors. Despite new laws and regulations, however, control over and accountability of PMCs continues to be controversial. Even though PMC personnel have effectively had immunity from Iraqi prosecution for any offences committed, enough accusations have been made to make people ask exactly who has jurisdiction over them, and exactly what laws can be

---

[17] For examples of past GAO reports see Problems with DoD's and Interior's Orders to Support Military Operations, GAO-05-201, April 2005; and Actions Needed to Improve Use of Private Security Providers, GAO-05-737, July 2005.

[18] A Review of ICITAP's Screening Procedures for Contractors Sent to Iraq as Correctional Advisors, Office of the Inspector General, US Department of Justice, February 2005, <http://www.usdoj.gov/oig/special/0502/final.pdf>.

used to prosecute them, if necessary. Which statute, regulation, and common law—for example, the Military Extraterritorial Jurisdiction Act, War Crimes Acts, Anti-Torture Statute, Foreign Corrupt Practices Act—is most applicable is a question that is hotly debated.[19]

The ambiguity of many of the laws relevant to PMCs, and the relative immunity granted to them thanks to CPA directives, help explain many of the incidents between them and Iraqi civilians. Private military contractors have been involved in scores of shootings in Iraq, but none have been prosecuted despite findings in at least one fatal case that the men had not followed proper procedures.[20] Instead, contractors suspected of reckless behaviour are sent home, sometimes with the knowledge of US officials, raising questions about accountability and stirring fierce resentment among Iraqis.

There have also been tensions between contractors and regular military forces. One of the better-known ones took place in May 2005 when a group of armed American guards from a security convoy from Zapata Engineering, a company hired to destroy enemy ammunition, were taken into custody on suspicion of shooting at the Marine tower. Subsequently the contractors were set free but each side tells a different story. Contractors and their families feel they were unfairly arrested and, once in the military prisons, they say they were treated with disrespect. Some say they were subjected to humiliating treatment and were abused. The marines say they were treated professionally.

Rules of engagement

In the early stages of the Iraqi reconstruction efforts the Pentagon lacked standardized rules for most issues involving private contractors accompanying US forces in Iraq, including whether they could carry arms.[21] Although the US military had compiled an extensive list of service and departmental regulations, doctrine, and field manuals to govern contractors' behaviour on the battlefield, they were more oriented to those providing logistical services and did not cover the new activities of PMCs.[22]

---

[19] Private Security Firms: Standards, Cooperation and Coordination on the Battlefield, Subcommittee on National Security, Emerging Threats, and International Relations, House Government Reform Committee, 13 June 2006.

[20] T Christian Miller, 'The Conflict In Iraq: Private Security Guards in Iraq Operate With Little Supervision,' *Los Angeles Times*, 4 December 2005.

[21] Jim Wolf, 'US Lacks Standardized Rules for Iraq Contractors,' *ABC News*, 24 June 2004.

[22] For example see 'Contractors on the Battlefield,' *Air Force Journal of Logistics*, Oct 1999; Deploying With Contractors: Contracting Considerations, Air Force General Counsel Guidance Document, Department of the Air Force, November 2003; HQ AFMC Contingency Contracting Web Site <https://www.afmc-mil.wpafb.af.mil/HQ-AFMC/PK/pko/gotowar.htm>; Contracting Support on the Battlefield, Army Field Manual 4-100.2 (FM100-10-2), 4 Aug 1999; Contractors Accompanying the Force, Army Regulation 715–9, 29 October 1999: AMC Contracts and Contracting Supporting Military Operations, Army Materiel Command Pamphlet 715–18, 16 June

Nevertheless these rules of engagement (ROE) applied to security contractors and coalition forces military personnel alike. It was common for newly recruited PMC personnel to be handed a complete copy of the ROE set forth by the theatre commander and prepared by the regional judge advocate general (JAG) office, which the employee had to study and sign. They were typically briefed on any changes or updates to the ROE and during each operations order and convoy brief the convoy leader or team leader reviewed the ROE.

One proposed provision to a Defense Department regulation required deployed contractors to follow combatant commanders' orders as long as those actions did not require the contractor employee to engage in armed conflict with an enemy force.[23] Those orders would supersede any existing contract terms or directions from a contracting officer.[24] The draft regulation also banned contract personnel from carrying privately owned weapons unless authorized by a military commander and from wearing military uniforms. The policy nevertheless allowed the combatant commander to issue weapons and ammunition to contractor employees.[25]

On 3 October 2005 the Pentagon released DoD Instruction 3020.41 'Contractor Personnel Authorized to Accompany the US Armed Forces'. This regulation was issued pursuant to a provision in the 2005 Defense Authorization Act and tied together nearly 60 Pentagon directives and Joint Staff doctrinal statements that relate to the role of contractors on the battlefield. The 33-page document clarified the legal status of civilians hired to support US military forces in a contingency. The new instruction also explained when contractors can carry weapons in areas where US troops operate—places like Iraq, where armed contractors have been operating for more than two years without clear regulatory guidance.

From the viewpoint of firms like Blackwater or Triple Canopy the new regulation was important because it established detailed criteria for civilian contractors to carry weapons, which are to be used only in self-defence. It also set forth detailed procedures for arming contingency contractor personnel for security services. The question now is how it will be implemented. Reportedly a number of Defense

---

1999; Concept for Managing Weapon System Contractors During Military Operations, Draft, 16 June 1999; Contractor Deployment Guide, Department of the Army Pamphlet 715–16, 27 February 1998; Contractors On The Battlefield, Army Field Manual 3-100.21 (FM100-21), March 2000; 'Institutionalizing Contractor Support on the Battlefield,' *Army Logistician*, vol 32, no 4 (July–August 2000) 12–15, 22; Joe A Fortner, 'Managing, Deploying, Sustaining, and Protecting Contractors on the Battlefield,' *Army Logistician*, vol 32, no 5 (September–October 2000) 3–7; PL106-523, Military Extraterritorial Jurisdiction Act of 2000; and OMB Circular No A-76, Performance of Commercial Activities, 4 August 1983 (Revised 1999); and the bibliography *Contractors on the Battlefield*, Library Notes, Naval War College, October 2003, vol 32, no 2, available at <http://www.nwc.navy.mil/library/3Publications/NWCLibraryPublications/LibNotes/libContractors.htm>.

[23] Ibid.
[24] David Phinney, 'DoD Rule Would Permit Arming of Contractors,' *Federal Times*, 29 March 2004, 1. See also Federal Register: 23 March 2004 (Volume 69, Number 56) [Proposed Rules] [Page 13500–13503] SUMMARY: DoD is proposing to amend the Defense Federal Acquisition Regulation Supplement (DFARS) to address issues related to contract performance outside the United States. The proposed rule contains a clause for use in contracts that require contractor employees to accompany a force engaged in contingency, humanitarian, peacekeeping, or combat operations. [25] Ibid.

Federal Acquisition Regulations are being modified to reflect the guidance in the new instruction. But it may be too difficult to retroactively implement all of the rules and regulations spelled out in the policy to cover all of the contracts already in effect in Iraq.

Congressional oversight

During the first couple of years of PMC activity in Iraq—aside from those who have grandstanded on the issue, focusing on the misdeeds by Halliburton and KBR—there has not been a lot of sustained attention paid by Congress to the issue of control and accountability of PMCs. This is unfortunate because most firms say privately that they would welcome reasonable proposals.

While only a handful of PMCs publicly voiced support for Congressional oversight, these tend to be the companies with the majority of people on the ground. According to David Claridge, managing director of the British company Janusian Security, 'Most of the serious players are quite supportive of bringing in some degree of regulation. It is traditionally globally an unregulated industry except with a few exceptions. Iraq is forcing the industry to grow up and consider how the industry should be regulated.'[26]

In 2004 the US Congress, as part of its annual military authorization bill, directed the Pentagon to develop new management guidelines for defence contractors in Iraq and to provide a report on their activities.[27] The House version of the Bill for the 2005 defence budget required Secretary of Defense Donald Rumsfeld to implement a process for collection of information on contractors providing security services in Iraq within 30 days. He would have 90 days to issue rules on managing contractors.

The Senate version also required the Defense Department to supply information on contractors.[28] Two amendments were proposed. One prescribed new limitations so that contractors could only be used if DoD military or civilian personnel 'cannot reasonably be made available to perform the functions'. Among

---

[26] Peter Brownfeld, 'Military Contractors Shoulder Heavy Burden in Iraq,' 16 April 2004, <http://www.foxnews.com/story/0,2933,117239,00.html>.

[27] See section 1205 of the House version of the 2005 Defense Authorization Act (HR 4200) on 'guidance and report required on contractors supporting deployed forces in Iraq,' <http://www.fas.org/sgp/congress/2004/defauth-cont.html>.

[28] Edmond Lococo, 'US Congress Seeking More Information on Contractors in Iraq,' *Bloomberg*, 21 May 2004, <http://quote.bloomberg.com/apps/news?pid=10000103&sid=aHT5mc1ZzE5s &refer=us>. S. 2400, [Report No. 108-260] To authorize appropriations for fiscal year 2005 for military activities of the Department of Defense, for military construction, and for defense activities of the Department of Energy, to prescribe personnel strengths for such fiscal year for the Armed Forces, and for other purposes. In the Senate of the United States, 11 May 2004. The relevant language was in Sec 865, which called for a report on contractor performance of security, intelligence, law enforcement, and criminal justice functions in Iraq.

other activities, those functions include supervising contractor performance and performing all inherently government-related functions. The other amendment would prohibit the use of contractors in interrogation of prisoners and for use in combat missions.

But the US Congress thus far seems ambivalent to the amendments. On 16 June 2004, soon after the Abu Ghraib revelations, the Senate defeated the attempt to ban private contractors in military interrogations. The plan to bar private interrogators within 90 days and translators within a year was rejected on a 54–43 vote; the tougher criminal penalties, of as much as 20 years, were defeated 52–46.[29] To date they have not been reintroduced.

Problems with PMC operations in Iraq, however, will not be solved by passing a few new laws. With the benefit of hindsight it seems clear that a lack of strategic planning affected private sector operations in Iraq in the same way it affected the regular US military. Co-ordination of PMCs was deficient and they were not given sufficient early warning before the war about how much their service would be needed. Even without hindsight it is clear that some things should have been done that were not. The US Project and Contracting Office, set up in 2004, should have been established before the war. Similarly, the contract awarded to Aegis Defence to provide security on all major Iraqi government projects should have been foreseen before the war.

One of the benefits of involving the private sector is that it can scale up and adapt faster than the regular military; a problem confronted in Iraq, however, was that the Pentagon's oversight mechanisms could not be scaled up quickly enough to keep pace. The shortened timeframe meant hasty tendering of contracts, which denied both the contracting PMC and the awarding organization the necessary time to make careful decisions. In addition, with the explosion of companies within the industry in Iraq, and the reduced timeframes for tenders, those awarding contracts had insufficient information about the companies tendering for contracts. This was exacerbated by that fact that those awarding the contracts often had little experience of the industry or of their own organization's security needs.[30]

Iraq also shows that some flexibility in contract pricing and delivery is required. Fixed-price contracts, for example, encourage underbidding by less reputable companies, while their more reputable counterparts include costs to cover deterioration in the security situation.[31] There have also been several cases where security contractor personnel in Iraq turned out to be unqualified, both professionally and ethically. Though there were far fewer of these cases than casually asserted in media reports, there were enough to warrant concern.

---

[29] Carl Hulse, 'Senate Rejects Harder Penalties On Companies, And Ban On Private Interrogators,' *New York Times*, 17 June, 2004.
[30] This point comes from William Moloney, *What has been the experience of the Private Military Industry in Iraq and what are the possible lessons for future deployments?*, Masters Dissertation-2004, War Studies Department, Kings College, London, unpublished research paper, 15.   [31] Ibid.

Measures to address such concerns would include increasing the number of regulators and earlier screening of PMC personnel. If PMCs were required to keep a register of their staff, some form of periodical review by government inspectors would be possible, with less intrusive oversight for those companies maintaining a good record—something similar currently happens with export licensing. Alternatively, a purely voluntary regulatory approach might be considered, with companies solely responsible for carrying out their own background checks, but with a system of financial and criminal penalties in place as a 'backstop' for when transgressions come to light. Other methods that rely on the contractual arrangement are discussed by James Cockayne and Laura Dickinson in chapters eleven and twelve. Lawmakers should also address the concerns raised by outsourcing inappropriate activities, such as the use of contractors for interrogations. The key consideration should be whether someone is qualified and operating within the law, but some positions may be simply too sensitive to be outsourced. Operationally, Congress should bring in auditors from other governmental agencies, such as the inspector general offices of the various military services. If past GAO reports tell us anything it is that that too few contract officers are trying to manage vast numbers of contracts worth billions of dollars, with predictable results.

To deal with abusive behaviour, the loopholes in the Military Extraterritorial Jurisdiction Act (MEJA) must be closed. No less importantly, government lawyers must be bold enough to start prosecuting cases using MEJA. To date they have been reluctant to do so, sometimes citing insufficient precedent on which to rely. But unless they start trying cases there will never be precedent.

A promising, if partial, step forward is the development of industry standards, which need to be enhanced and enforced. The formation of new trade associations in Britain and Iraq, in addition to the International Peace Operations Association, is a welcome step. Internationally, the involvement of groups like the International Committee of the Red Cross, which is working with the Swiss government to promote standards for the use of PMCs on the battlefield, is also a welcome development.[32]

The most basic tool for shaping PMC behaviour is, of course, economic. The lifeblood of PMCs is profit. Shaping financial incentives and disincentives should therefore be a high priority. For example, banning the hiring of firms that have overcharged government in the past or have committed crimes in the contracting process would be desirable. The guilty verdict against Custer Battles for fraud and fines against the company of over $10 million, although subsequently overturned by a federal judge, may therefore be an encouraging precedent.[33]

---

[32] Swiss Government, Swiss Initiative in Cooperation with the International Committee of the Red Cross to Promote Respect for International Humanitarian Law and Human Rights Law with Regard to Private Military and Security Companies Operating in Conflict Situations, see <http://www.eda.admin.ch/etc/medialib/downloads/edazen/topics/intla/humlaw.Par.0025.File.tmp/PMSCs%20-%20Outline%20-%20engl.%20(1.3.07).pdf>.

[33] Charles R Babcock, 'Contractor Bilked US On Iraq Work, Federal Jury Rules,' *Washington Post*, 10 March 2006, 14; 'Jury fines defense contractor in Iraq $10M,' Laura Parker, *USA Today*, 10 March

Conclusion

The use of PMCs in Iraq represents both a challenge and an opportunity. Their activities in Iraq have made public a number of issues that were previously of interest only to academics, some journalists, and people inside the industry itself. These include the complications of working both for and with regular military forces, recruiting qualified personnel, maintaining high standards of training, not undercutting civil-military relations, ensuring proper competition in awarding contracts, auditing contracts, and ensuring public control and accountability over the activities of PMCs, especially when it comes to the use of lethal force.

PMC personnel in Iraq have shot their weapons in hundreds of incidents but to date not a single contractor has been prosecuted. Either every single use of force has been beyond reproach or someone is looking the other way. Effective public accountability, despite the increase in the number of new laws and regulations on the books that at least theoretically apply to PMCs, is still lacking.

There are, however, things that can be done to improve the situation. Other chapters in this volume outline creative ways of enhancing the applicable norms, or using market-based tools to improve behaviour and punish abuse. Additional creative possibilities might include extending court-martial jurisdiction to civilian contractors.[34] The Uniform Code of Military Justice (UCMJ) details procedures for prosecuting members of the military should they commit a crime abroad. Article 2 of the code provides jurisdiction over 'persons serving with or accompanying an armed force in the field,' but only 'in time of war,' which the courts have held to mean a war formally declared by the Congress. The status of the 'global war on terror' is a key element of this.

While states and PMCs disagree over the specifics of various regulatory proposals ultimately they understand that the current state of affairs benefits no one. Companies understand that increased oversight and regulation protect them from the relatively few unsavoury types who periodically crop up in the PMC world. At the same time, oversight offers them credibility and increased business opportunities.

2006, 3A; and T Christian Miller, 'US Contractor Found Liable for Fraud in Iraq,' *Los Angeles Times*, 10 March 2006.

[34] William C Peters, 'On Law, Wars and Mercenaries: The Case for Courts-Martial Jurisdiction over Civilian Contract Misconduct in Iraq,' Brigham Young University Law Review (2006) 367.

6

Transitional states in search of support

Private military companies and security sector reform

Elke Krahmann

Security sector reform and private military assistance have become booming businesses for private military companies (PMCs).[1] In Afghanistan alone the US government expects to spend up to $7.2 billion by 2009 on training the new National Army and approximately $600 million annually to sustain security sector reform over the coming years.[2] In Iraq, contracts over $50 million and $48 million were awarded for the training of the military and police forces respectively to DynCorp International and Vinnell (with MPRI as its subcontractor), and an additional $18.4 billion worth were approved by US Congress for further security sector reforms in 2004.[3]

Western nations are also spending an increasing amount on the reform and training of security sector personnel in Africa. US military training programmes under the Pan Sahel Initiative have been established in Chad, Mali, Mauretania, Niger, Algeria, Morocco, Senegal, Tunisia, and Nigeria, and a new Global Peace Initiative by the State Department plans to train and equip peacekeepers for the African Union and other regional organizations.[4] In Liberia the United States is committed to helping with security sector reform by the training of a newly recruited and vetted armed force of 2,000 and by providing Liberia with training assistance administered by the UN Mission in Liberia (UNMIL) for civilian police

---

[1] This chapter takes the view that the line between military assistance and security sector reform is fluid. In particular, contemporary military assistance programmes in Africa include elements of security sector reform. See Andrew Cottey and Anthony Forster, *Reshaping Defence Diplomacy: New Roles for Military Cooperation and Assistance*, Adelphi Paper 365 (Oxford: Oxford University Press, 2004).

[2] United States Government Accountability Office (GAO), Afghanistan Security: Efforts to Establish Army and Police Have Made Progress, but Future Plans Need to Be Better Defined, GAO-05-575, June 2005, 3.

[3] Andrew Rathmell, Olga Oliker, Terrence K Kelly, David Brannan, and Keith Crane, 'Developing Iraq's Security Sector. The Coalition Provisional Authority's Experience,' RAND National Defense Research Institute, Report, 2005, 34.

[4] Samantha L Quigley, 'EUCOM Leader Calls Africa Global Strategic Initiative,' *American Forces Press Service*, 8 March 2006, available at: <http://www.defenselink.mil/news/Mar2006/20060308_4428.html>.

forces.[5] Under the contracts, which are administered by the State Department and are projected to cost $95 million, DynCorp is in charge of vetting, recruitment, and basic military training, while PAE supplies specialized advanced training services, equipment, and logistics.[6]

Meanwhile, the transformation and professionalization of national armed forces, police, and judiciary in Central and Eastern Europe is far from complete. The new members of and applicants to NATO and the European Union are expected to show that they are willing and able to participate fully within both organizations and contribute to international operations. As a result, PMCs such as Cubic Applications Inc, MPRI, and DynCorp have assisted security sector reforms in Hungary, the Czech Republic, Slovakia, Romania, Albania, Lithuania, Bulgaria, Croatia, Bosnia, and Kosovo.[7]

This survey suggests that there are two forms of private military assistance to security sector reform programmes. The first is the employment of private contractors by donor states, predominantly the United States, seeking to improve security sector governance in transitional societies through specific national or regional programmes. The second is the hiring of PMCs by transitional states, such as Croatia, Bosnia, and Romania, themselves. Each is faced with distinct challenges. Each also proceeds under different conditions that determine whether there are alternatives to private military assistance. While donor states would in theory be able to use uniformed personnel instead of private contractors, transitional states frequently have no other way of obtaining the necessary expertise when donors are lacking. Crucially, in most transitional states security sector reform is believed to be essential for the long-term success of the transformation to a peaceful and stable society.[8]

This chapter examines the challenges posed by the involvement of PMCs in military assistance and security sector reform. It argues that not all of these challenges can be addressed through improved legislation because some are due to the inherent disadvantages of private security sector reform assistance in comparison with military-to-military exchange and education programmes. The chapter first outlines the nature of security sector reform and the role of PMCs in the past two decades. The second section discusses why transitional and donor states are employing private contractors. Sections three and four consider the diverse challenges faced respectively by transitional and donor states that hire private contractors. The fifth section examines how these challenges have been or might be resolved. The chapter concludes that the question of whether to employ private contractors in

[5] Nicolas Cook, *Liberia's Post-War Recovery: Key Issues and Developments*, CRS Report for Congress, Washington, DC: Congressional Research Service, Library of Congress, 13 December 2005, 6. [6] Ibid.

[7] Cubic, at <http://www.cubic.com/cai1/force_enhance.html>; MPRI, at <http://www.mpri.com>; DynCorp, at <http://www.dyn-intl.com/subpage.aspx?id=42>.

[8] Jeremy King, A Walter Dorn and Matthew Hodes, 'An Unprecendented Experiment: Security Sector Reform in Bosnia and Herzegovina,' Bonn International Center for Conversion (BICC) and Saferworld, September 2002, 8.

security sector reform cannot be reduced to issues of accountability and control. It rather proposes that we need to ask first whether private military and security sector reform programmes are indeed as or more efficient and effective than uniformed military assistance and co-operation.

Security sector reform

Before one can turn to an analysis of the growing role of private contractors in the provision of security transition programmes, it is necessary to explain what is meant by security sector reform. According to Heiner Hänggi, security sector reform is aimed at establishing 'the efficient and effective provision of state and human security within the framework of democratic governance'.[9] It contains two elements, which may be of varying importance depending on the country-specific context: efficiency and effectiveness, and democratization and civilian control.[10] In post-authoritarian states the primary objective is the democratization of existing military and police forces and the supporting state apparatus. In developing states, improving the effectiveness and efficiency of the security sector is of foremost concern. In post-conflict societies, public security is frequently neither effective nor democratic, but requires the establishment of a new security apparatus.[11] In the latter cases, it may be more appropriate to speak of security sector transformation rather than merely reform.[12] Improving the effectiveness and efficiency of the security sector involves the creation of public agencies that are able to safeguard public security at the domestic level and to protect national borders from incursion. This allows citizens to engage in social, political, and economic activities without fear of violence.[13] Democratization suggests the establishment of public accountability, transparency, control, and participation in relation to the security sector.[14]

Recent models of security sector reform emphasize that the security sector needs to be viewed in holistic terms. It is not sufficient to focus exclusively on reforming the military, for example. Rather, security sector reform must incorporate the transformation of all political and societal forces that either legitimately or illegitimately control collective means of violence. In post-conflict societies,

---

[9] Heiner Hänggi, 'Conceptualizing Security Sector Reform and Reconstruction,' in Alan Bryden and Heiner Hänggi (eds), *Reform and Reconstruction of the Security Sector* (Münster: Lit 2004) 3.

[10] Timothy Edmunds, 'Security Sector Reform: Concepts and Implementation,' in Wilhelm N Germann and Timothy Edmunds (eds), *Towards Security Sector Reform in Post Cold War Europe* (Baden-Baden: Nomos, 2003) 16.

[11] Hänggi, 'Conceptualizing Security Sector Reform and Reconstruction' (n 9 above) 10.

[12] Adedeji Ebo, 'Security Sector Reform as an Instrument of Sub-Regional Transformation in West Africa,' in Alan Bryden and Heiner Hänggi (eds), *Reform and Reconstruction of the Security Sector* (n 9 above) 66.

[13] Edmunds, 'Security Sector Reform: Concepts and Implementation' (n 10 above) 17.

[14] Hänggi, 'Conceptualizing Security Sector Reform and Reconstruction' (n 9 above) 7.

these mechanisms may not be restricted to state institutions, but also include non-state actors such as local militias and warlords. In addition, the agents of public security include armed forces, police, customs, border and coastal guards, gendarmeries, paramilitary forces, secret services, and justice and penal agencies.[15]

Furthermore, security sector reform can neither be understood nor implemented without consideration of the global security environment in which transitional states are placed. The ability and willingness of transitional societies to engage in security sector reform is influenced by factors such as the global supply of arms, the emphasis on coercion in international interventions, as well as favourable or unfavourable trade relations such as structural adjustment programmes and aid dependence.[16]

Accordingly, security sector reform must involve both national and international responses in order to be effective. At the national level, security sector reform has focused on organizational and political change. Depending on national circumstances, organizational change may include the demobilization of illegitimate armed units, the reduction or expansion of national armed and police forces, the restructuring of the military and the police, the establishment or reform of judiciary agencies such as courts and penal institutions, and the reform or creation of ministries charged with the execution of security sector policies. Political transformation refers to the establishment of democratic control over these agencies. It is frequently referred to in terms of 'good governance', which includes principles such as the promotion of human rights, law, public accountability, and transparency.[17] At the international level, security sector reform can be supported by efforts to control the export of weapons to conflict and post-conflict regions, the creation of legal regimes that seek to limit the use of force in dispute resolution, and the provision of international aid and assistance.[18]

PMCs contribute to security sector reform through a variety of services ranging from consulting and institutional reform to police and military training. In terms of the policies outlined above, PMCs have so far been primarily engaged in organizational reform and transformation at the domestic level. However, within these areas the scope of their activities has been extensive. Private contractors have provided expertise on the design and structure of defence and police ministries, national armed and police forces, future force levels and strategy. In addition, they have helped with the training of these forces and offer long-term mentoring to ensure the effective implementation of the proposed changes. Moreover, there is a growing potential for the employment of PMCs by international organizations for global or regional programmes in support of security sector reform. The United

[15] Ibid, 6.

[16] Neil Cooper and Michael Pugh, Security Sector Transformation in Post-Conflict Societies, London: Centre for Defence Studies King's College London, The Conflict and Development Group Working Paper No 5, February 2002, 6, 9.

[17] Hänggi, 'Conceptualizing Security Sector Reform and Reconstruction,' (n 9 above) 3–5.

[18] Cooper and Pugh, 'Security Sector Transformation in Post-Conflict Societies' (n 16 above).

Nations, for instance, uses private contractor DynCorp as part of the US contribution to its security sector reform programme in Liberia.[19]

Private contractors are equally interesting for the kinds of services they cannot or do not offer. These omissions give an indication of the limitations of using PMCs for security sector reform. Specifically, PMCs are rarely involved in the political side of security sector reform, such as democratization projects, the fostering of civil society, and the establishment of good governance. Programmes designed to improve civilian accountability of the security sector and promote democratic civil-military relations are typically provided by donor governments, international organizations, and non-governmental organizations. Privatization can thus create or exacerbate tensions between organizational and political reforms. Similarly, military and police training frequently take precedence over judicial and administrative transformations.[20]

Reasons for privatization

Any assessment of the use of PMCs in security sector reform programmes has to start with the question of why both transitional and donor states choose to hire private contractors in the first place. What are the reasons for employing private contractors?

There are numerous advantages of employing PMCs for security sector reform programmes. Among them are contractors' flexibility, including their ability to deploy on short notice under existing contracts and their capacity to hire personnel with specific expertise and language skills in response to customers' needs. In addition, private contractors bring with them a high level of experience, as most contractor personnel have trained in the military or the police. Finally, contractors offer reliability and continuity because contractors are not subject to rotation or redeployment to other, more pressing, missions.[21]

In spite of these advantages, however, both transitional and donor states view PMCs as a second choice when compared to using uniformed military or police forces. As one US State Department official argued: 'In the best of all worlds, we would prefer if all of our training would be done by uniformed military. They are the most current experts and it is our view ... that our partners would prefer uniformed military.'[22] This is confirmed by Christopher Shoemaker, Senior Vice

[19] United Nations Mission in Liberia (UNMIL), Weekly Press Briefing, 25 January 2006, available at <http://www.unmil.org/article.asp?id=1004>.

[20] Jeremy King, A Walter Dorn and Matthew Hodes, 'An Unprecendented Experiment: Security Sector Reform in Bosnia and Herzegovina' (n 8 above) 7.

[21] Interviews with State Department officials, 22 and 24 May 2006; Richard Roan and John Sevold, 'African Contingency Operations Training and Assistance Program (ATCO),' PowerPoint presentation at Conference 21st Century Marines in Africa: West and Central Regions, Center for Emerging Threats and Opportunities, 18–19 January 2006.

[22] Interview with State Department official, 22 May 2006; see also PW Singer, *Corporate Warriors: The Rise of the Privatized Military Industry* (Ithaca: Cornell University Press, 2003) 122.

President for Strategic Planning of MPRI, who admits that 'initially [recipient states] would prefer to have uniform wearing military personnel' because the latter provides 'tangible evidence of US commitment'.[23] However, for transitional states the hire of private contractors is frequently a necessity because of a lack of donor states which are willing and able to send personnel with the appropriate training and expertise from their national armed and police forces. According to Enes Becirbasic, a Bosnian military official who managed the training of the Bosnian army: 'I would have preferred direct cooperation with state organizations like NATO or the Organization for Security and Cooperation in Europe. But we had no choice. We had to use MPRI.'[24] Even if international donors directly or indirectly pay for the contractors, as in Bosnia or in Liberia, transitional states would prefer co-operating with uniformed international personnel.[25] National military and police forces not only represent the short- and long-term engagement of their home countries and the international community, but also help to establish important direct contacts between the donor's and the recipient's armed forces and governments.[26]

Similarly, the US government's employment of PMCs for security sector reform programmes overseas appears to have little to do with the touted advantages of contractors in terms of deployability, efficiency, and effectiveness. It has rather been the result of persistent government pressure on the US armed forces to focus on combat functions and to outsource military and support services to commercial providers. The Clinton administration, which initiated the current policy of military privatization and outsourcing in the mid-1990s, identified military training as one of the first candidates for a transfer to the private sector. It thereby reduced the number of uniformed personnel with the relevant expertise for security sector reform programmes. According to US military officers, the increased operational tempo under George W Bush, with simultaneous missions in Afghanistan and Iraq, has put further strain on personnel and has thus 'forced program managers to hire contractors' for security sector reform projects.[27] Moreover, as the government faces increasing public demands to withdraw its national armed forces from Afghanistan and Iraq, security sector reform programmes have had to be cut short or accelerated.

The 'war on terror' has at the same time led to greater US and international demand and support for security sector reform in Africa, Central Asia, and the Caucasus. One of the primary concerns is to train effective military and counterterrorism forces in order to gain local support for the fight against global terrorist networks. The US National Security Strategy policy on Africa specifically identifies

[23] Interview with Dr Christopher Shoemaker, 30 May 2006.
[24] Ian Traynor, 'The Privatization of War,' *Guardian*, 10 December 2003.
[25] Liberia National Dialogue on Security Sector Reform, Summary Report, Corina Hotel, Monrovia, Liberia, 3–4 August 2005, 7, available at <http://www.dcaf.ch/awg/ev_monrovia_050803report.pdf>.   [26] Interview with US State Department official, 22 May 2006.
[27] General Alfred M Gray, '21st Century Marines in Africa: West and Central Regions,' Center for Emerging Threats and Opportunities, Conference report, 18–19 January 2006, 14.

security sector reform as a means by which to promote stability and fight terror-ism on the continent. Objectives include defence reform, the development of professional armed forces in African nations and helping regional security organ-izations to develop indigenous capabilities for the 'war on terror' and regional peacekeeping.[28]

Transitional states' hire of PMCs

In spite of the growing emphasis on security sector reform as a means to fight ter-rorism and as a condition for stability and peace, transitional states may find it difficult to obtain international uniformed military or police assistance. In particu-lar, post-authoritarian states with functioning but not fully democratic security sectors are rarely a top priority for potential donors and international organiza-tions. Developing and post-conflict states where effective military and police forces are lacking are more likely to receive direct assistance. This reflects a general pre-occupation with organizational rather than political reforms, although most governments and agencies in theory accept that security sector reform has to be approached holistically and cannot be limited to one or the other.[29] In practice, resource constraints determine which states receive security sector assistance and in what form, with the aim of achieving basic levels of security taking precedence over accountability.

As a consequence, many recent examples of transitional states directly hiring PMCs for assistance in security sector reform can be found in Central and Eastern Europe. The perhaps best-researched cases include the private military assistance and security sector reforms in Bosnia and Croatia.[30] However, most of the new NATO and European Union members have hired PMCs for specific training pro-grammes and to advise them on the restructuring of their armed forces.

In the overwhelming number of these cases, private contractors have shown themselves to be experienced and professional, and they have made significant contributions to security sector reforms. However, particularly in the early years of the security sector reform boom, companies were still developing the necessary expertise. In Bosnia, MPRI was thus criticized because it only provided training for the Federation Army and not that of the Republika Srpska, thereby undermin-ing integration efforts and 'polarising the state military'.[31]

[28] General Alfred M Gray, '21st Century Marines' (n 27 above), Foreword by RA Gangle.
[29] David Law, 'Security Sector Reform in the Euro-Atlantic Region: Unfinished Business,' in Alan Bryden and Heiner Hänggi (eds), *Reform and Reconstruction of the Security Sector* (n 9 above) 26.
[30] PW Singer, *Corporate Warriors* (n 22 above); Deborah D Avant, *The Market for Force. The Consequences of Privatizing Security* (Cambridge: Cambridge University Press, 2005).
[31] King, et al, 'An Unprecedented Experiment: Security Sector Reform in Bosnia and Herzegovina,' (n 20 above) 13; Marina Caparini, 'Security Sector Reform and Post-Conflict Stabilization: The Case of the Western Balkans,' in Alan Bryden and Heiner Hänggi (eds), *Reform and Reconstruction of the Security Sector* (n 9 above) 151.

Nevertheless, a number of problems continue to characterize the direct hire of private contractors for military assistance and security sector reform. Few of these problems are attributable to any fault on the side of the companies. They are rather a consequence of their nature as a private and commercial security provider, and the capabilities of their employers. Specifically, the direct control of the transitional state over the contract has positive as well as negative aspects. On the one hand, it might be argued that the hiring of private companies by transitional states themselves ensures a state's ownership over its security sector reforms and increases their chances of long-term success. On the other hand, the example of Croatia suggests that states that are in need of security sector reforms, in particular of improved democratic control, are not well positioned to implement these reforms independently. Contractors lack the authority to enforce security sector reforms and, with the old structures and personnel still in place, can be led to cater to entrenched interests. It has therefore been suggested that MPRI, which was hired in 1995 for Croatia's Democracy Transition Assistance Programme and strategic long-term capability planning, provided strategic training rather than support for democratic reform.[32] Although these allegations have been denied by MPRI, the offensive Operation Storm, which was launched a few months after contract work commenced, was characterized by both US-style military operations and serious human rights atrocities, raising questions about MPRI's schooling.[33]

A second issue is the question of long-term funding for security sector reform programmes. Not only do they come without the automatic financial support of a particular donor, such as the US International Military Education and Training (IMET) programme, private contractors are also essentially profit-oriented. Unlike donor states' uniformed military and police trainers, PMCs will only be available as long as a transitional state can fund a particular project. Since developing and post-conflict states often have limited resources, private military and security assistance might have to be constrained to a few select programmes, with the transformation to democratic security sector governance often considered less important than short-term safety and stability.

Central and Eastern European states have thus hired PMCs primarily for programmes aimed at improving the effectiveness and efficiency of their armed forces, including force structure modernization, logistics restructuring, doctrine, training, as well as personnel development and management.[34] The danger of this approach is that it in fact destabilizes a transitional state by 'providing a military that is capable, well resourced, well led, which is out of kilt with everything else in the country.'[35] Security sector reform needs to be comprehensive.

The situation has been worse in African states such as Sierra Leone and Angola, discussed by Taya Weiss and Angela McIntyre in chapter four. Rather than for security

[32] Avant, *The Market for Force* (n 30 above) 101–109.
[33] Singer, *Corporate Warriors* (n 22 above) 126.
[34] Cubic, available at <http://www.cubic.com/cai1/force_enhance.html>.
[35] Interview with British military officer, 25 May 2006.

sector reforms, the Sierra Leonean and Angolan governments employed PMCs such as Executive Outcomes and Sandline International to help restore basic security in national crises. Controversially, both states were only able to afford private assistance by granting mining concessions to international extractive corporations associated with the PMCs.[36] Moreover, soon after the end of these private interventions, violence re-erupted in the two states since the fundamental problems and weaknesses within their national security sectors had not been addressed. According to David J Francis the intervention in Sierra Leone failed to 'address the permanent security concern of the government because of the undisciplined army and the collapse of the state apparatus ... and functioned as a quick fix security at whatever price'.[37]

Fortunately, Sierra Leone has since obtained international assistance from the British government for a long-term security sector transformation programme. Britain has signed a 10-year memorandum with the Sierra Leone government on political, economic, and security sector reform, including a commitment of £15 million annually for an International Military Advisory Training Team (IMATT). The goal of the IMATT is to transform the 'Republic of Sierra Leone armed forces into an accountable, self-sustaining, and professional force'.[38] Unlike the United States, however, Britain is relying mostly on uniformed personnel to implement its military assistance and security sector reform programmes. According to a British military officer, who commanded a Sierra Leonean battalion as part of the British training, close interaction between military trainers and their students is crucial for instilling the moral components of effective and democratic armed forces not only in theory but also in practice.[39]

Finally, the direct hire of private military contractors fails to establish the important transnational military-to-military relations which help to integrate transitional states and their armed forces into the broader international community and its norms. One of the key reasons why transitional and donor states prefer uniformed personnel to help with security sector reforms is that foreign military and police forces are their direct counterparts. They not only serve as role models for the conduct of effective, efficient, and democratic security forces, but also provide access to military and government officials who can help provide long-term international support for security sector reforms.

[36] David J Francis, 'Mercenary Intervention in Sierra Leone: Providing National Security or International Exploitation?' *Third World Quarterly*, vol 20, no 2 (1999) 322–3; Gerry Cleaver, 'Subcontracting Military Power: The Privatization of Security in Contemporary Sub-Saharan Africa,' *Crime, Law & Social Change*, vol 33, no 1–2 (2000) 139–41.

[37] Francis, 'Mercenary Intervention in Sierra Leone,' (n 36 above) 330. See also Herbert M Howe, 'Private Security Forces and African Stability: The Case of Executive Outcomes,' *The Journal of Modern African Studies*, vol 36, no 2 (1998) 321.

[38] UK Foreign and Commonwealth Office, Africa—Security Sector Reform, available at <http://www.fco.gov.uk/servlet/Front?pagename=OpenMarket/Xcelerate/ShowPage&c=Page&cid=1094236372310>.   [39] Interview with British military officer, 25 May 2006.

Donor states' hire of PMCs

The challenges faced by donor states that hire PMCs to implement their foreign military assistance and security sector reform programmes overseas are somewhat different. To some degree they are determined by the distinct conditions under which donor states hire contractors. These conditions include the availability of an alternative, namely the use of uniformed personnel, against which private contractors must be measured. They also concern the normative and administrative structures that delimit the employment of PMCs. Finally, there is the issue of multiple principals—that is, the obligations of private contractors towards the donor as well as the recipient state—which is discussed in chapter eleven by James Cockayne. The resulting challenges can be divided into two categories. The first category concerns questions of transparency, accountability, and control that are related to the fact that, in most countries, the normative and administrative structures for the provision of military assistance and security sector reform are designed for the use of uniformed personnel and not private contractors. The second category concerns the efficiency and effectiveness of PMCs in comparison to national military and police forces. Because of these challenges, most countries have so far chosen to rely on their national armed and police forces to implement security sector reform programmes overseas. Only the US government has in the past decade systematically turned to private contractors for assistance; a few other countries, notably Britain, occasionally hire PMCs for training purposes overseas.[40] While focusing on the US experience, the following analysis is illustrative of the problems that may be faced by donor states when using private military and security sector support.

The lack of public information and transparency regarding the employment of PMCs in security sector reform and military assistance programmes funded by the United States is astonishing. Although the US Department of State lists in great detail military assistance and training provided to third countries in its annual reports to Congress, these reports fail to specify whether particular programmes are implemented by the armed forces or by private contractors.[41] In fact, the Defense Security Cooperation Agency, which is tasked with supervising the implementation of foreign security assistance, does not have any centralized information about the involvement of private contractors in training or education programmes. Since all foreign training projects are managed by the respective services, the Army, Navy,

---

[40] UK Ministry of Defence, Operations in Iraq: Key Facts & Figures, available at <http://www.mod.uk/DefenceInternet/FactSheets/OperationsFactsheets/OperationsInIraqKeyFactsFigures.htm>.

[41] Department of State, Bureau of Political-Military Affairs, Foreign Military Training—Joint Report to Congress, Fiscal Years 2000–2005, available at <http://www.state.gov/t/pm/rls/rpt/fmtrpt/>.

Marines, or Air Force decide individually whether to use uniformed personnel or hire private companies for a particular programme.[42] Moreover, while the Department of Defense is responsible for military reform projects, the Department of State manages the reconstruction and training of foreign police forces such as in Afghanistan and Iraq.[43]

According to Francesco Mancini, it is the lack of collective information regarding the use of private contractors that 'makes it difficult for donor agencies to root out bad practices, and there is also a danger of them being ineffective purchasers of private sector [security sector reform] services.'[44] Since there is no centralized collection or exchange of information regarding the cost, use, and performance of particular PMCs between the three services and government departments, important 'lessons learned' are not shared and may in fact be lost.

The problems of transparency and clear chains of accountability are compounded by the existence of multiple principals, the donor government and the recipient state, that may try to control the content and implementation of security sector reform programmes. Since the donor government maintains the primary authority over the contractor through the contract, PMCs can 'become the agents of unwanted change, delivering the wishes of donors without the consent of recipient governments.'[45] At a 2005 workshop on security sector reform in Liberia, participants thus criticized that 'the Liberian people had no role in choosing DynCorp,' which had been hired by the United States to train the new Liberian Army and voiced their concern about the suitability of the company.[46] Specifically, the involvement of DynCorp employees in sex trafficking in Bosnia was mentioned as a reason for the potential exclusion of the company because of Liberia's particular vulnerability in this area. Although there had been no accusations against DynCorp in this respect, tensions emerged between the Liberian Defence Minister Samukai and DynCorp when the company decided to employ a Lebanese company to provide meals for the new Liberian army. The decision showed particular disregard for the new Liberian government's efforts to rebuild the local economy after years of conflict and, according to Samukai, violated the terms of the contract which stipulated that, where possible, DynCorp should use local sources.[47]

It is less likely that private companies are used by the recipient state for their own purposes. As MPRI's Shoemaker argues: 'If we have done this right, we are ... embedded in the [donor] government team.... It usually tends to work out pretty

[42] Phone conversation with the Public Affairs Office, US Defense Security Cooperation Agency, 17 May 2006. See also Defense Security Cooperation Agency, Frequently Asked Questions, available at <http://www.dsca.mil/PressReleases/faq.htm#What%20is%A0Security%20Cooperation>.
[43] Interview with US State Department official, 24 May 2006.
[44] Francesco Mancini, *In Good Company? The Role of Business in Security Sector Reform* (London: DEMOS, 2005) 15–16.   [45] Ibid, 19.
[46] Liberia National Dialogue on Security Sector Reform, Summary Report, Corina Hotel, Monrovia, Liberia, 3–4 August 2005, 7, available at <http://www.dcaf.ch/awg/ev_monrovia_050803report.pdf>.
[47] Charles Crawford, 'Samukai Detests Awarding of Feeding Contract of New Army to Foreigners,' *The Inquirer*, 22 August 2006.

well in the sense of us understanding what the US government wants to accomplish, and then our counterparts on the ground work with us to make any adjustments that need to be made.'[48] If there are conflicting objectives, a company will always follow the wishes of the government that pays the bill. However, where donor governments are indirectly funding private security sector reform assistance, as was the case in Bosnia, it seems possible that donors may have insufficient oversight over programme contents.

A second challenge is the ability of donor states to control the behaviour of private contractor personnel overseas. Although the donor maintains control over security sector reform contractors through the contracts, the legal conditions of PMCs and their employees operating for the US government abroad are less clear. In many cases, US military contractors are exempted from prosecution under foreign national laws through Status of Forces Agreements (SOFAs). In Iraq, where there was no SOFA, Coalition Provision Authority Order 17 unilaterally granted the Multinational Forces and contractor personnel immunity from Iraqi law.[49] At the same time, the US has been slow to assert its legal authority over contractors accused of misdemeanours abroad. Since the passing of the Military Extraterritorial Jurisdiction Act in 2000, only one contractor has been prosecuted.[50] Moreover, PMCs employed for security sector reform are not usually part of military operations. They therefore do not fall under the Military Extraterritorial Jurisdiction Act or any other regulations which have been developed by the US and British defence departments for 'contractors accompanying the armed forces'.[51]

Very few accusations have been made against private military and security contractors engaged in security sector reforms. The best known is the case of DynCorp Aerospace Technology UK Ltd employees involved in illegal prostitution and human trafficking in Bosnia. The contractors were part of the United Nations International Police Task Force which was formed to monitor, advise, and train law enforcement personnel in Bosnia.[52] The accusations were made by another DynCorp employee, Kathryn Bokovac, who was subsequently fired by

---

[48] Interview with Dr Christopher C Shoemaker, 30 May 2006; also interview with State Department official, 24 May 2006.

[49] Coalition Provisional Authority Order Number 17 (Revised), Status of the Coalition Provisional Authority, MNF-Iraq, Certain Missions and Personnel in Iraq, available at <http://www.cpa-iraq.org/regulations/20040627_CPAORD_17_Status_of_Coalition__Rev__with_Annex_A.pdf>.

[50] James J McCullough and Courtney J Edmonds, Contractors on the Battlefield Revisited: The War in Iraq and Its Aftermath, Briefing Papers, Second Series, No. 04-6, 2004, Washington, DC: Thomson West, 6.

[51] US Headquarters Department of the Army, Contractors on the Battlefield, FM 3-100.21, January 2003; US Office of the Under Secretary of Defense for Acquisitions Technology and Logistics, Defense Federal Acquisitions Regulations Supplement (DFARS), Subpart 225.74—Defense Contractors Outside the United States, available at <http://www.acq.osd.mil/dpap/dars/dfars/html/r20060512/225_74.htm>; UK Ministry of Defence, Contractors on Deployed Operations, available at <http://www.ams.mod.uk/ams/content/docs/toolkit/gateway/guidance/condo.htm>.

[52] United Nations Mission in Bosnia Herzegovina, available at <http://www.un.org/Depts/DPKO/Missions/unmibh_p.htm>.

DynCorp, but won a lawsuit for wrongful contract termination.[53] While DynCorp dismissed the implicated personnel, no formal charges were brought forward by Bosnian, British, or US authorities. Uniformed peacekeepers were also accused, but a US Department of Defense Office of Inspector General case report noted that 'contract employees, while considered members of the SFOR and KFOR community, are not subject to the same restrictions that are placed on US Service members'; this included permission to live outside military installations and some companies' lack of monitoring of employee behaviour and misconduct.[54] As a consequence, the likelihood of misconduct is greater among private military contractors than uniformed personnel.

Other accusations include private contractors' participation in offensive action in Iraq.[55] Contracts very clearly state that private military and security personnel employed for the reform and training of the new Iraqi Armed and Police Forces must not become involved in fighting. However, contractors retain the right to self-defence and, in particular when private contractors are accompanying newly-trained police or armed forces on patrol, the line between training and fighting can be crossed. In fact, contractors risk being unconvincing as trainers and mentors if they have to stand back while their students are being attacked. To avoid putting contractors in situations where they would have to defend themselves, private military and police personnel mentoring newly-trained forces on patrol should normally be accompanied by military escorts.[56] Given the competing demands on uniformed military personnel in Afghanistan and Iraq, this means limiting the degree to which private mentors can operate in the field.[57] As an alternative, the State Department has begun to hire additional contractors as security escorts.[58]

The legal constraints on PMC employees can thus impinge upon their effectiveness. Contractors, unlike national armed forces personnel, cannot engage in combat alongside local troops. It would be impossible for a private contractor to be seconded to command a foreign military battalion, as British military officers do as part of the security sector reform programme in Sierra Leone. Yet military officials assert that close daily interaction and 'sharing the same conditions to the maximum extent possible' is essential for conveying not just technical military training, but also the norms underlying democratic armed forces.[59] Moreover, private contractors cannot act as an example of democratic armed forces and their

[53] US Department of the Defense Office of the Inspector General, Assessment of DoD Efforts to Combat Trafficking in Persons, Phase II—Bosnia-Herzegovina and Kosovo, Case Number H03L88433128, 8 December 2003, 9; Anthony Barnett and Solomon Hughes, 'British Firm Accused in UN "Sex Scandal",' *Observer*, 29 July 2001.

[54] US Department of the Defense Office of the Inspector General, Assessment of DoD Efforts to Combat Trafficking in Persons, (n 53 above) 2.

[55] T Christian Miller, 'A Journey that Ended in Anguish,' *Los Angeles Times*, 27 November 2005.

[56] Interview with US State Department official, 24 May 2006.

[57] Inspectors General US Department of State and US Department of Defense, Interagency Assessment of Iraq Police Training, 15 July 2005, 3.

[58] Interview with US State Department official, 24 May 2006.

[59] General Alfred M Gray, '21st Century Marines in Africa: West and Central Regions' (n 27 above) 15. Also interview with British military officer, 25 May 2006.

relations with civil society and other government agencies. Yet according to US State Department officials, foreign military training is most effective 'when training is conducted by uniformed military personnel, who in addition to conducting training can also serve as role models.'[60]

Another factor decreasing the effectiveness of private assistance is the fragmentation of security sector reform projects among multiple public and private providers.[61] Recent security sector reform programmes such as in Afghanistan and Iraq included national and international donors, multiple countries, different government departments, uniformed military and police forces, as well as private contractors from a number of companies. Although academic and government experts emphasize that a holistic approach based on close interagency co-operation is crucial for the success of security sector reform initiatives,[62] current practice seems often to the contrary.

In Afghanistan security sector reform is implemented by five lead nations which each have responsibility for a separate sector. The United States is in charge of training the new Afghan National Army, Germany of the police, Italy of the judiciary, Britain of combating the drugs trade, and Japan of disarmament, demilitarization, and reintegration.[63] When disagreements over the speed of police training provided by the German government led the United States to hire DynCorp to take over part of the training of the Afghan police forces, Germany continued to rely on uniformed police for its schooling of higher-ranking police officers.

In the same way that transitional states are missing an opportunity to build up transnational military-military linkages by employing PMCs, so are donor states. Such linkages between the donor and transitional state are important for long-term monitoring and reinforce the effectiveness of training and other security sector reform programs. The use of private military contractors also limits the ability of the armed forces and other donor agencies to learn and improve its security sector reform programmes. Finally, it inhibits the gathering of information about the progress of reforms in the recipient nation and the development of national military expertise in order to address the growing demand for security sector reform assistance.

Regulation and its limits

As the preceding section illustrates, many problems arising from the use of private contractors in military assistance and security sector reform have little to do with the behaviour of private companies. Many are due, instead, to the inherent

---

[60] General Alfred M Gray, ibid 14. Also interview with Christopher Shoemaker (MPRI), 30 May 2006.

[61] Inspectors General US Department of State and US Department of Defense, Interagency Assessment of Iraq Police Training, 43–4.

[62] General Alfred M Gray, '21st Century Marines in Africa: West and Central Regions' (n 27 above) 4.   [63] GAO, Afghanistan Security (n 2 above) 5.

normative, legal, and practical limits of private military and security advisors when compared to uniformed personnel. Accordingly, regulation can address only some of these problems. Regulation can play a role in improving the accountability of private contractors in security sector reform, but it should not distract from the question of whether PMCs are as efficient and effective as national military and police forces in the assistance of security sector reforms.

Regulation may specifically help to enhance the transparency, accountability, and control of transitional and donor states using private military and security contractors. A first step would be to improve the collective gathering, assessment, and publication of information regarding the use of private military and security contractors for military assistance and security sector reform programmes. For transitional states, which are in the process of reforming their security sectors, this can be particularly difficult as they can lack the capability and structures to ensure the democratic accountability of contractors. Theoretically, it can therefore be an advantage if donor states are involved in managing private contractors employed for security sector reforms. Donor states can also play a role in monitoring the behaviour of national PMCs abroad. In practice, however, neither the United States nor Britain have made serious attempts to oversee their private military and security industries. Both governments themselves lack centralized information about the use and performance of private contractors for their own projects.[64] Only recently have the US and British governments come under pressure to submit their employment of PMCs in Afghanistan and Iraq to greater public scrutiny. The hiring of contractors for security sector reform initiatives is part of the issue. However, compared to more controversial uses of private contractors in military operations such as security convoys and armed protection, private security sector assistance is in danger of being left out of emerging regulatory frameworks.

A second step to enhance the accountability and control over private contractors involves clarifying the legal conditions for their engagement in military assistance and security sector reforms abroad. In 2006 the US Department of Defense took a number of steps towards this aim, although these efforts pertained exclusively to contractors working for the government. Most important is section 552 of the National Defense Authorization Act for Fiscal Year 2007 which expands the application of the Uniform Code of Military Justice to civilians 'accompanying the force' from declared wars to 'wars or contingency operations'.[65]

In addition, the Department of Defense amended the Defense Federal Acquisition Regulation Supplement (DFARS) in two areas. The first amendment clarifies that 'contractor personnel are not authorized to use deadly force against enemy armed

---

[64] British House of Commons Hansard, Written Answers to Questions, Private Security Contractors, 8 June 2004, Vol 422, Part No 597, Column 305W, available at <http://www.publications.parliament.uk/pa/cm200304/cmhansrd/vo040608/text/40608w09.htm>; Phone conversation with the Public Affairs Office, US Defense Security Cooperation Agency, 17 May 2006.

[65] National Defense Authorization Act for Fiscal Year 2007, *Public Law*, 109–364, 17 October 2006, 109th Congress, 120 STAT 2217.

forces other than in self-defense' or 'when necessary to execute their security mission to protect assets/persons, consistent with the mission statement contained in their contract'.[66] Moreover, it states that the 'Military Extraterritorial Jurisdiction Act ... and some other statutes may apply to contractor personnel who commit offenses outside the United States'.[67]

The second amendment modifies the human trafficking rule contained in the Defense Federal Acquisition Regulation 'to include those labor areas that we feel are vulnerable to trafficking practices outside the United States ... supply, construction, and commercial service contracts'.[68] The regulation now gives the 'overseas commander the contract management tools necessary to hold contractors accountable for their labor practices and their employees' actions'.[69] Moreover, DynCorp itself has begun to require employees to sign a letter of agreement regarding a prohibition on human trafficking and requiring personnel to inform management of violations.[70]

While movements in the right direction, there are obvious limitations to the new US controls with regard to contractors hired for security sector reform. The most important is that contracts involving police reforms overseas are awarded and managed by the Department of State and not the Department of Defense. Contractors providing police training are thus not subject to the Military Extraterritorial Jurisdiction Act. Another limitation regards the phrasing of the National Defense Authorization Act for Fiscal Year 2007 which fails to clarify whether civilians 'accompanying the force' also includes personnel not contracted by the Department of Defense.[71]

Finally, there are few national and international safeguards to protect transitional states that hire private military and security contractors from potential exploitation and misconduct. Although the United States is one of the few states in addition to South Africa and Sweden that requires licences for the export of private military and security training, transitional states have to apply their own laws to the companies they hire. In the case of failed states, the ability to prosecute foreign private military and security contractors is questionable. Improved international regulation, specifically the introduction of basic standards and codes of practice for PMCs, would therefore be useful. However, so far all attempts to achieve international regulation of the sector have failed. More effective would be greater involvement of donor states in the management and provision of security

[66] Department of Defense, Defense Acquisitions Regulations System, Contractor Personnel Authorized to Accompany US Armed Forces (DFARS Case 2005-DO13), Interim Rule, Federal Register, Vol 17, No 116, 16 June 2006, 34826.　　　　　　　　　[67] Ibid, 34827.

[68] Steven Donald Smith, 'Defense Department Combats Human Trafficking,' *American Forces Press Service*, 22 June 2006, available at <http://www.defenselink.mil/news/Jun2006/20060622_5481.html>.

[69] Ibid.

[70] US Department of the Defense Office of the Inspector General, Assessment of DoD Efforts to Combat Trafficking in Persons (n 53 above) 10.

[71] McKenna Long & Aldridge Attorneys of Law, 'Civilians Accompanying Forces in the Field Now Subject to US Military Justice,' *Government Contracts Advisory*, vol V, no 4, 29 January 2007.

sector reforms. As has been argued above, most recipient states would prefer uniformed military and security sector reform assistance over private contractors and many rely on the foreign financing of security sector reform programmes.

In addition, there are those challenges that cannot be addressed by regulation. They primarily regard the efficiency and effectiveness of privatized military assistance and security sector reform. Both transitional and donor states believe that uniformed military and police forces have major advantages over private contractors. These advantages include the ability of uniformed personnel to be seconded to foreign armed forces and to participate in local operations, to serve as role models, to establish military-military networks, to directly co-ordinate with other donor agencies involved in security sector reform such as foreign and interior ministries, and to facilitate the long-term commitment of donor governments to security sector reforms abroad. Private contractors can attempt to address these disadvantages and might to some degree be able to ameliorate them, but they will never be equivalent to uniformed personnel.

For donor governments who want to improve the efficiency and effectiveness of foreign military assistance and security sector reform projects, the challenge is therefore to build up national or international pools of uniformed personnel who are specialized in security sector reform. Given the importance of a holistic approach to security sector reform, donor governments will also want to strengthen interagency co-operation through new institutional channels. The British government has already made an attempt to do so by setting up two interdepartmental conflict prevention budgets, one for sub-Saharan Africa and one for global operations, which are jointly funded and managed by the Foreign Office, the Ministry of Defence and the Department for International Development.[72] Moreover, efforts need to be made to enhance international collaboration in order to share the cost and improve co-ordination of multinational security sector reform programmes such as in Afghanistan.

For these changes to happen, donor governments have to accept security sector reform as a new 'core' task of their national armed and police forces. While the United States and other Western governments have recognized the importance of foreign military assistance and security sector reform as a contribution to the global 'war on terror' and regional stability, policy-makers and the military have been slow to draw the conclusion that these policies can only be effectively implemented through a redirection of resources and personnel. Reports about the failure of military and police reforms in Iraq have illustrated that training projects based on a limited number of private contractors are insufficient to achieve and sustain a fundamental transformation of corrupt and undemocratic armed and police forces. Already in 2004 the US Army took charge of the training of the new Iraqi Armed

---

[72] United Kingdom Foreign and Commonwealth Office, Conflict Prevention Pools, available at <http://www.fco.gov.uk/servlet/Front?pagename=OpenMarket/Xcelerate/ShowPage&c=Page&cid=1091891937471>.

Forces after contractors failed to meet projected targets. By 2006 police training in Iraq made it into the newspaper headlines because of allegations that the new Iraqi police forces were 'operating death squads for powerful political groups or simple profit.'[73] The failure of the army and police reforms can be linked to the low number of (contracted) trainers, the unwillingness of the US government to invest sufficient funds in security sector reform, and the limitations of private versus uniformed personnel. DynCorp's police training programme in Iraq, for instance, involved only 500 field mentors for a projected police force of 135,000. Moreover, initially, DynCorp personnel 'were not even getting out of their camps because of security concerns'.[74] The US government's intention was to increase the number of private and uniformed police trainers to 3,000 in 2006. However, the student to trainer ratio would still be significantly lower than in Kosovo.[75]

Conclusion

The growing realization of the importance of security sector reform in the 'war on terror' and for national, regional, and global peace and stability is leading many transitional and donor states to turn to PMCs for assistance. This chapter has examined the challenges that emerge from the privatization of military assistance and security sector reform. It has sought to show that regulation cannot address all of these challenges. The majority of private military and security contractors are professional and efficient. Private contractors have developed considerable expertise in security sector reform, and they have demonstrated their commitment and reliability in many countries. Although there is room for additional regulations in order to improve the accountability of contractors and the governments which hire them, the main challenge appears to lie in the efficiency and effectiveness of security sector reform programmes. This challenge does not arise from the faults of private contractors, but from the failure of donor governments to take security sector reform seriously.

Even before the end of the Cold War, major donor states such as the United States cut back the size of their armed forces with the aim to focus on the 'core' task of combat fighting. Since then, the emergence of new and increasing security demands has forced their armed forces to rely on private contractors for support. Rather than reforming and re-expanding their national armed and police forces to accommodate new tasks such as international peacekeeping, civilian policing, and security sector reform, governments such as the United States and Britain have turned to private military contractors. However, PMCs have a number of inherent

---

[73] Michael Moss and David Rohde, 'Law and Disorder: Misjudgements Marred US Plans for Iraqi Police,' *New York Times*, 21 May 2006. See also Simon Freeman, 'US Troops Arrest Iraqi Police Death Squad,' *Times Online*, 16 February 2006. [74] Ibid.
[75] Ibid.

disadvantages compared to the use of uniformed personnel. They do not have the same direct linkages with other government and international agencies which are necessary for a holistic approach to security sector reform that involves organizational as well as political transformation; they do not have the same authority and legitimacy to direct and implement reforms; and they fail to establish direct military-to-military relations between the donor and the recipient states.

While the current shortage of personnel and expertise in security sector reform among the armed and police forces of donor states suggests a continued role for PMCs, governments should assess their options more carefully in the long term. Given the persistent and growing demand for security sector reform assistance in Central and Eastern Europe, Central Asia, and Africa, donor states would do well to investigate the positive role that their own national armed and police forces can play in preventing conflict through a global support of security sector transformations.

PART III
NORMS

7

Private military companies under international humanitarian law

Louise Doswald-Beck

Private military companies (PMCs) frequently operate in situations of armed conflict, whether international or non-international. They are sometimes hired by a state party to a conflict, less often by a non-state party to an internal armed conflict or by a company seeking to protect its operations in a country where a conflict is taking place. Although PMCs are a relatively new phenomenon, the participation in armed conflicts of persons who are not officially members of the regular armed forces is far from new. International humanitarian law (also known as the 'law of war' or the 'law of armed conflict') has extensive rules relating to such persons, whether it be their status and treatment upon capture, the use of force by or against them, or state or individual responsibility for their actions.

Though there is specific reference to mercenaries in international humanitarian law (IHL), there is no such reference to PMCs in IHL treaties, nor are they specifically regulated in customary international law. It is true, then, to say that there is no discrete regulation of PMCs as such, but not accurate to say that there is no law applicable to them at all. Depending on the circumstances, specific aspects of established law will apply. Some issues, however, remain unclear in the law, which future state practice may resolve.

This chapter will examine existing law and its application to PMCs. Certain issues commonly raised when considering regulation are not actually relevant to IHL. These are, in particular, the classification of the company—in particular whether it calls itself a private military or a security company—and whether such companies are involved in so-called 'offensive' or 'defensive' operations.[1] Any attempt at differentiating between companies on this basis would be counterproductive for IHL. Therefore this chapter will explain the rationale of the relevant parts of IHL in order to have a better sense of how unresolved issues could or should be settled in a way that is coherent with the philosophy of this body of law.

---

[1] See, eg, Protocol I of 1977 additional to the 1949 Geneva Conventions (Additional Protocol I) art 49, which describes 'attacks' for the purpose of IHL as 'acts of violence against the adversary, whether in offence or defence'.

First it is necessary to examine the fundamental issue of which persons are entitled to take part in conflict and benefit from certain privileges when captured. In this context the issue of mercenaries will be discussed. The chapter then turns to the situation of PMC employees considered to be civilians and what this means from the point of view of possible attacks on them as well as treatment on capture. Finally the issues of state responsibility and individual criminal responsibility that are peculiar to IHL will be briefly addressed.[2]

'Combatants' and 'civilians'

International humanitarian law makes a fundamental distinction between members of the armed forces and civilians. The purpose of this distinction is not only to limit civilian casualties, but also to reflect an important facet of traditional interstate relations: members of the army are organs of state and, when captured, are expected to benefit from this official status. Hence, like diplomats, they may not be subjected to prosecution by the capturing state for taking part in the conflict. In particular, they may not be tried for activities normally associated with the conflict—namely killing, inflicting grievous bodily harm, carrying firearms, and so on. This is what 'prisoner-of-war status' means. This privilege, which stemmed from being a state official, historically did not apply to any civilians.[3] Additionally, the concept is not part of the law governing non-international armed conflicts, because conflicts between a government and rebels or between rebels do not have this interstate character.

Major powers have always sought to keep prisoner-of-war (POW) status limited to the official army as, by definition, they have large powerful armies and do not want to favour guerrilla activities. Smaller countries, however, and others who perceive themselves to be at a military disadvantage, have regularly resisted this. The first significant argument over this occurred during the first attempt, in 1874, to codify in treaty form the rules regulating POW status.[4] The result of this effort was adopted at a later conference in 1899.[5] It was a compromise enabling certain groups that do not officially belong to the army, as well as civilians spontaneously resisting an invading army, to benefit from POW status. The argument of the weaker nations was that they had the right to resist invasion and that persons genuinely fighting for their nation should not be tried as common criminals. The rules thus adopted remained with minor adjustments until the negotiation of

---

[2] On state responsibility and PMCs generally see chapter eight in this volume by Chia Lehnardt.

[3] This was first changed in 1899, as will be explained below.

[4] Arts 9–11 of the Project of an International Declaration concerning the Laws and Customs of War, Brussels conference, 1874. This document did not enter into force as a treaty.

[5] In arts 1 and 2 of the Regulations Respecting the Laws and Customs of War on Land annexed to Hague Convention II of 1899 and repeated in the same articles of the Regulations annexed to Hague Convention IV of 1907.

the first Additional Protocol to the 1949 Geneva Conventions. This conference, which began in 1974, plunged into arguments identical to the ones fought a century earlier, only this time it was newly created states that wished to relax the rules in order to give POW status to persons fighting for independence from colonial powers. The issue was the same: persons at a military disadvantage fighting for their nation should not be treated as common criminals. The rules were further adjusted to enable persons fighting in an occupation-type situation to benefit from this status, primarily by relaxing the requirement that a uniform must be worn. A complication that arose during the Protocol negotiations was the desire by newly-independent African states to outlaw POW status for mercenaries. Their experience was that such persons undermined those fighting for independence and that mercenaries by definition do not fight for their nation but for personal gain. Therefore, in the view of these African states, there was no moral reason why mercenaries should have such status. The result of the discussion was a new provision denying entitlement to POW status to mercenaries, together with a strict definition.

The Third Geneva Convention in 1949 already included extra categories of civilians that are entitled to POW status. These were essentially persons associated with the army in one form or another but who were not actual combatants.[6] The decision to accord POW status in this context was primarily to ensure decent treatment of persons thus captured—that is, the same treatment as that hitherto enjoyed by prisoners of war.

In addition to protecting the armies of states, a further purpose of the distinction between the armed forces and civilians was to limit civilian casualties. For this purpose, it was traditionally understood that, with minor exceptions, members of the armed forces are 'combatants'. This means that they are entitled to take part in hostilities (with the privilege of POW status) and may also be directly targeted by the adversary. Other persons—civilians—may not be targeted by the adversary, unless they 'take a direct part in hostilities'. What this expression means, precisely, and whether certain members of PMCs can be seen as falling into this category, will be discussed further below.

The increasing use of PMCs raises three fundamental questions. First, can they be combatants and therefore both use force and be targeted? Secondly, are they entitled to POW status? Thirdly, even if considered civilians, can they be targeted? The answers to these questions affect not only the treatment of such persons during hostilities and when captured, but also state responsibility for their actions. The legal provisions that developed as a result of the concerns explained above do not articulate those concerns but are written in the form of factual conditions. Many of the discussions that have begun to take place in relation to unclear issues often reflect views that are based not only on the letter of the law but also on doubts as to whether PMCs ought to benefit from provisions that were not developed with such companies in mind.

---

6 This is explained further below in the section on 'Non-combatants entitled to POW status'.

Prisoner-of-war status

The question of whether PMCs are entitled to POW status is relevant only to PMCs operating in an international armed conflict, including occupation of one state by another's armed forces. The question of whether PMCs benefit from combatant or POW status is complicated by the fact that those states that have not ratified Additional Protocol I of 1977[7] are still bound by the rules as they are set out in the Third Geneva Convention of 1949. Both of these treaties' provisions need to be analysed.

Combatants

Under Article 4 of the Third Geneva Convention, persons belonging to three categories of groups are entitled to POW status as a result of recognition of their right to use force. The first category embraces 'Members of the armed forces of a Party to the conflict as well as members of militias or volunteer corps forming part of such armed forces'.[8] The same Article makes it clear that armed forces belonging to a government not recognized by the capturing state are nevertheless covered by this provision.[9] If PMCs are formally incorporated into the army, then there is no doubt they would be covered by this provision. However, this is typically not the case as the purpose of hiring such companies is often to avoid the various employer's responsibilities that members of armies and their dependents enjoy.

A second category includes '[i]nhabitants of a non-occupied territory, who on the approach of the enemy spontaneously take up arms to resist the invading forces'.[10] This is clearly irrelevant for PMCs.

The third and most relevant category is defined as follows:

Members of other militias and members of other volunteer corps, including those of organized resistance movements, belonging to a Party to the conflict and operating in or outside their own territory even if this territory is occupied, provided that such militias or volunteer corps, including such organized resistance movements, fulfil the following conditions:

(a) that of being commanded by a person responsible for his subordinates;
(b) that of having a fixed distinctive sign recognizable at a distance;
(c) that of carrying arms openly;
(d) that of conducting their operations in accordance with the laws and customs of war.[11]

This provision actually contains five conditions. The first, belonging to a party to the conflict, presupposes some link with the state for which the group is fighting,

---

[7] 27 states have not yet ratified this treaty; the most significant are Afghanistan, India, Indonesia, Iran, Iraq, Israel, Pakistan, Turkey, and the United States.
[8] Third Geneva Convention 1949, art 4.A(1).　　[9] Ibid, para 3.　　[10] Ibid, art 4.A(6)
[11] Ibid, art 4.A(2).

although it is not part of that state's army.[12] The sort of link that is required is important when establishing whether PMCs could benefit from this provision. The wording of the 1949 text reflects the desire at the negotiating conference to give the benefit of POW status to resistance movements in occupied territory, an important factor in the Second World War. However, the entire provision is not limited to such resistance movements. The International Committee of the Red Cross (ICRC) commentary to the meaning of the words 'belonging to a party to the conflict' states that 'It is essential that there should be a *de facto* relationship between the resistance organization and the party [to the conflict], but the existence of this relationship is sufficient. It may find expression merely by tacit agreement, if the operations are such as to indicate clearly for which side the resistance organization is fighting.'[13]

It should be noted that this provision is very similar to the one agreed to in 1899 and incorporated into the Hague Regulations of 1899 and 1907, which did not refer to resistance movements. That provision did not specify 'belonging to a party to the conflict' but only reproduced the other four conditions.[14] Commentators on these texts have made it clear that the wording was intended to allow the granting of POW status to groups without formal authorization by the government, which had previously been required.[15]

This background makes it abundantly clear that a PMC is not precluded from falling within this provision because it is not part of the army or does not have formal authorization from the state. In practice, many PMCs that are hired by a state do have a card that confers a certain recognition and, in this author's view, should satisfy the existence of a *de facto* link.[16] Less clear is the case of PMCs that are sub-contracted by another company.

As regards the other conditions, they could in principle be respected by PMCs if they choose to operate in this fashion. Typically, however, they do not. The first condition presupposes that the head of the group both commands and accepts responsibility for wrongdoings of subordinates.[17] The second requires some sort of

---

[12] The addition of a specific reference to resistance movements in occupied territory in 1949 was motivated by the contribution of such movements during the Second World War.

[13] Jean S Pictet (ed) *Commentary, Geneva Convention relative to the treatment of prisoners of war* (Geneva: ICRC, 1960) 57.   [14] Hague Regulations, 1899 and 1907, art 1.

[15] Ibid and L Oppenheim *International Law Vol II*, 7th ed (Harlow: Longman, 1952) 256–7, para 80.

[16] The US Department of Defense has issued cards with its logo on them and a text stating that the individual concerned is a DoD contractor, according to a PMC representative in a meeting convened in 2005 by the University Centre for International Humanitarian Law (renamed in September 2007 'Geneva Academy for International Humanitarian Law and Human Rights'), as part of an effort undertaken by the Swiss Foreign Ministry to achieve a suitable regulation of PMCs. The meeting comprised specialists in IHL, including military legal advisers, as well as Foreign Ministry personnel, from several countries. The meeting took place under Chatham House Rules in order to enable free discussion. Report on Expert meeting on private military contractors: status and state responsibility for their actions; organized by the University Centre for International Humanitarian Law, Geneva, 29–30 August 2005, section B.1.a); <http://www.ucihl.org/communication/Private_Military_Companies_report.pdf>.

[17] This issue will be looked at more carefully below.

uniform, although it does not need to be a full one. The third is self-explanatory. The fourth assumes that the group will normally act in accordance with the basic provisions of international humanitarian law—clearly this would require either some training in this law or general respect of its provisions by the group.[18] It is not at all self-evident that this is the case for most PMCs.

Before moving on to what would be the status of members of PMCs if they do not fall into this category of the Third Geneva Convention, their situation under Additional Protocol I needs considering. At present 167 states are party to this treaty. The Protocol spells out which persons are to be considered combatants and which of these are entitled to POW status. The most significant change from the 1949 Geneva Convention is that there is no longer a difference, for the purposes of combatant status, between the regular armed forces and other armed groups. The relevant provision is Article 43, which reads as follows:

1. The armed forces of a Party to the conflict consist of all organized armed forces, groups and units which are under a command responsible to that Party for the conduct of its subordinates, even if that Party is represented by a government or an authority not recognized by an adverse Party. Such armed forces shall be subject to an internal disciplinary system which, *inter alia*, shall enforce compliance with the rules of international law applicable in armed conflict.

2. Members of the armed forces of a Party to the conflict (other than medical personnel and chaplains . . .) are combatants, that is to say, they have the right to participate directly in hostilities.

3. Whenever a Party to the conflict incorporates a paramilitary or armed law enforcement agency into its armed forces it shall so notify the other Parties to the conflict.

Article 44 specifies that any combatant, as defined in Article 43, who falls into the power of an adverse party shall be a prisoner of war. This provision goes on to specify that combatants are required to distinguish themselves from the civilian population with some sort of external sign; where this is not possible, combatants must carry their arms openly during the preparation and commission of each military engagement. If they do not do so, they forfeit their right to POW status.

There is no unanimity amongst specialists in IHL of whether members of PMCs could be entitled to POW status by virtue of these provisions.[19] One view is that the terms 'belonging to a Party to the conflict', or 'under a command responsible to [a Party to the conflict]' requires the state concerned to be able to have criminal jurisdiction over such forces. However, this is frequently not the case. An even narrower interpretation of these provisions is that the members of the PMCs need to be within the army's chain of command. This interpretation would require the state to formally incorporate a PMC into its armed forces by adopting domestic legislation which places the PMC under the command of the state's armed

---

[18] See Pictet, *Commentary*, (n 13 above) 61.

[19] This was abundantly clear during a discussion of this issue in the expert meeting on PMCs (n 16 above).

forces.[20] Under such an interpretation PMCs, as presently used, would not fall within these provisions.

Another view, which this author shares, is that such formal incorporation is not required. This is because Article 43 was intended to be a fusion of Article 4.A(1) and (2) of the Third Geneva Convention—that is, that the 'militias and volunteer corps' which do not formally belong to the army are considered to be 'armed forces' for the purpose of combatant status. These 'militias and volunteer corps' were meant to be groups that are not necessarily officially authorized by the government and are not part of the formal army. A commentary written by participants at the diplomatic conference states that Article 43 was aimed at including as 'armed forces' all groups which have some sort of factual link to the regular armed forces 'if the independent force acts on behalf of the party of the conflict in some manner and if that party is responsible for the group's operations'.[21]

It is clear that if a PMC is hired by a belligerent state, it is acting 'on behalf of the party to the conflict'. The crucial issue is whether the group is 'responsible' to the state. 'Militias and volunteer corps' were not part of the army and not subjected to the normal chain of command. Such a condition would therefore exceed what both the Third Geneva Convention and the Additional Protocol require for combatant (and therefore POW) status. Presumably there would be a form of responsibility to the state in that non-performance of the contract would result in liability in the form of breach of contract. Another issue is whether responsibility needs to include criminal jurisdiction by a state over such groups. This is not clear,[22] although the negotiators of both these treaties probably presupposed that this was so because typically such groups would have consisted of persons of their nationality fighting for their country. This is not necessarily the case for PMCs. Not only may its members not be of the hiring state's nationality, but also the group itself could be incorporated in another state, or in a part of a state enjoying specific jurisdictional exemptions, precisely in order to escape its jurisdiction (primarily for tax avoidance purposes). This could also create difficulties for exercise of jurisdiction for breach of contract. If the hiring state could exercise jurisdiction, whether civil or criminal, then the PMC could be more easily seen as being 'responsible' to the party to the conflict.

If the members do fall within the category of combatants, then the remaining condition under the Protocol to benefit from POW status would normally be the

[20] Michael N Schmitt, 'War, International Law, and Sovereignty: Reevaluating the Rules of the Game in a New Century: Humanitarian Law and Direct Participation in Hostilities by Private Contractors or Civilian Employees,' Chicago Journal of International Law, vol 5, no 2 (winter 2005) 511.

[21] Michael Bothe, Karl Josef Partsch, and Waldemar A Solf, *New Rules for Victims of Armed Conflict: Commentary on the Two 1977 Protocols Additional to the Geneva Conventions of 1949* (The Hague: Martinus Nijhoff Publishers, 1982) 234.

[22] Commentaries to Additional Protocol I do not address this directly (Bothe et al, *New Rules*, n 21 above) and that of the ICRC: Y Sandoz, C Swinarski, B Zimmermann (eds) *Commentary on the Additional Protocols of 8 June 1977 to the Geneva Conventions of 12 August 1949* (Geneva: Martinus Nijhoff Publishers, 1987) 511–13.

wearing of a uniform (unless they happen to be fighting for an occupied state's forces, in which case carrying arms openly would suffice).

Mercenaries

Even if PMCs could be seen as part of the 'armed forces' (within the meaning of Additional Protocol I) or 'militias or volunteer corps' (within the meaning of the Third Geneva Convention), they might still face the problem of falling within the definition of a 'mercenary'.

Two international treaties provide that mercenaries are not entitled to POW status, the most significant of which is Additional Protocol I of 1977.[23] Article 47 defines a 'mercenary' as any person who:

(a) is specially recruited locally or abroad in order to fight in an armed conflict;
(b) does, in fact, take a direct part in the hostilities;
(c) is motivated to take part in the hostilities essentially by the desire for private gain and, in fact, is promised by or on behalf of a Party to the conflict, material compensation substantially in excess of that promised or paid to combatants of similar ranks and functions in the armed forces of that Party;
(d) is neither a national of a Party to the conflict nor a resident of territory controlled by a Party to the conflict;
(e) is not a member of the armed forces of a Party to the conflict; and
(f) has not been sent by a state which is not a Party to the conflict on official duty as a member of its armed forces.

As all these conditions have to be met, the definition is very narrow. Two of these requirements are the most problematic for PMCs.[24]

The first is the requirement to be 'recruited to fight'. It is not necessarily the case that a PMC considers that it is 'recruited to fight', even if its members end up doing so, when the contract specifies that it is to guard a place or installation or to provide military training. A logical approach to this issue, from the point of view of IHL, would be that, whatever the contract might state, PMCs should be seen as being 'recruited to fight' if they are to defend a military objective against enemy forces—as opposed to being able to use force merely in self-defence and in defence of the object against common criminals. In this regard, whether the operations are seen as 'offensive' or 'defensive' makes no difference provided that the activity falls within an armed conflict situation and with sufficient nexus to the conflict itself. The rules of engagement issued to the PMC would be important here. Even if the contract is stated to be merely one of training military personnel, what is important is the actual activity undertaken. It has been stated, for example, that a US

---

[23] The other one is the OAU Convention for the Elimination of Mercenaries in Africa 1977. Both this convention and the 1989 UN Convention Against the Recruitment, Use, Financing, and Training of Mercenaries make mercenarism a crime.
[24] See Report on PMCs, (n 16 above), section B.3.(a).

company, MPRI, essentially planned and commanded military operations for Croatia during its war with Serbia, although the contract stated that the firm was to provide training in civil-military relations.[25]

A second issue is the condition of being 'neither a national of a Party to the conflict nor a resident of territory controlled by a Party to the conflict'. It is not at all clear whether this condition applies to the PMC's state of incorporation (in which case all its members would be treated as having that nationality) or the nationality of the individual member or both. When the Protocol was adopted PMCs were not an issue. A commentary to Article 47 notes that in 1977 it was 'implicit in both custom and conventional international law that the combatant's privilege and entitlement to prisoner-of-war status did not extend to members of armed groups which operate essentially for private ends and do not belong to a Party' to an international armed conflict.[26] Although this statement shows that it may be possible to speak of a 'mercenary company', the point made in the commentary does not apply to a situation where a PMC is hired by a Party to the conflict because in this case the link with the state is clear, even if the company is incorporated in another state. Given this difficulty, another approach could be to consider only the individual's nationality or residence so that certain members of a given PMC may be considered mercenaries and others not. In this hypothesis, a German working for a US PMC during the international conflict in Iraq would fall within Article 47, whereas his American and British co-workers would not.[27] Much will depend, therefore, on how states will actually implement this provision.

Finally, if a member of a PMC is captured by a state party to the OAU Convention on the Elimination of Mercenaries in Africa or the UN Convention Against the Recruitment, Use, Financing, and Training of Mercenaries, he or she risks not only being denied POW status and therefore tried for national crimes such as murder and carrying of arms, but also being tried for the specific crime of mercenarism.[28]

Non-combatants entitled to POW status

The Third Geneva Convention includes two categories of civilians that are entitled to POW status, the relevant one for our purposes being Article 4.A(4). This provision gives such status to:

Persons who accompany the armed forces without actually being members thereof, such as civilian members of military aircraft crews, war correspondents, supply contractors,

[25] Ibid, section B.3. (a) (iii). As one of the participants in this meeting put it: 'none of the members of this PMC thought that they were hired to make PowerPoint presentations'!

[26] Bothe et al, *New Rules* (n 21 above) 268.

[27] Report on PMCs (n 16 above), section B.3.(a) (i).

[28] The same is true for states that have included this crime in their national legislation whether or not they have ratified one of these treaties, as the lack of POW status means that they are subject to any national crime.

members of labour units or of services responsible for the welfare of the armed forces, provided that they have received authorization from the armed forces which they accompany, who shall provide them for that purpose with an identity card.

This category of persons reflects the fact that all armies, from time immemorial, have been accompanied by persons to supply its various needs, even though such persons are not part of the army. Typically, such persons did not have any fighting role. It is generally accepted that many PMCs will fall within this category of persons that supply armies with a service but are not expected to fight. Therefore, if members of PMCs are expected to fight, the general view is that they would not benefit from this provision.[29]

The other issue is that since this provision speaks of 'persons accompanying the armed forces', it is not clear whether this means that members of the armed forces have to be physically present where the PMC is operating. However, if one looks at the purpose of the provision, rather than the literal wording, the better view is that the PMC will fall within this provision if it is providing some sort of service to the army and not merely performing a contract for the state.[30]

Members of a PMC might, therefore, be entitled to POW status in an international armed conflict either as combatants or as persons accompanying the armed forces, but only if specific conditions are met and, in the case of combatants, if they do not fall within the definition of a mercenary.

Treatment of captured members of 'civilian' PMCs

International armed conflicts

Persons that do not fall within the legal classification of 'combatants' are 'civilians' for the purposes of international humanitarian law, whatever their behaviour. Even if civilians take part in hostilities, they technically remain a 'civilian'. This has been made crystal clear by Additional Protocol I which defines 'civilians' as persons not members of the armed forces or fighters that have not been specifically listed as being entitled to POW status.[31] Persons protected by the 1949 Fourth Geneva Convention Relative to the Protection of Civilian Persons in Time of War are those persons that are not covered by the other three Conventions—that is, they are not members of the armed forces or otherwise prisoners of war.[32] Article 5

[29] There is a view in the US to the effect that PMC members would retain their POW status, provided that they conformed to the conditions in art. 4.A(2). The preponderant view, however, is that there is no basis for this and that this article cannot be interpreted in such a strange fashion. For a full discussion of this see Report on PMCs (n 16 above), section B.2 (a), and ICRC/Asser Institute Report (n 59 below), section VI.3.   [30] Report on PMCs (n 16 above), section B.2.(a).
[31] Additional Protocol I, art 50(1), defines as a 'civilian' a person who does not belong to one of the categories of persons referred to in art 4.A(1), (2), (3), and (6) of the Third Geneva Convention nor in art 43 of Protocol I.
[32] Fourth Geneva Convention, art 4(3).

reinforces this interpretation by specifically referring to spies, saboteurs, and other persons undertaking activities hostile to the security of the state.

A major confusion that can occur is to label these persons as 'unlawful combatants', and thereby try to categorize them as falling outside both the Third and Fourth Geneva Conventions. The best study of why such a categorization is historically and legally incorrect remains that written by Richard Baxter back in 1951.[33] He explained why the reference to 'unlawful combatants' by the US Supreme Court in *Ex parte Quirin et al*[34] (and decades later used by the US government for persons held in Guantánamo Bay after the conflict in Afghanistan) was based on a fundamental misunderstanding by the court of the law of armed conflict. His analysis in that article is directly relevant today in relation to the debate surrounding whether members of PMCs should be seen as combatants who can benefit from POW status or whether they should be categorized as civilians. He pointed out that certain categories of persons—namely spies, saboteurs, and guerrillas—were not given POW status (for various reasons) even though states used such persons in armed conflict and did not consider this unlawful under international law. Therefore it was inaccurate to label such persons 'unlawful' combatants and he preferred the term 'unprivileged'—that is, without the privilege of POW status. As regards civilian PMCs, the question remains whether their participation in hostilities (whether in offence or defence) should not only have the effect of their members being 'unprivileged' but also be seen as a violation of international law by the state hiring them. Generally speaking this is not the case at present, except for the limited number of states that have ratified the OAU or UN Conventions.[35] There is some discussion as to whether states ought to adopt regulations that would make it clear that PMCs cannot be involved in hostilities. Either way, such civilian PMCs taking a direct part in hostilities would not benefit from POW status.

Those that do not benefit from POW status under the Third Geneva Convention are protected by the Fourth Geneva Convention of 1949[36] unless they are nationals of a neutral state or a co-belligerent state that has normal diplomatic representation in the state in whose hands they are.[37] Given the number of nationalities found in PMC membership, some may well fall outside those protected by the Fourth Convention. However, such persons would still have the benefit of fundamental customary rules relating to the prohibition of torture, inhumane treatment, and hostage-taking, as well as the right to a fair trial.[38] Persons covered

---

[33] Richard Baxter, 'So-called "Unprivileged Belligerency": Spies, Guerrillas and Saboteurs,' *British Yearbook of International Law*, vol 28 (1951) 324–45.   [34] Ibid, 320–31.

[35] OAU Treaty (n 23 above) arts 1(2) and 6; UN Treaty (n 23 above) art 5.

[36] This is clearly stated in the ICRC Commentary to the Fourth Convention, Pictet (ed) *Commentary Geneva Convention relative to the Protection of Civilian Persons in Time of War* (Geneva: International Committee of the Red Cross, 1958), 50–51.

[37] Fourth Geneva Convention 1949, art 4. Such persons were excluded because participants at the negotiating conference assumed that their country of origin would be able to protect them.

[38] These basic rights are codified in art 75 of Additional Protocol I which applies to all persons in the power of the adversary in an international armed conflict.

by the Fourth Geneva Convention are referred to as 'protected persons'. The principal advantage is that if they are interned, they have, like POWs, protection stemming from the fact that their details must be registered with the Central Tracing Agency[39] and they have the right to be visited by representatives of the ICRC.[40] This may help prevent forced disappearance, torture, and inhumane treatment. They would similarly benefit from provisions enabling them to correspond with their families.[41]

Unlike POWs, they may be tried, of course, for national offences linked with their activities with the PMC and if this involved fighting they may well face charges of murder. In the case of occupation, the Fourth Convention does have certain restrictions on the use of the death penalty—in particular, occupation authorities may not reintroduce the death penalty if the occupied state had abolished it[42] and should the death penalty be pronounced, it may not be carried out for at least six months.[43] However, it is unlikely that a PMC will be fighting for an occupied population and therefore in practice will have to rely on whatever human rights law relating to the death penalty is applicable to the state in question.

Members of PMCs may also be subject to internment without trial if 'the security of the Detaining Power makes it absolutely necessary'[44] and are entitled to have such action reconsidered as soon as possible by 'an appropriate court or administrative board designated by the Detaining Power for that purpose'.[45] It should be noted that reconsideration by a court is consistent with requirements under human rights law, but an administrative board would not be as it does not have the requisite independence. States bound by one of the human rights treaties would therefore have stricter obligations in this regard than those in the Fourth Geneva Convention.

One possible advantage of being a detainee under the Fourth Geneva Convention rather than as a POW is that a detainee 'shall be released by the Detaining Power as soon as the reasons which necessitated his internment no longer exist',[46] whereas, with narrow exceptions, POWs may be kept until the end of active hostilities.[47]

Non-international conflicts

There is no POW status in non-international conflicts and therefore any captured member of a PMC will be subject to national law unless the company benefits from an agreement with the state conferring on its members immunity from local courts.

International humanitarian law is less detailed as regards treatment of captured persons in non-international conflicts than in international ones. Unlike POWs

---

[39] Fourth Geneva Convention, art 140.   [40] Ibid, art 143(5).   [41] Ibid, arts 68–77.
[42] Ibid, art 68 (2).   [43] Ibid, art 75.   [44] Ibid, art 42.   [45] Ibid, art 43.
[46] Ibid, art 132. Article 133 adds that in any event internment shall cease as soon as possible after the close of hostilities except in the case of persons subject to criminal proceedings or still serving a sentence.
[47] Third Geneva Convention 1949, art 118.

or protected persons under the Fourth Geneva Convention, the ICRC does not have an absolute right of visit and the detaining state does not have a legal duty to send details of detainees to the Central Tracing Agency. In practice, however, both ICRC visits and such registration do occur as the ICRC has a 'right of initiative' under Article 3 common to the Geneva Conventions[48] and in practice most states do allow it to undertake similar functions to those practised in international conflicts.

Both common Article 3 and Additional Protocol II provide for basic protective treatment of anyone captured or otherwise not or no longer participating in hostilities. This includes a prohibition of murder, torture, inhuman or degrading treatment, the taking of hostages, and the passing of sentences without a fair trial, as well as decent treatment in detention.[49] Neither document addresses the issue of detention for security purposes without a criminal procedure being envisaged. The applicable law, therefore, is that of human rights, in particular the right to take proceedings to check the lawfulness of detention (*habeas corpus*), in principle by a court or, at a minimum, by an independent body. For states not party to human rights treaties, the view of this author is that all persons are entitled, as a minimum, to an independent supervisory procedure[50] to ensure that detention is not arbitrary, such detention being contrary to customary international law.[51]

May members of PMCs be attacked?

International armed conflicts

If members of PMCs are combatants in international armed conflicts,[52] then there is no doubt that they can be specifically targeted for attack (unless they are *hors de combat*).[53] As we have seen, however, members of PMCs are more likely in practice to be considered civilians under IHL. This does not necessarily mean that they are immune from attack as civilians who 'take a direct part in hostilities' lose

---

[48] The relevant part of art 3 reads as follows: 'An impartial humanitarian body, such as the International Committee of the Red Cross, may offer its services to the Parties to the conflict.'

[49] For a fuller description of fundamental guarantees applicable to all civilians and others not or no longer participating in hostilities, see Jean-Marie Henckaerts and Louise Doswald-Beck, *Customary International Humanitarian Law*, Vol I (Cambridge: Cambridge University Press, 2005) 299–383.

[50] See, eg, the UN Body of Principles for the Protection of all Persons under any Form of Detention or Imprisonment 1988, Principle 11.3.

[51] Henckaerts and Doswald-Beck, *Customary International Humanitarian Law* (n 49 above), Rule 99, p 344. See also the Report of the UN Working Group on Arbitrary Detention on the Situation of Detainees at Guantanamo Bay, 15 February 2006, UN Doc E/CN.4/2006/120.

[52] ie they belong to a group described in art 4.A(1), (2), or (6) of the Third Geneva Convention or art 43 of Additional Protocol I.

[53] That is, they can no longer fight because they have surrendered, are sick, wounded or shipwrecked, have bailed out of aircraft in distress, or have been captured.

this immunity.[54] A difficult issue is to establish in which circumstances a civilian can be considered to be taking 'a direct part in hostilities', other than in the simple scenario of the moment during which a person is in the process of using a weapon against the adversary.

In the context of an international armed conflict, it is clear that the persons whose conduct is to be analysed are those that are not 'combatants'. Article 51(3) of Additional Protocol I provides that: 'Civilians shall enjoy protection [from attack] unless and for such time as they take a direct part in hostilities'. The ICRC Commentary to this Article states that:

"direct" participation means acts of war which by their nature or purpose are likely to cause actual harm to the personnel and equipment of the enemy armed forces. It is only during such participation that a civilian loses his immunity and becomes a legitimate target.[55]

The Commentary also refers to the fact that during the negotiations, several delegations stated that the expression 'hostilities' in this Article included 'preparations for combat and return from combat'.[56]

At first sight this might seem straightforward, but on closer inspection the terms are far from clear. Do 'acts likely to cause actual harm to personnel and equipment' include loading bombs on aircraft, or providing co-ordinates for an attack? Could the causative link be even weaker? What do 'preparations for' or 'return from' combat include? What is clear is that mere participation in the war effort is not meant to be included.[57] During the research process for the study on customary IHL carried out by the ICRC, it became clear that state practice on these issues did not clarify what states consider 'direct participation in hostilities' to include. Most state legislation and military manuals are silent on what behaviour warrants attack under this principle, and those which do give a view reflect differing positions. Some include such activities as acting as guards or intelligence agents or even providing logistical support in some contexts, whereas others limit the concept to acts of violence.[58] Attempts at arriving at some sort of comprehensive definition have so far proved futile as all possibilities, such as referring to 'hostile activity' or 'military activity' could be seen as either too broad or too narrow depending on the context.[59]

---

[54] Additional Protocol I, art 51(3). This is also recognized as a customary rule.

[55] Sandoz et al, *Commentary on the Additional Protocols*, (n 22 above), 619, para 1944.

[56] Ibid, p 618, para 1943.   [57] Ibid, p 619, para 1945.

[58] Henckaerts and Doswald-Beck, *Customary International Humanitarian Law*, (n 49 above), commentary to Rule 6, 22–3. As a result of this finding, the ICRC and the Asser Institute have begun a series of expert meetings to try to clarify the precise meaning of this notion. A summary of these meetings as well as a copy of the reports are available at the following website address: <http://www.icrc.org/web/eng/siteeng0.nsf/iwpList575/459B0FF70176F4E5C1256DDE00572DAA>.

[59] For a summary of the difficulties in attempting a general definition beyond the direct use of violence, ie use of weapons, see the Report of the Third Expert Meeting on the Notion of Direct Participation in Hostilities, Geneva, 23–25 October 2005, ICRC and TMC Asser Institute, 6, available at <http://www.icrc.org/Web/eng/siteeng0.nsf/htmlall/participation-hostilities-ihl-311205/$File/Direct_participation_in_hostilities_2005_eng.pdf>.

In addition to the possibility of PMCs engaged in direct fighting in hostilities (which would clearly be considered to be direct participation), they also play a variety of supporting roles. Which of these could be considered 'direct participation' becomes critical in evaluating whether members of PMCs can be attacked. If the support role of a PMC is of the nature described in Article 4.A(4) of the Third Geneva Convention (persons accompanying the armed forces), it would be difficult to see such activities as being 'direct participation in hostilities' as this group is perceived as being civilian and benefiting from civilian immunity (with the possible exception of 'civilian members of military aircraft crews') although, being near the actual armed forces it risks being subject to collateral death or injury.

It would also be hard to envisage the use of force in personal self-defence or in defence of an object against common criminals as 'participation in hostilities'. This is not so clear, however, if the object to be defended is considered to be a military objective. Also drawing the line between activities against common criminals, on the one hand, and hostilities on the other, would be particularly difficult in the case of defence of an object for an occupying state against persons using force in occupied territory.

This author would prefer the expression 'direct participation in hostilities' to be narrowly defined in the context of international armed conflicts—that is, limited to acts of violence, given that combatants can be attacked and the purpose of the law is to avoid deliberate attacks on civilians. Civilians who choose to be in the vicinity of the armed forces take the risk of being 'collateral damage' in any event. To widen the definition risks losing the impact of the principle of distinction which was so carefully included in Additional Protocol I.[60] If this results in an unrealistic protection of PMCs that in practice undertake what is recognizably military work (which is, after all their chosen profession), then, in this author's view, the solution ought to be to categorize such PMCs as combatants, rather than weakening the protection of regular civilians.

Non-international armed conflicts

Additional Protocol II of 1977 repeats the same formula as Protocol I, namely, that 'civilians shall enjoy protection [against attack] unless and for such time as they take a direct part in hostilities'.[61] Yet the situation is far more complicated in non-international conflicts—precisely the sort of conflicts in which many PMCs find themselves. This is because civilians cannot be simply defined as persons that are not 'combatants'. There is no official combatant status in non-international conflicts. The issue, therefore, concerns whether 'armed groups' may be attacked as such, whatever the functions or activities of each of their members and at any

---

[60] There is a good case to be made that the drafters of the Protocol intended 'direct participation' to be narrowly defined; see Schmitt, *Humanitarian Law and Direct Participation* (n 20 above) 11.
[61] Protocol II of 1977 Additional to the Geneva Conventions of 1949, art 13(3).

time. If so, then this would certainly be wider than 'direct participation' by civilians in international armed conflict situations. The alternative approach is to state
that there is no difference between the two types of conflict as regards the meaning
of 'direct participation': all persons that are not members of the state's armed
forces are to be considered as civilians and no civilian may be attacked unless he or
she is directly taking part in hostilities, narrowly defined.

The theory that all members of armed groups are to be considered as valid targets for attack, whatever their individual function and whatever they are doing at
any particular moment, does have a basis for support. Article 3 common to the
Geneva Conventions gives specific protection to 'persons taking no active part in
the hostilities, including members of armed forces who have laid down their arms
and those placed *hors de combat*'. Additional Protocol II also refers to armed forces
and armed groups, not in the context of the rules relating to the use of force, but
rather the need for their existence in order for there to be a non-international
armed conflict within the meaning of the Protocol.[62] Further, the ICRC Commentary to this Protocol states that persons 'who belong to armed forces or armed
groups may be attacked at any time'.[63]

There is no provision in these treaties that would make it impossible for a PMC
being considered such an 'armed group' or even an independent party to a non-
international conflict. If one accepts this theory, then all members of PMCs
would be subject to attack whatever their individual function or activity (except
religious and medical personnel and those *hors de combat*). This would be trans-
posing an exact equivalent into a non-international armed conflict situation of the
situation of combatants in an international armed conflict.

However, in the context of non-international armed conflicts, where the IHL
lex specialis relating to combatant status is inapplicable, human rights law clearly
applies. Under this law it would be unlawful to kill someone who could be arrested
without risk.[64] The 'armed group' approach presents additional serious difficulties. Attacking on the basis of membership of a group is likely to lead to targeted
killings and to wide-scale abuses because of inaccurate presumptions as to who is a
member of the group, especially given the fluid nature of activities carried out for
rebel groups, either willingly or not. Accuracy can only be achieved if attacks are
limited to persons who are actually carrying out hostilities, although both this
term and the temporal scope still need to be defined. The motivations for this

---

[62] Additional Protocol II 1977, art 1(1) refers to 'armed conflicts ... which take place in the territory of a High Contracting Party between its armed forces and dissident armed forces or other organized armed groups ...'.

[63] Sandoz et al, *Commentary* (n 22 above), p 1453, para 4789.

[64] This is because human rights law prohibits arbitrary deprivation of life and there is extensive case
law from the United Nations and regional human rights treaty bodies specifying that force may not be
used unless arrest is not reasonably possible. See for a discussion of this practice in an armed conflict
context: Report of the Expert meeting on the right to life in armed conflicts and situations of occupation, University Centre for International Humanitarian Law, Geneva, 1–2 September 2005, Section F,
available at: <http://www.ucihl.org/communication/Right_to_Life_Meeting_Report.pdf>.

approach are not really relevant for PMCs which are distinct groups that know-ingly put themselves into a hostile and unstable situation. However, in this author's view, it would be inappropriate to extend the category of who can be attacked, merely in order to be able to include PMCs, given the implications for the rest of the population.

Given that PMCs regularly operate in non-international conflict situations, this lack of clarity places them in a confused legal situation. What is clear is that those members who are in the process of using force against the government forces or against a party to the conflict are subject to attack under either theory. This should come as no surprise and one must assume that PMCs knowingly under-take this risk. What is less obvious, however, is the situation of members of the group who do not have a combat function. The membership of an armed group theory would make them legally subject to attack even when not in the process of using force.

Given that the situation is not clear in IHL applicable to non-international conflicts, it would be unreasonable to interpret this law in a way that is incoherent with existing human rights law. Therefore, even if one accepts the theory that in non-international conflicts all members of armed groups can be attacked, an excep-tion should be made for members of the group who are in a situation in which they could easily be arrested.

State responsibility

State responsibility for actions of PMCs, depending on their status, function, and authorization is discussed in chapter eight by Chia Lehnardt. The most relevant norms for the purpose of evaluating state responsibility are reflected in Articles 5 and 8 of the Articles on State Responsibility prepared by the International Law Commission[65] and states will be responsible for many of their actions by virtue of these norms.[66] For the purposes of this chapter, discussion will be limited to cer-tain aspects of state responsibility that are specifically provided for in IHL.

Obligations and responsibility of the state hiring the PMC

The most important provision is the requirement that states 'ensure respect' of IHL 'in all circumstances'. This is laid down in Article 1 common to the Geneva Conventions and is considered to be customary law. As states have undertaken

---

[65] Report of the International Law Commission on the work of its fifty-third session, 2001, UN Doc A/56/10, and commended to the attention of governments by the United Nations General Assembly in Resolution 56/83, 12 December 2001.

[66] This issue was explored in depth during the expert meeting on PMCs (n 16 above), section E. State responsibility on the basis of status, function, and due diligence under human rights law are in other sections of the report.

certain duties under humanitarian law, these cannot be avoided by giving them to PMCs. It logically follows, therefore, that states should ensure that PMCs are properly trained and that their contract contains clear rules of engagement.

If PMCs are members of the armed forces, states are required to instruct them in IHL[67] and such armed forces are also required to have legal advisers available.[68] If they are not members of the armed forces, a requirement to train them would need to be found in other provisions. Specific provisions relating to persons that are not members of the armed forces do exist in the Third and Fourth Geneva Conventions. Article 127(2) of the Third Convention provides that: 'Any military or other authorities, who in time of war assume responsibility in respect of prisoners of war, must possess the text of the Convention and be specially instructed as to its provisions.' Article 144(2) of the Fourth Convention is similar: 'Any civilian, military or other authorities, who in time of war assume responsibilities in respect of protected persons, must possess the text of the Convention and be specially instructed as to its provisions.'

The question as regards these Articles is whether the term 'other authorities' implies governmental bodies, or whether one should concentrate on the expression 'assume responsibilities'. When these were drafted governments did not have PMCs in mind. On the one hand, governments cannot be responsible for any private person that undertakes some activities that governments are required to do, such as relief shipments. On the other hand, it would be in keeping with the spirit of these provisions to require them to be applied to PMCs hired to undertake these responsibilities.

The Conventions also refer to the civilian population generally. The First and Second Geneva Conventions of 1949 provide that the state must disseminate the Conventions such that 'the principles thereof may become known to the entire population, in particular to the fighting forces, the medical personnel and the chaplains'.[69] The Third and Fourth Conventions provide that states are to include the study of the Conventions 'in their programmes of military and, if possible, civil instruction'.[70] In practice, states do not consider themselves under an obligation to ensure that all persons are instructed in IHL and tend to leave it to other actors, such as Red Cross societies and specialized academic centres to do so. However, PMCs hired by a state can hardly be considered as part of the general civilian population. Many governments emphasize the need to train especially

---

[67] This requirement is contained in many treaties. See, eg, Hague Convention IV 1907, art 1, Hague Convention for the Protection of Cultural Property in the Event of Armed Conflict, 1954, art 7(1), Additional Protocol I, art 80(2), Convention on Certain Conventional Weapons 1980, art 6, as well as in all four of the 1949 Geneva Conventions. See also Henckaerts and Doswald-Beck, *Customary International Humanitarian Law*, commentary to Rule 142 (n 49 above) 501–505.

[68] Additional Protocol I 1977, art 82; Henckaerts and Doswald-Beck, *Customary International Humanitarian Law*, Rule 141 (n 49 above) 500.

[69] First Geneva Convention 1949, art 47; Second Geneva Convention 1949, art 48.

[70] Third Geneva Convention 1949, art 127; Fourth Geneva Convention 1949, art 144.

relevant personnel such as the judiciary, police, and prison personnel.[71] It would be in keeping with this approach to ensure that PMCs hired by states are so trained.

It is probably not necessary to fit the training of PMCs into a specific treaty provision as such training flows from the general requirement of states under Article 1 of the Geneva Conventions to 'ensure respect' of the law and training anyone they hire is inevitably part of this requirement. It is arguable that there is even no need to make reference to Article 1 as obligations under humanitarian law treaties are obligations of result. Therefore, if there is a violation by a PMC hired by the government and the government did not train it, or ensure that it knew the rules, then it will be responsible for that reason: for its own omission in not properly fulfilling any specific requirement in the treaties.[72]

Another avenue to explore is a possible duty of due diligence by parties to a conflict so that a lack of such diligence would make them responsible for the actions of private actors. Until recently, obligations and subsequent responsibility of states for violations by private actors have not been directly provided for under IHL. The only reference to such a concept is to be found in the ICRC Commentary to Article 91 of Additional Protocol I. This Article provides that a party to a conflict which violates the Geneva Conventions or Protocol is required to pay compensation. The Commentary provides, but without much authoritative support, that a state will similarly be responsible for the violations of a private actor if the state 'has not taken such preventive or repressive measures as could reasonably be expected to have been taken in the circumstances'.[73]

However, in the context of the obligations of an occupying power at least, this dearth of material has recently changed. In the judgement of the International Court of Justice in the Congo against Uganda case, the Court found that Uganda, as an occupying power in the Ituri district, was responsible for actions of private actors. The Court stated that as Uganda had the duty under Article 43 of the Hague Regulations of 1907 to 'ensure, as far as possible, public order and safety ... Uganda's responsibility is engaged ... for any lack of vigilance in preventing violations of ... international humanitarian law by other actors present in the occupied territory, including rebel groups acting on their own account'.[74]

Such reasoning would clearly also cover the actions of PMCs. It is uncertain, however, whether this statement was made only because of the specific responsibility of occupying states which is very similar to the responsibility of states under human rights law for persons within their jurisdiction.

[71] Henckaerts and Doswald-Beck, *Customary International Humanitarian Law* (n 49 above) 507.
[72] Report on PMCs (n 16 above), section E.1.b.
[73] Sandoz et al, *Commentary* (n 22 above), p 1057, para 3660.
[74] ICJ, *Case Concerning Armed Activities in the Territory of the Congo (Democratic Republic of the Congo v Uganda)*, judgment, 19 December 2005, ICJ Reports 2005, paras 178–9.

Obligations and responsibility of other states

The interpretation of the term 'ensure respect' in Article 1 common to the Geneva Conventions has in practice taken on a meaning that places some duties on states other than the hiring state. This is not an obligation of result, which would be unreasonable for third parties. On the basis of state practice, the study on customary international law has articulated this requirement as prohibiting the encouragement of violations by parties to a conflict and the requirement of third states to 'exert their influence, to the degree possible, to stop' such violations.[75] In practice the latter has taken the form of diplomatic protest and various forms of collective measures.

The question here is whether states of incorporation or states in which there are PMC offices are required to do something by virtue of this legal norm. State practice in the application of this norm thus far does not include a lack of regulation or training amounting to a violation of this norm by such a state. However, such an activity would be a very good means of 'ensuring respect' for the law and therefore any future practice regarding PMCs ought to envisage such actions as part of this requirement.

Criminal responsibility

All serious violations of IHL are war crimes[76] subject to universal jurisdiction.[77] This means that any state can give itself jurisdiction over such crimes irrespective of the nationality of the perpetrator or where the crime was committed. Particularly serious war crimes committed in international conflicts, known as grave breaches, are subject to obligatory universal jurisdiction under the Geneva Conventions,[78] although this is an obligation that has not been well observed.

War crimes can be committed not only by members of the armed forces but also by civilians.[79] Therefore members of PMCs who commit serious violations of IHL will be guilty of war crimes, whether such crimes occur in international or non-international armed conflicts. Theoretically, therefore, such persons could be prosecuted in any state or before any international tribunal that has jurisdiction. However, not all states have adopted legislation enabling them to prosecute persons on the basis of universal jurisdiction and even those who have done so have adopted conditions such as residence or some other specific connection with the

---

[75] Henckaerts and Doswald-Beck, *Customary International Humanitarian Law*, Rule 144 (n 49 above) 509.   [76] Ibid, Rule 156, p 604.

[77] Ibid, Rule 157, p 604.

[78] First Geneva Convention, art 49; Second Geneva Convention, art 50; Third Geneva Convention, art 129; Fourth Geneva Convention, art 146; Additional Protocol I, art 85 (1).

[79] See Knut Doermann, *Elements of War Crimes under the Rome Statute of the International Criminal Court* (Cambridge: Cambridge University Press, 2003) 34–7.

state.[80] A political unwillingness to try another state's nationals for activities that took place in another country has in practice had a significant dampening effect. Although there have been some trials on the basis of universal jurisdiction,[81] these are very few and none yet of members of PMCs.

Another difficulty is that even if the legislation allows for prosecution of crimes committed abroad, either on the basis of universal jurisdiction or nationality of the offender, the authorities may not be willing to undertake it because the collection of evidence and hearing of witnesses from another country are both difficult and very expensive. PMCs may have been granted immunity of jurisdiction by the courts of the state where the crime was committed or such local courts may not be functioning in a situation of armed conflict. This can lead to impunity. It has been suggested that one way to overcome this difficulty would be for states of PMC nationals to use transportable courts in the theatre of operations.[82]

If members of PMCs commit war crimes, there are two aspects peculiar to war crimes trials that may be problematic. The first is the doctrine of command responsibility and the other is the issue of superior orders; both are intimately linked to a regular army's command structure.

Command responsibility

The rule that commanders are responsible for crimes they have ordered to be committed[83] may be seen as comparable to incitement to commit a crime. However, there is also a rule that makes commanders and superiors criminally responsible for war crimes committed by their subordinates if such commanders or superiors knew, or had reason to know, that the subordinates were about to commit or were committing such crimes and did not take all necessary and reasonable measures to prevent them. Commanders are also liable if, once war crimes have been committed by their subordinates, they do nothing to investigate, report, or punish the persons responsible. It is generally accepted that such superiors can be civilian persons providing that they are effectively acting as a military commander.[84] The issue that would arise, as regards PMCs, is which person within the organization would be considered to be such a commander. If there were no particular hierarchy then the question would have to be one of fact in the circumstances at the time of the commission of the offence. This has yet to be tested.

The other issue is in which circumstances, if any, an individual state official, whether military or not, might be criminally responsible for war crimes committed

---

[80] For a description of the legislation and case law of states relating to the exercise of jurisdiction over war crimes, see Henckaerts and Doswald-Beck, *Customary International Law* (n 49 above) Vol II, 3894–931. A continually updated database of such national practice is to be found in the following ICRC website: <http://www.icrc.org/ihl-nat>. [81] Ibid.

[82] Report on PMCs (n 16 above), section G.1.

[83] See, eg, art 25.3(b) of the Statute of the International Criminal Court.

[84] See, eg, art 28 of the Statute of the International Criminal Court. Also, Henckaerts and Doswald-Beck, *Customary International Humanitarian Law*, Rule 153 and commentary (n 49 above) 558–63.

by a member of a PMC. Could this be the person organizing the contract, especially if he or she knew that the PMC has committed offences before and is being sent on an assignment where such offences could well occur again? The International Criminal Tribunal for the Former Yugoslavia (ICTY) has identified as crucial the *de facto* control over the actions of subordinates.[85] Generally speaking, this will not be the case for someone hiring a PMC. If a command relationship exists, then practice also shows that the superior does not actually have to know of the existence of crimes. Constructive knowledge is sufficient—that is, the superior is criminally responsible if he or she should have known or consciously disregarded information that clearly indicated that a crime is about to be committed.[86] It would be unfortunate in the scenario just described to be able to clear oneself of all criminal responsibility that would normally accrue to a commander, by simply arranging a PMC to carry out certain tasks whilst knowing that violations are likely. For example, it would be a strange result if a commander would be guilty by virtue of command responsibility because he or she put officers known to be sadists in charge of interrogations, whereas a state official who hired a PMC that has allegedly 'robust' techniques would not be. However, because of lack of *de facto* control in the latter case, this may well be the situation at present.

Superior orders

The other issue of interest is that of superior orders, which used to be a defence for a soldier, given the military duty to obey orders. This has not been available as a defence for some time, however, and the present rule is that obeying a superior order does not relieve a subordinate of criminal responsibility if the subordinate knew that the act ordered was unlawful or should have known because of the manifestly unlawful nature of the act. This means, on the contrary, that if the subordinate did not know that the order was unlawful and its unlawful nature was not manifest, then obeying a superior order would be a defence. In domestic criminal law ignorance of the law is no defence. The issue again arises, therefore, of whether there can be a commander-subordinate relationship within a PMC, or whether this issue is totally irrelevant for any criminal prosecution concerning an employee of a PMC. Does it depend on whether a PMC can be seen as part of the armed forces, as discussed earlier in this chapter? Again, there is no precedent to directly answer this question.

Conclusion

As the legal situation of PMCs under IHL will depend so much on circumstances, both governments and the companies themselves must consider carefully into

---

[85] International Criminal Tribunal for the Former Yugoslavia (ICTY), *Delalic and Others Case*, Judgment, 16 November 1998 (IT-96-21-T), para 370.
[86] Art 28(b)(i) of the Statute of the International Criminal Court.

which legal categories they would like their activities to fall. It is unlikely that most PMCs are aware of their legal situation, although most must certainly be aware of the dangers associated with being considered a mercenary, especially in certain countries. The first issue to consider is if they wish to benefit from POW status. Although they might technically be considered members of the armed forces of a hiring state that is a party to an international armed conflict, provided that certain conditions are met, the need to ensure that they are subject to the civil and criminal jurisdiction of the state is paramount. Even more effective would be to be brought within the regular army's chain of command, although it is not the universal view that this is strictly necessary for this purpose. It is interesting to note that regular army members generally do not favour PMCs as they are seen as something akin to loose cannons that can cause more trouble than they are worth. A disinclination to perceive them as 'combatants' unless they are brought within the chain of command is the natural off-shoot of this view.

The other element to take into account is that the relaxing of the rules, that had originally only granted POW status to members of the army, was undertaken to prevent people fighting for their country from being seen as common criminals. This patriotic sentiment is hardly appropriate for PMCs. Therefore, the question will be whether governmental decision-makers will interpret the treaties' provisions on the basis of the letter of the law or whether they will do so on the basis of their feelings of whether such companies have the moral right to benefit from such status. At a minimum, states hiring such companies ought to indicate how they view their legal situation.

A similar unfavourable view of persons not fighting primarily for their country is what lies behind the provisions denying the right to POW status for mercenaries. Although the conditions to be a mercenary are numerous and strict, members of PMCs may well qualify for this dubious status if they are not incorporated into the army and if either the company, or individual members, or both are not of the same nationality as, or resident in, a state party to a conflict. The latter point may be clarified through further state practice, but members with the 'wrong' nationality should be aware of the additional danger.

PMCs should also be aware that the predominant view at present is that they may well benefit from POW status if they are persons that accompany the army, but only provided that they do not fight. If they do so, not only will they be considered as no longer falling within the relevant provision of the Third Geneva Convention, but also increase the likelihood of being seen as a mercenary as they were 'recruited to fight'. Although they would still be subject to the benefits of the Fourth Geneva Convention, losing immunity from the criminal jurisdiction of the adversary can be serious.

Companies involved in hostilities in a non-international armed conflict also need to be aware that even members not actually having a fighting role may well be lawfully subject to attack. There is not much that such companies can do about this, other than warn persons working for them, as the law itself is not clear.

States that hire PMCs need to be aware that in most situations they will be responsible, under the doctrine of state responsibility, for violations of the law committed by such companies. Certain officials might even be criminally responsible for war crimes committed by PMC members, although this is much more unlikely. States need, therefore, to ensure that PMCs are trained in IHL or at a minimum insist on strict rules of engagement within the contract that are in conformity with that law. They also need to warn such companies that their members could well be tried as war criminals, in any state that has given itself jurisdiction, for violations committed in international or non-international conflicts.

Whatever position one takes on the morality of PMCs participating in conflict, it is important that the legal position of members of PMCs in any particular situation is clear to them in order to ensure that any risks they take are taken in full awareness of the potential consequences. Basic decency and the rule of law require this, as well as the basic protection that all human beings are entitled to under fundamental human rights law and applicable humanitarian law. It is also important that civil and criminal responsibility for war crimes, and any other international crimes, is not lost through a lack of proper regulation and a lack of enforceable jurisdiction. Though it is incorrect, therefore, to suggest that PMCs operate in a legal vacuum, the interpretation of many of the norms as applied to PMCs will be clarified only through practice.

8

Private military companies and state responsibility

*Chia Lehnardt**

One of the principal differences between private military companies (PMCs) and mercenaries is the fact that the activities of PMCs are often sanctioned openly, in one way or another, by states. States hire, licence, or permit the activities of PMCs, as these entities augment or even replace functions that have traditionally been performed by states. Through such legal arrangements, PMCs provide services that such states are either unwilling or unable to provide: offering security, military advice and training, interrogation of prisoners, and, in extreme cases, combat forces.

Indeed, one of the greatest concerns about the expanding role of PMCs is that military capacities are developed outside the state and put into practice in an inherently volatile setting. While there is no empirical evidence that PMCs are more likely to engage in misconduct than their public counterparts, PMCs can, of course, violate interests protected by international law. Understandably, discussion typically focuses on alleged and proven wrongdoing by PMC employees—charges levelled against PMCs include abuses of prisoners,[1] sex trafficking,[2] violating UN arm embargoes,[3]

* Many thanks to William Abresch, Simon Chesterman, Antje Pedain, and the anonymous reviewers for helpful comments on an earlier draft.

[1] Both the Taguba Report and the Fay Report found that three employees of CACI Int and Titan Inc were implicated in the abuses at Abu Ghraib; MG Antonio M Taguba, Article 15-6 Investigation at the 800th Military Police Brigade (henceforth Taguba Report), available at <http://news.findlaw.com/nytimes/docs/iraq/tagubarpt.html>, and MG George R Fay, AR 15-6 Investigation of the Abu Ghraib Detention Facility and 205th Military Intelligence Brigade (August 2004) at 7, 47–48, available at <http://fl1.findlaw.com/news.findlaw.com/hdocs/docs/dod/fay82504rpt.pdf> (henceforth Fay Report).

[2] Jamie Wilson and Kevin Maguire, 'American Firm in Bosnia Sex Trade Row Poised to Win MoD Contract,' *Guardian*, 29 November 2002.

[3] House of Commons, Foreign Affairs Committee, Second Report Sierra Leone, HC 116-I (February 1999) (about Executive Outcomes' operations in Sierra Leone); Antony Barnett and Patrick Smith, 'US Accused of Covert Operations in Somalia,' *Observer*, 10 September 2006 (alleging that a US PMC, Select Armor, prepared undercover operations in Somalia against the Supreme Islamic Courts Council in support of the transitional government with the knowledge of the CIA and in violation of the UN arms embargo).

and indiscriminate shootings at civilians.[4] Troubled by these developments, it is frequently asserted that there is a legal vacuum in which those firms operate,[5] with many commentators emphasizing the need to address the lack of accountability of contractors. Surprisingly little attention, however, has been paid to another dimension of the problem. Since these incidents are either tacitly or explicitly sanctioned by governments and have resulted from the transfer of functions from the public to the private sector, the question of accountability is also very much one of accountability of the state. An important question in the discussion on accountability is therefore: When does the hiring state, the host state, or the exporting state bear international responsibility for the conduct of PMCs?[6]

The fact that PMCs are often staffed by former military personnel and retain tight links to a certain state is often assumed to mean that such entities will be wary of acting against the interests of that state, or that it will act in a state's interest for commercial reasons.[7] Some writers even speak of 'foreign policy by proxy' or 'covert wings of governments'.[8] Similarly, PMCs seek to dispel suspicions by arguing that they will work only for legitimate governments.[9] Nevertheless, what states perceive to be in their interest is not necessarily in line with international law; nor do 'legitimate' governments always act in accordance with international law. If PMCs are a convenient tool to pursue foreign policy ends without the appearance of state involvement, the incentive for states to use PMCs to circumvent international obligations—or to save the costs of abiding by them—is apparent.

It is frequently assumed that the transfer of functions to PMCs involves a transfer of responsibility as well. First, there appears to be little effort to maintain effective control over their activities.[10] The US General Accounting Office (GAO) has

---

[4] Jonathan Finer, 'Security Contractors in Iraq under Scrutiny after Shootings,' *Washington Post*, 10 September 2005.

[5] Peter Singer, 'War, Profits and the Vacuum of Law: Privatized Military Firms and International Law,' Columbia Journal of Transnational Law, vol 42 (2004) 521; Thomas Catan, 'Private Armies March into a Legal Vacuum,' *Financial Times*, 10 February 2005.

[6] Exceptions are Christian Schaller, 'Private Sicherheits- und Militärfirmen in bewaffneten Konflikten: Völkerrechtliche Einsatzbedingungen und Kontrollmöglichkeiten,' SWP Studie 2005/S24, available at <http://www.swp-berlin.org>; University Centre for International Humanitarian Law, Expert Meeting on Private Military Contractors: Status and State Responsibility for their Actions, available at <http://www.ucihl.org/communication/Private_Military_Companies_report.pdf>, and the intergovernmental process initiated by the Swiss government in collaboration with the ICRC, see <http://www.eda.admin.ch/eda/en/home/topics/intla/humlaw/pse/psechi.html>.

[7] Foreign and Commonwealth Office, Private Military Companies: Options for Regulation, HC 577, February 2002, para 45 (henceforth FCO Green Paper); Juan Carlos Zarazate, 'The Emergence of a New Dog of War: Private International Security Companies, International Law, and the New World Disorder,' Stanford Journal of International Law, vol 34 (1994) 149. A prominent counterexample is the closing of Baghdad airport in September 2005 over disputes over pay; Patrick Cockburn, 'Baghdad Airport Closed by 'Unpaid' UK Security Firm,' *Independent*, 12 September 2005.

[8] Thomas Adams, 'The New Mercenaries and the Privatization of Conflict,' *Parameters*, vol 29 (2) (1999) 110; Kevin O'Brien, 'PMCs, Myths and Mercenaries: The Debate on Private Military Companies,' *Royal United Services Institute for Defense Studies*, vol 1 (2000) 145. See also FCO Green Paper (n 7 above), para 50.   [9] 'We're the Good Guys These Days,' *Economist*, 29 July 1995.

[10] See PW Singer, *Corporate Warriors: The Rise of the Privatized Military Industry* (Ithaca: Cornell University Press, 2003) 152.

pointed to a significant lack of oversight on the part of the hiring agencies over PMCs in Iraq.[11] During the occupation, no US agency kept track even of the number of PMCs operating on the ground.[12] Elsewhere, legislators frowning on the idea of commercial firms performing military activities have contributed to a continuing absence of formal control mechanisms: in Britain, another major PMC-exporting country, debate on regulation has been stalled because of the indignation with which parliamentarians received the FCO's Green Paper outlining options for regulation.[13] Secondly, on those occasions where it has been alleged that international obligations have been violated, governments have explicitly or implicitly denied any responsibility for such wrongdoing, not on the basis that no breach of international law has occurred, but because any connection to the perpetrators is denied.[14] Thirdly, although the domestic enforcement of international obligations is often a necessary means for fulfilling them, misconduct of contractors is rarely prosecuted through the state,[15] whether this is a consequence of confusion as to whether and how existing legal regimes apply or indeed of a sense that, once private firms are in play, the point at issue is not the conduct of the state. Abu Ghraib provides a stark illustration of the different responses to violations of international law depending on whether the misconduct was carried out by state organs or PMCs: none of the contractors named in the Taguba and Fay Reports as 'directly or indirectly responsible for the abuses' has been charged with any crime,[16] whereas their counterparts from the Army and the Marines have been sentenced to prison time by military courts.[17] As a result, the implicated

[11] GAO, 'Military Operations—Contractors Provide Vital Services to Deployed Forces but Are Not Adequately addressed in DOD Plans,' GAO-03-695, June 2003, p 20, available at <http://www.gao.govnew.items/d03695.pdf>. See also Taguba Report, Findings and Recommendations (Part II), para 30; Steven L Schooner, 'Contractor Atrocities in Abu Ghraib: Compromised Accountability in a Streamlined, Outsourced Government,' Stanford Law & Policy Review, vol 13 (2005) 549.

[12] US Congressional Research Service, 'Private Security Contractors in Iraq: Background, Legal Status, and Other Issues,' May 2004, p 2; Caroline Holmqvist, 'Private Security Companies—The Case for Regulation,' SIPRI Policy Paper No 9, January 2005, p 24.

[13] A member of the Commons Foreign Affairs Select Committee found it 'breathtaking in the extreme' that the Foreign Minister 'should even contemplate giving such companies a veneer of respectability'; Paul Waugh/Nigel Morris, ' "Mercenaries as Peace-keepers" Plan under Fire,' *Independent*, 14 February 2002.

[14] See, eg, 'Arms to Africa Affair,' House of Commons, Foreign Affairs Committee, Second Report Sierra Leone (n 3 above), para 52; MPRI's provision of military training to the Croatian force enabling the US to appear neutral, Zarazate, 'The Emergence of a New Dog of War' (n 7 above) 92; Clive Walker and David Whyte, 'Contracting Out War?,' International & Comparative Law Quarterly, vol 54 (2005) 661–2.

[15] The only case known to the author is one prosecution for alleged abuse: a security contractor who worked for the CIA in Afghanistan got charged for involvement in the beating to death of a detainee. The charge was brought under the PATRIOT Act. Section 804 of the Act, later codified as 18 USC Section 7(9), provides jurisdiction over crimes committed by or against any US national on lands or facilities designated for use by the United States government, Department of Justice; US Department of Justice Press Release of 17 June 2004, available at <http://www.usdoj.gov/opa/pr/2004/june/04_crm_414.htm>.

[16] GAO, 'Rebuilding Iraq: Actions Needed to Improve Use of Private Security Providers,' GAO-05-737, 28 July 2005, 21, n 18.

[17] Peter Spiegel, 'No Contractors Facing Abu Ghraib Abuse Charges,' *Financial Times*, 9 August 2005.

contractors faced trial only after the Iraqi victims had filed a class action on the basis of tort law.[18]

As private commercial actors emerge as significant military actors serious questions are raised about the viability of a legal system premised on the assumption that states conduct war, provide internal and external security, and organize their military. This conceptual discord might explain the current tendency to dismiss international law as largely irrelevant[19] and to move on to discuss voluntary instruments or contracts as the more promising means to regulate the use and conduct of PMCs.

This chapter seeks to shift the focus back to the traditional focus of international lawyers: the responsibility of the state. This is not to suggest that viewing the issue through the lens of state responsibility alone will adequately address accountability and control problems. The weak enforcement of state obligations is well known, and other mechanisms, such as contract law, may provide more effective tools to enforce international values, as Laura Dickinson shows in chapter twelve. While it is true that PMCs occupy an uncertain position in international law, however, speaking of a 'legal vacuum' ignores the numerous state obligations that apply in the environment in which PMCs operate. The mere fact that a state conducts its policies through proxies, rather than through state organs, does not render international law inapplicable. The existence of and consequences following from a breach of an international obligation are determined by principles of state responsibility, whose underlying conceptual premise is that states are the primary actors on the international plane. The question, then, is to what extent the law of state responsibility can reflect the quantitative and qualitative shift in the activities of PMCs—if it fails to take account of the altered military landscape, the capacity of international law to regulate the impact of both state and non-state actors on international security, conflict resolution, and human rights is gravely diminished.

International law and the concept of state responsibility, while state-centred, allows some flexibility to address accountability of states for the misconduct of PMCs. The ability of this approach to regulate military affairs, however, is hamstrung by weak enforcement and its very nature as a state-centred concept, which does not endeavour to address actual power-relationships between states and non-state actors. Relying on the responsibility of states alone is thus a necessary but insufficient tool for addressing the problems accompanying the expanding role of PMCs.

---

[18] *Saleh et al v Titan Corporation et al,* Case No 04 CV 1143 R (NLS), class action filed in the US District Court for the Southern District of California (transferred in June 2006 to the District Court for the District of Columbia), available at <http://www.ccr-ny.orgv2/legal/september_11th/sept11Article.asp?objID=8tzsXQmAh2&content=423>.
[19] See, eg, GAO, 'Actions still needed for improving the use of Private Security Contractors,' GAO 06- 865T, 13 June 2006, 4, 16, suggesting that 'no ... international standards exist for establishing private security provider and employee qualifications.'

State responsibility for conduct of private actors

The concept of state responsibility is based on a distinction between public and private conduct. In principle only the 'internationally wrongful act of a State entails the international responsibility of that State'.[20] Only conduct attributable to the state is an 'act of state'.[21] Since the state as an abstract construct does not act as such but through its officials and authorities, the presumption is that the acts of state organs are the acts of states.[22] This includes the acts of members of the armed forces of a state. In most cases contractors are not part of the armed forces. State responsibility can be generated also by private conduct, however. Under exceptional circumstances, private acts are attributed to the state; where no such attribution exists the state can still be internationally responsible if it failed to take appropriate measures to prevent the violation of international law, or to ensure that the wrongdoer makes suitable reparation or is punished. These possibilities will be considered in turn.

Private conduct that is state conduct: a question of attribution

The deliberate use of private proxies in international relations as a means to conduct foreign policy is not new. Mercenaries were used by former colonial powers to destabilize established governments; states in the Cold War relied on private groups as a more or less covert means to pursue foreign policy goals hoping they would escape both domestic and international scrutiny. This section will discuss the circumstances under which courts have attributed conduct of private actors to a state, and subsequently assess to what extent the developed principles apply to PMC conduct. Relevant for present purposes are the cases in which private conduct is deemed as state conduct because the private actor has been authorized by the state to exercise governmental powers,[23] or where the state has instructed, controlled, or directed the private conduct.[24]

Attribution de iure: *the exercise of elements of 'governmental authority'*

Courts have attributed private conduct to the state where the private entity was authorized to exercise elements of governmental authority. The focus is on the

---

[20] ILC Articles on State Responsibility, art 1 (henceforth ILC Articles).

[21] ILC Articles, art 2(a).

[22] International Court of Justice (ICJ), *LaGrand (Germany v United States)*, Judgment, 27 June 2001, ICJ Reports 2001, para 81; ILC Articles, art 4. See now ICJ, *Case Concerning the Application of the Convention on the Prevention and the Punishment of the Crime of Genocide (Bosnia and Hercegovina v Serbia and Montenegro)* Judgment, 26 February 2007, paras 391–395, 397 (referring to persons that should be 'equated with state organs *de facto*' due to their 'complete dependence' on the state, of which they are 'merely the instrument'). See also James Crawford, *The International Law Commission's Articles on State Responsibility—Introduction. Text and Commentaries* (Cambridge: Cambridge University Press, 2003), art 4, para 11 (henceforth *ILC Commentary*).

[23] ILC Articles, art 5. See also Report of the Special Rapporteur on Extrajudicial Summary and Arbitrary Executions, UN Doc E/CN.4/2005/7, para 70.   [24] ILC Articles, art 8.

nature of the activity involved; not decisive is the public or private character of the entity that exercises that function and its link to the state.[25] The commentary of the International Law Commission (ILC) on its Articles on State Responsibility notes that the principle is, in fact, meant to address the phenomenon of public corporations that have been privatized yet continue to exercise public functions, as well as para-statal entities exercising 'state functions'.[26] The rationale behind this attribution is that a state cannot evade its responsibility simply by transferring its functions to a private entity. This principle is dictated by logic and well acknowledged in international law:[27]

when, by delegation of powers, bodies act in a public capacity, eg, police an area ... the principles governing the responsibility of the State for its organs apply with equal force. From the point of view of international law, it does not matter whether a State polices a given area with its own police or entrusts this duty, to a greater or less extent, to autonomous bodies.[28]

This attribution occurs regardless of whether the non-state actor has exceeded its competences or contravened instructions.[29]

While the principle underlying this rule is obvious, its application is difficult for two reasons. The conceptual reason is that attribution hinges on the vague notion of governmental authority. The practical reason is that it is difficult to determine what PMC activities can be attributed to the state due to the uncertainty surrounding the range and nature of services offered by PMCs.

There is no international consensus as to what constitutes the exercise of governmental authority. In the context of state immunity, the complexity and perhaps impossibility of determining the precise scope of inherently 'sovereign', 'governmental', or 'public' activities is well known.[30] Understandings of these concepts are not only different in different societies, but also in constant flux: in 1971 the former ILC Special Rapporteur Robert Ago referred in this context to private persons driving vehicles used to carry troops to the front, but also 'postal communications' alongside 'military functions' and 'volunteers' supporting an insurrectional movement in a neighbouring country.[31] It is doubtful whether today these assessments

---

[25] Robert Ago, Third Report on State Responsibility, UN Doc A/CN.4/246, YILC 1971 II (1), para 191. [26] ILC Commentary (n 22 above) art 5, para 1.

[27] Report of the International Law Commission to the General Assembly, UN Doc A/9610/Rev 1, YILC 1974 II (1) Chapter III, para 17.

[28] German government, League of Nations, Conference for the Codification of International Law, Bases of Discussion for the Conference drawn up by the Preparatory Committee, Vol III: Responsibility of States for Damage caused in their Territory to the Person or Person of Foreigners (Doc.C. 75.M.69.1929.V.), p 90 (cited in *ILC Commentary* (n 22 above) art 5, para 4).

[29] *Yeager v Iran*, 17 Iran-USCTR 92, 110–111 (1987-IV); ILC Articles, art 7.

[30] See James Crawford, 'International Law and Foreign Sovereigns: Distinguishing Immune Transactions,' *British Yearbook of International Law*, vol 54 (1983) 83, 89–90.

[31] Third Report on State Responsibility (n 25 above), paras 189–90.

would be shared. More useful is considering the content of a state obligation itself. For example, if an occupying power is obliged to 'restore and ensure' public order and safety in the occupied territories,[32] it could be argued that international law thereby assumes that this responsibility entails the exercise of governmental authority. Such wording is not conclusive, however, as other provisions might impose an obligation on the state to 'ensure' the enjoyment of the right to education or employment, yet it is clear that providing the same does not constitute an intrinsic state function.[33]

The ILC endeavoured to give some guidelines noting that the content of the delegated powers, the way in which they were conferred, the purpose for which they are to be exercised, and the extent to which the non-state entity is accountable to government for their exercise are of particular relevance.[34] These criteria are, however, only of limited use. The first criterion—content of the competence in question—is essentially circular. Similarly, it is unclear how the means by which the power was transferred should affect its classification as governmental: can it have an impact on the classification of a competence whether it was granted through contract, order, or statute? Furthermore, taking into account the extent of accountability to government as a pertinent factor would result in undesirable consequences. Where a PMC has been authorized to interrogate prisoners but is not held accountable by the government, it would appear that its misconduct would not be attributed to the state and consequently the state is not responsible for it. As a result, the state would have no incentive to hold the PMC accountable—a result that would undermine one of the rationales of attribution of private conduct to the state.

The criterion of the purpose for which the transferred competences are exercised seems to be more useful and is echoed in attempts by different US government agencies to circumscribe the notion of 'governmental authority' or 'governmental function'. Well before the use of contractors in conflict zones became a prominent issue, the GAO and the US Office of Management and Budget (OMB) purported to define 'governmental functions' in order to facilitate determination of which functions are appropriate for outsourcing. Similarly to the ILC, both agencies found no definition but placed emphasis on the purpose of the conferred powers: the GAO referred to the 'basic principle ... that the government should not contract out its responsibilities to serve the public interest or to exercise its sovereign powers'.[35] The OMB counts an activity as a governmental function 'that is so

---

[32] Annex to Hague Convention IV, Regulations Respecting the Laws and Customs of War on Land, art 43.

[33] University Centre for International Humanitarian Law, 'Expert Meeting' (n 6 above) 19.

[34] *ILC Commentary* (n 22 above), art 5, para 6.

[35] GAO Report, Government Contractors—Are Service Contractors Performing Inherently Governmental Functions?, GAO-GGD92-11, November 1991, p 4.

intimately related to the public interest that it must be administered by government employees'.[36] Of course, the very fact that responsibilities related to military operations, previously regarded as core state functions, are now performed by private firms indicates that pinning down the precise degree of public interest in a given activity is an equally insurmountable task.

In the absence of a definition, some guidance might be drawn from court findings and discussions in the ILC. The ILC commentary in fact refers to private security firms acting as prison guards, qualifying detaining and disciplining individuals as exercising elements of governmental authority.[37] Other examples are powers related to immigration control or quarantine, or the identification of property for seizure.[38] The Iran-United States Claim Tribunal had to deal with the issue of attribution of conduct of para-statal forces, such as the Komitehs and Islamic Revolutionary Guards before they were formally recognized by the Islamic Republic of Iran, in a number of cases. In both *Rankin v Iran*[39] and *Yeager v Iran*,[40] detention and subsequent expropriation were regarded as the exercise of governmental powers, as was the seizure of property in *Hyatt v Iran*.[41]

As can be seen from the ILC Commentary and the above cases, although there is little prospect of a clear definition of the concept of governmental authority some activities are arguably so commonly regarded as 'core governmental functions' that their performance by PMCs can be said to constitute the exercise of governmental authority. Among them are law enforcement, engaging in combat, seizure of money,

---

[36] See OMB Circular A-76 (revised), 29 May 2003, available at <http://www.whitehouse.gov/ombcirculars/9076/976_incl_tech_correction.pdf>, stating that only 'commercial activities should be subject to the forces of competition' and that government agencies 'shall perform inherently governmental activities with government personnel'.

These activities require the exercise of substantial discretion in applying governmental authority and/or in making decisions for the government. Inherently governmental activities normally fall into two categories: the exercise of sovereign government authority or the establishment of procedures and processes related to the oversight of monetary transactions or entitlements. An inherently governmental activity involves: ... (2) determining, protecting, and advancing economic, political, territorial, property, or other interests by military or diplomatic action, civil or criminal judicial proceedings, contracts management, or otherwise; (3) significantly affecting the life, liberty, or property of private persons(...).

However, an 'activity may be provided by contract support where the contractor does not have the authority to decide on the course of action, but is tasked to develop options or implement a course of action, with agency oversight'. The US DoD aims at outsourcing as many activities as possible except for 'core government' or 'mission critical functions', the first being defined as 'directly related to war fighting', see *Quadrennial Defense Review Report*, September 2001, p 53, available at <http://www.defenselink.mil/pubs/qdr2001.pdf>. See also DoD Instruction No 3020.41, 3 October 2005, para 6.1.5., and DoD Instruction No 1100.22, 7 September 2006, in particular paras 4.1, 6.1.2, E2.1.1, E2.1.3.1, E2.1.3.3, E2.1.4, E2.1.6, E2.5.1.

[37] See also Gregory Townsend, 'State Responsibility for Acts of De Facto Agents,' Arizona Journal of International & Comparative Law, vol 14 (1997) 635.

[38] *ILC Commentary* (n 22 above), art 5, para 2.

[39] *Rankin v Iran*, 17 Iran-USCTR 135 (1987-IV).

[40] *Yeager v Iran*, 17 Iran-USCTR 92, 101 (1987-IV).

[41] *Hyatt International Corporation v Iran*, 9 Iran-USCTR 72 (1985-II).

detention and interrogation, expropriation, and border and immigration control. Consequently, the conduct of CACI and Titan at Abu Ghraib, of Executive Outcomes and Sandline International in Angola, Sierra Leone, and Papua New Guinea, and of the contractors guarding the Erez crossing in Gaza[42] would be attributed to the states that hired them.

Yet even with such a tentative list it is difficult to establish whether the activities in which PMCs are actually engaged correspond to the exercise of governmental authority. With regard to combat, it is not clear whether this is an activity undertaken by PMCs. From the perspective of the hiring governments and the industry it is clearly not. The care with which the Coalition Provisional Administration (CPA) in Iraq avoided even the appearance of PMCs engaging in 'military' or even 'offensive' activities was notable. It stated in 2004 that the PMCs with which it had direct contracts provided services that 'are defensive in nature': 'personnel security for senior civilian officials, non-military site security (buildings and infrastructure), and non-military convoy security'.[43] In the same vein, the US Department of Defense claims that 'PSCs are not being used to perform inherently military functions'[44] and that contractors are utilized to free up troops for offensive combat operations—not to perform such operations themselves. The Sierra Leone or Angola scenario where firms have acted as force multipliers or even fought the war on behalf of the governments is thus explained as an aberration. Indeed, very few firms today appear to be willing to engage directly in combat operations.[45]

Such claims are difficult to verify. There are reports of PMC personnel actively engaging in combat as commonly understood.[46] With regard to all other activities, the lack of clarity of mandate might result in PMCs taking on activities not explicitly foreseen in their contracts. Ambiguous and open-worded contracts that lend themselves to liberal interpretation by both contract parties, combined with disregard for internal policies and lack of oversight, facilitate this kind of mission creep.[47] In one instance, a firm was contracted for assistance in law enforcement; on the ground the mandate translated into participating in raids carried out by the Iraqi police.[48]

Furthermore, although it may now be unlikely that a PMC is contracted to fight a war on behalf of or alongside a national army, many conflicts do not correspond to this model of 'war'. PMC employees operating in an environment where

[42] 'Erez Crossing Will Be Operated by Private Company Starting Thursday,' *Haaretz*, 18 January 2006.
[43] US Congressional Research Service, 'Private Security Contractors in Iraq' (n 12 above) 3.
[44] Daniel Bergner, 'The other Army,' *New York Times Magazine*, 14 August 2005, p 32; see also DoD Instruction No 1100.22 (n 36 above) para E2.1.3.1.
[45] However, Patrick Toohey, vice president for government relations at Blackwater, described how his employees 'fought and engaged every combatant with precise fire' and that they were 'conducting a security operation', David Barstow et al, 'Security Companies: Shadow Soldiers in Iraq,' *New York Times*, 19 April 2004.　　[46] Singer, *Corporate Warriors* (n 10 above) 208.
[47] Schooner, 'Contractor Atrocities at Abu Ghraib' (n 11 above) 564; Holmqvist, 'Private Military Companies' (n 12 above) 25; see also chapter twelve in this volume by Laura Dickinson.
[48] Renae Merle, 'DynCorp took part in Chalabi raid,' *Washington Post*, 4 June 2004.

they may be fired upon by non-state actors who may indiscriminately attack both military and non-military targets[49] frequently contradict the assertions of government officials. Private contractors described their activity in Iraq as 'working in and amongst the most hostile parts of a conflict or post-conflict scenario';[50] 'Security in a hostile fire area is a classic military mission'.[51] It is likely that this is a more realistic description of their work in low-intensity conflicts, such as Iraq or Colombia, where without a clear frontline protecting individuals or buildings can easily slide into participating in the hostilities. Contractors guarding reconstruction projects or escorting supply convoys through hostile territory are as much in the battlefield as US troops. Even providing security for food delivery can result in being drawn into combat situations, as the death of four Blackwater employees in Fallujah, Iraq, illustrated.[52] The distinction between security and military, defensive and offensive operations appears, therefore, rather artificial.[53] The use of sophisticated weapon systems is another change in warfare that adds to this haziness and might require rethinking the notion of combat. Contractors are hired to maintain and operate those systems that can have as much impact on the battlefield as troops fighting on the ground, thus being equally 'mission critical'.[54]

The ambiguities surrounding both the notion of governmental authority and the nature of activities of PMCs make it difficult to apply a principle of attribution based on the performance of governmental functions.[55]

Attribution de facto: *control and instructions*

Where the conduct in question cannot be said to constitute the exercise of governmental authority, or where no authorization exists, private conduct is also attributed to the state when it is carried out on the instructions of the state or where the private actor is under the state's direction or control.[56] A state hiring a firm and instructing it to abuse prisoners is a fairly clear-cut case. Much more complex is the situation in which no such instructions exist, but where the state played a role

---

[49] PMC personnel have become an explicit target of Al Qaeda, 'Australians Targeted in Baghdad Blasts: al-Qaeda,' *Sydney Morning Herald*, 26 October 2005.

[50] Michael Battles, co-founder of the PMC Custer Battles, cited in David Barstow et al, 'Security Companies: Shadow Soldiers in Iraq' (n 45 above).

[51] Senator Jack Reed, member of the US Armed Service committee, in a letter to Defense Secretary Rumsfeld, cited in David Barstow et al, ibid.

[52] David Barstow, 'Iraqi Escorts Lured US Contractors into Ambush, Security Firm Says,' *New York Times*, 10 April 2004.   [53] See also FCO Green Paper (n 7 above), para 11.

[54] Singer, *Corporate Warriors* (n 10 above) 90.

[55] For a different conclusion see University Centre for International Humanitarian Law, 'Expert Meeting' (n 6 above) 20.

[56] ILC Articles, art 8. Note that in the *Genocide* case (n 22 above) the ICJ is ambiguous as to whether the question of control in this context concerns responsibility of the state for the conduct of one of its organs controlling private conduct and therefore being "the cause of the comission of acts in breach of its international obligations" or for the private conduct which is attributed to the state by virtue of control, para 397. The analysis following that paragraph would suggest the latter.

in the preparation and in the implementation of the operation by directing or controlling it. When the ILC drafted the article laying down the principle of attribution by virtue of control, direction, or instructions it meant to address those cases where the state supplements its actions by recruiting private actors acting as 'auxiliaries' without integrating them in the state apparatus,[57] though it also noted that mere recruiting is not sufficient: a 'real link' between the private group or person and the state is required.[58] The extent to which the state must 'control' the private actor and its operations is, however, subject to debate.

The International Court of Justice (ICJ) considered this question in 1986 in the *Nicaragua* case:

> What the Court has to determine at this point is whether or not the relationship of the *contras* to the United States Government was so much one of dependence on the one side and control on the other that it would be right to equate the contras, for legal purposes, with an organ of the United States Government, or as acting on behalf of that Government. Here it is relevant to note that in May 1983 the assessment of the Intelligence Committee ... was that the contras 'constitute(d) an independent force' and that the 'only element of control that could be exercised by the United States' was 'cessation of aid'. Paradoxically this assessment serves to underline, *a contrario*, the potential for control inherent in the degree of the *contras'* dependence on aid. Yet despite the heavy subsidies and other support provided to them by the United States, there is no clear evidence of the United States having actually exercised such a degree of control in all fields as to justify treating the *contras* as acting on its behalf ... even the general control of the respondent State with a high degree of dependency on it, would not in themselves mean, without further evidence, that the United States directed or enforced the perpetration of the acts contrary to human rights and humanitarian law alleged by the applicant State. For this conduct to give rise to legal responsibility of the United States, it would in principle have to be proved that the State had effective control of the military or paramilitary operations in the course of which the alleged violations were committed.[59]

Consequently, from the ICJ's perspective, 'effective control' had to be established, which Judge Ago, in his Separate Opinion, specified as involving specific instructions to commit a particular act or to carry out a particular task of some kind.[60] Even though the Court acknowledged that the Contras were dependent on US funding, the lack of control on the part of the United States over the specific operations prevented the judges from attributing their activities to the United States. Under this reading, if a state hired a PMC but did not exercise control over all its operations, even if the PMC would have to discontinue an operation upon cessation of payment, their conduct would not be deemed as attributable to the hiring state, less so to the exporting state.

---

[57] *ILC Commentary* (n 22 above), art 8, para 2.

[58] *ILC Commentary* (n 22 above), art 8, para 1.

[59] ICJ, *Case concerning Military and Paramilitary Activities in and against Nicaragua (Nicaragua v United States)*, Judgment (Merits), 27 June 1986, ICJ Reports 1986, paras 109–15. But see *Genocide* case (n 22 above), paras 393, 397, 400.

[60] *Nicaragua* case (n 59 above), 189–90.

An obvious issue in this context is that PMC personnel hired by US agencies in Iraq fall outside the military chain of command unless they enter a US military facility.[61] The relationship between PMCs and the military is described as one of 'informal co-ordination', consisting of regular meetings to share information and co-ordinate and resolve conflicts in operations. Contractors have reportedly erected unauthorized checkpoints and claimed to have the power to detain and confiscate identity cards, apparently without the knowledge of the commander in the theatre.[62] In some cases, the control relationship is reversed: according to the Fay Report, the contractors implicated in the Abu Ghraib abuses might have 'supervised' governmental personnel.[63] Contract officers, who have the competence to administer the contracts between the hiring US agency and the firm, appear to be rarely on site.[64] PMC personnel would thus not be deemed as acting on behalf of the United States.

Even less can PMCs be said to act on behalf of a state if the only connection is the fact that a licence has been granted. Three key exporting states—the United States, South Africa, and Israel—operate licensing regimes controlling the commercial export of military services.[65] Yet systematic post-licensing verification mechanisms are lacking—even the US licensing regime as the most sophisticated one fails to adequately monitor PMCs once a licence is issued.[66] Without any systematic monitoring and oversight mechanism there is very little control over PMC conduct; not even a minimum of control exists where a licensing regime is absent in the first place, as is the case in Britain.

In 1997 the ICTY revisited the question of attribution by virtue of control. In *Tadic*, the Trial Chamber admitted that the *Nicaragua* test was a 'particularly high threshold test' but ultimately applied a similarly restrictive method along the lines of the ICJ.[67] Its decision, however, was overturned by the Appeals Chamber, which was less favourably disposed towards the ICJ approach. The judges dismissed the, in their view, overly strict test and established a more flexible approach according to which requirements could vary under different circumstances.[68] Where the private actors in question are organized and hierarchically structured—as opposed to a single private individual—more lenient guidelines apply according to which 'overall control' over the group would suffice for attribution of conduct of individuals:

Under international law it is by no means necessary that the controlling authorities should plan all the operations of the units dependent on them, choose their targets, or give specific instructions concerning the conduct of military operations and any alleged violations of

---

[61] Army Field Manual 3—100.21, 'Contractors on the Battlefield', (Chapter 1, 'Military of Contractor Employees'), available at <http://www.globalsecurity.org/military/library/policy/army/fm/3-100-21/chap1.htm>; GAO, 'Actions Needed to Improve Use of Private Security Providers,' GAO-05-737, July 2005, pp 20–21.

[62] 'The Baghdad Boom: Mercenaries,' *Economist*, 27 March 2004.

[63] Fay Report (n 1 above) 51.   [64] Fay Report (n 1 above) 52.

[65] See chapter nine in this volume by Marina Caparini.

[66] See Deborah Avant, *The Market for Force: The Consequences of Privatizing Security* (Cambridge: Cambridge University Press, 2005) 147.

[67] ICTY, Trial Chamber, *Prosecutor v Tadic*, Judgment, 7 May 1997, IT-94-1-T, paras 588, 605, 606.

[68] ICTY, Appeals Chamber, *Prosecutor v Tadic*, Judgment, 15 July 1999, IT-94-1-A, para 117.

international humanitarian law. The control required by international law may be deemed to exist when a State ... has a role in organizing, coordinating or planning the military actions of the military group, in addition to financing, training and equipping or providing operational support to the group.[69]

If the issuing of specific orders or its direction over individual operations is not required, PMC conduct can be attributed more readily to both the exporting or hiring state, depending on the role played in the planning and financing of their activities.

It might be argued that the Appeal Chamber's more flexible approach is a response to the increasing significance of non-state actors in international law. Some support for this assumption can be found in its reasoning as to why the ICJ test was too strict. The judges reconfirmed the rationale for attribution of conduct of *de facto* agents, which is

to prevent States escaping international responsibility by having private individuals carry out tasks that may not or should not be performed by State officials, or by claiming that individuals actually participating in the government authority are not classified as State organs under national legislation and therefore do not engage State responsibility.[70]

However, the circumstances of the case and the reason why the court examined the question of attribution caution against reading too much into the decision for present purposes. The Chamber addressed this issue in order to determine the existence of an 'international conflict' for the purpose of establishing jurisdiction. Recently, the ICJ reaffirmed its own *Nicaragua* approach.[71]

On the other hand, the difference between the *Nicaragua* scenario and the situation in which PMCs operate in conflict zones with the consent of the respective government might justify a departure from the ICJ test. Both the *Nicaragua* and the *Congo* cases dealt with 'mercenary' or 'volunteer' groups that intruded into foreign territory without the knowledge and against the will of the 'host' state. If the private actor operates without the knowledge and acceptance of the 'host' state, or if the hiring or exporting state is different from the state where the private actors carry out their activities, the potentially increased difficulty of directing the tactics or course of an operation and the lack of permanent territorial control[72] might necessitate proof of a greater degree of control over the conduct of those groups.

The latter appears to have been an important factor in the deliberations of the ICTY Appeals Chamber:

Of course, if, as in Nicaragua, the controlling State is *not the territorial State* where the armed clashes occur, or where at any rate the armed units or groups perform their acts,

[69] Ibid, para 137.   [70] Ibid, para 117.
[71] ICJ, *Case Concerning Armed Activities in the Territory of the Congo (Democratic Republic of the Congo v Uganda)*, Judgment, 9 December 2005, ICJ Reports 2005, para 160; *Genocide* case (n 22 above), paras 402–06 (but see Vice-President Al-Khasawneh's dissent, paras 36–9).
[72] See ICJ, *Legal Consequences for States of the Continued Presence of South Africa in Namibia (South West Africa) Notwithstanding Security Council Resolution 276 (1970)*, Advisory Opinion, 21 June 1971, ICJ Reports 1971, para 118.

more and compelling evidence is required to show that the State is genuinely in control of the units and groups not merely by financing and equipping them, but also by generally directing or helping plan their actions ... Where the controlling State is the adjacent State with territorial ambitions on the State where the conflict is taking place, and the controlling State is attempting to achieve its territorial enlargement through the armed forces which it controls, it may be easier to establish the threshold.[73]

According to the Appeals Chamber, the extent of control required decreases with the increasing proximity of the controlling state to the territory where the private conduct takes place, as it then can be more readily presumed that the controlling state can produce effects outside its own territory. This would suggest that where PMCs are hired by the state on whose territory they operate or by the state present in the territory where they operate (as was the case in Iraq), only overall control over the firm as such through the state is required; depending on the proximity of the exporting state to the host state a greater degree of control is necessary. The appropriateness of relying on the criterion of proximity alone is open to question: physical distance is certainly not conclusive as to the degree of control actually exercised if the controlling state has sophisticated means of communication at its disposal enabling it to control the course of an operation. However, the reference to the motivation of the controlling state (territorial ambition) might point to the more general idea that the fact that the government of the host state knows and approves of the presence of PMCs makes it easier for the controlling government to direct the private conduct. This is even more so where the hiring state is also the host state. Therefore, there is some basis for the view that the degree of control required for the purposes of attribution may vary according to the circumstances of the situation.[74]

Private conduct is private conduct but still gives rise to state responsibility: a question of due diligence

Where conduct of PMC personnel is not attributed to the state, it might still be taken into account in determining state responsibility if it is accompanied by certain actions or omissions on the part of the state, as confirmed by the ICJ in the *Corfu Channel* case. Although it was not certain whether mines laid in Albanian waters and damaging British vessels were laid by Albanian officials or by private individuals, the ICJ found that since 'nothing was attempted by the Albanian authorities to prevent the disaster', these 'grave omissions involve the international responsibility of Albania'.[75] Similarly, the ICJ held Iran responsible for the hostage-taking at the US embassy in Tehran for, inter alia, failure to take appropriate steps

---

[73] ICTY, Appeals Chamber, *Prosecutor v Tadic* (n 68 above), paras 138–40, confirmed in *Prosecutor v Delalic*, Judgment, 20 February 2001, IT-96-21-A, para 47.
[74] See Vice-President's Al-Khasawneh's dissent in the *Genocide* case (n 22 above), para 39.
[75] *The Corfu Channel* case *(United Kingdom v Albania)*, Judgment (Merits), 9 April 1949, ICJ Reports 1949, 4, 23. See also *Noyes (United States) v Panama*, 22 May 1933, RIAA vol VI, 308, 311.

either to prevent the militants from invading the Embassy or to persuade or compel them to withdraw.[76] In other words, if the state fails to show due diligence in attempting to prevent or respond to the violation of international law, it is not the private conduct itself but its omission or insufficient effort to prevent or respond to it that might generate its international responsibility.[77] However, an omission or failure to take certain action as such is not relevant for the purposes of state responsibility. There must be, at a minimum, a conventional or customary obligation to endeavour to control private conduct.

Here a note of caution must be made. The concept of due diligence has been discussed primarily in the context of injuries to aliens, in very few instances with regard to diplomatic and consular relations[78] and the law of neutrality.[79] In the context of environmental and space law the required conduct is often specified in the respective treaty.[80] The lack of jurisprudence in other fields of law cautions against an assumption that this is a general principle of international law.[81] For example, Article 1 of the Geneva Conventions and the First Additional Protocol establishes a positive obligation for states 'to ensure respect' for international humanitarian law, but it could be argued that it is related merely to an overall policy, rather than imposing specific obligations on states to train or instruct PMCs.[82]

However, on the basis of Article 43 of the Hague Regulations the ICJ recently found Uganda, as the occupying power in the Ituri district in the Democratic Republic of the Congo, responsible for its 'lack of vigilance in preventing the violation of human rights and international humanitarian law and not to tolerate such violence by a third party'.[83] The matter is also fairly established in the case law of human rights bodies. Conventions oblige states to 'ensure', 'protect', or 'secure' rights.[84] These obligations have been interpreted as requiring states to take positive steps in order to prevent the violation of rights through private actors.[85] In doing so, it was recognized that a concept solely focusing on public authorities as potential violators of human rights would result in a significantly diminished protection. This problem is particularly underscored in the case of 'disappearances', where it is often difficult to establish whether state organs or private individuals

---

[76] *United States Diplomatic and Consular Staff in Tehran (United States v Iran)*, Judgment, 24 May 1980, ICJ Reports 1980, paras 63, 67.

[77] See *Alabama Claims* arbitrations (United States-Britain, Claims Arbitration, 1872, summarized in Herbert W Briggs, *The Law of Nations* (New York: Appleton-Century-Crofts, 1947) 866–71.

[78] *Tehran Hostages* case (n 76 above); Robert Ago, Fourth Report on State Responsibility, UN Doc A/CN.4/264, YBIL 1972 II (1), p 97, para 65.   [79] *Alabama Claims* (n 77 above).

[80] See, eg, Convention on Environmental Impact Assessment in a Transboundary Context (Espoo Convention); see also *Genocide* case (n 22 above), para 429.

[81] But see Robert Ago, Fourth Report on State Responsibility (n 78 above), p 126, para 145.

[82] University Centre for International Humanitarian Law, Expert Meeting (n 6 above) 44.

[83] ICJ, *Case Concerning Armed Activities in the Territory of the Congo* (n 71 above) para 178.

[84] See, eg, International Covenant on Civil and Political Rights, art 1(2); American Convention on Human Rights, art 1; European Convention on Human Rights, art 1.

[85] See August Reinisch, 'The Changing International Framework for Dealing with Non-state Actors,' in Philip Alston (ed), *Non-State Actors and Human Rights* (Oxford: Oxford University Press, 2005) 79–80.

are responsible for the abduction, and if the latter is the case, what relationship that individual has with the state. This issue was explicitly addressed by the Inter-American Court of Human Rights in the *Velasquez Rodriguez* case, where the Court found that the disappearance of Velasquez Rodriguez gave rise to Honduras' responsibility although it could not be determined whether he had disappeared at the hands of or with the acquiescence of Honduran officials,[86] not 'because of the act itself, but because of the lack of due diligence to prevent the violation or to respond to it as required by the Convention'.[87] Human rights protection would similarly lose meaning if states could evade responsibility by shifting responsibilities to the private sector. Therefore, the European Court of Human Rights held that 'the State cannot absolve itself from responsibility by delegating its obligations to private bodies or individuals'.[88]

Of course, this begs the question just what diligence is due—the mere fact that interests protected by international law through a positive obligation have been violated by private actors does not suffice in itself to generate international responsibility. Although the existence of the concept is not disputed, a clear-cut definition has not emerged so far and is probably impossible to articulate.[89] Rather, the precise degree will vary according to the circumstances[90] and the level of protection provided by applicable norms.[91] However, it is possible to determine factors to be taken into account, such as the risk of violation of international law, which would be assessed, inter alia, on the basis of what private actors are in play—whether, for instance, they are armed or not, as well as the protected group.[92]

What this suggests is that where PMC personnel act in violation of human rights or international humanitarian law, their conduct can generate the responsibility of the host or the hiring state for failure to prevent or adequately respond to such conduct even if it is not clear what role state organs have played in the specific operation.[93] Furthermore, the state must in principle be able to exercise its authority over the private actor. This is at least the case in its own territory and if it

---

[86] Inter-American Court of Human Right, *Velasquez Rodriguez v Honduras*, Judgment, 29 July 1988, Ser C, No 4, para 148.   [87] Ibid, para 172.

[88] ECtHR, *Costello Roberts v United Kingdom*, Judgement, 23 February 1993, Series A, No 247-C (1995), 19 EHRR 112, para 27.

[89] Francisco V Garcia Amador, 'Second Report on State Responsibility,' YILC 1957 II, 104.

[90] Alwyn V Freeman, 'Responsibility of States for Unlawful Acts of their Armed Forces,' 88 RdC 1955 II, 278; see also *Genocide* case (n 22 above), paras 429–431.

[91] For instance, the protection afforded to diplomatic agents and missions is particularly high, see Arts 22 II and 29 of the Vienna Convention on Diplomatic Relations and Arts 31 III and 40 of the Vienna Convention on Consular Relations; *Tehran Hostages* case (n 76 above) paras 61–2; Art 10 of the Harvard School's 1929 draft.

[92] Astrid Epiney, *Die völkerrechtliche Verantwortlichkeit von Staaten für Rechtswidriges Verhalten im Zusammenhang mit Aktionen Privater* (Baden-Baden: Nomos-Verlag, 1992) 249.

[93] With regard to human rights obligations of the state that is not the host state, however, it must be established that those rights apply outside the territory of the hiring or exporting state. For the European Convention of Human Rights see England and Wales Court of Appeal, *Al-Skeini and others v Secretary of State for Defence*, (2005) EWCA Civ 1609.

occupies another state.[94] Consequently, the host state or the occupying power might be internationally responsible for failing to exercise due diligence with regard to PMCs. The exporting state is under an obligation to prevent actions of the PMC directed against the territorial integrity of another state;[95] less clear, however, is whether this principle also applies where the PMC is hired or its presence accepted by the other state. While one might argue that this is desirable and possible in theory, it is important to note that to date no court has found a state to be responsible for failing to control its companies or nationals abroad under such circumstances.

Manifestations of failure to exercise due diligence may be found in domestic legislation that proves inadequate to secure and protect rights: where domestic legislation does not take into account the obligation to 'secure to everyone within its jurisdiction the rights and freedoms defined ... in the Convention' and this results in a violation of those rights and freedoms,[96] or in the lack of oversight, adequate training, and background vetting of PMC personnel.[97] If the lack of adequate response is a consequence of deficient execution of an existing legal regime or the lack of competence of authorities to prosecute, this might result in international responsibility as well.[98]

Conclusion

The above analysis demonstrates that there is no legal vacuum in which PMCs operate. States are internationally responsible where PMCs engage in law enforcement or interrogation of prisoners, or where their conduct is controlled by a state. Where states do not directly control PMCs, but rather give a quiet nod to risk prone or abusive conduct, the same reasons why their conduct is not attributed to the state for lack of control can generate state responsibility for lack of due diligence at least on the part of the host or the hiring state. At present, it appears that the diligence shown with regard to PMCs in conflict zones falls significantly short of what is required under international law. It is open to question whether states are willing to implement an effective oversight and monitoring system: costs are considerable and might raise the costs for retaining PMCs to such an extent that the economic rationale for retaining PMCs' services is called into question.[99] The

---

[94] ICJ, *Case Concerning Armed Activities in the Territory of the Congo* (n 71 above) paras 172, 178, 179.

[95] Ian Brownlie, *International Law and the Use of Force by States* (Oxford: Clarendon Press, 1963), chapters 20, 21, 24; UN GA Res 2625 (XXV), 24 October 1970 (Friendly Relations Declaration).

[96] ECtHR, *Young, James and Webster v United Kingdom*, Judgment, 13 August 1981, Series A, No 44 (1981), 4 EHRR 38, para 49.

[97] See Fay Report (n 1 above) 49; Schlesinger, Final Report of the Independent Panel to Review DoD Operations, available at <http://www.defenselink.mil/news/Aug2004/d20040824finalreport.pdf>.

[98] *Neer (United States) v Mexico*, 15 October 1926, RIAA vol IV, 60–1.

[99] See Fay Report (n 1 above) 52; Singer, *Corporate Warriors* (n 10 above) 153.

fact that the US government responded to the communications and co-ordination problems in Iraq between PMCs on the one hand and between PMCs and the Coalition Forces on the other by hiring yet another PMC[100] suggests that prospects are rather bleak.[101]

A second finding of the analysis is that considerable uncertainties remain. The question of what does—or should—constitute governmental functions is unlikely to be resolved in the near future; according to the ICJ, the degree of control necessary to establish state responsibility is a high one and would essentially require a structure allowing the hiring or host state to control the course of the operation. Yet a departure from this test might be justified in certain situations. Indeed, in coping with the changing role of PMCs, at least in the short term, a repositioning of the public-private parameters that determine state responsibility for private conduct might be the most viable solution. Within the limitations set by the state-centeredness of international law, there is room for manoeuvring by lowering the threshold for attribution, and increasing due diligence requirements where the private activity is inherently risk prone, or fundamental rights at stake.

Of course, shifting conceptual boundaries will not render international law a sufficient tool to regulate the use and conduct of PMCs. The enforcement problems of international law are well known. PMCs thrive in weak and failing states, which have little bargaining power and are unlikely to be in a position to monitor and restrict PMC conduct, or to enforce the responsibility of another hiring state. Even where states are willing and in principle able to monitor the activities of PMCs, the private nature of PMCs provides them with means of protection from scrutiny not available to public actors, such as arguments of privacy and client confidentiality. Issues of extraterritorial jurisdiction compound the problem.

An inherent limit is the very nature of state responsibility as a state-centred concept: PMCs are outside its radar even where they are allowed to reverse control relationships vis-à-vis the state, as outlined by James Cockayne in chapter eleven. It does not endeavour to address the responsibility of PMCs as such, nor do the consequences of state responsibility directly target actors other than the state: as a result, the public-private divide underpinning the concept of state responsibility does not reflect the convoluted relationships between the exporting, the hiring, the host state, the PMC and its non-state clients. This is particularly problematic where PMCs do not merely implement policy or concrete decisions, but shape them.[102] Suppose a PMC, authorized or even sent by a Western government, advises a war-torn country or trains its military. While it might act as a proxy of the exporting state, it is conceivable that vis-à-vis its client the roles are reversed,

---

[100] Tracey Boles, 'Dog of War builds Pounds 62m business on Iraq,' *Sunday Times*, 5 February 2006.

[101] See also GAO, Statement of William Solis, Director Defense Capabilities and Management, 'Rebuilding Iraq: Actions Still Needed to Improve the Use of Private Security Providers,' June 2006.

[102] See Anna Leander, 'The Power to Construct International Security: On the Significance of Private Military Companies,' *Millenium*, vol 33 (2005) 803, and her chapter three in this volume.

either because of its superior expertise or because of conditions set by the export-ing government. Particularly troubling is the possibility that the decision over the use of force, although formally in the hands of the states, is essentially made by the firm. For instance, even where state agents pull the trigger or push the button, if the identification of the target depends to a large extent on the PMC contracted to gather intelligence, holding the state responsible alone addresses only one dimension of the problem, or indeed obscures the real issue.[103] By definition the law of state responsibility does not consider the roles of private and public actors in the decision-making process; merely re-interpreting it will not suffice to take into account the potentially crucial impact of private commercial interests on state conduct.

While acknowledging these limits of international law, this chapter argues that in considering a regulatory framework for dealing with PMCs more attention must be paid to the responsibility of states. Failure to do so would ignore an important dimension of the phenomenon: PMCs go where their presence is either requested or accepted by the state. Some states have an interest in retaining PMCs as a flexible tool by which their continuing influence in regions that are not of immediate strategic relevance is ensured, or where sending uniformed military is politically unpalatable, and in keeping the costs for doing so low. Perhaps more importantly, ignoring the law of state responsibility is to dismiss the central role of states in the context of force and might ultimately result in an abdication of responsibility for peace, international security, and the protection of the individ-ual. The monopoly of states to control violence is a consequence of the realization that governance through states is the most effective means to place limits on the use of force. Viewed in this light, in the context of military affairs the state-centeredness of the concept of state responsibility might be seen not as a reflection of its failure to keep pace with changes in the military landscape, but as an institu-tionalization of this insight.

---

[103] In 2003, two AirScan employees helped the Colombian military to bomb a village, killing 18 civilians, by identifying potential targets, Christian Miller, 'US Pair's Role in Bombing Shown,' *Los Angeles Times*, 16 March 2003.

9

Domestic regulation

Licensing regimes for the export of military goods and services

Marina Caparini

Since the end of the Cold War there has been a marked increase in the reliance by states and non-state actors on a broad array of contract security services provided by private entities. These services are provided in both conflict and non-conflict areas, often transnationally by Western firms that recruit globally. The inadequacy of existing international law in dealing with mercenarism, let alone the rapidly expanding domain of transnational private military and security services, has under-scored the difficulties of developing an effective international regulatory regime.[1] Domestic regulatory frameworks provide another means of bringing greater con-trol and accountability to this domain. As yet, however, there are very few states that explicitly regulate the sale of security-related services abroad.[2]

Regulation can be narrowly understood as a set of authoritative rules that include a mechanism, often a public agency, for monitoring and promoting com-pliance with those rules.[3] This chapter will examine national systems regulating the sale of private contract military and security services abroad in the United States and South Africa. It will examine the laws and processes by which such sales are approved by state authorities and the effectiveness of each in fulfilling its object-ives. Although both national approaches are tied to existing arms export control regimes, they differ in the underlying objectives of regulation, the extent of state control exercised, the nature of relations that they foster between the industry and the state, and their impact on development of the industry more generally. The chapter concludes with insights that the contrasting experiences offer for other

---

[1] Christopher Kinsey, 'Challenging International Law: A Dilemma of Private Security Companies,' *Conflict, Security & Development*, vol 5, no 3 (2005) 281–6.

[2] See chapter eleven in this volume by James Cockayne for an overview of approaches of the US, South Africa, Iraq, France, and Britain in licensing or otherwise authorizing PMCs.

[3] Robert Baldwin, Colin Scott, and Christopher Hood, 'Introduction' in R Baldwin, C Scott, and C Hood (eds), *A Reader on Regulation*, Oxford Readings in Socio-Legal Studies (Oxford: Oxford University Press, 1998) 3–4.

states considering the establishment of similar export control-based regimes to regulate the sale of commercial defence and security services to foreign governments and other actors.[4]

The United States: direct commercial sales and foreign military sales

The United States is a major source of commercial firms providing defence and security-related services abroad and its regulatory approach to controlling the export of those services is thus far the most developed and comprehensive. This approach is based on the assumption that defence exports are a primary component of security assistance and should support US foreign and national security policy objectives.[5] Legislation regulates the sale of 'defence services',[6] which reflect some of the activities of private military companies (PMCs) as understood in this volume. The export of commercial military services by PMCs offers various potential benefits to the government, including freeing up US forces from non-essential tasks (such as commitments to train foreign troops or police), delivering training and other services to countries that might provoke controversy at home or abroad if carried out by the state's forces, and spreading US approaches and concepts to actual and potential partners. The US approach to regulation allows it to retain control over the deployment of military- and security-related services overseas by private providers and helps to ensure that sales of services abroad serve US foreign policy and national security interests.

The United States has two systems for commercial transfers of defence articles and services to foreign entities. These transfers occur through (1) direct commercial sales (DCS) in which companies sell directly to foreign entities on the basis of an approved export licence; or (2) through the government-to-government program known as the Foreign Military Sales (FMS) program, for which a licence is not required.

The ITAR licensing system

The Arms Export Control Act (AECA) is the main legislative instrument governing sales of defence articles and services, and expressly states that the President 'is

---

[4] This chapter does not address the issue of regulating outsourcing, ie the engagement of private military or security companies to accompany and support home-state armed forces and/or other governmental departments or agencies, whether operating at home or abroad.

[5] US Department of Defense, Defence Security Cooperation Agency, *Security Assistance Management Manual (SAMM)*, DoD 51015.38-M, 3 October 2003, Chapter One, 'Security Assistance Overview,' 29, available at: <http://www.dsca.mil/samm>.

[6] A 'defence service' is defined as: '... (3) Military training of foreign units and forces, regular and irregular, including formal or informal instruction of foreign persons in the United States or abroad or by correspondence courses, technical, educational, or information publications and media of all kinds, training aid, orientation, training exercise, and military advice.' See ITAR §120.9

authorized to control the import and the export of defence articles and defence services and to provide foreign policy guidance to persons of the United States involved in the export and import of such articles and services'.[7] The AECA is implemented through the International Traffic in Arms Regulations (ITAR), which defines defence services and establishes general policies. It establishes registration and licensing policies and procedures that must be followed by those looking to export defence articles and services. It also sets out compliance and enforcement measures, including penalties for violations of the ITAR.[8] On behalf of the President, the Department of State exercises control over exports and imports of arms and is responsible for overseeing the implementation of ITAR through the Directorate of Defense Trade Controls (DDTC).[9]

The ITAR requires those seeking to sell defence services to a foreign government to obtain prior approval through a licence from the State Department. These are categorized according to the US Munitions List (USML), which constitutes part of ITAR. US companies looking to export defence services are required to first register with the DDTC, after which the company can apply to obtain a licence for a specific sale. Companies exporting defence services would seek a licence under a Technical Assistance Agreement (TAA), which is valid for up to 10 years.

DDTC reviews contract proposals to ensure that the entity applying for the licence is legitimate and reliable, and that the proposed export will not undermine US policy. Proposed defence exports to embargoed countries are automatically denied a licence. Those licence requests concerning sales to NATO allies and friendly countries generally encounter few obstacles, and measures have been implemented to expedite the licensing process.[10] While the majority of licence requests are determined internally by DDTC, in about one-third of cases the application undergoes a 'staffed' or interagency review that is co-ordinated by DDTC. The staffed review constitutes a risk assessment on the basis of national security and foreign policy considerations, including the impact of the proposed transfer on aspects such as regional stability and human rights.[11] Different offices from within the State Department and Department of Defense(DoD) represented by the Defense Technology Security Administration (DTSA), and other federal offices such as the National Security Council may be involved. Furthermore, information may be shared with law enforcement agencies such as the Department of

---

[7] 22 USC, chapter 39, subchapter III, §2778 'Control of Arms Exports and Imports,' (a)(1).

[8] The ITAR can be found in subchapter M, title 22, Code of Federal Regulations, Parts 120 through 130 (22 CFR 120-130). See the Electronic Code of Federal Regulations (e-CFR) at: <http://www.pmddtc.state.gov/consolidated_itar.htm>.   [9] 22 CFR §120.1.

[10] For example, an expedited licensing procedure exists on the basis of bilateral agreements with Britain and Australia. See Final Rule, 'Amendments to the International Traffic in Arms Regulations': Part 126, 70 Fed Reg 39919 (12 July 2005).

[11] Nancy Meyer, Directorate of Defense Trade Controls, Bureau of Political–Military Affairs, Department of State, PowerPoint presentation delivered to the ITAR Seminar Series, Australian Department of Industry, Tourism and Resources, February–March 2006, available at <http://www.industry.gov.au/content/itrinternet/cmscontent.cfm?objectID=FC567D6E-B920-7AA9-D426676F7B872793>.

Homeland Security or Customs in order to flag potential problems regarding eligibility or past violations of export laws.[12]

DDTC applies a pre-licence check to the proposed foreign end-user of US defence articles or services, aimed at establishing their reliability and determining whether they are suitable to receive the defence services and are likely to comply with end-use restrictions. To that end it maintains a watchlist of suspicious organizations and individuals it consults when considering export licence applications. DDTC has four options in dealing with an export licence application: it can approve a licence; approve it subject to provisos or limiting conditions; deny a licence; or return it without action due to missing information. Conditions attached to a licence may be very specific in nature. For example, reviews of contracts for military or police training of foreign forces may require the alteration of course curricula, training manuals, and other supporting material such as specific information contained in PowerPoint presentations.[13] The State Department is also required to monitor the end-use of commercially exported licensed defence articles and services, to ensure that the recipient is complying with the requirements set out and that the articles and services are being used for the purposes for which they were provided. It must submit an annual report on its monitoring programme to Congress.[14]

DDTC holds responsibility for enforcement of ITAR and can conduct investigations of suspected ITAR violations. It has the authority to suspend, deny, or revoke licence approvals and can undertake criminal prosecutions and civil action. Penalties for ITAR violations can be severe: criminal penalties may include fines up to $1 million per violation for corporations and up to 10 years imprisonment for individuals. Civil penalties of up to $500,000 per violation may also be assessed, and multiple violations may be identified in a programme or transfer. The violator may also have its export privileges suspended or be debarred from contracting with the government for up to three years. The imposition of penalties may additionally result in negative publicity for the firm and individuals involved, and corporations that have incurred penalties may also be subject to enhanced scrutiny in future transactions.

The 'Blue Lantern Program' was introduced in 1990 to enforce end-use restrictions of commercial defence exports, employing pre-licence checks and monitoring end-use of exported articles and services with the assistance of overseas embassy personnel. In 2004 about 500 checks occurred on some 60,000 licensed transactions, of which 18 per cent yielded unfavourable results.[15] However, a lack of detailed

---

[12] US Department of State, '2006 Summary Privacy Impact Assessment,' Defense Trade Application System, October 2004.

[13] Author's telephone correspondence with DDTC agreement officer, 17 October 2006.

[14] AECA, chapter 3A, section 40A 'End-Use Monitoring of Defense Articles and Defense Services.'

[15] DDTC, End Use Monitoring of Defense Articles and Defense Services: Commercial Exports FY04, available at: <http://www.fas.org/asmp/resources/govern/109th/StateEUMfy04.pdf>.

reporting information leaves it unclear how systematically the State Department monitors the actual provision of defence services and to what extent conditions attached to the export licence are respected. In practice, the Blue Lantern Program appears to be targeted on those articles most susceptible to diversion or misuse into the grey arms trade, such as firearms, ammunition, spare parts for military air-craft, and electronics and communications equipment.[16] Information published on debarred firms and individuals has not provided indications of serious misconduct by firms supplying defence services such as military training. However, due to the lack of detailed information in the public domain, it is unclear whether that is because companies exporting military training and other defence services generally comply with the conditions of their licensed agreements in delivering military- and security-related services, or because monitoring tends to focus more on the end-use of defence articles than of services. Moreover, while US embassy officials in the contracting country are charged with general oversight, no official has a dedicated responsibility to monitor the firms or their activities,[17] and some embassy officials have reportedly been unwilling to take on an oversight role vis-à-vis US firms and their employees working in-country.[18]

While the ITAR regulatory regime appears rigorous, there are problems with transparency. The licensing process is largely hidden from public view, making it difficult to examine how the regulatory structure functions in practice and on what grounds decisions are taken. While the DDTC must provide annual and quarterly reports of authorizations to Congress, there is little information publicly available with regard to specific types of defence services that have been authorized. For example, while Category IX of the USML refers to military training, defence services may also be classified under various other categories based on the articles or materiel they may involve. Moreover, there is very limited information that firms must legally make publicly available. ITAR specifies that the name of the country in which an approved contract is performed and which services were exported can only be withheld if determined by the President (in practice the State Department) to be contrary to the national interest. The State Department applies a strict inter-pretation of that requirement, with the result that these are the only types of infor-mation that are released via Freedom of Information Act procedures.[19]

Similarly, there is a lack of detailed information publicly available in reports to Congress on licensed commercial exports of defence services. According to sec-tion 655 of the Foreign Military Assistance Act, the DDTC must produce an

[16] Ibid.

[17] PW Singer, 'War, Profits, and the Vacuum of Law,' Columbia Journal of Transnational Law, vol 42 (2004) 539.

[18] Deborah D Avant, *The Market for Force: The Consequences of Privatizing Security* (Cambridge: Cambridge University Press, 2005) 151.

[19] Laura Peterson, 'Privatizing Combat, the New World Order,' Center for Public Integrity, Washington DC, 28 October 2002, available at <http://www.publicintegrity.org/bow/report.aspx?aid=148>.

annual consolidated report for Congress on licensed exports and FMS.[20] But in contrast to the government-to-government FMS system (described below), data on licensed exports is not systematically collected, and so is incomplete and less precise, both in terms of contracts concluded and the actual deliveries of goods and services. Given that companies have up to ten years to act once they are granted an export licence for defence services covered by a TAA, the figures in section 655 reports to Congress cannot be construed as representing actual trade in defence articles and services for the reporting period.[21] Once approved and granted a commercial licence, the company is under no requirement to provide information about the sales contract that results (if it results), nor about whether the contract was subsequently reduced in scope or cancelled. The State Department has also been criticized for the systematic miscoding of licence applications at DDTC (especially overuse of the generic code 'various' when more precisely applicable codes were available), which has thrown into question the reliability of annual reports on licensed commercial sales.[22]

There remains a significant lack of clarity in ITAR reporting. The category of 'defence services' covers a wide range of activities that may include international joint ventures, co-production, and licensed manufacturing in addition to military training. Activities surrounding the development of defence articles by the traditional defence industry are not clearly differentiated from those that concern training and advice provided to foreign actors by PMCs. The aggregate totals often include activities for multi-year periods since technical assistance agreements exceed the four-year limit applied to export licences for defence articles. There is no separate category under defence services for training provided by PMCs, and there is no public listing of precisely which firms have been licensed to provide private military or security training, for what purposes, or to whom.

Legislative oversight of the sale of defence services is another problem with the ITAR licensing process, being more robust on paper than in practice. The State Department is required to notify Congress of requests for licences for sales that exceed certain threshold levels, specifically proposed sales of defence services exceeding $50 million to non-NATO and non-allied countries.[23] Congressional notification can trigger much greater scrutiny, lengthening the review process and incurring a greater risk of opposition to granting a licence. Congress may request

---

[20] See DDTC website, Section 655 Annual Military Assistance Reports for the years 1999–2005 at: <http://www.pmddtc.state.gov/rpt655intro.htm>.

[21] DDTC, Report by the Department of State Pursuant to Sec 655 of the Foreign Assistance Act: Direct Commercial Sales Authorizations for Fiscal Year 2004, 2.

[22] US Government Accountability Office (GAO), 'State Department Needs to Resolve Data Reliability Problems that Led to Inaccurate Reporting to Congress on Foreign Arms Sales,' GAO-05-156R, 28 January 2005, 16.

[23] A two-tier system was introduced in 2005 based on country of destination in which the threshold levels were raised to $25 million for major defence equipment and $100 million or more for other defence articles and services sold to NATO countries, Australia, New Zealand, and Japan. See Final Rule, 'Amendments to the International Traffic in Arms Regulations,' 70 Fed Reg 35652 (15 June 2005).

a highly detailed assessment from the State Department concerning various aspects of the proposed sale such as the reasons behind it, how it would support US national interests, and its implications for the military capabilities of the country, regional stability, arms control, international terrorism, and the chance of outbreak or escalation of conflict.[24] If dissatisfied with the proposed sale, members of Congress can block it by means of a joint resolution of disapproval within 30 days for non-NATO and non-allied countries. If Congress does not make an objection within the prescribed time period, the DDTC can proceed with approving the proposed sale.[25]

In practice, Congress has never successfully blocked an arms sale in this way, although it once came close.[26] A major obstacle is the time limit established for marshalling a joint resolution of disapproval, which has proven extremely difficult to meet.[27] Even if both the House and Senate managed to pass a joint resolution in time, the President would presumably veto the legislation, which could only be overridden by a two-thirds majority in Congress. Lack of awareness among US lawmakers of proposed individual arms sales and the difficulty of successfully blocking a sale have made this a rarely-used procedure for congressional review of arms sales.[28] Also, many contracts for the sales of defence articles and services naturally fall under this amount and thus avoid triggering the requirement for congressional notification, while larger contracts can be broken up into multiple components to avoid reaching the threshold and thereby circumvent this form of congressional oversight. While Congress can also block or modify a proposed sale of defence articles and services by passing freestanding legislation prohibiting or modifying the sale to the recipient country, it is only likely to be successful given a strong majority in both Houses of Congress.[29]

Lobbying may also influence the licensing of overseas sales of defence services just as it does with domestic procurement decisions. In 2001, ten US PMCs spent more than $32 million on lobbying and invested $12 million in financing election campaigns.[30] Beyond the injection of money into party coffers, PMCs often hire former senior military and administration officials (a phenomenon known as the 'revolving door'), whose prestige and professional networks are obvious assets

[24] For a full list of possible topics that Congress can request to be included in the assessment, see 22 USC §2776 (b) (A)–(P).

[25] However, the President may waive the Congressional opposition by asserting 'that an emergency exists which requires the sale in the national security interest of the United States'. The notification must accordingly contain a detailed justification and description of the emergency.

[26] Richard F Grimmett, 'Arms Sales: Congressional Review Process,' Report for Congress, Congressional Research Service (CRS), 20 December 2002, 6–7.

[27] See Richard F Grimmett, 'Foreign Policy Roles of the President and Congress,' CRS Report to Congress, 1 June 1999.

[28] Lora Lumpe and Jeff Donarski, 'Congress' Role' in *The Arms Trade Revealed* (Washington, DC: Federation of American Scientists Fund, 1998), available at: <http://www.fas.org/asmp/library/handbook/cover.html>.

[29] Grimmett, 'Foreign Policy Roles of the President and Congress' (n 27 above) 6.

[30] Barry Yeoman, 'Soldiers of good fortune,' *Independent* (UK), 23 July 2003.

when seeking to influence licensing decisions. One case of successful lobbying concerned MPRI's 1998 application to conduct an evaluation of the Equatoguinean defence system for President Teodore Obiang and to create a 'national security enhancement plan'. MPRI's application for a licence was rejected by the State Department because of objections from the Bureau of African Affairs and the Bureau of Democracy, Human Rights, and Labor concerning the Obiang government's record on human rights violations. An intense lobbying campaign ensued, targeting the State Department, Congress, and the Pentagon. These efforts proved successful and resulted in a U-turn in which MPRI was granted a licence in 2000.[31]

Although defence industry officials and some academic observers view the ITAR system as unnecessarily restrictive, recent changes have aimed at speeding up the licensing process, especially for proposed transfers to allied and friendly countries. Consequently, the median processing time for licence applications declined from 26 days in 1999 to 13 days in 2002. Moreover, procedures can be put into place to flag and fast-track licence applications for high priority areas in US foreign policy: licence applications for Operation Enduring Freedom in Afghanistan and Operation Iraqi Freedom now have a targeted processing time of two days for unstaffed applications, and four days for those subject to interagency review.[32] Additionally, conditions may be altered or waived across a group of cases in order to more effectively facilitate transfers in areas deemed to be of clear priority in US foreign policy. For example, contrary to its usual policy, DDTC is authorizing the export of fully-automatic weapons to US private security companies operating in Afghanistan and Iraq.[33]

The Foreign Military Sales programme

Aside from the ITAR licensing procedures, the other means by which defence services are sold to foreign purchasers is through the Foreign Military Sales (FMS) programme. FMS is a government-to-government system and forms part of security assistance, authorized by AECA,[34] in support of US foreign and national security policy. FMS involves the negotiation and purchase by eligible governments of US defence articles and services, using the Pentagon as intermediary. Once a Letter of Offer and Acceptance (LOA) has been signed, the Defense Security Cooperation Agency, which oversees Department of Defense security assistance

---

[31] Sunday Dare, 'The Curious Bonds of Oil Diplomacy,' *Making a Killing: The Business of War Project*, Center for Public Integrity, International Consortium of Investigative Journalists, 6 November 2002, available at <http://www.publicintegrity.org/bow/report.aspx?aid=151>.

[32] GAO, 'Defense Trade: Arms Export Control System in the Post-9/11 environment,' February 2005, 20, 25.

[33] See Directorate of Defence Trade Controls, Guidance for Iraq and Afghanistan Cases, revised 01/11/06, available at: <http://www.pmddtc.state.gov/docs/OEF_OIF_License_submission_guidelines.doc>.   [34] See section 3 of the AECA.

programmes, directly purchases the item or service from US defence firms. Selling specific defence articles and services through the FMS programme is exempted from needing an ITAR licence during the period in which the LOA and implementing contracts and sub-contracts are in effect.[35]

Under FMS, the Pentagon negotiates with a contractor on behalf of the customer country to obtain the most advantageous terms and prices. Since customer purchases are grouped with US government purchases whenever possible, better conditions and lower costs from economies of scale can be obtained than if the customer were to purchase the services independently. A base three per cent surcharge is applied when using FMS procedures in order to help recoup costs of administering the programme, which is seen by some as a disincentive. However the customer country is often well served by this arrangement, which is administered by the Defense Department and draws on the experience of its negotiators and acquisitions personnel. FMS tends to foster closer relationships between officials in the customer country and their US counterparts. FMS thus offers tangible and intangible benefits from the links and implicit legitimacy granted by the ties it fosters with the US government.[36]

Such contracts are held to the same requirement of congressional notification if an intended LOA exceeds certain dollar thresholds as the ITAR licensing system. FMS is a more transparent system than the ITAR licensing system, but the amount of information publicly released about contracts remains limited. Commercial or financial information provided to the US government by an individual, a US or foreign business, or a foreign government may be exempt from public disclosure under the Freedom of Information Act if it is of a type of information not usually released to the public; if disclosure is likely to cause 'substantial competitive harm to the originator'; if disclosure would impair the ability of the US government to obtain necessary commercial or financial information in the future; or if disclosure is likely to impair some other legitimate US government interest.[37]

Thus, the US regime regulating the commercial sale of defence services abroad consists of a dual system that retains considerable executive branch control to ensure that such sales support US interests and policy objectives. The opacity of the ITAR licensing process reinforces executive branch power vis-à-vis other actors who may seek to influence the process, such as the Congress, media, or members of the public. Bureaucratic actors tend to have an interest in maintaining the opacity of the regulatory process especially in view of the 'revolving door'

---

[35] 22 CFR subchapater M, §126.6 (c) (1), as amended by 70 Fed Reg 50966, 29 August 2005. See also Defense Trade Security Initiative, 'Fact Sheet—ITAR Exemption for FMS Defense Services,' 24 May 2000, available at: <http://www.dsca.mil/dtsi/itarexemp4fmsdefsvcfact.pdf>.

[36] An example of an FMS programme contract was MPRI's contract to train the Macedonian and Bulgarian militaries. See Peterson, 'Privatizing Combat' (n 19 above).

[37] Department of Defense, DOD Freedom of Information Act Program, DoD 5400.7-R, section C3.2.1 'FOIA Exemptions,' paragraph C3.2.1.4, exemption (b)(4), available at: <http://www.dtic.mil/whs/directives/corres/pdf/540007r_090498/54007r.pdf>.

phenomenon whereby many former senior administration and military officials, including members of regulatory offices, tend to work directly for PMCs and defence industry firms once they leave government service or sell their advice and expertise to the industry via legal and consultancy firms. Long documented in the study of regulation in the US, the revolving door draws not only on the professional networks and knowledge of bureaucratic procedures of former 'regulatory insiders', but on their inside knowledge of how the policy-making system works and their ability to predict the outcome of policy debates.[38] Close links fostered by the movement of individuals, money, and information between the state and industry through the revolving door is especially prominent in the contemporary defence and security sphere.[39] These factors have resulted in a regulatory system that encourages an industry that is closely in sync with government and its foreign policy objectives.

Congressional oversight of sales of defence articles and services, while appearing robust on paper, has proven rather weak in practice. It is easy to evade the Congressional notification requirement, and in practice Congress allows the executive arm broad discretion in regulating the licensed export of commercial military services. There is little detailed information made publicly available on the licensed activities of PMCs, since commercial training contracts are exempt from disclosure under the Freedom of Information Act. The lack of publicly available information and transparency make it difficult to assess how the system works in practice and the extent to which compliance with conditions attached to licences for exported defence services is monitored and enforced.

The US regulatory system promotes a close alignment of firms exporting defence services with US foreign policy. The government constitutes a major client of US-based PMCs, including in support of its foreign military assistance programs. Given the extent to which security functions are outsourced by the US government, there are strong incentives for US PMCs to maintain close ties to government and to ensure their commercial interests remain closely aligned with US foreign policy objectives while retaining a good image in the eyes of policy-makers, officials, and publics;[40] as recognized within the industry, undermining US government interests could well spell the end of US government contracts for a particular contractor.[41]

---

[38] Anthony G Heyes, 'Expert Advice and Regulatory Complexity,' *Journal of Regulatory Economics*, vol 24, no 2 (2003) 119.

[39] Michael Monahan, 'The Business of Warfighting: Ethical Implications of the Industry-Government Relationship in the Development of Defense Technology,' paper presented to the International Symposium on Technology and Society (ISTAS) Conference, Loyola Marymount University, Los Angeles, CA, 8–11 June 2005.

[40] For a discussion of how a state's purchasing power can influence the behaviour of PMCs see chapter ten in this volume by Deborah Avant.

[41] According to Chris Taylor, vice president for strategic initiatives and corporate strategy for Blackwater USA, 'If we went against US government interests we would never get another contract.' See Ted Koppel, 'These Guns for Hire,' *New York Times*, 22 May 2006.

South Africa: the FMMA and its successor

South Africa's approach to regulating the export of private military and security services is a product of its past experiences under the highly militarized apartheid regime. Lingering socio-economic legacies include a large number of former soldiers and ex-combatants who constitute a pool of potential recruits for mercenary activities as well as private military and security firms.[42] Some 30 per cent of former apartheid-era South African Defence Force (SADF) Special Forces personnel are working in the private military and security industry. Further, as a result of ineffective disarmament, demobilization, and reintegration efforts, ex-combatants tend to face high levels of unemployment and social marginalization. According to one study, two-thirds of former liberation fighters—veterans of the African National Congress' armed wing Umkhonto we Sizwe and the Azanian People's Liberation Army—are unemployed and lack suitable housing.[43] As discussed by Kevin O'Brien in chapter two of this volume, failed re-education and training programmes have contributed to a general problem with mercenaries in Africa; in South Africa the problem is even wider and more complex.

The participation of South African nationals in armed conflicts across the continent is a source of embarrassment to the South African government, which has sought to assert a firm commitment to democratic principles, human rights, and regional security in its foreign policy.[44] The initial catalyst for regulation was the controversial South Africa-based PMC Executive Outcomes (EO). EO employed former elite soldiers of the SADF, many of whom had spent the previous decade fighting the African National Congress and its allies. The involvement of EO and other groups in armed conflicts in Papua New Guinea, Sierra Leone, Angola, and Zaïre led the National Unity government under President Nelson Mandela to formulate legislation banning mercenary activity and asserting state control in authorizing and approving the sale of private military and security services abroad. The following section will outline the resulting legislation and some of the reasons why the law went largely unenforced. It will then examine recent efforts to correct the flaws and establish a more effective system of regulation.

---

[42] Jacklyn Cock, "'Guards and Guns': Towards Privatised Militarism in Post-Apartheid South Africa,' *Journal of Southern African Studies*, vol 31, no 4 (2005) 796–7; Sasha Gear, 'Wishing Us Away: Challenges facing ex-combatants in the "new South Africa",' Centre for the Study of Violence and Reconciliation, Violence and Transition Series, vol 8, 2002. Available at: <http://www.csvr.org.za/papers/papvtp8a.htm>.
[43] 'Two-thirds of vets jobless,' Radio 702, Johannesburg, in English, 1055 GMT, 19 March 2004.
[44] Chris Alden and Garth le Pere, *South Africa's Post-Apartheid Foreign Policy—from Reconciliation to Revival?*, Adelphi Paper 362 (Oxford: Oxford University Press for the International Institute for Strategic Studies, December 2003).

The Foreign Military Assistance Act (FMAA)

South Africa's system for regulating the sale of commercial military assistance and security services abroad has been based on the Regulation of Foreign Military Assistance Act (FMAA) of 1998,[45] which grounds itself on the constitutional principle that 'the resolve to live in peace and harmony precludes any South African citizen from participating in armed conflict, nationally or internationally, except as provided for in the Constitution or national legislation'.[46] The application of the FMAA is triggered by an official declaration of an area of armed conflict. First, it prohibits mercenarism, making it an offence to recruit, use, or train persons for, or finance or engage in mercenary activity, defined as 'direct participation as a combatant in armed conflict for private gain'.[47] And second, the FMAA seeks to regulate the provision of 'foreign military assistance' to a party involved in an armed conflict. This is defined as the provision of advice and training; personnel, financial, logistical, intelligence, and operational support; personnel recruitment; medical or paramedical services; or procurement of equipment.[48]

The FMAA establishes a two-stage process in which nationals, permanent residents or firms first seek authorization to enter into negotiations to offer such assistance. Requests are scrutinized by the National Conventional Arms Control Committee (NCACC), an interdepartmental cabinet committee set up in 1995 to provide political oversight of arms trade policy in South Africa. The NCACC is chaired by a minister from a government department having no direct links or line function responsibilities leading to the defence industry, and is composed of ministers and deputy ministers and other persons appointed by the president. The NCACC makes a recommendation about whether to grant or refuse the request to the minister of defence, who then takes the final decision. The minister may attach conditions, and may also withdraw or amend an authorization that has already been granted.[49] Only after being granted authorization to offer foreign military assistance can the person or company proceed to the second stage and submit an application for *approval* of the contract or agreement to render the military assistance once it has been negotiated.[50] The procedure is the same as for the authorization stage outlined above.

The FMAA sets out the criteria on which decisions for authorization and approval are to be based. Circumstances under which a licence will not be granted include foreign military assistance that is deemed to: conflict with South Africa's obligations under international law; infringe human rights and fundamental freedoms; endanger peace by introducing destabilizing military capabilities or

---

[45] Republic of South Africa, Regulation of Foreign Military Assistance Bill, Bill 54D-97 (GG), 1997, available at <http://www.gov.za/gazette/bills/1997/b54-97.pdf>.

[46] See chapter 11, section 198 (b), of the Constitution of the Republic of South Africa, 1996.

[47] FMAA, §2.   [48] FMAA, §1 (iii).

[49] FMAA, §4, 'Authorization for rendering of foreign military assistance.'

[50] FMAA, §5, 'Approval of agreement for rendering of foreign military assistance.'

otherwise contribute to regional instability and negatively influence the balance of power in a region; support or encourage terrorism; contribute to the escalation of regional conflicts; prejudice South Africa's national or international interests; or 'be unacceptable for any other reason'.[51] South African courts have the authority to try South African citizens, companies, and permanent residents if their alleged conduct in contravention of the law occurs in South Africa or abroad, and foreign citizens who commit an offence within South Africa.[52] The Act includes penalties (a fine or imprisonment or both) for those who act in violation of its provisions.

The FMAA has been minimally enforced as only a handful of cases have been brought under it, all settled by plea bargain. Some problems concerning enforcement had been anticipated from the beginning, as suggested by Kader Asmal, drafter of the FMAA and former chairperson of the NCACC, who noted that South Africa would have to rely on journalists to help it enforce the FMAA.[53] Serious flaws include its overly-broad definitions of 'foreign military assistance' and 'security services' and the loopholes these have created in the legislation; its vague and subjective criteria for refusing authorization; the lack of a monitoring mechanism; and the challenges of collecting evidence to support a successful prosecution. This has resulted in general flouting of the FMAA, with thousands of South African citizens and several firms having sold military and security-related services abroad to actors in conflict zones without seeking authorization.

Weak enforcement of the FMAA and low penalties imposed on the few individuals who were convicted of contravening its provisions diminished its potential deterrent effect. The fines imposed on the first two individuals convicted under the FMAA in 2003 were so low that they could not reasonably be considered to have acted as a deterrent to involvement in the lucrative private military and security trade.[54] Although no one was ever jailed under the Act, a handful of individuals were charged and fined under the FMAA for mercenary activities, most recently key individuals linked to the attempted coup in Equatorial Guinea in August 2004. Two individuals implicated in the coup attempt returned to South Africa to face charges of violating the provisions of the FMAA. They agreed to a plea bargain and were fined 350,000 Rand ($48,800) in exchange for testifying at Mark Thatcher's trial.[55] Mark Thatcher, who pleaded guilty to violating the FMAA in January 2005 by financing the lease of a helicopter he suspected might be used for mercenary purposes, received the heaviest fine—three million Rand ($418,000).

[51] FMAA, §7 (1), 'Criteria for granting or refusal of authorizations and approvals.'

[52] FMAA, §9, 'Extraterritorial application of Act.'

[53] 'South Africa will look to journalists to enforce new mercenary law,' Agence France Presse, 19 August 1997.

[54] The first two people convicted under the FMAA were Richard Rouget and Carl Alberts, linked to mercenary activity in Côte d'Ivoire. Rouget had recruited South Africans to fight as mercenaries and pled guilty to mercenary activity; he was fined 10,000 Rand (about $1400) in 2003. Alberts also admitted to mercenary activity and was fined 20,000 Rand; he was freed after paying a 10,000 Rand fine. See Tisha Steyn, 'War hero: I was a mercenary,' News 24.com, 13 February 2004.

[55] 'South Africa: Authorities target alleged mercenaries,' IRINnews.org, 4 February 2004.

The FMAA has been further criticized for granting the executive broad discretionary powers by giving contract sanctioning power to the minister of defence, and failing to provide for adequate parliamentary oversight.[56] While the NCACC is required to submit a report to parliament each quarter on the authorizations and approvals issued by the minister and thus is to some degree accountable to parliament, the parliament has no decision-making or advisory role in the authorization and approval process. A related point of criticism is that by requiring the South African government to approve each contract, the FMAA 'results in the official sanctioning of the contract'.[57] In other words, the requirement that every contract of South African PMCs for activities abroad be approved by the South African government could make the government responsible for the actions of these firms. (The question of state responsibility is examined by Chia Lehnardt in chapter eight of this volume.)

Due to various definitional loopholes and concerns about the willingness and the ability of the prosecuting authority to marshal sufficient evidence to conduct successful prosecutions under the Act, the number of prosecutions has been very low and the FMAA is considered to be too weak to be able to secure convictions in most cases. One of the main loopholes in the FMAA is its blanket exclusion of humanitarian assistance from requiring the NCACC's authorization and approval.[58] Some South African firms consequently registered as de-mining companies or claimed to be delivering humanitarian assistance in Iraq in order to avoid the remit of the FMAA.[59] Another problem with the FMAA is its definition of security services as services 'provided for the protection of individuals involved in armed conflict or their property', which has proven too general. Neither the FMAA nor any other piece of legislation has effectively regulated the sale of security services abroad. South Africa's extensive domestic private security industry, comprising over 4,600 registered companies employing around 300,000 people, is regulated by SIRA (the Private Security Industry Regulatory Authority). Although SIRA does have extraterritorial powers,[60] SIRA cannot in practice monitor the activities of South African PSCs that conduct business outside the country due to its small budget, few monitors, and reliance on third parties for information even for monitoring within the state.[61]

In 2004 the South African government designated Iraq a 'theatre of armed conflict'. In consequence, the FMAA took effect and any South African resident, citizen, or firm is required to seek authorization before going to Iraq and providing

---

[56] Singer, 'War, Profits, and the Vacuum of Law' (n 17 above) 539.   [57] Ibid.

[58] FMAA, §1(iii)(d).

[59] Beauregard Tromp, 'Hired Guns from SA Flood Iraq,' *Cape Times*, 4 February 2004.

[60] See Private Security Industry Regulations Act 2001 (Act No 56, 2001), section 39(1), according to which 'Any act constituting an offence in terms of this Act and which is committed outside the Republic by any security service provider, registered or obliged to be registered in terms of this Act, is deemed to have been committed in the Republic.'

[61] 'Private Security Industry under Scrutiny,' SABC News Online, 4 November 2005. See also 'Thorburn Security Solutions Security Review,' 31 October to 6 November 2005.

military services. However, the law has been widely ignored and South Africa is one of the key sources of PMC personnel working in Iraq. An estimated 1,500 to 8,000 South Africans are performing security functions without authorization in the stabilization and reconstruction of Iraq.[62] By 2004 at least ten South African firms were active providing security services in Iraq, but only two—Meteoric Tactical Solutions and Grand Lake Trading 45 (Pty) Ltd—had submitted applications to the NCACC.[63] Neither were ultimately granted approval, but continued to work in Iraq. Meteoric Tactical Solutions received contracts to provide protection services in Iraq, including for staff of the British Department for International Development in 2003 and for the Swiss Federal Department of Foreign Affairs to protect its missions in Iraq in 2004, as well as a contract for training new Iraqi police and security forces.

According to the NCACC, only two companies had submitted applications to work abroad and these were refused in 2003. Another two cases were referred to the National Prosecution Authority (NPA) in 2003 for prosecution for violations of the Act, however these could not be prosecuted because of difficulties in obtaining evidence.[64] Erinys Iraq, an affiliate of the joint British–South African company Erinys and headed by a South African national, received a $40 million contract in August 2003 from the Coalition Provisional Authority to protect Iraq's oil infrastructure (subsequently enlarged to a $100 million contract which Erinys shared with several other firms).[65] Erinys never applied for authorization from the NCACC.[66]

In each of the handful of cases ever brought under the FMAA, plea agreements were struck and the perpetrators were widely perceived to be getting off lightly with fines and suspended sentences. Some legal observers criticized the repeated resort to plea bargaining by the prosecuting authority and especially the failure to allow the Cape High Court in the Thatcher case to interpret the legislation, including its purpose and prohibitions.[67] The NPA defended its decision to conclude a plea bargain with Thatcher as the most strategically sound approach when taking into account the nature of the case, the prospects of success, and the cost of prosecution: the NPA claims that it would have been extremely difficult to prosecute Thatcher under the provisions of the FMAA and the case would have dragged on at great public expense. By securing a plea bargain, their view was at least they had started to develop some case law around the FMAA.[68]

---

[62] Tromp, 'Hired Guns' (n 59 above); Andy Clarno and Salim Vally, 'Iraq: The South African Connection,' ZNET, 6 March 2005; 'South Africa to Open Iraq Embassy,' BBC News, 9 March 2006.
[63] Tromp, 'Hired Guns' (n 59 above).
[64] 'South Africa: New Mercenary Law to Put Squeeze on Soldiers of Fortune,' *Africa News*, 3 August 2005.
[65] David Isenberg, 'Protecting Iraq's Precarious Pipelines,' *Asia Times*, 24 September 2004.
[66] Tromp, 'Hired Guns' (n 59 above).
[67] Shehnaz Seria, 'SA Jurisprudence Poorer as a Result of Easy Let-off in Mark Thatcher Case,' *Sunday Times* (South Africa), 13 February 2005.
[68] Wyndham Hartley, 'NPA Defends "Strategic" Deal with Thatcher,' *Business Day* (South Africa), 4 November 2005, 3.

The Prohibition of Mercenary Activities and Regulation of Certain Activities in Country of Armed Conflict Bill 2005

In addition to the flow of former South African military and police to work as private military and security contractors in Afghanistan and Iraq, the failed attempt to overthrow the government of Equatorial Guinea in 2004 proved a further embarrassment to the South African government. Most of those implicated in the coup attempt were travelling on South African passports and included a number of former members of the notorious 32 (Buffalo) Battalion of the apartheid-era SADF. The event highlighted the contradiction between the new regime's foreign policy aimed at promoting peace, stability, and a united Africa, and the destabilizing actions of certain of its citizens. The South African government acknowledged that it had stumbled in its resolve to end the country's reputation as a major supplier of mercenaries, and that the gaps and loopholes in the existing legislation had to be closed in order to more effectively curb mercenary activities and regulate the activities of South Africans in areas of armed conflict.[69]

The failed coup attempt served as a catalyst to the government's efforts to tighten up legislation, and resulted in the Prohibition of Mercenary Activity and Prohibition and Regulation of Certain Activities in Country of Armed Conflict Bill of 2005.[70] The Bill received cabinet approval in September 2005 and immediately provoked controversy among a variety of foreign and international actors that included foreign PMCs, diplomats, and humanitarian organizations. Three of its provisions were considered especially problematic. First, the drafters sought to close the loophole that had enabled firms to claim to be delivering humanitarian assistance and thus enjoy the blanket exemption for authorization of such activities. The Bill widened the definition of military activities to include humanitarian assistance, which would require specific authorization from the NCACC. This provision was widely criticized by South African and international humanitarian organizations for its potential to impede the delivery of humanitarian aid, and also its potential to undermine the autonomy, independence, and operational effectiveness of humanitarian efforts by actors such as the International Red Cross, the United Nations High Commissioner for Refugees, and Doctors without Borders. Humanitarian aid organizations objected to the Bill's implication that their operations would be subject to the approval of the NCACC and South African executive.[71]

Secondly, the Bill asserted extraterritorial application to non-South African nationals who have provided security or other support services in a designated area

---

[69] 'Lekota Concedes Problems in Bill on Mercenary Activity,' *Africa News*, 9 November 2005.

[70] The Prohibition of Mercenary Activities and Prohibition and Regulation of Certain Activities in Areas of Armed Conflict Bill, B42-2005, available at <http://ipoaonline.org/php/images/documents/southafricalegislation/sa_leg_bill_original.pdf>.

[71] South African National Halaal Authority, written submission to the Defence Portfolio Committee, 24 October 2005, available at <http://ipoaonline.org/php/images/documents/southafricanlegislation/safelegbap.pdf>.

of armed conflict, meaning that non-nationals could find themselves subject to arrest and prosecution if they were to visit South Africa, even if their activities were considered legal both in their home country and in the country in which they were providing such services. The extraterritorial application was heavily criticized as inconsistent with international law, and became a focus of pressure by US and British diplomats and private security industry representatives.[72]

Thirdly, the Bill made a specific exemption for acts 'committed during a struggle waged by peoples in the exercise or furtherance of their legitimate right' to national liberation, self-determination, independence against colonialism or 'resistance against occupation, aggression or domination by alien or foreign forces'.[73] This exemption, which had also been added to South Africa's anti-terrorism legislation in 2004, stemmed from recognition of the role foreigners played in supporting the ruling African National Congress when it was outlawed as a terrorist group under apartheid but identified itself as a liberation movement. Critics maintained that this exemption for 'freedom fighters' or those joining liberation movements would enable, for example, South Africans to take part in the anti-US insurgency in Iraq whilst requiring those seeking to work for private military or security companies in Iraq to apply for authorization. These concepts were also criticized for lacking any basis in or being contested under international law.[74]

Domestic critics also faulted the government on procedural grounds for drafting the Bill secretly and in haste, consulting only government departments while excluding industry, non-governmental organizations and humanitarian agencies, and academic security experts. The government was also accused of attempting to fast-track the Bill through parliament without due regard for proper parliamentary procedure, and allowing minimal time for interested parties to make written submissions on it.[75] While public hearings on the Bill were held in May 2006, the low number of submissions received by the Portfolio Committee on Defence on the draft bill indicates limited public participation in the debate over amending the FMAA.[76]

The Bill was then re-drafted, and the controversial provisions for extraterritorial application to non-South Africans and the exemption for freedom fighters were dropped, without diluting the intent of the legislation.[77] The revised Bill was

[72] See submission to the Defence Portfolio Committee by the British Association of Private Security Companies, 31 October 2005. Available at www.ipoaonline.org. See also Cillian Donnelly and Darren Ennis, 'EU Industry Facing South Africa Bill,' *EU Reporter*, 10 November 2005.

[73] Stephen Fidler, 'Mercenaries Face New S African Curbs,' *Financial Times* (London Edition), 14 October 2005.

[74] Laurie Nathan, ' "Tightening and Loosening the Screws": Submission on the Bill Governing Mercenary Activity and other Activities in an Area of Armed Conflict,' 25 October 2005, available at <http://ipoaonline.org/php/images/documents/southafricanlegislation/safelegnathan.pdf>.

[75] 'Mercenaries Bill "Being Rushed",' News24.com, 18 October 2005.

[76] Submissions from organizations on the draft bill of 2005 are posted on the IPOA website at <http://ipoaonline.org/en/gov/southafrica.htm>.

[77] The Prohibition of Mercenary Activities and Regulation of Certain Activities in Country of Armed Conflict Bill, B42B-2005. Available at http://www.ipoaonline.org/en/gov/sa_leg_bill_revised.pdf.

deliberated in the defence committee, and was subsequently passed in parliament at the end of August 2006. As of March 2007, the Bill had yet to gain the assent of the second parliamentary chamber, the National Council of Provinces, which is normally easily achieved especially given the large African National Congress majority in parliament. However the Bill appears to be stuck in the second chamber, suggesting the possibility of further amendments.

If the Bill becomes law in its current form, all South African citizens looking to work abroad in military and security services in a regulated country will be required to register with the NCACC and obtain authorization to engage in such work. Critics expect that this process will cause considerable delays and act as a disincentive to firms operating in the sector, and will eliminate a lucrative source of revenue for South African individuals and firms.[78] In order to address one of the flaws of the FMAA, the Bill provides an extensive list of activities under the definition of security services. The revised Bill also restricts the scope of the legislation to South African humanitarian organizations, which will be required to register with the NCACC in order to carry out humanitarian work in a given country. It remains unclear, however, whether organizations such as the South African branch of the Red Cross would fall under the jurisdiction of the Bill. Still valid are concerns raised about the earlier version of the Bill that the broad definition of 'assistance' and 'service' could encompass non-governmental organizations and individuals providing advice and assistance in areas such as disarmament and arms control, demilitarization, demobilization, human rights monitoring, security sector and justice reform.[79]

The Bill also establishes that no South African citizen or permanent resident may enlist with any foreign armed force, including an armed force of any state, unless he or she has been authorized by the NCACC. That authorization may end if the person to which it has been granted takes part in an armed conflict as a member of a foreign armed force when that conflict does not concord with South Africa's foreign policy or otherwise contravenes the authorization criteria set out in the bill. This provision is seen as targeting some 780 South African citizens who have joined the British armed forces, which are currently experiencing overstretch with their deployments in Iraq and Afghanistan, and have difficulty in meeting recruitment targets. Despite strenuous efforts, British diplomats failed to secure an exemption for those serving in the British armed forces in the revised version of the Bill. If the Bill becomes law, the soldiers will have six months to apply for authorization. British sources have suggested that if South Africans serving with

[78] Clare Nullis, 'South Africa Assembly OKs Mercenary Bill,' *Seattle Post-Intelligencer*, 29 August 2006.

[79] See submissions by Amnesty International, SaferAfrica, Safenet Group, and the Ceasefire Campaign to the Portfolio Committee on Defence on the Prohibition of Mercenary Activity and Prohibition and Regulation of Certain Activities in an Area of Armed Conflict Bill, October–November 2005, available at <http://ipoaonline.org/php/index.php?option=com_content&task=view&id=99&Itemid=107>.

the British armed forces are forced to choose between leaving the British armed forces or dropping their South African citizenship, they may be offered British citizenship as an inducement to remain.[80]

Conclusion

Both the US and South African systems of regulating the export of private military and security services are motivated by concerns that the commercial export of such services should not undermine their respective foreign policies. Both systems are based on existing arms export control regimes, and involve a form of registration and application for licence or authorization to carry out activities. Both systems threaten penalties for non-compliance. Both systems give the executive considerable discretion in authorizing such sales. And although the US system offers a potentially greater role for Congress in overseeing such sales, in practice the legislative role in each is minor.

However, these national regulatory systems also differ in several important ways. The US regime for licensed and non-licensed defence exports is underpinned by the view that such exports should promote US foreign policy interests, and the system is increasingly structured to facilitate trade to allies, partners, and areas of foreign policy priority. The ITAR and FMS regimes apply whether or not the military and security services are being exported to a conflict zone, in contrast to the South African legislation, which hinges on an official declaration that an area is considered an area of armed conflict and, therefore, regulated. There is more profound acceptance in the US context of outsourcing generally, and specifically of using PMCs to deliver services formerly provided by state institutions, including military and police training assistance. The existence of a 'revolving door' between the defence industrial and services sector and government, as illustrated by the presence of numerous high-ranking former military and government officials on the boards and in management of US firms selling commercial defence services, suggest an entrenched symbiotic relationship between state and private sector. Further, due to the extent of outsourcing and therefore US government business that the private military and security industry can potentially tap, there is a strong incentive for those firms to remain closely aligned with US interests and policies, and this is further supported by the 'good faith' atmosphere between regulators and industry. These factors underpin a convergence of interests between government and the private military and security industry.

In comparison, the South African system was initially created in reaction to the activities of EO and certain individuals—typically former members of repressive apartheid-era security forces—who sold their military skills in unstable regions

---

[80] David Blair and Peta Thornycroft, 'South African Ban Could Hit British Forces' Recruitment,' *Daily Telegraph*, 31 August 2006.

throughout Africa. The regulatory system emerged from the view that the sale of private military and security services was a negative phenomenon linked to mercenarism and the lingering social legacies of apartheid-era forces and policies, and was undermining new South Africa's foreign policy of promoting regional stability, human rights, democracy, and good governance across the continent. The ANC government has viewed the industry more as an embarrassment and a potentially harmful influence on the reputation of the state than as an asset or potential partner. This is reflected in the regulation of the sale of private military and security services under the same body of legislation as that prohibiting mercenary activity, an approach found both in the FMAA and the subsequent draft Bill now awaiting final approval. Whereas relations between the private military and security industry and government in the US system are characterized by an atmosphere of 'good faith', relations within the South African system tend more towards the antagonistic than co-operative. South African PMCs that operate abroad have fewer incentives to conform to the preferences of the South African government. This contrasts with the influence wielded by the US government, which outsources domestic and external functions extensively and is a vital client of most US PMCs.

Thus regulatory systems may be based on divergent principles and underlying motives, and these are likely to affect other aspects of the system and the object being regulated. The double system for authorizing commercial export of defence services under the US AECA encompasses both formal and informal means of ensuring that such sales support US foreign policy and national security interests. While it has sometimes been argued that South Africa and other states should look closely at the US licensing system and follow it as a model, doing so would require a shift in the underlying principles of regulation, since the US system tends to proactively promote private defence and security interests, whereas the South African stance has tended to be more defensive and driven by concerns to protect South Africa's international reputation and commitment to a more responsible foreign policy. The differing principles underlying the South African and the US regulatory approaches are based on their respective patterns of historical development, foreign policy objectives, and the nature of relations between the state and corporate sector. The process involved in authorizing foreign military sales by private US firms would be less feasible in a country with fewer administrative and budgetary resources for evaluating requests for licences and monitoring compliance, even with smaller PMCs attracting fewer contracts.

Beyond these essential differences in approach, the US and South African experiences provide insights on a practical level for other governments considering building similar regulatory systems. A state that seeks to regulate the commercial export of military and security services from its territory needs effective compliance and enforcement mechanisms, including the capacity to monitor compliance and investigate apparent transgressions, suspend or revoke licences, and apply strict civil and criminal penalties for non-compliance. In the South African case, problematic definitions in the legislation, very limited human and budgetary resources for monitoring compliance extraterritorially, and doubts about the viability of investing time and financial resources in prosecutions have resulted in under-enforcement of the law. Further, civil society actors in South Africa have underde-veloped capacities to engage with defence and security issues, a legacy of the secrecy that shrouded such matters under the former apartheid regime. Whereas the United States has a robust community of non-governmental organizations, acade-mic and research institutions, and advocacy groups that contribute to public scrutiny of both security policy and corporate actors including PMCs and PSCs, South African civil society is much more limited in its present capacity to scrutinize the activities of South African PMCs operating abroad.

States may lack the capacity, resources, or the will to enforce regulation, especially extraterritorially. Undertaking to implement an effective regulatory mechanism thus requires an investment of sufficient economic resources, skilled personnel, and political will. The South African FMAA was weakly enforced due to difficulties collecting evidence and doubts about the ability to successfully prosecute cases due to legal loopholes. Failure to enforce legislation and regulatory regimes may result in emboldening those seeking to engage in prohibited activities.

While there are valid arguments for protecting business confidentiality and other proprietary information in order to maintain the competitiveness of national firms, some degree of transparency is essential for accountability of both regulators and the industry, and this can be imposed by legislation. Effective oversight espe-cially requires an actively engaged legislative body and an adequately resourced monitoring and enforcement capacity in the executive branch. Legislative over-sight is minimal in both the US and South African regulatory systems. In the United States, executive control is reinforced by the lack of transparency, 'revolving door' practices in which government employees subsequently work for private industry and government contractors, and a convergence of interests between industry and the state. In the South African case, the executive also dominates the regulatory process but lacks a 'revolving door' phenomenon and experiences much more antagonistic relations between industry and government, greatly reducing the likelihood that PMCs will view it as in their self-interest to operate within the boundaries of the South African government's foreign policy interests.

PART IV

MARKETS

10

The emerging market for private military services and the problems of regulation

Deborah Avant

A 'market' implies a free interchange where profit-maximizing producers seek to meet the demands of consumers. Savvy consumers choose to purchase what they want and competition among producers yields 'goods' that best satisfy consumer demand. The stylized market is frequently contrasted with the more directed, hierarchical organization within states where superiors set up bureaucracies to carry out tasks according to specific instructions.[1] Truly free markets are, of course, quite rare, and many features of state policy and social life more generally figure into the outcomes of any particular market exchange.[2] Thinking about the differences between markets and hierarchies, however, can generate insights into how we should expect shifting a service from a state military to Private Military Companies (PMCs) to affect its control.[3] More important for the purposes of this volume, investigating the character of different markets and attendant regulatory efforts can suggest a variety of challenges and opportunities for regulating the emerging market for force in the current era. This chapter first describes the emergence of the market for force and the factors that shape its character, suggests a variety of challenges issued by this character and, given this, the efforts that are most likely to be successful.

The market for force

The initial increase in private security can be tied to supply and demand. In the 1990s, the supply factors came from both domestic (the end of apartheid in South Africa) and international (the end of the Cold War) phenomena that caused

---

[1] Oliver Williamson, *Markets and Hierarchies: Analysis and Antitrust Implications* (New York: The Free Press, 1975).
[2] Douglass North, *Structure and Change in Economic History* (New York: WW Norton, 1981).
[3] Deborah D Avant, *The Market for Force: the Consequences of Privatizing Security* (Cambridge: Cambridge University Press, 2005).

militaries to be downsized in the late 1980s and early 1990s. Military downsizing led to a flood of experienced personnel available for contracting.[4] Concomitant with the increase in supply was an increase in the demand for military skills on the private market—from Western states that had downsized their militaries, from countries seeking to upgrade their militaries as a way of demonstrating credentials for entry into Western institutions, from rulers of weak or failed states no longer propped up by superpower patrons, and from non-state actors such as private firms and non-governmental organizations (NGOs) operating in the territories of weak or failed states.

In a globalizing world market pressures, technology, and social change created demands for 'security' that states had difficulty supplying or fostering because the scale of the security people demanded was often different from the scale of the nation state.[5] This was partly a result of the variety of ways people came to see security, including environmental and economic well-being, which could not be guaranteed by one state alone.[6] It was also a consequence of how disorder in one part of the world, combined with information technology and the speed of travel, fed insecurity in another. Security became increasingly diffuse and borders more complicated to defend, at least within the bounds of what many saw as acceptable political constraints.[7]

The fact that global trends demonstrated a mismatch between security concerns and national military institutions, however, did not necessitate privatization. In fact, the pursuit of goals associated with public goods on a 'greater than national scale' had been increasingly facilitated by multilateral institutions. In the immediate wake of the Cold War, some argued that reaching new security goals required

---

[4] Looking to history, it is often the case that the downsizing of militaries (for whatever reason) leads to a rise in private military activity as skilled military personnel look for places to sell their talents. See Peter Lock, 'Africa, Military Downsizing and the Growth in the Security Industry,' in Cilliers and Mason (eds), *Peace, Profit or Plunder?* (Pretoria: Institute for International Studies, 1999).

[5] Philip Cerny, 'Globalization and the Changing Nature of Collective Action,' *International Organization*, vol 49, no 4 (autumn 1995) 597. See also Susan Strange, *Retreat of the State: The Diffusion of Power in the World Economy* (Cambridge: Cambridge University Press, 1996); David Held, Anthony McGrew, David Goldblatt, and Jonathan Perraton, *Global Transformations: Politics, Economics and Culture* (Stanford: Stanford University Press, 1999) 137–43; E Skons, 'The Internationalization of the Arms Industry,' *Annals of the American Academy of Political and Social Sciences*, 1994; D Silverberg, 'Global Trends in Military Production and Conversion,' *Annals of the American Academy of Political and Social Sciences*, 1994.

[6] For the debate about how to define security, see Joseph Nye and Sean Lynn Jones, 'International Security Studies: Report of a Conference on the State of the Field,' *International Security*, vol 12, no 4 (spring 1988); Jessica Tuchman Mathews, 'Redefining Security,' *Foreign Affairs*, vol 68, no 2 (spring 1989) 162–177; Barry Buzan, 'New Patterns of Global Security in the 21st Century,' *International Affairs*, vol 67, no 3 (1991); Stephen Walt, 'The Renaissance of Security Studies,' *International Studies Quarterly*, vol 35, no 2 (June 1991) 211–240; Edward Kolodziej, 'Renaissance of Security Studies? Caveat Lector!,' *International Studies Quarterly*, vol 36 (December 1992) 421–38; David Baldwin, 'Security Studies and the End of the Cold War,' *World Politics*, vol 48, no 1 (October 1995) 117–41; Roland Paris, 'Human Security: Paradigm Shift or Hot Air?,' *International Security*, vol 26, no 2 (fall 2001) 87–102.

[7] Peter Andreas, 'Redrawing Borders and Security in the 21st Century,' *International Security*, vol 28, no 2 (fall 2003).

greater capacity for multilateral security organs[8] and many predicted the growth
and strengthening of multilateral institutions to meet new security concerns.[9] The
possibility that the United Nations should be arranged to provide security tools
(such as peace enforcement) for this new world was debated as was the possibility
that NATO or other regional security organizations might be strengthened to do
the same. Funding, activism, and research on multilateral organizations like the
United Nations, NATO, the European Union, and the Organization for Security
and Cooperation in Europe (OSCE) increased in the 1990s.[10] Even financial institutions like the World Bank and International Monetary Fund (IMF) began to
think about the security consequences of their actions.

Ideas about the benefits of privatization suggested an alternative response to the
scale mismatch. In the United States and Britain, the privatization movement
began with the arguments of British academics and Conservative party officials
who articulated a sweeping privatization agenda as Margaret Thatcher took office
in 1979.[11] Arguing that social programmes generated massive inefficiencies and
financing them required incentive-sapping levels of taxation and inflationary
budget deficits, Conservatives 'viewed retrenchment not as a necessary evil but as
a necessary good'.[12] Initially, these ideas were associated with the powerful Conservative coalitions in the United States and Britain in the 1980s, but the collapse of
the Soviet bloc, the ensuing privatization of state-owned industries across Europe,
and the endorsement of these principles by international financial institutions like
the IMF and the World Bank led privatization to be endorsed much more widely.
Privatization was often associated with comparative advantage and competition,
and said to generate efficient and effective market responses as contrasted with
staid, expensive, and backward-looking bureaucratic responses.[13]

Thus far it is the market rather than multilateral alternatives that have thrived.
This is in part because multilateral institutions have encountered operational difficulties. The United Nations experimented with peace enforcement missions in
Somalia, Bosnia, and Rwanda, but was beset with problems.[14] Though the operational issues are potentially overcome, the political issues that underlie them are

[8] See, eg, John G. Ruggie, *Constructing the World Polity* (London: Routledge, 1998).

[9] See Held et al, *Global Transformations* (n 5 above) 44; John G Ruggie (ed), *Multilateralism Matters* (New York: Columbia, 1993); James Goldgeier and Michael McFaul, 'A Tale of Two Worlds: Core and Periphery After the Cold War,' *International Organization*, vol 46, no 3 (spring 1992).

[10] See for instance, Ruggie, *Constructing the World Polity* (n 8 above); Celeste Wallender, 'NATO After the Cold War,' *International Organization*, vol 54, no 4 (autumn 2000) 705–36; Walter Mattli and Anne-Marie Slaughter, 'Law and Politics in the European Union,' *International Organization*, vol 49, no 1 (winter,1995) 183–190; John Duffield, 'NATO's Functions after the Cold War,' *Political Science Quarterly*, vol 109, no 5 (winter 1994–1995) 763–87.

[11] See Madsen Pirie, *Dismantling the State* (Dallas: National Center for Policy Analysis, 1985); John Donahue, *The Privatization Decision: Public Ends, Private Means* (New York: Basic Books, 1989).

[12] Paul Pierson, *Dismantling the Welfare State* (Cambridge: Cambridge University Press, 1994) 1.

[13] Harvey Feigenbaum, Jeffrey Henig, and Chris Hamnett, *Shrinking the State: the Political Underpinnings of Privatization* (Cambridge: Cambridge University Press, 1998), ch 1.

[14] For an analysis of the difficulties, see Lakhdar Brahimi, Report of the Panel on United Nations Peace Operations, 21 August 2000, UN Doc A/55/305-S/2000/80.

more daunting. It is often the case that all agree that *something* should be done in a particular instance, but cannot agree on what that something is. In these situations, the United Nations has been increasingly seen in the same framework as government bureaucracies only worse: unresponsive, expensive, *and* unaccountable. The United States, under President George W Bush, has been especially contemptuous of the UN's legitimacy, arguing that some of the governments are either illegitimate representatives of their people or inappropriate guardians of rights they routinely violate within their borders. Even within institutions such as NATO, where countries are arguably held to greater standards of legitimacy than among the UN General Assembly, agreement on intervention and strategies for intervention have been hard to reach. This was an issue in Bosnia and then in Kosovo.[15] Other regional organizations, particularly in Africa, have manifested greater problems with operational capacity, legitimacy, and agreement.[16]

When the political agreement necessary to field multilateral forces was not forthcoming, PMCs provided an alternative tool that many see as more effective. To the degree that they are more effective, or at least more easily deployable, it is often precisely because their deployment is not contingent on the same level of political agreement. The growth of the current market was neither natural nor inevitable then, but grew in a context where states were reluctant to take on the variety of missions that people felt moved to respond to and multilateral options appeared to perform poorly—often because their rules precluded action where there was no political agreement.

Almost two decades after the end of the Cold War the supply push evident in the 1990s has largely ended, but the demand for military and other security skills on the private market continues to swell. The demand is led by the United States. Its pursuit of the 'Global War on Terror' has created a surge of spending, exacerbated strain on existing forces, and demanded new skills, all of which have enhanced the use of PMCs. As the United States is seen as a leader in military innovation, other Western states have increasingly looked to privatization of military and security services as the wave of the future even though they have approached privatization in different ways, as James Cockayne's discussion of the differences between the French and Anglo-Saxon models of control in chapter eleven illustrates. Demand from weak and transitional states has also continued; sometimes funded by Western training dollars, other times by natural resources. Finally, demand from non-state actors such as private firms and NGOs that work in ungoverned parts of the world, has continued to grow as it has become more and more commonplace for these organizations to see security as something crucial to the pursuit of their goals.

---

[15] Ivo H Daalder and Michael E O'Hanlon, *Winning Ugly: NATO's War to Save Kosovo* (Washington, DC: Brookings, 2000); Wesley Clark, *Waging Modern War: Bosnia, Kosovo, and the Future of Conflict* (New York: Public Affairs, 2001).

[16] Herbert Howe, *Ambiguous Order: Military Forces and African States* (Boulder: Lynne Rienner, 2001), ch 4.

Market characteristics and challenges to regulation

Private security offers opportunities to states and non-state actors. As both have taken advantage of these opportunities, the market for force has grown and begun to alter the terrain on which violent forces are controlled.[17] Generally, the change has not eroded the control of force but changed who controls force and how by diffusing control among a wider body of consumers and enhancing the importance of market mechanisms of control. These changes have redistributed power within states, between states, and among states and non-state actors and pose challenges for regulatory efforts. These challenges are enhanced by the character of the industry: its transnational nature, low capitalization, fluid structure, and the lack of commitment to territory all decrease the usefulness (or raise the costs) of traditional single state regulation.

Diffusion of control

Though private security sometimes strengthens elements of an individual state's control over force, the growth of the market for force simultaneously diffuses control over violence among a variety of non-state entities, undermining states' *collective* monopoly over the control of force. It enhances the roles for non-state actors in shaping decisions about the use of force and presents states and non-state actors with additional tools for accomplishing their goals. As power is redistributed to a variety of actors with different constituents, roles, and claims to authority, it makes co-ordination among powerful actors more difficult. By increasingly calling into question existing international laws and simultaneously making co-ordination to create new standards more difficult, the market's diffusion of control offers significant hurdles to regulation.[18]

States do participate in the market and can use their purchasing power to enhance their influence over PMCs (states can both affect the behaviour of PMCs with their procurement and give firms incentives to abide by regulation to preserve their government contracts). The market's availability to non-state actors, however, as well as the political flexibilities it offers to states, both increase the difficulty of co-ordination. The sheer number and variety of customers present three kinds of problems. First, the breakdown of state monopoly over violence may allow violence to be used for a wider variety of rationales than in the state system, including the use of violence by wealthy customers for purely private gain. Secondly, as the proliferation of PMCs are also a tool with which states can more easily avoid their international (and domestic) commitments, their use may exacerbate state co-operation to regulate violence. If what is rewarded by one state is undermined by another, or by other non-state customers, the ability of consumer

---

[17] Avant, *Market for Force* (n 3 above).   [18] Ibid.

demand to be an effective tool for supporting a particular standard of behaviour is weakened. Finally, when different authorities with different motivations and interests share in the direction of an agent, the agent is often able to evade direction or carve out spheres of discretion. This 'multiple principal' problem can occur even within a state when different agencies or constitutional authorities direct military organizations or contracts.[19] In the case of consumer direction of private security the multiple principal problems are much more extreme and have within them dynamics that make co-ordination difficult.

The variety of entities that are consumers in the market introduces hurdles to regulation. Private financiers may use violence for private gain. Even if they claim to be acting in the public good (such as claiming to be protecting private property to insure that economic development—beneficial to all—can move forward), the mechanisms by which private financiers are held accountable as well as who they are accountable to (stock holders or boards of trustees, for example) may hold them to very different standards than state entities and through different processes. In the worst instances, this offers possibilities for opportunism and rent-seeking. Even under the best circumstances, however, it may lead agents to focus on short run goals such as ensuring that property is intact without attention to the long-term viability of their solution. For an example of the latter, when Executive Outcomes operated in Sierra Leone, its use and training of Kamajors to protect mines in the interior of the country was effective in the short run but also enhanced the capacities of a parallel force that in the long term frustrated effective governance. Also consider recent revelations that the Erinys-trained Facilities Protection Force in Iraq has been a tool for strengthening militia forces in that country.

Furthermore, when one PMC serves many different authorities, it can increase the costs of strict state regulation. As illustrated by South Africa's efforts to regulate its industry, so long as there are other customers, individual state efforts can be frustrated. Multiple principals can also encourage states to, in effect, free-ride on collective state responsibilities to develop or enforce international standards, potentially avoiding legal obligations and encouraging a race to the bottom. There is some tension between the goals of individual customers and overarching attention to professional and ethical goals. Though all may wish that PMCs abide by standards generally, in particular instances consumers often prefer that PMCs bend the standards to suit their individual interest. This is especially true because PMCs are often used to undertake action that does not generate the level of agreement within states or international organizations required to use military forces. The very kind of activities that have led to their rise ensures that their use is more likely

---

[19] See chapter eleven in this volume by James Cockayne. See also Deborah Avant, *Political Institutions and Military Change: Lessons from Peripheral Wars* (Ithaca: Cornell University Press, 1994); Alexander Cooley and James Ron, 'The NGO Scramble,' *International Security*, vol 27, no 1 (summer 2002) 5–39. In highly institutionalized settings, some have referred to this as a problem of a collective principal. See Mona Lyne, Daniel Nielson, and Michael Tierney, 'A Problem of Principals: Common Agency and Social Lending at the Multilateral Development Banks,' unpublished manuscript.

when there is not agreement within conventional authority structures for missions that are seen as new, on the fringe or at the political extreme.

Finally, so many different authorities can allow individual PMCs (or the industry as a whole) opportunities for evading control altogether or shaping the demands of consumers rather than the reverse. This is made more likely by the fact that there are not even forums within which the different customers that might hire PMCs can come together. While there are forums for state co-operation (international organizations or bilateral or multilateral talks) and even some kinds of industry co-operation (among industry groups), finding an appropriate forum in which states, corporations, international organizations, and NGOs can come to agreement is complicated.

Market mechanisms

Aside from simply diffusing control, the growth of the market should lead us to think of the control of violence differently. Instead of accruing to superiors in a hierarchical sense (in the manner that civilian leaders nested in electorates direct military organizations), control accrues to consumers. The mechanism through which individual values and interests are aggregated to make 'consumer demand' is based on purchases. Consumers are those who can pay—suggesting that political power over the control of private violence will be distributed according to access to wealth rather than, say, votes.[20] As discussed above, in the current market, wealthy customers include states as well as corporations, NGOs, and individuals. Some have claimed that this will lead to a 'commodification' of security. Those who can afford it will protect their property and other interests and those who cannot afford to pay will do without.[21]

The structure of the industry should only enhance the prospects for commodification. Typical of the transnational service industries in general, a PMC frustrated with one state's rules can simply move abroad, or melt and reconstitute itself differently to avoid them.[22] The ability of individual states to regulate the market under these circumstances is tied to their consumption. PMCs are less likely to run afoul of a good customer likely to spend in the future but may dismiss the rules of states that are not consumers. For example, the United States, as a large consumer

[20] The simultaneous growth of vigilantes and militias suggests a different alternative for those who cannot afford other private options. See C Ero, 'Vigilantes, Civil Defence Forces and Militia Groups,' *Conflict Trends*, vol 1 (2000) 25–9.

[21] See Elke Krahmann, 'The Commodification of Security,' Research Project, University of Bristol. See also Ian Loader, 'Consumer Culture and the Commodification of Policing and Security,' *Sociology*, vol 33, no 2 (1999) 373–92.

[22] Jeffrey Herbst, 'The Regulation of Private Security Forces,' in Gregor Mills and John Stremlau (eds), *The privatization of security in Africa* (Johannesburg: SIIA Press, 1999), 107–27; Michael E Porter, *Competitive Advantage of Nations* (New York: Free Press, 1990) 239–76; Peter F Drucker, 'Trade Lessons From the World Economy,' Foreign Affairs, vol 73, no 1 (1994) 99–108; Geza Feketekuty, *International Trade in Services: An Overview and Blueprint for Negotiations* (Cambridge: Ballinger, 1988); Michel Kostecki, *Marketing Strategies for Services* (Oxford: Pergamon Press, 1994).

in this market, gives PMCs incentive to attend to US regulation while the South African government, which has chosen to eschew its reliance on the private sector for security, has also reduced PMCs incentives to comply with its wishes.

The most extreme implications of the commodification argument, however, ignore important social underpinnings of markets. Under many conditions, the protection of wealthy customers' interests requires action that also affects the security of those around them—for good or ill. Different strategies for security among the wealthy may generate greater or lesser efforts to take account of the interests of others. Some oil companies, for instance, believe that the long-term protection of their interests requires taking into consideration the interests of the populations that live around oil facilities or pipelines.[23] In other words, the way wealthy customers conceive of their interests and develop strategies to pursue them are important factors that shape the way the market affects the security of 'non-consumers'. Anticipating how the market will unfold, then, requires some understanding of ideas (or norms) about what is typical, proper, and likely to work. Norms can arise in many different ways, out of an accidental pattern of action (path dependency), through intentional behaviour by norm entrepreneurs, out of the preferences of the powerful, or through some combination, just to name a few.[24] Norms are more likely to be stable and impact behaviour, however, when they are agreed upon, enforced, and seen to be not only 'good' but also 'effective'.[25]

The market could impact the potential for norm emergence and stability in several ways. One could imagine customers upholding existing norms. As Jeff Herbst has argued, 'in industries where the barriers to entry are low and where, as a result, companies probably cannot compete on price alone, firms will necessarily attempt to differentiate themselves in other ways'.[26] He predicted that a distinction would emerge between upscale, professional firms (that appeal to the UN, NGOs, and other upstanding members of the international community by virtue of their willingness to abide by international law) and downscale, unprofessional firms (that appeal to non-lawful elements). If there are a variety of PMCs, companies are worried about their reputation and prospective employers can easily know what they are likely to be buying, consumers can exercise effective control with purchasing decisions. If customers—particularly wealthy customers—agree on norms and abide by them in their purchasing decisions, customer decisions could uphold these norms.

A variety of features of the current market may interrupt this result, however. First, as discussed above, when there are many types of consumers with different needs and interests, they may not agree upon the professional norms they want to

---

[23] Jane Nelson, *The Business of Peace* (London: Prince of Wales Business Leader's Forum, 2000).

[24] Martha Finnemore and Katherine Sikkink, 'International Norm Dynamics and Political Change,' *International Organization*, vol 52, no 4 (autumn 1998) 909–15.

[25] Deborah Avant, 'From Mercenary to Citizen Armies: Explaining Change in the Practice of War,' *International Organization*, vol 54, no 1 (winter 2000) 41–72.

[26] Jeffrey Herbst, 'The Regulation of Private Security Forces' (n 22 above).

uphold or abide by through similar purchasing practices. Different customers hire private security companies with different priorities in mind. Though humanitarian NGOs may want to hire PMCs committed to behaviour that respects human rights, large oil industry giants may have as their first concern PMCs that can guarantee the security of pipelines. Even among states the attention to professional norms may differ or they may use various interpretations of norms in their hiring decisions. States sometimes hire PMCs rather than using their own military for particular tasks precisely because it may allow action that would otherwise be politically infeasible.[27] This may include action that violates professional norms in one way or another. If PMCs believe that wealthy customers demand a variety of approaches to security, some more attentive to professional norms and some less, they have incentives to speak loudly about being 'professional' but quietly pursue quite different behaviour for different clients.

Secondly, the capacity of customers affects their ability to make choices that reflect their interests. In some instances customers may not have enough competence to make good choices. This can be true when customers are states and the contract is issued through an agency with inadequate security training. For instance, the US Department of the Interior contracted for interrogators and interpreters at Abu Ghraib prison in Iraq with little knowledge of what such a setting required. It can also occur when NGOs or corporations with little training in security are suddenly faced with making decisions about security contracts. NGOs focused on rhino conservation in the Democratic Republic of Congo, for example, did not have the requisite expertise to evaluate different private security plans.[28] Lack of competence on the part of customers increases the opportunities for 'slack' among PMC agents and the ability of agents to shape customer preferences rather than the reverse.[29]

Thirdly, customers may not have enough information to make good choices. Even if customers have a clear sense of what professional means and want to hire a PMC that behaves according to professional norms, the information they need to make this judgment may be difficult to obtain. To begin with it may be hard to distinguish between companies. Though some states have systems for approving companies, the links between approved companies and behaviour of the individuals working for that company on the ground may be tenuous. Most PMCs operate as databases from which to service contracts and these databases are non-exclusive (individuals often show up on the rosters of several different companies). Thus, someone working for one firm one week may be working for a different firm or

---

[27] Deborah Avant, 'The Implications of Marketized Security for IR Theory: the Democratic Peace, Late State Building and the Nature and Frequency of Conflict,' *Perspectives on Politics*, vol 4, no 3 (2006).

[28] Deborah Avant, 'Conserving Nature in the State of Nature: The Politics of INGO Policy Implementation,' *Review of International Studies*, vol 30, no 3 (2004) 361–82.

[29] Steven Tadelis, 'What's in a Name? Reputation as a Tradable Asset,' *The American Economic Review*, vol 89, no 3 (1999) 548–63.

simply as an independent consultant the next. The actual people working on a contract, then, may not vary with the PMC chosen. Also, even if companies espouse professional standards, their ability to communicate these to employees working on short-term contracts may be problematic. Finally, the fact that individuals can shift from one company to the next so easily makes monitoring by third parties (so called 'fire alarm' monitoring) in the field much more difficult. For instance, NGOs accused MPRI of training the KLA in the midst of the war in Kosovo. These claims were vociferously denied by MPRI. At the same time, however, persons who had worked for MPRI at one time were doing freelance consulting with the Albanian government and probably providing services to portions of the Kosovo resistance.[30] While there is a virtual cottage industry of reporting on the connections between individuals and various firms drawing attention to the suspicious links, and companies do appear worried about their reputations, the fluctuation in personnel makes it hard to track which individual behaviour is attributable to which firm.[31] This complicates the development of corporate reputation as a link to accountability or control by clouding the information available.

Fourthly, purchasing power is a blunt tool. It offers fewer pathways for consumers to explain their choices than hierarchies offer to superiors. The lesson that security service providers draw from different purchasing decisions may be quite different from what the customer intended. For example, when the United States hired Aegis to co-ordinate personal security in Iraq, there was a debate among analysts in the industry about the decision. Many looked at the decision to hire a company headed by someone who had been arrested for mercenary activity as problematic for the development of professional norms among PMCs. Some claimed that the US government simply made a bad decision based on lack of knowledge. Others, however, suggested that the United States knew just what it was doing and was seeking 'cowboys' who would do whatever it took (even including unprofessional or illegal behaviour) to accomplish US goals. The lesson the industry drew, then, was either that portions of the US customer were incompetent or that portions of the US customer were interested in performance rather than compliance with applicable laws. Regardless of whether either interpretation is true, the mere fact that this debate took place demonstrates the difficulty of communicating customer purchasing intent to a broad range of potential suppliers.

If features of the current market make consumer choices an unlikely stabilizer of professional norms, what about producer choices? Could producers affect the emergence and stability of norms? At first glance, this seems to fly in the face of market suppliers in desperate competition with one another. If international

[30] Personal interviews, December 1999, June 2001.
[31] See, eg, Khareen Pech, 'Executive Outcomes: A Corporate Conquest,' in Jakkie Cilliers and Peggy Mason (eds), *Peace, Profit, or Plunder: the Privatization of Security in War-Torn African Societies* (Pretoria: Institute for Security Studies, 1999); Ken Silverstein, *Private Warriors* (New York: Verso, 2000); Abdel-Fatau Musah and J Kayode Fayemi, 'Introduction,' in *Mercenaries: an African Security Dilemma,* (London: Pluto, 2000).

conditions have made what is appropriate and what is effective appear to diverge, competition among PMCs and between PMCs and militaries for services should lead to even greater violation of norms in the private sector. After all, it is through the delivery of an effective service that these companies are in the picture in the first place. Also, while serving in military organizations military personnel must respond to hierarchical organizational incentives and face military justice systems. The institutional sanctions faced by individuals slow the rate at which norms change. As the chapters in part three of this book describe, once individuals are working for a PMC the murkiness in their legal responsibilities should enhance the potential for violation of norms. Knowing that other personnel or other companies are available for hire if their 'customer' is dissatisfied with the outcome, PMCs and the personnel that work for them should be more likely to choose effective (rather than appropriate) action.

Economics textbooks are littered, however, with examples where suppliers do not compete but instead 'collude' to generate barriers to entry or to maximize prices and profits. Though these strategies are not frequently examined as tools for stabilizing norms, the market-driven emergence of professionalism in fields such as law, medicine, and architecture can be traced to just these strategies.[32] Professions and professionalism frequently developed precisely to impose structure and rules on particular occupations. One impetus to this was social and economic change, which led some kinds of work to be poorly situated within traditional forms of authority.[33] Another, however, was the economic gains to be had by those who successfully claimed to be professional. Systems of expert knowledge, ethical codes, and means of entry (such as licensing) were mechanisms by which a powerful few could capture more economic benefits by keeping out competitors.[34] Whereas professionalism often emerged in Europe as the result of state action, in Britain and (particularly) the United States, professions developed in the context of private initiatives with an eye toward markets.[35]

Professionalism is an effort to undertake collective action that limits individual entry, defines individual expertise in the name of the public good. Those advancing arguments based on professional standards may be strategically using the standards to limit entry and maximize profit, may believe that the standard is related

[32] See Millerson, *The Qualifying Associations* (London: Routledge, 1964); Caplow, *The Sociology of Work* (Minneapolis: University of Minnesota Press, 1954); Willensky and Lebeaux, *Industrial Society and Social Welfare* (New York: Russell Sage, 1958); TJ Johnson, *Professions and Power* (London: Macmillan, 1967); MS Larson, *The Rise of Professionalism* (Berkeley: University of California Press, 1977); Mike Sacs, *Professions and the Public Interest: Medical Power, altruism and alternative medicine* (London: Routledge, 1995).

[33] Elliott Krause, *Death of the Guilds* (New Haven: Yale University Press, 1999).

[34] For examples of the former see Geoffrey Millerson, *The Qualifying Associations*; Theodore Caplow, *The Sociology of Work*; Harold Willensky and Charles Lebeaux, *Industrial Society and Social Welfare*. For the latter, see TJ Johnson, *Professions and Power*; MS Larson, *The Rise of Professionalism* (all n 32 above).

[35] Rolf Torsendahl, 'Essential properties, strategic aims and historical development: three approaches to theories of professionalism,' in Michael Burrage and Rolf Torsendahl (eds), *Professions in Theory and History: Rethinking the Study of Professions* (London: Sage, 1990) 44–61.

to some overarching social good, or both. Regardless, these standards provide a tool for differentiating between individuals who can be called professionals and those who can not (and for removing individuals from the professional category based on some transgression). Thinking about private security providers as professionals, then, suggests that efforts to maximize profits among PMCs could simultaneously be mechanisms through which to stabilize norms.

Many associated with PMCs already use this language. They argue that proper behaviour is crucial to the legitimacy of the industry and the reputation of individual firms. In addition, standards for behaviour reduce uncertainty in ways that enhance the prospect for profitability by weeding out fly-by-night firms and 'mercenaries'—who may both drive down prices and endanger the legitimacy of the industry. As part of a larger movement where corporations in general have begun to focus on the long-term viability of their actions—or the 'triple bottom line', many companies claim to be governed by integrity, ethics, and professionalism. PMCs have participated in emerging regimes of corporate responsibility, offering to come up with standards for professional behavior and monitoring by objective groups.[36] As Andrew Bearpark and Sabrina Schulz suggest in chapter thirteen of this volume, there are also organizations for the 'self-regulation' of international PMCs.[37]

Looking at the way professionalism has worked historically, however, suggests that professions have been built on individuals. A profession typically channels individual achievement towards broader social goals through the definition of expert knowledge, ethical codes, and means of entry (such as licensing).[38] Thus far, many of the arguments about industry-led standards focus on the regulation and licensing of *companies*. Thinking seriously about private security *professionals* would require, first and foremost, a focus on *individuals*: what individuals should know, how individuals should be trained, and the boundaries of individual action.

Over the course of the last several decades, there has been increasing transnational discussion about what constitutes a security professional. Some of this has to do with the mastery of particular forms of expertise, which has spread across borders with security organizations and military-military contacts.[39] There is

[36] For instance, the 'Voluntary Principles on Security and Human Rights,' statement by the governments of the United States of America and the United Kingdom, 20 December 2000 was the result of efforts by PMCs, members of extractive industries, INGOs, and governments to regulate the behaviour of the private sector in unstable territories.

[37] Such as the International Peace Operations Association (<http://www.IPOAonline.org/>) and the British Association of Private Security Companies (BAPSC) (<http://www.bapsc.org.uk>).

[38] Andrew Abbott, *The System of Professions* (Chicago: University of Chicago Press, 1988) 8; Michael Dietrich and Jennifer Roberts, 'Beyond the Economics of Professionalism,' in Jane Broadbent, Michael Dietrich, and Jennifer Roberts (eds), *The End of Professions? The Restructuring of Professional Work* (New York: Routledge, 1997) 23.

[39] John W Meyer et al, 'The Structuring of a World Environmental Regime, 1870–1990,' *International Organization*, vol 51, issue 4 (1997) 623–51 argue that security is dominated by governments. Ronald Jepperson, Alexander Wendt, and Peter Katzenstein, 'Norms, Identity, and Culture in National Security,' in Katzenstein (ed), *The Culture of National Security: Norms and Identity in World Politics* (New York: Columbia University Press, 1999) however, suggest that even security is being affected by norms.

increasing agreement among security professionals across the globe about how one does a number of tasks and what individual skill is required to be effective at a variety of security-related tasks (military and policing). There is also a set of principles, growing in acceptance, about what appropriate individual behaviour is.[40] This began with the International Tribunal at Nuremburg, which found that when international rules protecting humanitarian values come into conflict with state laws, individuals are obligated to transgress the laws of their government (except when there is no room for 'moral choice'). Individual military personnel cannot escape criminal responsibility for actions that violate international law by citing civilian orders. There are similar standards for law enforcement personnel that can be gleaned from the training in peace missions and general standards for international civilian police.[41] The acceptance of a body of expertise and judgment about the proper role of security professionals is a step toward the definition of standard principles of behaviour among security professionals.[42]

Common among historically successful claims to a profession are also arguments about the public benefits of professional behaviour. Even when this accompanies efforts to curtail competitiveness in the market, the claims to public benefits are both important to a profession's legitimacy and place constraints on opportunistic action. The appeal to public benefits accords with other current arguments about the way in which private entities and private initiatives might bring about global public benefits. In his discussion of the normative practices that should underlie the generation of law, for instance, Benedict Kingsbury argues that any entity should accept the principles of public law (legality, rationality, proportionality, rule of law, and human rights) and should make a normative commitment to 'public-ness'.[43]

A necessary feature of a profession also includes an occupational organization that can test competence, regulate standards, and maintain discipline.[44] Here, of course, private security has quite a distance to travel. Examining successful and unsuccessful efforts among professionals in other fields may prove instructive. This is also an area where interested parties—states, NGOs, international organizations, corporations, and others—might pool efforts to generate or ratify steps

---

[40] See the discussion in Held et al, *Global Transformations* (n 5 above) 71–3. See also Y Dinstein, 'Rules of War,' in J Krieger, ed, *The Oxford Companion to the Politics of the World* (Oxford: Oxford University Press, 1993); J Vincent, 'Modernity and Universal Human Rights,' in AG McGrew and PG Lewis, *Global Politics* (Cambridge: Polity Press, 1992).

[41] David Bayley, *Changing the Guard: Developing Democratic Police Abroad* (Oxford: Oxford University Press, 2005); Jerome H Skolnick and David H Bayley, *Community Policing: Issues and Practices Around the World* (Washington, DC: National Institute of Justice, 1988).

[42] Margaret Keck and Katherine Sikkink talk about the importance of expertise for the building of networks. Though their focus is on advocacy networks, one could extend the analysis to other varieties such as security professionals. See Keck and Sikkink, *Activists Beyond Borders: Advocacy Networks in International Politics* (Ithaca: Cornell University Press, 1998), ch 6.

[43] Benedict Kingsbury, Nico Krisch, and Richard B Stewart, 'The Emergence of Global Administrative Law,' *Law and Contemporary Problems*, vol 68, no 3 (2005) 15–61.

[44] Krause (n 33 above) quotes The Monopolies Commission, London, 1970. See p. 5.

toward such an organization. Even if it initially generates only minimal standards, history suggests that such organizations often build and morph over time.

Conclusion

In considering how best to encourage proper behaviour by PMCs and the individuals they employ, a number of options have been raised, foremost among them intergovernmental legal co-ordination (to standardize contracting and legal mechanisms for retrospective justice) and global industry standards. Though these are both important options, neither of them address important elements of the industry and thus the pursuit of either alone, or even both together, is unlikely to prove effective. Intergovernmental co-ordination has been stymied by the different roles various governments play in the market. When what each government wants to control is very different, it is hard to get them to institute standard regulatory schemes together. Without standard regulatory schemes, it is easy for companies to take advantage of the global nature of the market to avoid the rules of any one government. Furthermore, intergovernmental co-ordination rarely addresses private financiers of private security and other stakeholders.

Corporate industry standards options have run into difficulties with finding ways to tie a company's stated policy to its behaviour on the ground. The contract-driven nature of the industry means that individuals may be on the rosters of many companies and work for several in quick succession within a single conflict zone. This leads to difficulty inculcating individuals with any corporate culture and also to problems accurately linking individual misbehaviour to the right corporation. Though some PMCs advertise themselves as ethical, what that means for action on the ground is uncertain. This complicates the development of corporate reputation as a link to accountability or control by clouding the information available.

In this volume, other options for regulation have been raised, including Kevin O'Brien's framework in chapter two, which aims to distinguish between security and military firms, between offensive and defensive services, and between contracts that aim to alter the strategic landscape and those that do not—and regulate or prohibit contracts at the national level on that basis. The market offers many challenges to national level regulation of these services, however, and the unfolding nature of conflict (and political uses of violence more generally) render many of these distinctions problematic. Also, the intergovernmental co-ordination that O'Brien admits is crucial to the effectiveness of his framework has been stymied by the different roles various governments play in the market.

An alternative approach would build on the interests of producers to socialize the market. The stated commitment of many PMCs to professionalism is a place to start. Interested stakeholders might push PMCs to avoid a purely ceremonial appeal to professionalism by establishing processes and organizations to articulate standards for global security professionals. The nascent conceptions of security professionals that have grown in the last several decades and are built largely around the framework of international humanitarian law should provide a reasonable place to start. Efforts to further develop standards could draw on other arenas where analysts have begun to outline standards for those non-state entities that are, in effect, governing.[45]

Standards for private security professionals might allow the use of litigation—as Cockayne discusses in the next chapter—to be a more effective tool for regulation. It could also provide the basis for a system of individual licensing for transnational private security professionals. The standards that Bearpark and Schulz propose for companies in chapter thirteen could be more easily achieved if these companies could designate their commitment to corporate social responsibility by agreeing to hire only licensed security professionals. Most importantly, a process for developing standards could also provide a focal point for customer education, agreement, and potential co-ordination. Though hardly a silver bullet for the myriad challenges presented above, building on producer attempts to differentiate themselves both works through market mechanisms and is attentive to the pressures that led to the market's rise in the first place—and is thus among the most promising steps toward its taming.

[45] Kingsbury et al, 'The Emergence of Global Administrative Law' (n 43 above).

11

Make or buy? Principal-agent theory and the regulation of private military companies

*James Cockayne**

Should states make their own security, or buy it on a global market? Private military companies (PMCs) seem to offer states the option of purchasing, rather than producing, security—perhaps even at reduced cost. Yet many commentators suggest such an approach risks under-regulation, endangering public security, or that PMCs operate in a regulatory 'vacuum',[1] recalling Machiavelli's warnings of the inadequacies of controls over mercenaries.[2]

The basic concern is that PMCs make bad agents, because they may: (a) supplant their principals, for example by usurping the power of a government that has engaged them; (b) co-opt their principals, by developing excessive 'epistemic power' over their principals' preferences;[3] and (c) allow their principals to circumvent legitimate constraints. Understanding how the existing system of fragmented but overlapping regulation through international law, national law, and market signals may lead to these outcomes requires careful analysis of the cumulative effect of regulatory arrangements across multiple jurisdictions. But how can we compare the social, legal, and financial controls which confront Aegis—London-based, stacked with British ex-military personnel and contracting with the US military—to the controls confronting the joint ventures spun off by Executive Outcomes with the assistance of numerous African officials in the late 1990s?[4] How can we contemplate global controls for PMCs without first understanding the different controls confronting DynCorp—close to the US foreign policy establishment,

    * Thanks to Benedict Kingsbury, Simon Chesterman, Chia Lehnardt, and anonymous reviewers for their comments on an earlier draft.
    [1] See, eg, PW Singer, 'War, Profits and the Vacuum of Law: Privatized Military Firms and International Law,' Columbia Journal of Transnational Law, vol 42 (2004) 532.
    [2] Nicolò Machiavelli, *The Prince* (1505, published 1515, trans WK Marriott, 1908), ch XII.
    [3] Anna Leander, 'The Power to Construct International Security: On the Significance of Private Military Companies,' *Millennium: Journal of International Studies*, vol 13 (2005) 803.
    [4] See Jakkie Cilliers, 'Private security in war-torn African states,' in Jakkie Cilliers and Peggy Mason (eds), *Peace, Profit or Plunder? The Privatization of Security in War-Torn African Societies* (Pretoria: Institute for Security Studies, 1999) 4.

high-profile and with an increasing emphasis on security sector reform work—and local start-ups providing residential compound security to NGO staff in Nairobi?[5]

Much existing discussion of PMC regulation obscures these differences. This literature tends to focus on the role of large, Western-based PMCs, rather than their less visible, often informally-organized local affiliates in developing countries. Such accounts are of limited utility in predicting future dynamics within the industry, or in understanding the complex interaction of international, state, market and self-regulation.

This chapter argues that principal-agent theory may provide a useful framework for such comparative analysis.[6] It is the uniquely trans-boundary, trans-regulatory nature of PMC activity that challenges both analysis and policy-making. The first section introduces principal-agent theory and adapts it to analyse PMC regulation. The chapter then argues that states attempt to harness three sets of regulatory tools (international law, national law, and market signals) to constitute PMCs as their agents. In some cases PMCs can play off multiple principals to their own advantage, raising concerns about the extent of PMC influence over national law-making. Litigation may yet discipline PMC conduct, aligning it with global human rights and *jus in bello* norms. Future PMC regulation may be more driven by industry consolidation, a desire for product differentiation, and the shadow of litigation: some PMCs and their state patrons may co-operate to generate global regulatory mechanisms rewarding socially responsible PMCs and driving others to the margins. The chapter concludes by describing the broader implications of these trends for the global organization of legitimate violence.

Applying principal-agent theory to PMCs

Principal-agent theory is an offshoot of transaction costs theory, which acknowledges that many economic transactions occur under conditions of uncertainty and asymmetric information. This forces principals to grant agents a level of independent discretion—'agency slack'—in turn affording agents the opportunity to pursue their own preferences, rather than those of their principal.[7] Principals must set off agent discretion against the possibility of agents 'shirking'. Principal-agent theory is thus centrally concerned with assessing hierarchical organization as a

---

[5] See Rita Abrahamsen and Michael C Williams, 'The Politics of Private Security in Kenya,' *Review of African Political Economy*, vol 32 (2005) 425–31; James Cockayne, 'Commercial Security in Humanitarian and Post-Conflict Settings: An Exploratory Study,' International Peace Academy, New York, March 2006, available at <http://www.ipacademy.org/pdfs/COMMERCIAL_SECURITY_FINAL.pdf>.

[6] For earlier discussion of principal-agent theory in this context see Deborah D Avant, *The Market for Force: The Consequences of Privatizing Security* (Cambridge: Cambridge University Press, 2005); P W Singer, *Corporate Warriors. The Rise of the Privatized Military Industry* (Ithaca: Cornell University Press, 2003); Eric J Fredland, 'Outsourcing Military Force: A Transactions Cost Perspective on the Role of Military Companies,' *Defence & Peace Economics*, vol 15 (2004) 205–19.

[7] Jonathan Bendor et al, 'Theories of Delegation,' *Annual Review of Political Science*, vol 4 (2001) 236.

format for service delivery, and identifying when consumers will (or should) 'make or buy' products—the very issue at stake in arguments over the relative merits of state and market regulation of PMCs.[8] The taboo surrounding commercial military activity, discussed in chapter one by Sarah Percy, might in a sense be understood as a norm encouraging consumers of security to produce their own security, rather than pay others to provide it, because the overall social costs of delegation—including the costs of PMC defection—are seen as insupportable. Machiavelli's warning can be similarly characterized.

Principal-agent theory is helpful in clarifying the costs and benefits of delegation to PMCs. Immediate benefits include reduced expertise acquisition costs, reduced expertise maintenance costs, reduced administration costs, and increased efficiency through specialization.[9] Longer-term benefits may include binding multiple principals to a common delegation arrangement, reducing negotiation costs, decision-making efficiencies, and blame-shifting, because agents—not principals—carry the consequences of unpopular decisions.[10]

We know less about the costs of hiring PMCs. The US experience with PMCs in Iraq suggests that governments have radically underestimated the secondary economic costs arising from reliance on PMCs, including personnel and contractor replacement costs, workers' compensation, increased insurance premiums, evacuation and rescue costs, and increased reconstruction costs.[11] Many clients also appear to know little about their own potential liability for PMC misconduct or their exposure to reputational risk as a result of that conduct.[12] But, broadly speaking, the costs involved in using a PMC as an agent fall into four categories, excluding secondary costs resulting from the arrangement: screening costs in selecting agents; negotiation costs, including building in institutional checks into principal-agent arrangements; monitoring costs, whether from police-patrol monitoring (direct monitoring by the principal) or fire alarm monitoring (relying on third party testimony or whistle-blowing);[13] and the costs of sanctions. These four control mechanisms (screening, institutional checks, monitoring, and sanctions) offer a basis for analyzing PMC regulation across a range of environments.

Before turning to that discussion, however, it is important to clarify the concepts of 'principality' and 'agency'—somewhat contested in the theoretical literature.[14]

---

[8] See Terry Moe, 'The New Economics of Organization,' *American Journal of Political Science*, vol 28 (1984) 757.   [9] For examples, see Cockayne, 'Commercial Security' (n 5 above).
[10] Jonas Tallberg, 'Delegation to Supranational Institutions: Why, How, and with What Consequences?', *Western European Policy*, vol 25 (2002) 26.
[11] See David Isenberg, 'A Fistful of Contractors: The Case for a Pragmatic Assessment of Private Military Companies in Iraq,' British American Security Information Council, Research Report 2004.4, September 2004, Washington DC, 25; US General Accounting Office (GAO), 'Rebuilding Iraq: Actions Needed to Improve Use of Private Security Providers,' GAO-05-737, 28 July 2005.
[12] Cockayne, 'Commercial Security' (n 5 above).
[13] Jonas Tallberg, 'The Anatomy of Autonomy: An Institutional Account of Variation in Supranational Influence,' *Journal of Common Market Studies*, vol 38 (2000) 843.
[14] Daniel L Nielson and Michael J Tierney, 'Delegating to International Organizations: Agency Theory and World Bank Environmental Reform,' *International Organization*, vol 57 (2003) 241–76.

In the approach adopted here, what makes each principal a principal—rather than a mere third party, however influential, such as a private investor—is the *binding legal authority* exerted by the principal in relation to the task at hand.[15] This has three significant implications. First, it facilitates application of principal-agent theory to situations in which public principals hire private agents.[16] Unlike public agents (such as parliamentary committees), private agents' capabilities are constituted partly by parties (such as shareholders) external to a particular contract. The nature of different stakeholders' relations with an agent—for example, whether they are likely to be repeat players or involved in a one-off transaction, or if they have strong social or legal sway over the agent—thus comes to the fore in determining their control over private agents, and whether they serve as 'principals'. Secondly, this approach highlights that private agents will work across multiple stakeholders, and may use this as an opportunity to subvert different principals' control.[17] Thirdly, this allows us to deal with a range of principal-agent relations at once, notwithstanding the fact that different principals exert different types of legal control over agents: through a contract, through regulation of their corporate personality, through permission to operate on their territory.

PMCs as state agents in the international system

In the existing international security system, states alone are authorized to organize legitimate violence; other groups (such as international organizations, private citizens, and non-state actors) may use force only with their permission. States, in other words, are the mutually recognizing, oligopolistic principals, each with a monopoly on legitimate violence within their own territory. This system is held together by a complex legal framework controlling violence between those states, in spaces not controlled by any one particular state, and by non-state actors. In this section, I argue that states have sought to use the regulatory tools (legal, social, and contractual) at their disposal to co-opt PMCs, constituting them as agents of their interests, while allowing them limited autonomy within the international security system.

PMCs as agents of the state system under international law

States have used international law to limit, control, and co-opt—but not eradicate—independent, transnational commercial military activity, subordinating it

---

[15] This is an unusually broad conception of principality. Existing accounts focus on *contractual* principals, but as a result fail to account for non-contractual forms of influence on agent (and principal) behaviour. I limit principality to *legal* control to distinguish it from mere influence.

[16] Compare Oliver Williamson, 'Public and Private Bureaucracies: a Transaction Cost Economic Perspective,' *Journal of Law, Economics and Organization*, vol 15 (1999) 320; Walter Mattli and Tim Büthe, 'Global Private Governance: Lessons from a National Model of Setting Standards in Accounting,' *Law and Contemporary Problems*, vol 68 (2005) 225.

[17] See Mattli and Büthe, 'Global Private Governance' ibid.

to and aligning it with the state system, while protecting its private, commercial character.

The international legal system has traditionally left the means of organizing violence within the state largely to states to decide for themselves, including by purchasing security services from commercial providers. Early modern European states relied heavily on mercenary forces in building, consolidating, and globalizing their own power,[18] and relics of earlier market forms—such as privateering, chartered companies, and foreign recruiting by commercial agents—long survived within the state system.[19] States did not outlaw this commercially-organized military activity *per se*: instead, international prohibitions developed and changed over time, reflecting changing assessments by states of their need and ability to control specific forms of private, commercial military organization. Rules have developed, often in response to social and technological change, attributing liability to states in certain cases for the acts of private groups with which they are associated, to ensure that private actors cannot destabilize or even unravel the state system, producing the complex situation of state responsibility described in chapter eight by Chia Lehnardt. In some cases, states have even adopted inter-state liability rules incentivizing effective enforcement of regimes for the control of non-state actors by state regulators within their own territories.[20]

States' attitudes to commercial military activity changed radically in the last century, responding to massive geopolitical, social and technological changes— but without outlawing state use of PMCs altogether. In 1907 the European colonial powers rejected a German proposal for a total ban on the service of foreigners in national militaries; they opted instead merely to require neutral states to prevent commercial recruiting on their territory.[21] Following the Second World War the 1949 Geneva Conventions afforded military contractors prisoner of war status—but only if they possessed a state-supplied identification card.[22] Commercial military activity was permitted, but forced towards state control.

In 1961 the Belgian government chose not to enforce laws against mercenary recruiting (required by the 1907 Hague Convention), allowing Belgian corporations to back an attempted secession by Katanga, a mineral-rich Congolese province, shortly after the exit of Belgian state armed forces from Congo upon Congolese independence. This signalled the arrival of a new fault-line in state

---

[18] Charles Tilly, 'War Making and State Making as Organized Crime,' in Peter Evans, Dietrich Rueschemeyer, and Theda Skocpol (eds), *Bringing the State Back In* (Cambridge, New York: Cambridge University Press, 1985) 169–91.

[19] See Janice Thomson, *Mercenaries, Pirates, and Sovereigns: State-building and Extraterritorial Violence in Early Modern Europe* (Princeton: Princeton University Press, 1994).

[20] Thomson, *Mercenaries, Pirates, and Sovereigns* (n 19 above) 80–81; Montgomery Sapone, 'Have Rifle With Scope, Will Travel: The Global Economy of Mercenary Violence,' California Western International Law Journal, vol 30 (1999) 32–3.

[21] Convention Respecting the Rights and Duties of Neutral Powers and Persons in Case of War on Land (Hague Convention No V), 18 October 1907, 1 Bevans 654–68, art 4.

[22] See Geneva Conventions (I) and (II), 75 UNTS 31 and 85, arts 13(4); Geneva Convention (III), 75 UNTS 135, art 4(4).

attitudes to the global military market, pitting former colonial states, where military entrepreneurs were often based, against newly decolonized states fearful of recolonization under a corporate veil.[23] Newly decolonized states quickly turned to the United Nations,[24] the Organization for African Unity,[25] and other multilateral treaty-negotiating forums[26] to develop norms further limiting commercial military activity, in particular by prohibiting its use in violation of the right to self-determination. But at the same time these states ensured they retained a free hand to use military entrepreneurs to consolidate their own hold on power against rebel movements.

These rules permit most of the commercial military activity that today's PMCs undertake.[27] States and commercial suppliers are aware of the legal loopholes and make use of them, as Sandline's contract with the Papua New Guinea government made clear.[28] The result is not so much a 'vacuum' as a 'patchwork' of international regulation that leaves states free to harness PMCs in a manner that renders them free agents within—but very much of—the state system. This focus on protecting systemic interests is also reflected in growing efforts to ensure alignment of PMC conduct with international rules protecting civilians. Thus the discussion of mercenarism initiated within the UN Commission on Human Rights in the mid-1980s by anti-market socialist and anti-colonial non-aligned states, in an attempt to ensure commercial military activity did not undermine their own state power,[29] has led to efforts to enforce PMC observance of human rights and humanitarian standards, both within the Commission framework (through a Special Rapporteur and a more recent Working Group) and beyond (especially in the Swiss-ICRC initiative[30] and in the ICRC's own work with PMCs).[31]

These efforts seek to harness a range of regulatory tools to ensure PMCs serve as agents of the state system as a whole. Such initiatives are needed because purely inter-state liability seems increasingly limited as a regulatory tool, as social and technological conditions facilitate trans-national organization of commercial

[23] Anthony Mockler, *The Mercenaries* (New York: Oxford University Press, 1969) 93–110.

[24] See, eg, GA Res 2131, 21 December 1965, UN Doc A/6014 (1965); International Convention Against the Recruitment, Use, Financing, and Training of Mercenaries, 4 December 1989, UN Doc A/44/49 (1989).

[25] OAU Convention for the Elimination of Mercenaries in Africa, 22 April 1985, reprinted in Gino J Naldi (ed), *Documents of the Organization of African Unity* (New York: Mansell, 1992) 58.

[26] Protocol Additional to the Geneva Conventions of 12 August 1949, and Relating to the Protection of Victims of International Armed Conflicts (Protocol I), 1125 UNTS 3, 7 December 1978, art 47.

[27] ICRC, *Commentary on the Additional Protocols of 8 June 1977 to the Geneva Conventions of 12 August 1949* (Geneva: ICRC, 1987), paras 1806 et seq.

[28] *Sandline International Inc v Papua New Guinea*, Queensland Supreme Court, *International Law Reports*, vol 117 (1999) 552–565, 565–593.

[29] See Leonard Gaultier et al, 'The mercenary issue at the UN Commission on Human Rights: the need for a new approach,' International Alert, 2001.

[30] See <http://www.eda.admin.ch/eda/en/home/topics/intla/humlaw/pse/psechi.html>.

[31] Claude Voillat, 'Private Military Companies: A Word of Caution,' *Humanitarian Exchange*, vol 28 (2005) 33.

military activity. Existing regulatory arrangements offer PMCs tools with which to protect the fruits of the trade from intrusive state regulation: limited liability; improved capital convertibility and mobility; reduced transaction costs; commercial confidentiality; and, perhaps most important, protection of profits through judicial enforcement of arbitral awards against states.[32] In addition, the adoption of corporate forms has allowed risk-sharing and economies of scale through organizational innovation, often producing inter-sectoral alliances between natural resource extractors, construction companies, risk consultants and military and security entrepreneurs. As a result, states may need to look beyond international law for the tools to ensure that PMCs can be made agents of state interests. State-based regulatory mechanisms take on a new salience.

PMCs as state agents under national law

States have used national law to control PMCs in two different ways: through direct or contractual agency, and through indirect or licensed agency.

Direct agency: contracting PMCs

We can analyse states' contracting of PMCs through the four control mechanisms identified earlier: screening, institutional checks, monitoring, and sanctions.

States seem to screen PMCs to identify agents that will be cost-efficient, rather than those likely to create negative externalities by, for example, engaging in human rights abuses. That seems unlikely to change, absent any exogenous incentive—although, as I discuss below, such incentives may develop out of third-party litigation. Even those states that do not engage in formal screening often rely on informal market signals such as PMCs' connections to special operations groups. The use of formal screening is apparently affected by bargaining power. Repeat players—such as the US Department of Defense—have access to more information about PMCs than single-shot players, such as a national government hiring a PMC to defend itself against an insurgency, so repeat players can more easily conduct screening. Additionally, desire for access to future revenues from repeat players makes PMCs more willing to submit to intrusive screening by those players than by single-shot players. PMCs that compete for single-shot contracts thus seem likely to prefer an opaque market, whereas PMCs that receive most of their revenues from repeat players will be more prepared to invest in brand and market signals by developing self-regulatory mechanisms like the British Association of Private Security Companies (BAPSC), the International Peace Operations Association (IPOA), or the Private Security Company Association of Iraq (PSCAI). What seems, therefore, to be emerging is a two-tiered system of screening, with large PMCs voluntarily subscribing to screening mechanisms patronized by large, repeat-player

---

[32] See D Sturzaker, 'The Sandline affair: illegality and international law,' International Arbitration Law Review, vol 3 (2000) 164.

clients, while smaller PMCs operate marginally, seeking high-value, high-risk, single-shot contracts.

States also use 'institutional checks' such as judicial review to control PMCs they contract. Again, bargaining power seems an important determinant of how judicial review is used. For example, US PMCs operating in Iraq are subject to judicial review by US courts, but not by Iraqi courts. Thus, Custer Battles was ordered to pay $10 million in damages and fines for civil fraud for services in Iraq[33]—but is immune from suit in Iraq.[34] Single-shot players are, again, at a disadvantage, since they may have to forego judicial review to secure the services they seek: thus Sandline contracted with Papua New Guinea under English law, and UNCITRAL arbitration rather than Papua New Guinean courts was the agreed dispute resolution forum.

In contrast, it is the nature and location of performance of services contracted for—rather than bargaining power—that seems to determine the use of monitoring mechanisms in direct contracts. In particular, contracts performed extra-territorially seem more weakly policed because of expense and difficulty.[35] Clients often rely on 'fire alarm' monitoring for information about contractual violations—including whistle-blowers, as in the Custer Battles case above, or the media or NGOs. Inevitably, monitoring breaks down when service benchmarks and provision are complex or when service delivery occurs in a conflict zone. Self-reporting may offer a valuable option, but contracts must be structured to create adequate incentives for self-reporting; few one-shot contracts will be so structured.

Principals seem to attempt to reduce monitoring costs in a number of ways, for example by employing PMCs to whom they have informal social ties—whether personal familiarity, common service in a particular armed force, language, or nationality. In fact, to some extent the talk of a 'global' PMC industry may be somewhat misleading: there may be a number of culturally distinct markets, which only minimally overlap and intersect: an Anglo-Saxon industry focused on the US and British defence establishments; a francophone industry; and a network of former Soviet and eastern European security providers. These industries may in fact be more closely integrated with local partners in conflict zones than with each other.

Of the four controlling mechanisms, it is sanctions which lie at the heart of concerns about state control over PMCs—or more precisely, the limited ability and willingness of states to impose sanctions. States' will to impose their own will on PMCs through coercion, in the form of individual criminal responsibility, is greatly limited by their reliance on PMC services, and their ability limited by the

[33] Laura Parker, 'Jury fines defense contractor in Iraq $10M,' *USA Today*, 10 March 2006.

[34] See Coalition Provisional Authority, Memorandum Number 17, available at <http://www.iraqcoalition.org/regulations/20040626_CPAMEMO_17_Registration_Requirements_for_Private_Security_Companies_with_Annexes.pdf>.

[35] See for example PW Singer, 'Warriors for Hire in Iraq,' *Salon.com*, 15 April 2004, available at <http://dir.salon.com/story/news/feature/2004/04/15/warriors/index.html>.

difficulty of gathering evidence in war zones—often overseas. As discussed below, states may in fact have incentives to bury evidence of PMC misconduct. Moreover, the threat of criminal prosecution is unlikely to secure specific performance. The result is that contracts often give PMCs greater security than states.[36] Beyond the criminal law, clients' sanctioning power depends primarily on their control of goods valuable to PMCs: PMC assets and financing, corporate personality, materiel, personnel—and future revenue streams. In a globalized economy, all of these production factors are highly mobile. Control of a fixed asset with a high future value to the PMC (such as natural resources and access to personnel) and high value future contracts therefore seem likely to increase a client's ability to impose its sanctioning power.

Accordingly, the establishment of an effective control system seems likely to require co-operative sanctioning arrangements amongst those clients—particularly US and European governments, but also other potentially significant players such as global resource extractors, the humanitarian community, and multilateral peacekeeping and peacebuilding organizations—that control such a preponderant proportion of market revenues that they are able to induce major PMCs to meet minimum behavioural thresholds. Over time, this may create a two-tiered system, involving a 'white' trade between major clients and sanctioned PMCs, and a 'black' market conducted off the books.

Indirect agency: licensing PMCs

In many cases, states exert control over PMCs not through directly contracting them as state agents, but by exerting (or refraining from exerting) regulatory power over PMCs' dealings with other clients, corporate form, and behaviour. States controlling PMCs' conduct, structure, and access to production factors through these 'licensing' regimes exercise a limited form of indirect principality over PMCs—because these controls can shape PMCs' roles and powers as agents. It is therefore worth considering how those regimes compare to the more 'direct' principal-agent relations just discussed.

This section explores how five countries—the United States, South Africa, Iraq, France, and, in a somewhat unorthodox categorization, Britain—use their 'licensing' power to render PMCs their indirect agents.[37] Each has adopted a different approach: the United States combines a global market outlook with strong national executive control; the Iraqi approach largely surrenders executive control;

---

[36] See, eg, Col Steven J Zamparelli, 'Contractors on the Battlefield: What Have We Signed Up For?,' *Air Force Journal of Logistics* vol 23, no 3 (fall 1999).

[37] Britain's *laissez faire* approach is not normally described as a 'licensing' regime, as it is hands-off and involves no statutory licensing regime. But this in fact provides a general permission or licence backed up by informal norms and social ties. Contrasting this informal arrangement with more formal licensing regimes helps illuminate the contours of such regimes—which are not limited to the five jurisdictions addressed here, but also used elsewhere, such as Israel and some eastern European states.

the South African approach unsuccessfully seeks to discourage exports by imposing strong executive control, but without adequate enforcement mechanisms or financial incentives;[38] the French model is decidedly *Étatist*; and the British model is informal and based on social ties and market norms. But despite these differences, all seem to seek to align the behaviour of PMCs contracted to private clients with the licensing state's security and foreign policy interests. The success of that policy, however, seems to depend on a state's control not only of legal but also other regulatory mechanisms, such as financial incentives and social networks.

In each of the five countries in question, screening and checks on PMC discretion are used primarily to ensure that PMC conduct aligns with the national executive's foreign or domestic security policy.[39] Other potentially relevant accountability standards, such as the prior criminal records of contractors[40] and evidence of respect for human rights[41] receive only minor, vague, and unenforceable mentions in the applicable administrative regimes.

In addition to these statutory controls, a number of jurisdictions impose informal screening and institutional checks on PMCs. The French regime combines a formal prohibition on mercenarism[42] with state control of the export market through the establishment of a government-controlled parastatal—Défense Conseil International—providing export opportunities to French military personnel. The French government has tolerated the formation of export-focused PMCs on the 'Anglo-Saxon' model, such as Barril and Secopex, but has taken steps to establish informal ties with these groups to impose the shadow of regulation and maintain informal controls. The British approach, rooted in a liberal economic orthodoxy,[43] provides a general permission for PMC activity; but Whitehall and Westminster have used personal and corporate connections with the City and Sandhurst to try to direct and control the trade—sometimes with disastrous results, as the so-called 'Arms to Africa' affair and more recent Equatorial Guinea coup plot have made clear.[44]

[38] The Regulation of Foreign Military Assistance Act 1998 (SA) was regularly flouted in Iraq: see chapter nine in this volume by Marina Caparini and Beauregard Tromp, 'Hired guns from SA flood Iraq,' *Cape Times*, 4 February 2004. The South African government subsequently revised the legislation, presenting the Prohibition of Mercenary Activity and Prohibition of Regulation of Certain Activities in an area of Armed Conflict Bill 2005, which was in the South African parliament at the time of writing.

[39] 22 USC § 2778(a)(1) (1994); Regulation of Foreign Military Assistance Act 1998 (SA) s /(f); Iraq: see CPA, Memorandum Number 17 (n 34 above), s 2(3).

[40] CPA, Memorandum Number 17 (n 34 above), s 2(4)–(6).

[41] 'Criteria for Decision-making on US Arms Exports,' White House Memorandum, 17 February 1995; Regulation of Foreign Military Assistance Act 1998 (SA) s 7; CPA, Memorandum Number 17 (n 34 above), s 2(6)(c).

[42] Loi n° 2003-340 du 14 Avril 2003 relatif à la répression de l'activité de mercenaire, JO n° 89 du 15 Avril 2003, 6636.

[43] Report of the Committee of Privy Counsellors Appointed to Inquire into the Recruitment of Mercenaries, Cmnd 6569 (August 1976) 10.

[44] Sir Thomas Legg KCB QC, Sir Robbin Ibbs KBE, Report of the Sierra Leone Arms Investigation (UK FCO, July 1998); Jamie Wilson, Paul Lashmar, and Andrew Meldrum, 'Archer Linked to Thatcher and Coup Scandal,' *The Sun-Herald*, 29 August 2004.

These licensing regimes are also characterized by weak post-licence monitoring and sanctioning arrangements. Embassy staff charged with oversight tend to consider that, as one Department of State official put it, 'Our job is to protect Americans, not investigate Americans.'[45] In Iraq, one Pentagon Inspector General's report found that Pentagon procurement rules were not followed in 22 of 24 deals awarded. France has secured a small number of convictions in recent years,[46] but in other jurisdictions, prosecutions for violating PMC licensing regimes are the exception, rather than the rule. The British Foreign Enlistment Act 1870 was not enforced against British citizens participating in either the Spanish Civil War, or the conflict in Afghanistan.[47] The same pattern is evident as far as India.[48] Prosecutions are also hampered by the failure of national executives to extend the jurisdiction of domestic courts to the extra-territorial activities of commercial suppliers. There is evidence of a trend by executives reluctantly to fill that gap,[49] though not completely.[50]

The costs of this weak post-licensing accountability may fall on communities where PMCs perform their contracts: not only those of direct violence, but also the discounted prices on national assets offered by governing elites to PMC business partners to achieve short-term security goals; crowding out of investment in public institutions; and the reduction of public security expectations to the minimum required to facilitate resource extraction and other core economic activities.[51]

State regulators explain the absence of monitoring and effective sanctions on the basis of cost, pointing to the difficulty of monitoring in war zones. Yet few attempts have been made to impose the administrative costs of monitoring on the suppliers, through licensing fees, by imposing annual reporting requirements, or by instituting spot-checks or self-reporting requirements. All of this tends to suggest that national executives may in fact see other benefits in PMC extra-territorial conduct being little-known at home. They may, in other words, see benefits in relying on the outsourcing of military tasks to private agents to reduce the control that other stakeholders—including democratic electorates—have over them.

---

[45] T Christian Miller, 'A Colombian Town Caught in a Cross-Fire,' *LA Times*, 10 March 2002.

[46] Paul Michaud, 'No More Mercenaries,' *New African*, issue 422 (2003) 29.

[47] See UK Foreign and Commonwealth Office, HC 577 Private Military Companies: Options for Regulation 2001–02, London: The Stationery Office, 2002, 20; Jason Burke, 'al Qaeda Britons feared to be back in UK,' *Observer*, 2 June 2002.

[48] See Agence France Press, 'India Probes Reports of Ex-soldiers Working Illegally in Iraq,' 3 May 2004.

[49] See, eg, Military Extraterritorial Jurisdiction Act (MEJA), 18 USC § 3261, 22 November 2000; Ronald W Reagan National Defense Authorization Act for Fiscal Year 2005, 108th Congress, 2d Session, S 2400, 28 October 2004, s 1088.

[50] MEJA does not cover US nationals working for foreign entities, foreign contractors ordinarily resident in the 'host nation,' or US contractors working for US government agencies not supporting military action.

[51] See especially Caroline Holmqvist, Private Security Companies: The Case for Regulation, SIPRI Policy Paper No 9, Stockholm, January 2005, 15–17.

Remote agency? Soft law, voluntary codes, and market signals

Beyond systemic arrangements through international law, and direct contracting and indirect licensing through national law, states seek to influence PMCs through the manipulation of market signalling mechanisms. As described above, some PMCs seeking access to the revenue streams offered by certain major, repeat-player clients are beginning to differentiate themselves by creating market signals and brands which serve as screening proxies, such as the International Peace Operations Association (IPOA) and the British Association of Private Security Companies (BAPSC). States appear to be moving towards buying into such an approach, promoting legalistic, 'soft' norms setting out minimum behavioural standards, which PMCs would bind themselves to voluntarily, following models adopted in other industries,[52] aligning their own behaviour with the preferences of states backing those codes. This is the outer bounds, however, of principality, because under each of these codes the screening powers, institutional checks, monitoring powers, and sanctions available to states (and other actors) are extremely weak. Any enforcement authority states wield over PMCs through such standards is extremely 'soft', any principality very 'remote'.

At present, however, such voluntary norms are not 'linked' to state enforcement power. Many in fact constitute simply entirely voluntary codes put forward by PMCs themselves, either individually or collectively. These appear to have had little impact to date on PMC conduct: CACI-supplied interrogators implicated in the abuse of prisoners at Abu Ghraib[53] (which included extensive sexual humiliation) were apparently unfazed by CACI's Standards of Ethics and Business Conduct, including injunctions against sexual harassment.[54] The Code of Conduct established by the International Peace Operations Association has not yet produced any significant sanctions for violating members, although IPOA is developing a significant and transparent Enforcement Mechanism to promote both self-regulation and fire alarm monitoring. The sanctions to be imposed by the new BAPSC on its members also remain unclear.

The danger of all such soft law and voluntary codes, disconnected from state enforcement powers, is that they mimic formal principal-agent accountability structures without their effect, thus 'ceremonializing' such regulatory controls. PMCs signal to the market that they are working in a socially responsible manner, but because of the weak enforcement mechanisms, may in fact be free to shirk,

---

[52] Voluntary Principles on Security and Human Rights; the OECD Guidelines for Multinational Enterprises; and the UN Norms on the Responsibilities of Transnational Corporations and Other Business Enterprises with Regard to Human Rights, approved in UN Doc E/CN.4/Sub.2/2003/L.11, 13 August 2003.

[53] Joel Brinkley and James Glanz, 'Contract Workers Implicated in February Army Report on Prison Abuse Remain on the Job,' *New York Times*, 4 May 2004.

[54] CACI, Standards of Ethics and Business Conduct, available at <http://www.caci.com/about/corp_gov/ethics.shtml>.

defecting from society's preferences.[55] Ceremonialization ensures the ongoing approval of the principal, while reducing compliance costs for the agent. The risk with many PMC codes of conduct and government-backed soft law is that they offer lip service to corporate social responsibility, without teeth.

However, if such codes begin to refer to or even incorporate existing control mechanisms—for example by referring to obligations under the Geneva Conventions, which can be enforced by any High Contracting Party—they may slowly develop teeth. Before returning to this, it is first necessary to consider the possibility that in some circumstances PMC agents may escape the control of their state principals altogether.

Towards principality? When agents seek to control their principals

If principal-agent relations are not carefully structured, principals can become dependent on their agents—or even, as Machiavelli warned his Prince, be usurped by them. Lessons from government contracting with defence materiel providers that indicate that over-specialization can lead to path dependence by creating prohibitive costs of changing agents, facilitating price-gouging, may also be applicable to the high-technology end of the PMC market, particularly where PMCs provide and operate weapons systems.[56] But such 'dependence' can also emerge at the low-technology end of the market, for example where humanitarian relief providers rely on convoy security, sometimes producing protection rackets.[57] But only in very few cases—for example in eastern Sierra Leone, where Executive Outcomes temporarily exercised such extensive and effective control that it operated local judicial tribunals, underpinned by the social legitimacy of local tribal authorities[58]—have PMCs supplanted a state. Asking PMCs to draft the rules which govern them—as has occurred in both the United States and Iraq[59]—falls far short of such a result, but also risks moving beyond appropriate industry consultation and invites blurring between the principal and the agent. PMCs rarely

---

[55] Compare Darren Hawkins and Wade Jacoby, Conceptualizing Agents as Important Actors: The Agent Side of Principal-Agent Theory, paper given at the Workshop *Delegation to International Organizations*, Weatherhead Center, Harvard University, 26 April 2003, 28–32; Darren Hawkins and Wade Jacoby, Why Agents Matter, paper given in the panel *Problems in State Delegation to International Organizations*. International Studies Association Meeting, Montreal, Canada, 19 March 2004, 15–17.

[56] Hawkins and Jacoby, 'Conceptualizing Agents' (n 55 above); PW Singer, *Corporate Warriors* (n 6 above) 164–6.   [57] Cockayne, 'Commercial Security' (n 5 above).

[58] AJ Venter, 'Privatising War,' manuscript on file with the author (detailing trials held by Colonel Roelf van Heerden of Executive Outcomes in the presence of tribal chiefs and elders).

[59] Jonathan Werve, 'Contractors Write the Rules: Army policy governing use of contractors omits intelligence restrictions,' Center for Public Integrity, 30 June 2004, available at <http://www.publicintegrity.org/wow/report.aspx?aid=334&sid=100>; David Isenberg, A Fistful of Contractors: The Case for a Pragmatic Assessment of Private Military Companies in Iraq, British American Security Information Council, Research Report 2004, September 2004, Washington DC, 35.

gain such a high level of control of law-making institutions, but instead rely on strategies playing off multiple principals to enlarge their slack.

The broad approach to principality adopted in this chapter means that PMCs in fact work almost constantly with multiple principals: their contractual client, their home state regulator, the host state regulator, and even others. These multiple principals in turn face three classic problems that PMCs can turn to their own benefit to enlarge slack: co-ordination, free-riding, and the need for a 'sociotropic' assessment rule.[60] In addition, these problems arise in a variety of configurations between multiple principals and a single PMC agent.

Problems for multiple principals

Multiple principals working with a single agent face three particular problems. First, multiple principals may compete to impose their own preferences on the agent, creating co-ordination costs, and allowing the agent to play principals off against each other.[61] The contending influence of multiple principals may lead to outcomes that none of them prefer.[62]

Secondly, even if their substantive preferences are co-ordinated, there will be competition amongst multiple principals *not* to bear the transaction costs associated with delegating, particularly monitoring and sanction costs. Every principal has an incentive to allow some other principal to bear those costs—that is, to free-ride. As a result, the agent is likely to be under-monitored, and able to increase her slack.[63]

Thirdly, where multiple principals join together to form a 'collective' principal, principal-agent theory suggests that an agent will only perform to the same level as it would with a single principal if the collective principal evaluates the agent's performance against some 'sociotropic' rule—a rule that measures the principal's individual well-being according to some socialized 'trope'.[64] Without such a 'trope', individual principals will assess agent performance against the provision of individual, rather than collective (or social) goods. This may be a particularly important problem in the context of *private* agents, because absent adequate incentives, private agents are likely to provide private goods, rather than public goods. Unless collective principals adopt a 'sociotropic rule' which measures agent performance against the provision of the public good—rather than satisfaction of their own individual interests—the agent is unlikely to provide that public good.

[60] Mona Lyne, Dan Nielson, and Michael Tierney, Principal Problems within International Organizations, paper prepared for workshop on Delegation to International Organization sponsored by the Radcliffe Institute at Harvard University, 13 December 2002, 18.

[61] Moe, 'The New Economics' (n 8 above) 768–9; B Douglas Bernheim and Michael D Whinston, 'Common Agency,' *Econometrica*, vol 54 (1986) 923.

[62] Lyne, Nielson and Tierney, 'Principal Problems' (n 60 above) 13–14.   [63] Ibid, 15.

[64] John Ferejohn, 'Incumbent Performance and Electoral Control,' *Public Choice*, vol 50 (1986) 5; Donald Kinder and DR Kiewiet, 'Sociotropic Politics,' *British Journal of Political Science*, vol 11 (1981) 129.

Configurations of multiple principals

Principals' preferences are not always independent: their relations with each other may affect their inputs to the agent's decision-making process. To date, most principal-agent literature addressing multiple principals assumes that preferences operate independently.[65] Three basic configurations between multiple principals and agents can be distinguished, referred to here as the hub-and-spoke, the chain, and the polygon.

In the hub-and-spoke configuration, an agent has a number of independent relations with different principals. In the chain configuration, the agent of the ultimate principal stands as a proximate principal to the next agent and so on. Thus, a national electorate stands as ultimate principal to a national legislature (its agent), which stands as a principal to a legislative committee (its agent), which stands as a principal to a bureaucratic agency (its agent). The preferences of the ultimate principal (the electorate) must be translated through a series of transactions, within each of which there is the potential for agency slack, before they reach the ultimate agent (the bureaucracy). Finally, in the polygon configuration, a chain closes up on itself, because the ultimate principal gains access to sources of information about or means of sanctioning the ultimate agent which are independent of the existing principal-agent chain. The most obvious example of such a relationship is the triangular organization of legitimate coercion within a democratic state: the electorate elects a government, which delegates power to the police—but the electorate monitors the police not only (or even primarily) through government reporting, but also through direct observation. Polygon configurations thus reduce agency slack—but at the price of increased monitoring costs for the ultimate principal. Moreover, third parties may play a key role in closing chains into polygons by providing ultimate principals with information about agent performance.

Implications for PMCs

With these analytical tools at our disposal, we can now turn to an investigation of the strategies PMCs use to maximize their agency slack when operating with multiple principals—and the limits of such strategies.

Hub-and-spoke configurations: free-riding and arbitrage problems

In a number of cases, PMC relations with principals appear to have been affected by free-riding and co-ordination problems confronting multiple principals.

In the mid-1990s in eastern Zaïre, UNHCR financed and equipped international military advisers, many seconded from national military contingents, to train and supervise Zaïrian armed forces guarding refugee camps following the Hutu refugee exodus from Rwanda. Reviews of the performance of these advisers

---

[65] Compare Mattli and Büthe, 'Global Private Governance' (n 16 above).

are mixed, with some suggesting that their lax supervision of security in the camps allowed the Interahamwe to re-establish social control and mount operations which ultimately destabilized the whole Great Lakes region.[66] With a number of principals (UNHCR, national governments, and the Zaïrian armed forces) involved in the establishment and operation of this commercial military group, it was open to each of them to pass the buck for the shortcomings of the group.

A similar buck-passing exercise occurred in early 2003, when a plane carrying four US contractors and one Colombian soldier was shot down over FARC territory in Colombia. Although the FARC called the three contractors it kept alive 'prisoners of war', the US government denied them such a status, calling them 'kidnapees'[67]—thus avoiding domestic legal obligations to secure their release. The Colombian and US governments both suggested it was the responsibility of the other government to secure the men's release, passing the buck on bearing the transaction costs associated with the contractors' service.

PMCs may also use the co-ordination problem to engage in regulatory arbitrage strategies. Different regulatory strategies in different jurisdictions allow PMCs to structure their operations to reduce their exposure to taxation, licensing controls, asset seizure and labour costs. When South Africa introduced a licensing regime in the late 1990s, Executive Outcomes (EO) dissolved into an informal network of local joint venture agreements between EO operators and local political and military figures, avoiding effective regulation. Most PMCs, however, will prefer *not* to dissolve their operations in this way, because of the investment they have sunk into the business and social networks which provide their comparative advantage, allowing them quickly and professionally to mount operations and because of a desire to continue working with the national militaries of the jurisdictions in which they are based.

Chain configurations: playing off multiple principals

In some cases, an ultimate principal's influence over a proximate principal may reduce the PMC's own room to manoeuvre, overriding the terms of the contract between the proximate principal and the PMC. In the Arms to Africa affair, Britain's dissatisfaction with Sandline's arms exports to Sierra Leone (apparently in contravention of British law and a Security Council arms embargo) forced the Sierra Leonean government to renege on its contract with Sandline. In Papua New Guinea, Sandline's agency discretion was reduced to zero when a *de facto* ultimate principal—in this case the Papua New Guinea armed forces—forced a change in the policy of Sandline's contractual principal, the national government.[68]

---

[66] Cockayne, 'Commercial Security' (n 5 above) 7.

[67] Avant, *Market for Force* (n 6 above) 233.

[68] S Dinnen, RJ May, and AJ Regan (eds), "Challenging the State: The Sandline Affair in Papua New Guinea," Canberra: Regime Change/Regime Maintenance Discussion Paper No 21, National Centre for Development Studies and Department of Political and Social Change, Research School of Pacific and Asian Studies, The Australian National University, 1997.

Yet in some situations the direction of influence reverses: proximate principals work with PMCs specifically in order to enlarge their own agency slack vis-à-vis the ultimate principal. This seems particularly prevalent in the turn by democratic executives to PMCs: by employing and deploying PMCs, rather than national militaries, national executives mask the extent and costs of overseas intervention. Principal-agent theory suggests principals will turn to agents in part to 'shift blame', particularly where the costs of their own poor performance outweigh the benefits of good performance, and where ultimate principals lack access to independent information about agent performance: both conditions which obtain in relation to foreign military expeditions. The risk is that elected officials will 'ceremonialize' democratic accountability mechanisms by relying excessively on PMCs.

In fact, the licensing regimes discussed above might all be interpreted as enlarging executive power at the expense of other arms of government and electoral accountability. In each of the licensing regimes discussed earlier, parliamentary oversight in particular is extremely weak: for example, in the United States, Congressional notification requirements are weakened by high quantitative thresholds, after-the-fact reporting requirements, and easy circumvention;[69] South Africa's Parliament is informed only once an export approval is granted and has no disapproval or even information-gathering powers;[70] Iraq's intra-governmental 'Oversight Committee' includes a judicial member, but no parliamentary involvement.[71]

The electoral benefits of executive use of PMCs are noted by a Pentagon official: 'The American public doesn't get quite as concerned when contractors are killed.'[72] Commercial suppliers have given US governments foreign policy options they probably would not otherwise have had if relying on US troops, such as intervention in Liberia and Croatia, allowing them repeatedly to exceed Congressionally-mandated troop ceilings.[73]

Outsourcing foreign military and security assistance activities to PMCs thus risks lowering a corporate veil over matters that were previously subject to public scrutiny: what was political and public becomes economic and private, with the result that the costs of military operations can be more easily externalized. The creation of a global market in military services alters foreign policy and domestic political processes, advantaging executives relative to legislatures, reducing transparency, and reducing the domestic political support required for foreign military expeditions.[74]

A polygon configuration? How litigation may socialize the market

Chain configurations allow proximate principals to enlarge slack at the expense of ultimate principals only until the ultimate principal accesses some independent

---

[69] 22 USC § 2776.   [70] Regulation of Foreign Military Assistance Act 1998 (SA), s 6.
[71] CPA Memo No 17 (n 34 above), s 8.
[72] Michael Duffy, 'When Private Armies Take to the Front Lines,' *Time*, World edition, 12 April 2004, 32.
[73] Carl A Buhler, 'When Contractors Deploy: A Guide for the Operational Commander,' Naval War College, Rhode Island, 8 February 2000, on file with the author, 4–5.
[74] Avant, *Market for Force* (n 6 above) 60, 68, 258.

monitoring or sanctioning mechanism, thereby closing the chain into a polygon. In the face of globalized civil society, media, and increasingly transnationalized legal argumentation, executives find that closure increasingly hard to avoid. Transnational NGOs serve as information providers and extra-territorial 'fire alarms';[75] but the key factor in transforming PMC regulation may turn out to be litigation.

Litigation is likely to come in the form of national prosecutors and private litigants seeking to enforce global public standards governing violence, including human rights, humanitarian law and international criminal law.[76] Enforcement is possible through national prosecutions,[77] but civil litigation in domestic courts may have quicker success, because of lower standards of proof than criminal prosecution, broader liability doctrines (particularly due diligence doctrines),[78] class actions, and broad remedies. In the United States, the Alien Tort Claims Act[79] and anti-racketeering legislation offer opportunities.[80] In the European Union, international human rights mechanisms are likely to play a key role.[81]

Activists and litigants currently applying ancillary and attributed liability to global arms transfers[82] will likely in time apply similar standards to global military service transfers, exploring issues of liability of government officials for PMC clients and PMC licensees under their 'effective control'. References to existing standards such as Geneva Convention obligations may also facilitate access to universal jurisdiction, reducing the protection offered PMCs by jurisdictional barriers, the commercial veil, and capital mobility. Nevertheless, jurisdictional barriers (such as sovereign immunity, act of state doctrine, and judicial deference to executives in foreign policy decision-making) and informational obstacles (such as Freedom of Information immunity) may make natural resource extractors, engineering and post-conflict reconstruction groups, and other private clients a more likely target for such litigation than states.

Private regulation may even occur outside the courtroom, through other forms of civil action, such as shareholder actions against PMCs and their corporate

[75] See Kal Raustiala, 'States, NGOs, and International Environmental Institutions,' *International Studies Quarterly*, vol 41 (1997) 719.
[76] See generally Alexis Kontos, ' "Private" security guards: Privatized force and State responsibility under international human rights law,' *Non-State Actors and International Law*, vol 4 (2005) 228–37.
[77] See BOFAXE, 'Prosecuting private contractors under US law for the mistreatment of detainees in Abu Ghraib,' No 272E, 17 May 2004, available at <http://www.ruhr-uni-bochum.de/lfhv/>.
[78] See FAFO and International Peace Academy, Business and International Crimes: Assessing the Liability of Business Entities for Grave Violations of International Law, FAFO Report 467, 2004, 26–7.
[79] Nathaniel Stinnett, 'Regulating the Privatization of War: How to Stop Private Military Firms from Committing Human Rights Abuses,' Boston College International & Comparative Law Review, vol 28 (2005), 211; Tina Garmon, 'Domesticating International Corporate Responsibility: Holding Private Military Firms Accountable under the Alien Tort Claims Act,' Tulane Journal of International & Comparative Law, vol 11 (2003), 325.
[80] See, eg, *Al Rawi et al v Titan Corp et al*, 05-CV-1165, United States District Court, District of Columbia, available at <http://www.cdi.org/news/law/Al-Rawi-v-Titan-Complaint.pdf> (9 June 2004).
[81] *Costello-Roberts v UK*, ECtHR, Series A, No 247C (1993), para. 27; *R (Al-Skeni and others) v Secretary of State for Defence* [2004] EWHEC 2911 (Admin), now on appeal.
[82] Alexandra Boivin, 'Complicity and Beyond: International Law and the Transfer of Small Arms and Light Weapons,' *International Review of the Red Cross*, no 859 (2005), 467–96.

clients.[83] This will be rare because of the high thresholds to success, particularly the co-ordination problems private shareholders face. But private actors may find support in unlikely places: the ICRC, for example, notes that the effect of its disapproval of specific conduct may in fact be stronger for a traded company than it would be for a state.[84]

Relying on the shadow of litigation as the driver for global regulation of PMCs contains numerous risks. In particular, private law may not be an adequate framework for addressing the long-term social costs of privately-ordered violence.[85] The remedies available to private actors, acting as public guardians, are likely to be narrowly framed and targeted, often relying on individual harms, individualized civil and criminal remedies, contractual enforcement, and the narrow terms of human rights or humanitarian law remedies. This provides limited scope for addressing long-term, social and strategic costs of the privatization of legitimate violence. In many cases, it will be the co-ordination costs resulting from fragmented regulatory arrangements which prevent private actors co-operating to reimpose on the market the externalized social costs of PMC activity. Regulatory harmonization will therefore be driven by those market players who have the most to gain from investing to overcome these transaction costs. Prominent among these benefits is the reduced risk associated with increased transparency and market stabilization—suggesting that insurers and PMC underwriters may be amongst those most likely to drive regulatory harmonization. Absent harmonized, socializing standards—or pressure for them from their clients and underwriters—PMCs may continue to point to free-rider problems as a justification for avoiding progressive unilateral action.[86] Regulatory fragmentation allows those actors that benefit from market opacity, including some of the largest PMC clients such as national executives, to resist improved regulation—which may threaten their own slack vis-à-vis their own ultimate principals. Consequently, serious harmonization of national PMC regulation seems unlikely absent a commercial lobby favouring global harmonization of PMC regulation. As we have seen, some PMCs favour harmonization for commercial reasons; but if litigation successfully targets national resource extractors, post-conflict reconstruction groups or other private clients, that lobby would likely develop more quickly and deeply.

If such a dynamic does emerge, it will have a number of remarkable features. It will serve to socialize the market, by reimposing the externalized social costs of PMC activity on the parties to the transaction giving rise to that activity. It would also, in a very rudimentary form, signal the direct assertion by citizens worldwide of their own ultimate principality in the global organization of legitimate violence;

---

[83] Stephen J Kobrin, 'Oil And Politics: Talisman Energy and Sudan,' New York University Journal of International Law and Politics, vol 36 (2004), 425.   [84] Author's interviews, July 2005.

[85] Clive Walker and Dave Whyte, 'Contracting Out War?: Private Military Companies, Law and Regulation in the United Kingdom,' International & Comparative Law Quarterly, vol 54 (2005) 689.

[86] Gilles Carbonnier, 'Corporate Responsibility and Humanitarian Action,' *International Review of the Red Cross*, no 844 (2001), 947–68.

in essence, this would represent a prototypical translation of the closed polygon configuration of accountability in the organization of legitimate violence in the state onto a global canvas. Equally remarkable, this system would give a role to private actors, alongside public actors, in regulating security services, as well as in providing them.

Towards hybrid regulatory harmonization?

The aim of this chapter has been to use the tools of principal-agent theory to think anew about the nature of the power wielded by PMCs, with a view to understanding how best they might be regulated, in particular through state and market regulation. This final section offers some brief policy conclusions focusing on how the regulation of PMCs may develop in the near future.

Three major factors are likely to drive regulatory harmonization in the coming years towards an internationalized hybrid model, combining state support with market incentives: trans-Atlantic industry consolidation; efforts by major British and US PMCs to improve their brand and drive out small operators by voluntarily surrendering to more stringent regulation signalling corporate social responsibility, in exchange for privileged access to US and British governmental revenues; and litigation by public prosecutors and private citizens (and other civil action such as shareholder actions) seeking to hold PMCs and their clients to international human rights, humanitarian law and international criminal law standards. Intergovernmental dialogue, such as the current Swiss-led initiative, as well as in other forums, such as the Council of Europe[87] and the Commonwealth of Independent States, will also push towards standardization of domestic due diligence obligations and linking PMCs into existing *jus in bello* enforcement mechanisms.

But regulatory fragmentation will persist, and likely continue to undermine public faith in the industry. One possibility that might help to secure long-term support for the industry would be to create an independent regulator, funded by PMCs, with significant screening, institutional checking, monitoring, and sanctioning powers delegated to it by multiple states. A single-state version of such an arrangement may already be in the pipeline in Britain, in the form of the BAPSC. In time, the BAPSC may work with its US counterpart, the IPOA, to harmonize or even merge their self-regulation models.[88] The larger global PMCs might see many benefits in such a move: reduced administrative costs, the promotion of industry consolidation, the increased barriers to entry for small players, and possibly increased public support—particularly if a transatlantic arrangement could secure backing

---

[87] Parliamentary Assembly of the Council of Europe, Democratic Oversight of the Security Sector in Member States, Report of the Political Affairs Committee, Doc 10567, 2 June 2005, para 10.
[88] Author's interviews, July 2005.

from the United States, Britain or even the European Union or NATO as a quality assurance mechanism. Others involved in the market, notably PMC clients, financiers—and especially insurers—would also reap benefits, including reduced risk, lowered transaction costs, and increased transparency.

Conclusion

This chapter has focused on how principal-agent analysis might improve our understanding of the regulation of PMCs. But it may also be of utility in a broader attempt to understand the changing organization of violence in contemporary global society. As Deborah Avant has commented, too much focus on whether we should regulate PMCs through state- or market-based solutions—whether we should make or buy public security—may lead us to 'miss what may be globalization's most important effects—changes in the practice of statehood'[89]—or, to put it another way, the changing organization of legitimate violence.

The analysis given here may offer some insights into the risks and opportunities posed in particular by the rising role of private authority in organizing legitimate violence. Private governance may, in some circumstances, risk breaking open the closed polygon of regulatory control present in states governed by the rule of law, creating opportunities for agents to maximize slack at the expense of ultimate principals. The implications in the case of private control of the production and distribution of security, particularly for already weak states, may be grave: access to security may become a product of purchasing power or social entitlement—not a legal right. Access to security—and even, in extreme cases, law-making power—risk becoming even more a matter of cash, capital, class, clan, club, creed, or colour, rather than citizenship, than they are in today's states. The significant presence of non-state, non-rational forms of authority in the supply chains that allow PMCs to deliver security and military services, particularly in Africa, may risk deepening the neopatrimonial tinge of much organized violence in weak states.

Yet the analysis here also points to ways that proxy action by third parties may help make PMCs—and their state clients—socially responsible, reimposing externalized social costs on private transactions organizing violence. This, in turn, may spur governments to work with market players to provide effective, hybrid, transnational regulation. The regulation of commercially organized violence will, just like its production and distribution, become the product of a hybrid state-market model: partially made, and partially bought.

---

[89] Avant, *Market for Force* (n 6 above) 258.

12

Contract as a tool for regulating private military companies

Laura A Dickinson

As a number of the essays in this volume make clear, private military companies (PMCs) do not inhabit a complete regulatory void, but rather operate in an environment regulated by a complex array of existing international and domestic legal provisions. Nevertheless, there can be little doubt that the increasing use of private military contractors does at least challenge the current international and transnational legal framework. For example, ambiguities persist as to the extent to which certain public law commitments, such as the international law prohibition on official torture,[1] apply to contractors because they are, at least nominally, non-state actors. In response to this challenge, scholarly and policy work focusing on military privatization has mostly emphasized the possible role of transnational litigation,[2] domestic and international licensing schemes,[3] treaty reform,[4] and industry self-regulation.[5] Yet, few scholars have homed in on the regulatory potential

[1] See Convention Against Torture and Other Cruel, Inhuman, or Degrading Treatment or Punishment, art 1 (defining torture as certain activities designed to inflict pain or suffering when such 'pain or suffering is inflicted by or at the instigation of or with the consent or acquiescence of a public official or other person acting in an official capacity'). Of course, this international 'state action' requirement can be challenged on a number of grounds. See, eg, Jordan J Paust, 'Human Rights Responsibilities of Private Corporations,' Vanderbilt Journal of Transnational Law, vol 35 (2002) 801ff; see also Laura A Dickinson, 'Public Law Values in a Privatized World,' Yale Journal of International Law, vol 31 (2006) 394ff (summarizing arguments that international 'state action' requirement is minimal).

[2] See, eg, Tina Garmon, 'Domesticating International Corporate Responsibility: Holding Private Military Firms Accountable Under the Alien Tort Claims Act,' Tulsa Journal of International and Comparative Law, vol 11 (2003) 325ff. Victims of abuse by contractors at Abu Ghraib prison in Iraq have brought suit under the Alien Tort Claims Act. See, eg, *Ibrahim v Titan Corp et al*, 04-cv-01248 (DDC 2004); *Al Rawi v Titan Corp et al*, 04-cv-1143 (SD Ca 2004).

[3] See, eg, chapter two in this volume by Kevin O'Brien; Juan Carlos Zarate, 'The Emergence of a New Dog of War: Private International Security Companies, International Law, and the New World Disorder,' Stanford Journal of International Law, vol 34 (1998) 75ff; see also PW Singer, *Corporate Warriors: The Rise of the Privatized Military Industry* (Ithaca: Cornell University Press, 2003).

[4] See, eg, Todd S Milliard, 'Overcoming Post-Colonial Myopia: A Call to Recognize and Regulate Private Military Companies,' Military Law Review, vol 176 (2003) 1ff.

[5] See, eg, chapter thirteen in this volume by Andrew Bearpark and Sabrina Schulz; see also International Peace Operations Association (IPOA) Code of Conduct, available at <http://ipoaonline.org/php/index.php?option=com_content&task=view&id=100&Itemid=109>.

of the government contracts themselves.[6] Contracts are, however, the vehicle of military privatization, and as such they could carry what we might call the norms and values of public international law into the 'private' sector.

I have argued elsewhere that there are many ways in which PMCs, government officials, and non-governmental organizations seeking to prevent military contractors from committing abuses can use governmental contracts to incorporate crucial public law values, including human rights, transparency, and anti-corruption norms.[7] Contracts could be drafted to explicitly extend relevant norms of public international law to private contractors, provide for enhanced oversight and enforcement, and include more specific terms such as carefully drafted training and accreditation requirements. Further, my analysis has drawn on insights from the scholarly literature on the long-standing trend within the United States to privatize domestic governmental functions, such as prison management, healthcare, welfare, and education.[8] In each of these contexts, scholars have noted efforts to incorporate various substantive and procedural accountability mechanisms into privatization contracts and I have argued that similar provisions could be included in contracts with PMCs.

This chapter explores the numerous objections that policymakers and scholars might make to such contractual provisions. To be sure, because few commentators have focused specifically on the role that contract might play in the arena of military privatization, no one has yet articulated a comprehensive set of objections. Nonetheless, it is possible to extrapolate from the debates about privatization in the domestic context. Drawing on those debates, I identify six objections to the idea of reforming contracts so as to make them a more effective tool for regulatory oversight. Critics might argue that: (1) reforming contracts is unnecessary because industry self-regulation or other non-governmental measures are more effective; (2) reforming contracts would be a costly venture that would eat up any cost savings from privatization; (3) neither government officials nor PMCs are likely to agree to such reforms; (4) the structure of the private military contractor market itself undermines the prospects of successful contractual regulation; (5) reforms that grant rights to third parties either to participate in contract design or to file grievances would be unwieldy; or (6) terms in governmental contracts are difficult to enforce, and expanding enforcement to include third parties would be impossible to manage. Each of these objections will be considered in turn, along with a

---

[6] One scholar who has is Steve Schooner, a government contracts expert who has identified problems in the Iraq military and reconstruction contracts. See Steven L Schooner, 'Contractor Atrocities at Abu Ghraib: Compromised Accountability in a Streamlined, Outsourced Government,' Stanford Law and Policy Review, vol 16 (2005) 549ff. Schooner has not, however, focused specifically on how contracts could be used to protect human rights.

[7] See Dickinson, 'Public Law Values in a Privatized World' (n 1 above).

[8] See, eg, Jody Freeman, 'The Private Role in Public Governance,' New York University Law Review, vol 75 (2000) 543 ff; Gillian Metzger, 'Privatization as Delegation,' Columbia Law Review, vol 103 (2003) 1367 ff.

response supporting both the viability and desirability of contractual provisions as a means of regulating PMC conduct.

The necessity of contractual reform

A number of commentators have suggested that self-regulation by the industry is likely to control PMCs more effectively than governmentally-imposed reforms of the contracting process or other measures. Deborah Avant, for example, would eschew most types of regulation other than efforts to professionalize the culture of PMC employees.[9] Andrew Bearpark and Sabrina Schulz, while potentially supporting a variety of mechanisms of control at the national level, argue in favour of industry self-regulation as the most viable means of curbing contractor abuses, at least in the near term.[10]

The current contractual framework is so ineffective, however, as examples from the US-led military and reconstruction efforts in Iraq demonstrate, that contractual reform must be part of any comprehensive oversight regime. In addition to violating human rights, Iraq contractors have also been implicated in fraud and other financial abuses. For example, Kellogg, Brown & Root's more than $10 billion in contracts with the US government in Iraq 'have been dogged by charges of preferential treatment, over-billing, cost overruns, and waste'.[11] Perhaps even more egregious was Custer Battles, a company that had received two $16 million contracts from the US Agency for International Development (USAID) to provide security for the Baghdad airport and distribute Iraqi dinars. Custer Battles employees reportedly chartered a flight to Beirut with $10 million in dinars in their luggage, set up sham Cayman Islands subsidiaries to submit invoices, and regularly overcharged for materials—in one case allegedly billing the United States $10 million for materials that it purchased for $3.5 million.[12] A jury issued a $10 million verdict against Custer Battles in connection with such abuses.[13] In a similar case, former

---

[9] See chapter ten in this volume by Deborah Avant.

[10] See chapter thirteen in this volume by Andrew Bearpark and Sabrina Schulz.

[11] Warren Hoge, 'UN Criticizes Iraq Occupation Oil Sales,' *New York Times*, 15 December 2004. In addition, the chief contracting officer for the Army Corps of Engineers has publicly accused the Army of granting preferential treatment to KBR (through its parent company, Halliburton) in awarding contracts in Iraq and the Balkans, in violation of US contracting regulations. Erik Eckholm, 'A Top US Contracting Official for the Army Calls for an Inquiry in the Halliburton Case,' *New York Times*, 25 October 2004.

[12] See 'Waste, Fraud, and Abuse in US Government Contracting in Iraq: Hearing Before the S Democratic Policy Comm,' 109th Cong 10 (2005) [hereinafter SDPC Hearing] 1–2 (statement of Alan Grayson).

[13] The suit was brought as a private enforcement action under the Federal False Claims Act, 31 USC § 3730 (2000). See Yochai J Dreazen, 'Attorney Pursues Iraq Contractor Fraud,' *Wall Street Journal*, 19 April 2006 (discussing the suit). In March 2006 a jury ordered Custer Battles to return $10 million in ill-gotten funds to the government. See ibid. Yet, though the district court judge in that case had permitted the suit to proceed, *United States ex rel DRC, Inc v Custer Battles*, LLC, 376 F Supp 2d 617 (E D Va 2005), it is unclear whether the verdict will ultimately hold up on appeal and whether such False Claims Act suits will be deemed sustainable in this context.

US occupation official Robert J Stein has pleaded guilty to charges of corruption and bribery in the award of reconstruction contracts.[14] Army reserve officers have also been arrested and indicted for charges in related proceedings, and a US businessman, Philip Bloom, has pleaded guilty to charges of conspiracy and money laundering.[15] At the core of the inquiry, prosecutors say, was a scheme in which Stein and other officials steered at least $8.6 million in reconstruction contracts to companies controlled by Bloom, in exchange for millions of dollars in bribes, jewellery and other favours.[16] Stein also pleaded guilty to federal weapons charges for having used the money to buy submachine guns, grenade launchers and other weapons in the United States. Investigators suspect that there may be a link between these cases and the death of human rights worker Fern Holland and press officer Robert Zangas.[17] Moreover, all indications are that the corruption that has come to light so far is only the tip of the iceberg. In short, corruption and fraud have been rampant in Iraq.

The existing governmental contracts have clearly not prevented these abuses. A careful examination of such agreements both highlights their deficiencies and at the same time suggests possible reforms. In a recent study, for example, I examined all publicly available Iraq military and reconstruction contracts entered into by the US government, and compared them to agreements between local state government contracts involving roughly analogous domestic governmental functions, such as prison management.[18] In contrast to the domestic agreements, the Iraq contracts are strikingly vague. And though some flexibility is undoubtedly necessary to cope with the exigencies and security concerns inherent in the sorts of environments where PMCs are likely to be used, the foreign affairs contracts (at least those that are publicly available) possess so few guidelines, requirements, or benchmarks that they effectively contain no meaningful evaluative criteria whatsoever. Drawing on the lessons from the domestic setting, these contracts could be reformed in a number of ways that would have a significant impact. Specifically, the contracts could resolve any lingering ambiguity about the applicability of international human rights and humanitarian law, include more specific terms, such as training and accreditation requirements, and provide for enhanced monitoring, oversight, and enforcement.

Making human rights and humanitarian law apply

Perhaps most importantly, the contracts could explicitly require that the contractors obey the norms that implement public law values. The terms of each agreement could provide that private contractors must abide by relevant human rights

---

[14] James Glanz, 'Two Years Later, Slayings in Iraq and Lost Cash are Mysteries,' *New York Times*, 9 May 2006.   [15] Ibid.
[16] Ibid.   [17] Ibid.
[18] See Dickinson, 'Public Law Values in a Privatized World' (n 1 above).

and humanitarian law rules applicable to governmental actors. Such contractual terms would obviate the need to show that the private actors were functioning as an extension of government so as to satisfy any state action requirement that might arise under domestic or international legal regimes. Instead, the norms applicable to governmental actors would simply be part of the contractual terms, enforceable like any other provisions, regardless of state action.

While such provisions are commonplace in the domestic setting,[19] the US government's military and foreign aid contracts in Iraq are woefully inadequate. To be sure, a 2005 Department of Defense (DOD) document providing general instructions regarding contracting practices does state that contractors 'shall abide by applicable laws, regulations, DOD policy, and international agreements'.[20] Nevertheless, of the sixty publicly available Iraq contracts,[21] none contains specific provisions requiring contractors to obey human rights, anti-corruption, or transparency norms.

The agreements between the US government and CACI to supply military interrogators starkly illustrate this point. The intelligence personnel were hired pursuant to a standing 'blanket purchase agreement' between the Department of the Interior and CACI, negotiated in 2000.[22] Under such an agreement the procuring agency need not request specific services at the time the agreement is made but rather may enter task orders as the need arises. In 2003 eleven task orders, worth $66.2 million, were submitted (none of which was the result of competitive bidding).[23] The orders specify only that CACI would provide interrogation support and analysis work for the US Army in Iraq, including 'debriefing of personnel, intelligence report writing, and screening/interrogation of detainees at established holding areas.'[24] Significantly, the orders do not expressly require that the private contractor interrogators comply with international human rights or humanitarian law rules such as those contained in the Torture Convention or the Geneva Conventions. Drafting contracts to include such provisions is an easy and obvious reform.

Making contractual terms more specific and requiring accreditation

The contracts with private military contractors could also include more specific terms. For example, contracts could explicitly require contractor-employees to

---

[19] As a term in their contracts with privately run prisons, for example, many states require compliance with constitutional, federal, state, and private standards for prison operation and inmates' rights.

[20] US Department of Defense Instruction, No 3020.41, § 6.1 (3 October 2005).

[21] See Center for Public Integrity, Contracts and Reports, available at <http://publicintegrity.org/wow/resources.aspx?act=resources> [hereinafter Contracts and Reports] (providing text of contracts).

[22] See Agreement Between the Department of the Interior and CACI Premier Technology, Inc, No NBCHA010005 (2004), available at <http://publicintegrity.org/docs/wow/CACI_ordersAll.pdf> [hereinafter DOI-CACI].

[23] Work Orders Nos 000035/0004, 000036/0004, 000037/0004, 000038/0004, 000064/0004, 000067/0004, 000070/0004, 000071/0004, 000072/0004, 000073/0004, & 000080/0004, issued under DOI-CACI (ibid), available at <http://publicintegrity.org/docs/wow/CACI_ordersAll.pdf>.

[24] Work Order No 000071/0004 (ibid).

receive training in international human rights and humanitarian law. Domestic contracts in the United States between state governments and private prison operators regularly include such terms.[25] Yet, while the 2005 DOD instructions require documentation of training concerning appropriate use of force,[26] none of the publicly available Iraq contracts appears to require such training. Indeed, although a few of the agreements require that contractors hire employees with a certain number of years' experience,[27] none specifies that the contractor must provide any particular training at all. Thus, it is not surprising that an Army Inspector General report on the conditions that led to the Abu Ghraib scandal concluded that 35 percent of CACI's Iraqi interrogators did not even have any 'formal training in military interrogation policies and techniques', let alone training in international law norms.[28]

Similarly, contracts might lay out more specific performance benchmarks. In the domestic context, commentators and policymakers have long urged that contracts include benchmarks, and rigorous performance standards regularly appear in contracts.[29] For example, under the model contract for private prison management drafted by the Oklahoma Department of Corrections, contractors must meet such delineated standards for security, meals, and education.[30]

In contrast, the Iraq contracts are again woefully inadequate. Indeed, it is striking that, of the publicly available Iraq contracts for military services, not one contains clear benchmarks or output requirements. For example, a contract between the US government and Military Resources Professionals Incorporated (MPRI) to provide translators for government personnel, including interrogators, simply provides that the contractors will supply interpreters.[31] The agreement says nothing about whether the interpreters must be effective or how effectiveness might be measured. Similarly, the CACI task orders for interrogators specify only that

[25] A standard term in state agreements with companies that manage private prisons, for example, requires companies to certify that the training they provide to personnel is comparable to that offered to state employees. See, eg, Oklahoma Department of Corrections, 'Correctional Services Contract' § 6.4, (on file with author) [hereinafter Oklahoma Contract]; Florida Corrections Privatization Commission, 'Correctional Services Contract with Corrections Corporation of America' § 6.5 [hereinafter Florida Contract].   [26] DOD Instruction (n 20 above), § 6.3.5.3.4.

[27] See, eg, Work Order No 000071/0001 (n 24 above), (requiring that human intelligence advisors must have at least ten years of experience and must be 'knowledgeable of Army/Joint Interrogation procedures'). Notably, this work order does not require the contractor to provide any training.

[28] US Department of the Army, Inspector General, 'Detainee Operations Inspection' (2004), pp. 87–89, available at <http://www4.army.mil/ocpa/reports/ArmyIGDetaineeAbuse/DAIG%20Detainee%20Operations%20Inspection%20Report.pdf>.

[29] See, eg, Harry P Hatry, Urban Inst, 'Performance Measurement: Getting Results' (1999) 3–10 (1999). Scholars have argued that, ideally, performance-based contracts should 'clearly spell out the desired end result' but leave the choice of method to the contractor, who should have 'as much freedom as possible in figuring out how to best meet government's performance objective.' William D Eggers, *Performance-Based Contracting: Designing State-of-the-Art Contract Administration and Monitoring Systems* (Los Angeles: Reason Public Policy Institute, 1997) 2.

[30] See, eg, Oklahoma Contract (n 25 above) § 5.

[31] Agreement Between DOD and MPRI, 'Iraq Interpreters,' No GS-23F-9814H (Apr 28, 2003), available at <http://publicintegrity.org/docs/wow/MPRI_Linguists.pdf>.

CACI will provide interrogation support and analysis work for the US Army in Iraq, including 'debriefing of personnel, intelligence report writing, and screening/interrogation of detainees at established holding areas'.[32] Other than these broad goals, the task orders say little more. To be sure, security imperatives may sometimes require some degree of vagueness. Nonetheless, the task orders could be much more specific about training requirements, standards of conduct, supervision, and performance parameters.

Furthermore, contracts could require that independent organizations accredit military contractors. Industry organizations have in fact begun to do so. In chapter thirteen of this volume Andrew Bearpark and Sabrina Schulz describe such an initiative in Britain.[33] The International Peace Operations Association (IPOA), another industry-based organization, has launched a similar effort.[34] Independent organizations without industry ties could establish a rating system as well. Yet amazingly, not one of the available contracts for aid or military services in Iraq requires that the entities receiving the contracts be vetted or accredited by independent organizations.

On this score, the domestic context provides a particularly rich set of models as to how an accreditation scheme might work. For example, in the healthcare field, state laws or contractual terms often specify that health maintenance organizations (HMOs) must receive accreditation by the National Committee for Quality Assurance (NCQA), an independent non-profit organization, before receiving public funding. Until recently, NCQA certification was primarily voluntary, offering HMOs an advantage when competing for contracts.[35] When states became managed care purchasers, however, they adopted NCQA as a benchmark of quality.[36] Similarly, many contracts with private prison operators require companies to receive accreditation by the American Correctional Association.[37] And because private investors come to view accreditation as an indicator of quality, an accreditation requirement creates significant compliance incentives.

Enhancing oversight

The Iraq contracts also fall far short in the arena of monitoring and enforcement.[38] It should go without saying that any effective contractual regime must include

---

[32] Work Order No 000071/0004 (n 24 above) 6.

[33] See chapter thirteen in this volume by Andrew Bearpark and Sabrina Schulz.

[34] See, eg, International Peace Operations Association Code of Conduct, (n 5 above).

[35] Although NCQA's accreditation programme is voluntary, almost half the HMOs in the nation, covering three quarters of all HMO enrolees, are currently involved in the NCQA Accreditation process. Significantly, employers increasingly require or request NCQA accreditation of the plans with which they do business. See National Comm for Quality Assurance, NCQA: Overview, available at <http://www.ncqa.org/Communications/Publications/overviewncqa.pdf>.

[36] Freeman, 'The Private Role in Public Governance' (n 8 above) 618–19.

[37] See, eg, Oklahoma Contract (n 25 above).

[38] For a searing indictment of the government's failure to oversee military contractors and that failure's role in the Abu Ghraib atrocities, see Schooner, 'Contractor Atrocities at Abu Ghraib' (n 6 above).

sufficient numbers of trained and experienced governmental contract monitors, along with a team of governmental ombudspersons: leaders of independent offices charged with providing enhanced oversight. Recently the government has moved in precisely the wrong direction, however, by dramatically *reducing* its acquisitions workforce.[39] And few contract monitors are trained in international human rights and humanitarian law standards.

An added problem is the prevalence of broad, standing purchase agreements, which agencies can use as a basis for issuing work orders. The use of such work orders enables government actors to avoid more stringent regulations that apply to negotiating contracts. In addition, because one agency can earn fees by facilitating another agency's contracts, there are incentives to sponsor other agencies' contracts but little incentive to supervise them.[40] These arrangements can lead to abuse, as occurred in the case of the Department of the Interior sponsorship of DOD's task orders for intelligence services at Abu Ghraib.

In addition, contracts should include terms allowing the government to take over contracts by degrees for failure to observe international human rights and humanitarian law norms. In the domestic context, states are turning to mechanisms such as graduated penalties, for example, to increase oversight of private nursing homes receiving public funding.[41] Although many of the US Iraq contracts do have termination provisions, outright termination is an extreme measure that the government rarely exercises. Indeed, after CACI employees were implicated in the abuse at Abu Ghraib, not only did government actors fail to terminate the contract, they actually *expanded* its terms. Graduated takeover provisions would help alleviate the problem by permitting a more moderate remedy short of outright termination.

Perhaps even more importantly, contracts should provide for enhanced whistleblower protections and third-party suit provisions. Currently, only the government or the contractor may enforce the terms of the agreement. Yet those who are subject to a contractor security action should be deemed third-party beneficiaries, either by statute or through contractual terms. Accordingly, third parties would be able to make private law claims under the contracts for non-compliance with international human rights and humanitarian law norms. Claims could be heard and adjudicated in courts or, alternatively, through grievance procedures established and run either by the contractor itself or by a professional association of contractors. Such privatized grievance mechanisms are commonplace in contracts

---

[39] Comptroller Gen, US General Accounting Office (GAO), Sourcing and Acquisition, Rep No GAO-03-771R (2003) 1; see also Laura Peterson, 'Outsourcing Government: Service Contracting Has Risen Dramatically in the Last Decade,' 30 October 2003, available at <http://publicintegrity.org/wow/report.aspx?aid=68>. For a detailed discussion of the depletion of the acquisition workforce, see David A Whiteford, 'Negotiated Procurements: Squandering the Benefit of the Bargain,' Public Contractor Law Journal, vol 32 (2003) 555–57.

[40] Schooner, 'Contractor Atrocities at Abu Ghraib' (n 6 above) 564–70.

[41] Freeman, 'The Private Role in Public Governance' (n 8 above) 608.

with private prison operators[42] or HMOs receiving federal funding to cover their treatment of Medicare beneficiaries.[43] And though, as discussed below, critics might worry that granting such rights might be unwieldy, third-party beneficiary provisions could be crafted to take account of the exigencies of various types of contracts.

These various reforms provide a menu of possible contractual provisions that, while by no means a panacea, would almost certainly improve the meagre contractual oversight that now exists. Thus, to argue that reforms are unnecessary or that they would inevitably be ineffectual lacks empirical support. And in any event, given the widespread abuses in the current contracting process, settling for the status quo is simply not a viable option.

The cost of reform

A second critique of contractual regulation is to cite the cost of contractual reform. One of the central rationales for privatizing governmental functions is the savings that privatization promises, although the extent to which privatization actually does result in such savings is not fully understood. Certainly there is some empirical work, particularly on domestic services such as prison management, that supports claims of cost-cutting.[44] Such savings may accrue because contractors are free from expensive civil service requirements. Indeed, proponents of military privatization have emphasized that freedom from such requirements enables greater 'nimbleness'.[45] And while contractors may earn more for a particular job, their pay is typically for a shorter term. They can be mobilized quickly on the front end and terminated quickly on the back end. Some proponents of privatization thus might argue that enhanced contractual requirements, such as human rights training provisions, self-evaluation, and accreditation would be costly ventures that would essentially re-bureaucratize the privatized work force, undermining the flexibility of private contractors and potentially reducing or even eliminating the very cost savings that provide the principal justification for privatization in the first place.[46]

---

[42] For examples of contracts with private operators that require grievance procedures, see Florida Contract (n 25 above), § 5.24; Oklahoma Contract (n 25 above), § 5.15.

[43] 42 USC § 1395mm(c)(5)(A) (2000).

[44] See, eg, Oliver Hart, Andrei Shleifer, and Robert W Vishny, 'The Proper Scope of Government: Theory and an Application to Prisons,' *Quarterly Journal of Economics*, vol 112 (1997) 1143 (claiming that their model 'explains why in some—arguably most—cases, private provision leads to both lower costs and higher quality'); see also Jody Freeman, 'Extending Public Law Norms through Privatization,' Harvard Law Review, vol 116 (2000) 1295–301 (summarizing pragmatic arguments that privatizing domestic services cuts costs).

[45] See Martha Minow, 'Outsourcing Power: How Privatizing Military Efforts Challenges Accountability, Professionalism, and Democracy,' Boston College Law Review, vol 46 (2005) 1004 (discussing nimbleness argument of military privatization proponents).

[46] For a comparable argument in the domestic prison privatization context, see Sharon Dolovitch, 'State Punishment and Private Prisons,' Duke Law Journal, vol 55 (2006) 437ff.

It is far from clear, however, that the costs of reforms would outweigh the savings they might generate, as there is a high price for *not* implementing some of the proposals suggested above. The argument that increased contractual requirements necessarily increase costs requires more empirical study, but at this point we do have evidence that the *failure* to incorporate certain requirements imposes hefty costs. Perhaps most notably, poor monitoring and oversight lead to corruption and waste that is itself quite expensive. Contractual terms that mandate comprehensive outside monitoring and require contractors to engage in self-evaluation, combined with increased resources for monitors, can therefore result in savings down the line.

The Iraq case provides some clear examples of the costs that arise from the failure to engage in serious contractual monitoring. As former Coalition Provisional Authority (CPA) official Alan Grayson has observed, 'contracts were made that were mistakes, and were poorly, if at all, supervised [and] money was spent that could have been saved, if we simply had the right numbers of people'.[47] Grayson has asserted that lack of employee screening and training, combined with poor government contract monitor oversight, led to the theft of millions of dollars.[48] Indeed, with regard to the Custer Battles fiasco described earlier, another former CPA official has argued that even devoting a single staff person to the two $16 million Custer Battles contracts would have saved at least $4 million.[49] The various other corruption examples described previously have cost US taxpayers further millions of dollars.

Moreover, government reports suggest that the abuses that have come to light are not isolated instances but rather stem from systematic problems in oversight and monitoring. A recent DOD Inspector General study concluded that more than half of the Iraq contracts had not been adequately monitored.[50] This fact is not surprising given that DOD reduced its acquisition workforce by more than half between 1990 and 2001, while the department's contracting workload increased by more than twelve per cent.[51] In addition, those who were assigned to monitor contract performance were often inadequately trained.[52] Indeed, in an ironic twist, private contractors themselves are often hired to write the procedural rules governing contracting rules and monitoring protocols: the DOD handbook on the contracting process, for example, was drafted by one of its principal military contractors.[53] Similarly, with respect to the CPA, a report notes that the CPA

[47] SDPC Hearing (n 12 above) (statement of Franklin Willis).
[48] Ibid (testimony of Alan Grayson).   [49] Ibid (statement of Franklin Willis).
[50] Office of the Inspector Gen, US DOD, 'Acquisitions: Contracts Awarded for the Coalition Provisional Authority by the Defense Contracting Command—Washington,' Report No D-2004-057 (2004), 24.
[51] GAO, 'Sourcing and Acquisition,' Rep No GAO-03-771R (2003), 1; see also Peterson, 'Outsourcing Government' (n 39 above). For a detailed discussion of the depletion of the acquisition workforce, see David A Whiteford, 'Negotiated Procurements: Squandering the Benefit of the Bargain,' Public Contractor Law Journal, vol 32 (2003), 555–7.   [52] Ibid.
[53] See Singer, *Corporate Warriors* (n 3 above) 123–4.

had not kept accounts for the hundreds of millions of dollars of cash in its vault, had awarded contracts worth billions of dollars to American firms without tender, and had no idea what was happening to the money from the Development Fund for Iraq, which was being spent by the interim Iraqi government ministries.[54] Thus, a strong case can be made that better monitoring and other contractual reforms would actually save far more money than they would cost.

Perhaps even more significantly, failure to implement contractual reforms can lead to human rights abuses that result in enormous costs, both economic and non-economic, that are difficult to measure but that impose serious liabilities on the government. The role of CACI and Titan in the torture and cruel treatment of prisoners at Abu Ghraib is just one example. The government has now tried a number of uniformed personnel for abuses at Abu Ghraib in proceedings that taxpayers must fund. If the Abu Ghraib victims succeed in their ATCA suits against CACI and Titan, either in court or in an out-of-court settlement, the litigation's costs presumably would ultimately be passed on to the government in higher contract fees. Indeed, even the fear of such litigation may result in expenses that companies such as CACI and Titan may factor into their bids. Beyond these economic costs, human rights abuse scandals cost the government untold amounts in reputation. These reputational losses impede the ability of diplomats to pursue not only human rights policies such as eradicating torture around the world in countries such as China, but also in building coalitions with other countries to engage in cooperative efforts—from trade to fighting terrorism.[55]

Rebecca Weiner has recently sought to identify, and to some degree quantify, many of the costs of military outsourcing.[56] She emphasizes that the general 'indefinite quantity/indefinite cost' framework of many of the contracts, in which contractors can simply charge the government a certain percentage above the price to them of the services they perform, has been quite expensive for the government (and for taxpayers). She also notes that insurance and workers' compensation are hidden costs not usually factored into the price tag for outsourcing. Contract reform might reduce some of these costs.

Finally, the privatization of domestic functions, such as prisons and healthcare, provides some evidence that contractual reforms do not eat up all of the cost savings of privatization. Indeed, state governments in the United States have long implemented many of the contractual reforms discussed above, which suggests that even with such reforms contracting remains cost-effective. For example, state governments' contracts with companies that manage private prisons routinely

---

[54] Ed Harriman, 'Where Has All the Money Gone?' *London Review of Books*, 7 July 2005.

[55] Cf Brief of Amicus Curiae Diplomats Morton Abramowitz, et al, *McCarver v North Carolina*, No 00-8727 (US Supreme Court, filed 8 June 2001), 8–9 (arguing that executing mentally retarded defendants strains diplomatic relations with allies, provides diplomatic ammunition to countries with demonstrably worse human rights records, increases US diplomatic isolation, and impairs other US foreign policy interests).

[56] Rebecca Ulam Weiner, 'Incorporating the Combat Zone: An Overview of the Military Service Provider Industry' (unpublished paper on file with the author).

require compliance with constitutional norms of human dignity, as well as training regarding these norms equivalent to the training state prison guards would receive. Similarly, state governments' contracts with HMOs routinely require accreditation, self-evaluation, and private grievance mechanisms for patients who believe they were not treated fairly. Thus, while much more research quantifying the costs of privatization is necessary, it is difficult to argue that contractual reform would necessarily eliminate all of the cost savings that may accrue.

Government and contractor resistance

A third critique of contractual reforms is that neither governments nor contractors would adopt them. Indeed, with respect to governmental actors, critics might claim that governments engage in privatization generally, and military privatization in particular, precisely to *avoid* the legal commitments that bind bureaucratic actors. According to this view, the US government used contractor interrogators and translators at Abu Ghraib prison in order to escape potential accountability for abuses. With respect to the contractors, critics might maintain that PMCs would not agree to more onerous contractual terms because the companies would view these measures as too expensive and cumbersome.

For both sets of actors, however, substantial evidence actually points in the opposite direction. To be sure, more research is needed to understand the motivations of governments' privatization decisions as well as the interests of contractors. But there is certainly a case to be made that government actors and contractors would not be nearly as reluctant to embrace these reforms as critics have supposed.

Government actors

To begin with, the argument that governments privatize to avoid accountability runs into some difficulties because government actors do not necessarily escape responsibility merely by outsourcing particular tasks. As Chia Lehnardt argues in chapter eight of this volume, while some existing ambiguities might enable contractors to slip through certain cracks in international law, contractors do not exist in a regulatory void.[57] In particular, the UN's Articles on Responsibility of States for Internationally Wrongful Acts aims to make clear that the 'conduct of any State organ shall be considered an act of that State under international law,' and that a person's conduct shall be attributed to the state if he or she is acting on the state's instructions or under the state's direction.[58] Likewise, courts and tribunals have at

---

[57] See chapter eight in this volume by Chia Lehnardt; see also Laura A Dickinson, 'Government for Hire: Privatizing Foreign Affairs and the Problem of Accountability Under International Law,' William & Mary Law Review, vol 47 (2005) 135ff.

[58] See, eg, Draft Articles on Responsibility of States for Internationally Wrongful Acts, arts. 4, 8, in International Law Commission, Report of the International Law Commission on the Work of Its Fifty-Third Session, UN Doc A/56/10 (2001).

times applied principles of state responsibility for instrumentalities to impute the liability of companies on to states.[59] Thus, privatization is not a fail-safe way for governments to avoid accountability.

At the same time, a decision *not* to privatize does not necessarily result in full accountability. Indeed, courts have not generally held large numbers of official governmental actors accountable for abuses under our existing legal regime. For example, in the wake of reports on widespread prisoner abuse in Iraq and Afghanistan, very few governmental officials implicated in the abuse have faced trial. Thus far, only eleven uniformed soldiers have been convicted for cruel treatment at Abu Ghraib, and all of those tried have been relatively low-level actors.[60] Moreover, the first officer was not charged until April 2006.[61] Therefore, to the extent that governmental actors want to avoid accountability for abuses, privatization is not particularly necessary. Moreover, because governments are not monolithic, even if some in any given administration seek to privatize in order to avoid accountability or funnel money to cronies, there are many who sincerely want to do their job and could spearhead efforts to reform the contract monitoring process.

Significantly, in the somewhat analogous arena of development and humanitarian aid, governmental and inter-governmental officials have voluntarily undertaken significant contractual regulation. For example, USAID has imposed extensive self-evaluation requirements and performance benchmarks on aid organizations.[62] Meanwhile, the UN High Commissioner for Refugees has begun to experiment with beneficiary participation in programme design and critiques of operations in refugee camps.[63] And the World Bank has established grievance mechanisms for people adversely affected by development projects, including public-private partnerships.[64]

While one might think that military privatization would be more resistant to such increased contractual regulation, even here some reforms have occurred. For example, some of the existing Iraq contracts now include terms requiring stakeholder notification and participation. And the DOD has begun to require more specificity in the terms of its military contracts. Its August 2005 contracting

[59] See, eg, *McKesson Corp v Islamic Republic of Iran*, 52 F.3d 346, 351–352 (DC Cir 1995) (holding Iran responsible for corporation over which it exercised control); *Foremost Tehran, Inc v Islamic Republic of Iran*, 10 Iran-US Cl Trib Rep 228, 241–242 (1987) (same); *Maffezini v Kingdom of Spain* (Rectification and Award), 5 ICSID (World Bank) 387, 412–413 (2001) (holding Spain responsible for the acts of its state entity); *Case Concerning Barcelona Traction, Light & Power Co Ltd (Belg v Spain) (Second Phase)*, 1970 ICJ 4, 39, 58 (Feb 5) ('[V]eil lifting ... is admissible to play ... a role in international law.').
[60] See David Dishneau 'Dog Handler Gets Split Verdict,' *Fort Worth Star-Telegram*, 2 June 2006.
[61] See 'Politics This Week,' *Economist*, 6 May 2006.
[62] See generally USAID, 'Results-Oriented Assistance: A USAID Sourcebook,' available at <http://www.usaid.gov/pubs/sourcebook/usgov>.
[63] See Tania Kaiser, 'Participation or Consultation? Reflections on a 'Beneficiary Based' Evaluation of UNHCR's Programme for Sierra Leonean and Liberian Refugees in Guinea, June-July 2000,' *Journal of Refugee Studies*, vol 17 (2004) 186.
[64] See, eg, David Hunter, 'Using the World Bank Inspection Panel to Defend the Interests of Project-Affected People,' *Chicago Journal of International Law*, vol 4 (2003) 201ff.

regulations require that agreements include terms stating that contractors are bound by international law and specifying that contractors must train their employees in applicable rules regarding the use of force.[65]

Perhaps most importantly, even if government actors are not particularly eager to initiate reforms, NGOs or international organizations can push for them, or indeed launch them independently. Such organizations can pressure governments to include various safeguards in their contracts by promulgating international guidelines and then exposing (or mobilizing diplomatic pressure against) governments that refuse to adopt the guidelines. Along these lines, Amnesty International made reform of military contracts a centrepiece of its annual human rights report and a leading advocacy project for 2006.[66]

In addition, NGOs can independently rate or 'accredit' PMCs according to human rights compliance and other values. As noted previously, NCQA began such an independent accreditation effort to assess HMOs in the United States. While these independent efforts are of course more difficult without full access to information, nonetheless, measurements can be used to give scorecards to different companies. These measures are then very easy for the government to later use as a contractual requirement (as has happened with NCQA). Moreover, NGOs can try to harness popular political pressure to get governments and companies to adopt their accreditation or evaluation metrics.

Private military companies

Although at first blush it might seem surprising, many private military contractors are both willing to accept, and in some cases are even leading the way toward, contractual reforms. Indeed, although contractors often grumble about enhanced regulation generally—arguing that such regulation increases costs and impedes flexibility—the reality is that they rarely refuse contracts on this basis, which is perhaps not so surprising given how lucrative these contracts are.[67] Moreover, as mentioned previously, PMCs are initiating extensive self-regulation efforts in both the United States and Britain. Interestingly, many PMCs are eager for more regulation and accreditation requirements because they want to distinguish themselves from what they view as 'rogue' outfits that give the industry as a whole a bad name. Moreover, contractual (as opposed to legislative) reform may be appealing to such companies because it is more flexible and project-specific. Thus, there is no reason to think that contractual reform is unrealistic.

---

[65] See US DOD Instruction (n 20 above).

[66] Amnesty International Report 2006, 'The State of the World's Human Rights' available at <http://www.amnestyusa.org/news/document.do?id=ENGPOL100042006.pdf>; see also Alan Cowell, 'Rights Group Criticizes US Over Outsourcing in Iraq,' *New York Times*, 24 May 2006; Peter Spiegel, 'US Is Faulted for Using Private Military Workers,' *Los Angeles Times*, 24 May 2006.

[67] See Steven Schooner, 'Fear of Oversight: The Fundamental Failure of Businesslike Government,' American University Law Review, vol 50 (2001), 668, n 137.

Market barriers to contractual regulation

Critics might also cite the varied nature of private military contractors as an impediment to contractual regulation. PMCs are a diverse group that include, depending on the definition of the term, military logistics firms, military strategy firms, and direct military provider firms. In addition, some companies, such as MPRI, are large, long-established, and highly professionalized, with generals from major western militaries on their boards, while others are newcomers without the level of expertise, experience, or in some cases the commitment to professionalism. A one-size-fits-all approach therefore is inappropriate, one might argue, because of the range of functions that the firms provide. Furthermore, the differences may mean that some firms, such as the more established companies, may be more amenable to contract-based reform than others. For example, some firms may be better able to comply with contractual terms such as training requirements or private grievance systems (which require greater administrative infrastructure) than others. Moreover, to the extent that contract enables tailoring of reforms to suit the particulars of a given company, results are likely to be piecemeal and therefore ineffectual. At the same time, critics might charge that regulating PMCs through contractual terms is the tail wagging the dog, as corruption and cronyism are rampant in the initial *award* of government contracts. Without addressing this corruption up front, one might think, reform of contractual terms can have little effect.

Nevertheless, despite the problems posed by the market's diversity and the potential for cronyism, the structure of the market for PMCs may, in fact, make contract the most effective regulatory approach. In a diverse market, contract has the advantage of flexibility. And there is no reason that contractual reforms cannot go hand-in-hand with other efforts to reduce corruption in the actual award of contracts.

Market diversity

One of the virtues of contract, as opposed to other forms of regulation, is that it is *not* a one-size-fits-all approach. As compared to treaty-based, statutory, or even regulatory reform, contractual reform can be implemented on a case-by-case basis and can be tailored to fit the particular type of firm. Contractual training requirements, could, for example, be moulded to suit the activities of the particular PMC in question. Thus, a government contract with a company such as Kellogg, Brown & Root that provides meals to troops might require employees to learn the limits of excessive force under international law, but would focus primarily on defensive use of force. A contract such as the CACI agreement providing military interrogators could require much more extensive training, homing in on the limits of proactive interrogation techniques. A contract with a company providing combat services, such as the Sierra Leonean government's agreement with the now disbanded Executive Outcomes, would require extensive training on offensive use of force on the battlefield. Similarly, contractual terms requiring companies to establish internal grievance mechanisms for those adversely affected by contractor actions could also vary according to the type of firm.

Moreover, the fact that contractual reform is inevitably piecemeal does not mean that such reform will necessarily be ineffectual. Indeed, although an estimated 90 different groups have entered the market for private military contracts,[68] only a very small number of firms, particularly in the United States, retain a significant market share.[69] These larger firms are likely to be the easiest to regulate. Even simply incorporating contractual reform in the most significant contracts with the largest firms would have important effects.

Cronyism and corruption

Many reforms to the terms of contracts at the back end may help address crony-ism and corruption in the bidding process at the front end. Thus, there is no reason to think that seeking reform of contractual provisions and monitoring impedes or excludes efforts to reform the process by which contracts are awarded in the first place. Improvements in contractual monitoring, for example, will increase transparency and help prevent abuses. Similarly, accreditation by independent, third-party organizations will help serve as a brake on awards to contractors with histories of corruption. Accreditation provides information to the public at large, which can enhance the political incentives to award contracts to entities that receive high marks. And performance benchmarks also have an information-forcing effect that can help deter cronyism. To the extent that contractual terms are more specific and result-oriented, there is less room for contractors to take advantage of cronyism.

Furthermore, reforming contractual terms certainly can, and should, proceed in tandem with efforts to reform the contract award process. Specifically, as com-mentators have urged,[70] the government should dramatically reduce the number of no-bid contracts it enters into and should reduce the number of Freedom of Information Act exemptions it issues, thereby allowing for greater transparency in the bidding process. In addition, third-party agencies should not be permitted to conduct the bidding process and secure contracts that other agencies will adminis-ter, because such bifurcation tends to reduce oversight and accountability. But in any event, such reforms, while necessary, do not eliminate the need to reform the contracts themselves.

[68] See Singer, *Corporate Warriors* (n 3 above) 78.
[69] See Weiner, 'Incorporating the Combat Zone' (n 56 above) 24.
[70] See, eg, Schooner, 'Contractor Atrocities at Abu Ghraib' (n 7 above). It is worth noting that, in a related setting, public outcry over the no-bid process resulted in quick reforms in the provision of disaster relief after Hurricane Katrina.

The feasibility of creating third-party beneficiary rights

A fifth critique might focus specifically on those contractual reforms that seek to give third parties rights either to be consulted in the contract design process or to bring grievances. Critics could argue that such third-party participation would be unwieldy at best. For example, it would be very difficult to identify the appropriate third-party 'beneficiaries' of a private military contract. Is a beneficiary anyone who is remotely affected by contractor actions? In the case of Iraq, for example, would any Iraqi citizen qualify as a beneficiary of a contract to train the Iraqi police? Are US citizens the beneficiaries of such contracts? The net could be drawn very widely indeed.

Yet the flexibility of the contractual form again provides a means of addressing this problem. Beneficiaries could be defined differently depending on the context. Both at the front end in the design of agreements, and at the back end if they go awry, contracts can enable certain groups of beneficiaries to have a voice without opening up the process to broad and virtually unlimited involvement.

With respect to shaping contractual terms, the government and contractors can identify relevant stakeholders and include them based on the degree to which they stand to benefit from, or be harmed by, the contractor's actions. For example, in the case of a contract to train Iraqi police, affected stakeholders or beneficiaries might include interim governmental officials responsible for security, existing Iraqi trade associations or groups likely to provide employees in the police force, as well as political leaders and civil society leaders in the communities subject to policing. The contract could require the company providing training to consult with each of these groups in designing its training plan, to notify them of the planned course of action, and to seek input from them about key issues, problems, or difficulties. Such a consultation process would have the added benefit of alerting contractor employees to any cultural issues or sensitivities that could impede training efforts.

In other contexts, the relevant beneficiaries or stakeholders would be different. For example, in the case of an agreement between the US government and a private company to feed troops stationed in Iraq, the beneficiaries are the US troops and, by extension, the US public at large. Iraqis might of course be affected by the actions of such a company, for example, if armed company employees responded defensively to a perceived attack. Nevertheless, because Iraqis are not the direct beneficiaries of the contract, they need not be included at the design stage. And though security concerns may make broad public notification in the United States problematic, some transparency is certainly possible.

With respect to grievance procedures, again different provisions could be made depending on the type of contract because some contracts are far more likely to lead to abuses that would require such grievance procedures than others. For example, military interrogation work, such as was performed at Abu Ghraib by CACI, obviously poses a fairly high risk of harm to the bodily integrity of Iraqi prisoners. These prisoners are, by definition, in detention and not free to leave. Even with well-trained interrogators, the risk of crossing the line between permissible and impermissible uses of pressure is ever-present. In such circumstances, grievance procedures are particularly appropriate.

By contrast, contractors supplying food to troops on the battlefield do not engage in work that is as likely to directly affect the bodily integrity of Iraqis or others. It is true, as noted above, that contractor employees may be armed to defend themselves, and inappropriate uses of force may occur. Nonetheless, the contractors' use of weapons is almost certain to be for defensive purposes only, and such uses of force are not at the core of the contractors' purpose. Thus, the risk of harm to bodily integrity is probably much lower, and provisions for grievance procedures would be less appropriate in such contracts.

Significantly, in analogous contexts governments and inter-governmental organizations have allowed for this type of beneficiary involvement, and line-drawing among different categories of beneficiaries has not proved unworkable. For example, some of the de-mining contracts between the US government and private companies in Iraq require stakeholder notification and participation. The agreement between the Army Corps of Engineers and Tetra Tech to provide munitions support and removal similarly includes a provision requiring 'public involvement'.[71] In this agreement, the contractor undertakes to 'assist in responsiveness summaries, public meetings, restoration advisory boards, community restoration planning, administrative record establishment and maintenance, and other stakeholder forums that facilitate public involvement'.[72] The contract between the Corps and Zapata Engineering to remove hazards in Iraq (and Afghanistan) to ensure that lands and waters can be used safely contains a virtually identical provision.[73] And an agreement between the former Coalition Provisional Authority and Washington Group International to improve power systems within Iraq provides for 'public participation in public outreach activities'.[74] Such provisions could become standard terms.

The World Bank has also required private companies to engage in such beneficiary consultation processes as a condition of receiving loan agreements for public-private development projects. For example, the Bank prompted Exxon, the lead company building an oil pipeline in Chad, to engage in extensive consultations with local groups during the research phase of the project, from 1993 until

[71] Contract No W912DY-04-D-0011, 8 April 2004, in Contracts and Reports (n 21 above).
[72] Ibid at § C.4.5.23.
[73] Contract No W912DY-04-D-0007, 27 February 2004, at § C.4.5.23, in Contracts and Reports (n 23 above) (requiring that contractors '[a]ssist in responsiveness summaries, public meetings, restoration advisory boards, community restoration planning, administrative record establishment and maintenance, and other stakeholder forums that facilitate public involvement').
[74] Contract No W905S-04-D-0010, 12 March 2004, at § 2.2.8, in Contracts and Reports (n 21 above).

1996. During this period, Exxon's subsidiary in Chad, known as Esso Tchad, sent sociologists, ethnologists, and various experts and consultants to the region.[75]

There are also models for third-party grievance procedures. As mentioned previously, the World Bank allows anyone affected by a Bank project to bring claims to an Inspection Panel or a Compliance Advisor Ombudsman. Similarly, in the United States, state government contracts with HMOs receiving Medicare and Medicaid reimbursement routinely require the HMOs to establish grievance procedures for individuals who believe they were adversely affected by HMO care. And again, though certain security considerations might require grievance procedures to be more circumscribed in the context of military contracts, there is no reason to believe that grievance provisions are completely unworkable.

Potential enforcement problems

Finally, critics of regulation by contract might point out that government contracts are particularly difficult to enforce, because generally only government actors (and the contractors) may enforce them. And government officials rarely do so. Indeed, as noted previously, in the wake of the Abu Ghraib prison abuse scandal, the government did not terminate the contract with CACI, the company that had hired interrogators implicated in the abuse. Moreover, litigation in courts is also rare, and the enforcement actions the government does bring usually focus on issues such as corruption rather than other public law values such as human rights. And litigation in the US runs up against the so-called 'government contractor immunity' defence, which may protect from litigation those companies acting under the direction of the US government.

While these enforcement difficulties undoubtedly exist, many of the contractual reforms proposed actually would help address them. For example, graduated penalties or government takeover of failing contracts might give the government more enforcement options when termination is politically difficult. Because such penalties are less extreme than outright termination, they are far more likely actually to be invoked by contract monitors, making them a more effective enforcement mechanism than the harsher (though rarely invoked) termination provisions. As noted previously, in the domestic context, states are using graduated penalties in their oversight of private nursing homes receiving public funding.[76] Scholars

[75] Luc Lampriere, 'Exxon in Chad' (unpublished manuscript on file with author). For example, according to Exxon an American sociologist conducted 129 Human Environment survey village meetings, with over 5,000 participants, in the oil region. One Exxon document states, 'the project has conducted one of the most extensive consultation efforts ever undertaken in Africa for an industrial development project. Few similar ... projects in Europe or North America have held so many village-level public consultation meetings over such a wide area.'

[76] Freeman, 'The Private Role in Public Governance' (n 8 above) 608.

and practitioners have also called for the use of such penalties in the private prison setting.[77]

Similarly, inclusion of standards regarding international law and training make enforcement of human rights values in litigation more feasible. For example, in a case brought in the US courts against a private company managing an Immigration and Naturalization Service detention centre, the training standards for employees served as the basis for a tort claim against the company and its employees.[78] The court found these standards relevant in evaluating whether the company and its employees breached applicable duties.

Furthermore, enforcement by individuals other than the government or the contractor is at least possible. As discussed above, third-party beneficiary suit provisions can be added to agreements to improve enforcement capabilities. At the same time, even without such reforms, the ATCA provides a means for non-citizens to bring suit against contractors for human rights violations.[79] The suits against CACI and Titan, for example, are proceeding under the ATCA. Plaintiffs will have to demonstrate that the substantive international law violations alleged, including torture, were claims similar in nature to those existing in 1789 when the statute was enacted.[80] And they will have to demonstrate 'state action' in order to make a successful claim for torture.[81] Nevertheless, such claims are viable.[82]

In addition, the actual employees of PMCs (or their families) can bring tort suits against the companies for wrongful death and fraud. One such case, *Nordan v Blackwater Security Consulting, LLC*, alleges causes of action for wrongful death and fraud arising from the 21 March 2004 murder and mutilation of four military contractors in Fallujah, Iraq.[83] Two other cases, *Fisher v Halliburton* and *Johnson v Halliburton et al*, allege that an employer knowingly used one convoy as a decoy for a second convoy in Iraq, resulting in the deaths of at least six drivers, and injuries to eleven others.[84] As in *Nordan*, plaintiffs in these cases have brought wrongful death and fraud claims, as well as a civil rights claim under 42 USC §1983. Although these cases have not yet reached an outcome, judges have made preliminary rulings in favour of the plaintiffs.[85]

---

[77] Alexander Volokh, 'A Tale of Two Systems: Cost, Quality, and Accountability in Private Prisons,' Harvard Law Review, vol 115 (2002) 1888; see also Alphonse Gerhardstein, 'Private Prison Litigation: The 'Youngstown' Case and Theories of Liability,' Criminal Law Bulletin, vol 36 (2000) 198.

[78] *Jama v INS*, 334 F Supp 2d 662, 683–685 (DNJ 2004).

[79] 28 USC § 1350 (conferring jurisdiction on the federal courts to consider claims by aliens for torts in violation of the law of nations). [80] *Sosa v Alvarez-Machain*, 542 US 692 (2004).

[81] Convention Against Torture and Other Cruel, Inhuman, or Degrading Treatment or Punishment (n 1 above). [82] See Dickinson, 'Government for Hire' (n 57 above).

[83] *Nordan v Blackwater Security Consulting*, LLC, 382 F Supp 2d 801 (EDNC 2005); see also Estes Thompson, 'Families Sue Over Workers' Slaying in Iraq,' *Washington Post*, 6 January 2005.

[84] Pls' Complaint, *Fisher v Halliburton*, 390 F Supp 2d 610 (SD TX, 2005); and Pls' Complaint, *Johnson v Halliburton et al*, No: EDCV05-265 (CD Cal filed 29 March 2005).

[85] Kateryna Rakowsky, 'Military Contractors and Civil Liability,' *Stanford Journal of Civil Rights and Civil Liberties*, vol 2 (2006) 365.

Finally, there are strong arguments that 'government contractor immunity' does not apply in this context. The case that establishes this doctrine, *Boyle v United Technologies, Inc*,[86] involved a products liability claim (not a claim regarding a services contract) and in any event limited the defence to circumstances in which the government set the design specifications with reasonable precision, leaving little discretion to the contractor. As noted previously, most of the Iraq contracts were not at all specific and left broad discretion to the contractor, thus removing the predicate for contractor immunity. Moreover, at least one court has concluded that the defence does not apply to international human rights claims in any event.[87]

Thus, enforcement is not impossible, particularly if reforms are implemented. And whatever deficiencies there may be, such reforms will at least be an improvement on the current system. Accordingly, we should try to implement such reforms instead of declaring them a failure in advance.

Conclusion

Based on the present state of military privatization, it is clear that some reform of the contracting process is sorely needed. Thus, none of the arguments in favour of doing nothing is convincing. Whatever the imperfections of contractual reform, we must at least make the effort. At the other extreme, some international law scholars, policymakers, and NGOs either resist privatization altogether or insist that the only useful reforms involve increasing the mechanisms for holding private actors directly responsible under international law. Such critics might equate a focus on contractual reform with capitulation.

Those concerned about abuses committed by PMCs cannot simply rail against privatization altogether, however, because the trend towards privatization will be difficult to reverse in the foreseeable future. Accordingly, energy is better spent seeking reform. There is, in any case, no reason that formal international legal instruments need to be the only possible regulatory mechanisms. After all, it is a perhaps regrettable, but nevertheless true, fact of international law that even state actors are only rarely prosecuted for human rights abuses. Thus, even if all international instruments were interpreted to apply to private military contractors, we would still need to seek additional alternative accountability mechanisms in order to achieve meaningful oversight.

Accordingly, the claim advanced here is only that reforming the terms of the contracts themselves should be one avenue of reform among many. In addition, unlike amending or reinterpreting formal international legal instruments, NGOs could create accreditation regimes without any official governmental support.

---

[86]   487 US 500, 512 (1988).
[87]   *In re Agent Orange Prod Liab Litig*, 373 F Supp 2d 7, 85–99 (EDNY 2005).

NGOs could identify those companies most committed to curtailing abuses and then mobilize political pressure to make sure only those companies are awarded contracts. And while such activities could be undertaken regardless of governmental approval, we might also find that governmental support (and even support from the PMCs themselves) is not as difficult to achieve as might first be supposed. In any event, my principal aim is to encourage broader thinking about the wide variety of possible accountability mechanisms that might be available in an era of military privitization.

13

The future of the market

Andrew Bearpark and Sabrina Schulz

As previous chapters have shown, the privatization of military and security services in the past decade encompasses a vast range of activities that defy any single explanation. Armed private actors, especially in Western states, now fulfil tasks ranging from military activities that used to be the prerogative of national armed forces to the support of humanitarian aid, disaster relief operations, and state-building.[1] At the same time the developing world, in particular Sub-Saharan Africa, has seen increasing privatization of predominantly domestic security services, such as policing. Although the two phenomena need to be distinguished analytically in that they are caused by different circumstances,[2] both trends are linked to structural changes in the social, economic, political, and strategic spheres that are truly global in nature. In other words, social forces penetrate national borders more easily, and models of controlling violence are therefore emulated across borders without major difficulties. At the same time, both the demand and the supply of private security services are becoming increasingly globalized. Private companies offer security personnel, risk management, and training services on a transnational basis. States as well as private actors—in theory—get value-for-money through a choice that is not limited by national boundaries.

Against this background, this chapter argues that only a multi-dimensional approach can achieve a reasonable degree of regulation of the private security industry. In other words, regulation has to be introduced at different levels simultaneously; it will have to consist of both national and international components and involve the industry through a degree of self-regulation. These different levels of regulation have to be complementary and must not arbitrarily diffuse control

---

[1] In the humanitarian community the term state-building is usually preferred to the term nation-building. In a recent publication James Dobbins defines nation-building as the use of 'military force to underpin a process of democratization'. This definition is endorsed here because it comprises phenomena like occupation, peacekeeping, peace-enforcement, stabilization, and reconstruction. See James Dobbins et al, *America's Role in Nation-Building: From Germany to Iraq* (Washington, DC: RAND, 2005) 1.

[2] Elke Krahmann, 'Security Governance and the Private Military Industry in Europe and North America,' *Conflict, Security & Development*, vol 5, 2 (2005) 247–68.

to multiple actors. They are necessary because there is no 'one size fits all' template to regulate the industries of several countries in exactly the same way.

The chapter will focus on the regulatory debate in Britain, one of the main suppliers of private security services worldwide. The British private security market is distinct in many respects. In contrast to many US firms, for instance, most British as well as other European private security providers refrain from services at the frontline of hostilities in conflict-zones. The British government therefore refers to them as private security companies (PSCs) rather than private military companies (PMCs), and this chapter will use the label PSCs for the same reason. The term PSC better expresses the wide range of services companies are offering, but its use also has to do with cultural reservations as to the term PMC. This is not least due to the fact that British companies rely heavily on contracts from the private sector rather than the British (or any other) government. Therefore, in Britain, reputation is a central factor in the acquisition of new business and distinguishes a company in a market that is growing and diversifying.[3]

Because of the increase of both supply and demand in the private security market regulation has become an issue in Britain. While PSCs are preparing themselves for a 'post-Iraq bubble' world they are exploring a wide range of new market opportunities. Anticipating that the market for private security may have reached a temporary peak and may undergo a process of consolidation in the near future, PSCs expect the number of major players in the industry to decrease, not least through buy-outs and mergers.

The British market is currently characterized by diversification or expansion in roughly four areas. Some companies try to cover all of them; others seek to find a niche market. These areas have emerged from a rather unique combination of factors that would not necessarily be found to the same extent in other countries. Such factors include a growing trend to introduce aspects of privatization in the public sector, a significant supply of expertise (including from retiring members of the armed forces), the reliance of the British industrial base on services and the export thereof, as well as internationalist business traditions. There might be similar market evolutions worldwide, but the dynamics differ significantly in every country.

The first area comprises more traditional security and risk management services for other private businesses. These include mainly strategic and operational risk management for companies operating in conflict, post-conflict, or risk-prone environments. Examples of services provided by PSCs include risk analysis, crisis management, consultancy, training, and security reviews, but also—on the operational side—protective security services such as close protection and asset protection by indigenous and expatriate professionals, convoy security, event security, evacuation planning, and travel security for individuals. Furthermore, PSCs offer

---

[3] For a critical view on reputation as a means of establishing standards of good behaviour in the industry see chapter ten in this volume by Deborah Avant.

business intelligence and investigation such as due diligence, asset tracing and recovery, brand protection, pre-employment screening, counter-surveillance and anti-surveillance, kidnap and ransom, and information security consultancy. More generally, they provide research, intelligence, advice on insurance, and international project security planning. In summary, this sphere of activities concerns the integrity of their clients' systems and the achievement of competitive advantage in new markets.

Secondly, PSCs support post-conflict reconstruction efforts, such as in Iraq and Afghanistan, and offer security services to non-military actors in regions characterized by instability. Humanitarian aid agencies, international organizations, and non-governmental organizations (NGOs) that are operating in these areas are increasingly seeking the advice and the services of PSCs for personal and site security. This is usually done with extreme caution, however, because the humanitarian actors sometimes fear that the use of PSCs may undermine their impartiality. There are also tendencies to privatize several tasks in peacekeeping operations. Although this field implies hardly any incentive for 'secrecy', only minimal data is available on the emergence of this challenging new set of actor-relations in conflict zones so far.

Related to the previous area is a third one: PSCs are trying to open up business opportunities by moving into new fields such as state-building, supporting and providing humanitarian and disaster relief, and development tasks. In particular, they are involved in infrastructure redevelopment, which includes logistics, communications, and energy services. These operations purportedly have an impact on capacity-building, governance, the promotion of democracy and the rule of law, as well as the empowerment of civil society. In order to succeed in these areas, PSCs recruit former expert staff from government departments, NGOs, and humanitarian organizations. Once a company has acquired a certain degree of expertise in one of these areas, such as security sector reform in the Balkans, it may want to use its expertise and apply similar principles to health sector reform in other post-conflict environments.

The fourth area of diversification concerns activities that were previously performed by national militaries and which are now being outsourced to private contractors. These tasks include the provision of personal security for senior civilian officials in post-conflict environments, military and non-military site and convoy security, and security sector reform including the training of police and military personnel. The range of training offered by PSCs—not only to foreign regimes but also to their home states' armed forces—comprises fields as diverse as conventional military training, special forces training, counter-terrorism training, surveillance and intelligence-gathering training, specialist police training, aviation security, and public security. PSCs also provide technical support, maintenance, and the operation of complex weapons systems as well as mine clearance services.

The sphere where most concerns regarding the activities of private security and military companies are raised falls into the same category. It involves the provision of full military employment and procurement, as well as military advice. This area of activities is extremely difficult to monitor and proves a likely field of criminal and unlawful behaviour. Moreover, it is virtually inviting accusations of war-profiteering and unethical behaviour in that it supposedly capitalizes on human suffering and uncontrolled violence. This point is stressed in a great deal of the academic literature on private security as well as more journalistic accounts of PSC or PMC activity.

In a similar vein, the privatization of security services that used to be the prerogative of the national armed forces is giving rise to fears that this will increasingly undermine the nation-state's monopoly of violence. Yet privatization is not necessarily the enemy of the state. The privatization of certain services supposedly ensures that 'the job gets done' despite the downsizing of the armed forces. In other words, the state itself has, in most cases, created a demand for private force, and private companies have been all too ready to respond to this demand. Lamenting the state's imminent loss of its monopoly of violence is thus to ignore that outsourcing and privatization are conscious political strategies. In many instances, the state seems to benefit from privatized security services.

This is particularly the case in the United States and to some extent in Britain where privatization is most developed. The reasons for this are manifold. First, the ideological climate in these two countries is clearly more favourable towards the privatization of public services than in many continental European countries and elsewhere in the world. A liberal economic order, in combination with cultural preferences for a slim state, generally facilitates efforts towards liberalization and privatization. Secondly, both the United States and Britain are likely to remain involved in operations requiring the projection of military force, particularly in the context of the 'Global War on Terror'. Since both countries are committed to the transformation of their armed forces, especially in military-technological terms, significant resources are committed to high-tech military hardware.[4] The United States and, although to a lesser extent, Britain will therefore continue to rely on private actors to support war-fighting proper, but also peacekeeping, state-building, and post-conflict reconstruction efforts. And thirdly, the professional armed forces in both countries offer a pool of highly trained personnel for the private sector. In Britain, members of the armed forces only serve for a limited period of time; sometimes they retire after ten to fifteen years of service when they are in

---

[4] At the core of military transformation lies the idea that advances in information technology lead to far-reaching changes in the organization, equipment, and training of military forces, the result of which will be an entirely new way of warfare for the participating nations. Transformation is therefore not the same as modernization which refers to the replacement of obsolete capabilities and equipment (Rob de Wijk, 'The Implications for Force Transformation: The Small Country Perspective,' in Daniel S Hamilton (ed), *Transatlantic Transformations: Equipping NATO for the 21st Century* (Washington DC: Center for Transatlantic Relations, Johns Hopkins University, 2004) 116. Transformation further implies a decisive focus on more high-tech in the armed forces, implying increased reliance on network centric warfare (NCW), C4ISR (ie command, control, communications, computers, intelligence, surveillance, and reconnaissance), and Precision-Guided Munitions (PGMs).

their early thirties. The qualifications they acquire during their military careers are sought after by PSCs, including the growing sector of risk management services.

Since military transformation and accompanying trends towards outsourcing bring about long-lasting changes in the armed forces we will possibly witness more rather than fewer of these activities in the near future. It seems, therefore, reasonable to assume that the private security industry in both the United States and Britain is not only here to stay, but is likely to grow, diversify, and become a 'mature' industry. The British government has clearly recognized this. The 1998 report on the Sierra Leone arms affair already stated that '[t]hese companies are on the scene and look likely to stay on it'.[5] The industry's current unregulated nature is therefore unsustainable. Regulation is indispensable for at least three reasons. First, the use of firearms by civilian PSC personnel in war zones and post-conflict environments raises concerns regarding the arbitrary or unlawful use of lethal force. Several incidents, notably in Iraq, have demonstrated this and tarnished the image of the entire industry. Respectable firms therefore have to pay the price for the misconduct of a few individuals. Secondly, the relationship between PSCs and the armed forces has to be formalized and requires a firm legal basis. Effective co-operation is frequently obstructed because of inadequate rules and procedures regarding issues such as the sharing of information or intelligence.

Furthermore, in the absence of regulation, the seemingly secretive nature of the industry and its lack of transparency prevent PSCs from becoming recognized and legitimate actors in conflict environments. This makes their co-operation with established actors, such as the military, international organizations, and NGOs, difficult and sometimes unproductive. Yet since the involvement of private companies in peacekeeping and post-conflict reconstruction is likely to grow rather then decrease, inter-agency relations are of immense importance. This means that regulation is also essential because of rising concerns that the outsourcing of tasks that used to be the prerogative of national armed forces has diminished the scrutiny, democratic accountability, and transparency of a wide range of security-related services.

Guidelines for regulation

The present moment is therefore a critical one to establish regulation or more accurately 'control' for the industry, not only on a national, but also—ideally—on an international level. Yet it is unrealistic to consider a large and expensive international regime, comparable perhaps to the International Civil Aviation Organization (ICAO) in 1944, for the private security industry. No grouping of global

---

[5] UK Foreign and Commonwealth Office, Report of the Sierra Leone Arms Investigation, 1998, available at <http://www.fco.gov.uk/Files/kfile/report.pdf>.

powers will be willing to invest large amounts of money and manpower in the creation and maintenance of a major regulatory body.

The introduction of regulation must therefore primarily be the task of national governments. They are the most credible actors to ensure that regulation is comprehensive, compatible with regulatory frameworks in other countries, and, most importantly, that it is enforceable. At present, very few countries have any regulatory schemes at all, and the existing ones—such as in South Africa and the United States—may need further amendment as the international environment changes and the industry develops. Thus, there is hardly any best practice to follow, not least because the industry, both nationally and internationally, is still in the process of diversifying and consolidating itself. This also implies significant uncertainties as to which issues should be covered by regulation and how it could best be enforced.

As to the first problem, what regulation should entail, it has to be kept in mind that we are dealing with an extremely broad range of activities and contracts. PSCs and PMCs do business with their home governments, foreign governments, international organizations, and NGOs, with other businesses, and with individuals. Depending on the nature of the service provided, individual contracts may be regulated by the applicable national and international business and contract law, by the respective rules for the use of force (RUF) and standard operating procedures (SOPs) in conflict environments, or by arms export licensing schemes. At the same time, however, the 'exceptional' nature of the industry—in the sense that it is both operating abroad and relying on the potential use of armed force—frequently makes it difficult to apply and enforce existing legal frameworks.

The regulatory debate usually focuses on the services that imply the use of armed force, and this is also the way it is understood here. Although individual RUF may give precise guidelines for the actual use of firearms in environments such as Afghanistan and Iraq they do not have the same quality as law. Thus, a wide range of issues needs to be regulated on a broader basis. Standards pertaining to the qualification of PSC and PMC personnel are fundamental. Not only do individual contractors need to receive appropriate weapons training, they also have to be given thorough instruction regarding their rights and duties under international humanitarian law (IHL) as well as human rights law. Moreover, it has to be ensured that they are accountable for their acts as soldiers who are subject to the chain of command and the military jurisdiction of their armed forces. Thus, although they are entitled to the use of lethal force in the context of battle, combatants are bound to respect the Geneva Conventions and their respective rules of engagement (ROE).

It seems to be reasonable to assume that the training as well as the working conditions for PSC and PMC employees and contractors are key factors when trying to rid the private security industry of irresponsible companies. It is therefore equally important to drive up standards covering health and safety provisions for PSC and PMC staff, their training, protection, and insurance policies. Improvements in these areas will, in the long term, benefit the level of professionalism in the industry as a whole.

A comprehensive regulatory framework will have to address a number of further issues through mechanisms that are covered in more depth in other chapters of this volume.[6] Their respective value will, however, differ significantly according to the specific situation in any country where they are applied. Generally speaking, these mechanisms concern the conformity of contracts in terms of national and international law as well as their legitimacy in terms of the foreign policy goals of the country where a company is registered. Licensing schemes for individual contracts or services, issued by a governmental agency, may be one way of realizing these goals. The effectiveness of licensing schemes depends, of course, on oversight and enforcement mechanisms requiring resources that governments may not want to commit readily. Regulation without a credible monitoring and enforcement mechanism would, however, forfeit the credibility of any regulatory scheme.[7]

A further pitfall that needs to be avoided in any regulatory scheme concerns the nature of contract acquisitions in the industry. Most tenders and bidding processes on the private market happen under severe time constraints. It will not be in any firm's interest to submit to any regulation that puts it into a disadvantageous position compared to its competitors who are not committed to similar restrictions. Regulation, therefore, has to take legitimate business interests into account if the majority of firms are expected to submit to it.

Thus, the regulatory process must strike a delicate balance. If voluntary regulation puts some firms at a disadvantage the regulatory framework is very likely to be circumvented and therefore to become meaningless. Business interests have to be taken into account so that firms will not be driven underground in an effort to escape regulation and control. The direct participation of the industry in the development of a regulatory framework seems to be a suitable way of ensuring compliance with international and national laws and standards. At the same time, however, there are legitimate concerns, in particular among the humanitarian community, about the introduction of regulation that would be too lax. It will, therefore, be difficult to accommodate these highly diverging interests among the stakeholders in the regulatory debate and to encapsulate them into unambiguous legal terms.

Enforcement

Regulation will not only have to deal with different interests: it will also have to embrace highly diverse activities meaning loopholes are to be expected in any

---

[6] See in particular the contributions by Deborah Avant, James Cockayne, Laura Dickinson, and Kevin O'Brien.

[7] Foreign and Commonwealth Office (2002), 'Private Military Companies: Options for Regulation,' 12 February 2002, London: The Stationery Office, 73 f. See also Christopher Kinsey, 'Regulation and

regulatory scheme. Further difficulties are to be expected from the international nature of most of the services provided by the industry. This allows individual companies to relocate their business at any time to avoid constraints on their operations and to select the least arduous national regulatory regime. What is more, firms are able to avoid the legal system of their owners' countries of origin by setting up their bases offshore. The companies may also operate their offshore subsidiaries under different names in different parts of the world. The global market that brought about the emergence of the private security industry in the first place may therefore also be the biggest obstacle to effective regulation.[8]

Further problems regarding the enforcement of regulation stem from the difficulties involved in the investigation of human rights violations or crimes according to IHL. It may simply not be realistic to assume that British or US officials would travel to Iraq or Afghanistan in order to investigate an incident, question witnesses, and conduct any forensic examinations.

The challenges pertaining to the enforcement of regulation suggest the need for more comprehensive regulatory schemes which go beyond national legislation. At the moment there are no adequate legal frameworks that fully address the activities of PSCs or PMCs on either a national or an international level. The only way of securing control of the private security industry in the long term consists of a matrix of international codes of conduct, national regulation, and industry self-regulation. Regulation is likely to become a very long and arduous process that needs to be co-ordinated across national borders in order to be effective. This will take a lot of political will and commitment on the part of national governments.

Self-regulation

The British government responded to the potential challenges posed by PSCs/PMCs as early as 2002 with the publication of its Green Paper entitled *Private Military Companies: Options for Regulation*.[9] The Paper outlined several options for the regulation of the industry comprising: (a) a ban on military activity abroad; (b) a ban on recruitment for military activity abroad; (c) a licensing regime for military services; (d) registration and notification; (e) general licences; and (f) self-regulation.[10] But the initiative lost its momentum relatively quickly. This is a

Control of Private Military Companies: The Legislative Dimension,' *Contemporary Security Policy*, vol 26, 1 (2005), 84–102.

[8] Kim Richard Nossal, 'Global Governance and National Interests: Regulating Transnational Security Corporations in the Post-Cold War Era,' Melbourne Journal of International Law, vol 2 (2001) 459–76.
[9] Foreign and Commonwealth Office, Options for Regulation (n 7 above).
[10] Self-regulation has become a central feature of Britain's economic and industrial policies. The majority of Western state bureaucracies have realized that the regulatory overload, in particular of the 1960s and 1970s, has not only become problematic, but has also had counterproductive effects. Further developments such as a shrinking tax base and an ideological move away from interventionist policies suggest a broad consensus in favour of self-regulation.

matter of concern insofar as, from 2003 onwards, the British government itself started to draw upon private companies to sustain its post-conflict reconstruction efforts in Iraq.

Yet, for the industry, regulation is a vital issue for several reasons. Most importantly, it can enhance its respectability and legitimacy by putting its operations on a firm legal basis. In order to create new markets and in order to increase their individual market shares the companies depend heavily on their public image. This is particularly true for British PSCs who, unlike their US counterparts, cannot rely on public contracts to remain in business. The relevant and respectable players in Britain's private security industry—comprising no more than 25 companies—are therefore keen to introduce regulation which may, in the long term, outlaw most of the disreputable competitors that mar the image of the entire industry.[11]

Against this background, self-regulation has become a viable and feasible option for the British industry, at least for the time being. It can be argued that the industry understands itself better than the government and can therefore apply sanctions that are better targeted. At the same time, the government does not have to expose itself to any reputation risks. If, however, the government was responsible for regulation and a company that it is supposed to be monitoring gets involved in illegal contracts, the government itself could be seen as condoning these actions. A further challenge for the government would be to commit the resources—both in terms of manpower and money—for regulation, monitoring, and sanctioning.

First steps towards self-regulation in the British industry have been taken through the creation of a trade association, the British Association of Private Security Companies (BAPSC), in February 2006. BAPSC, of which the authors of this chapter are Director General and Director of Policy, represents companies that are based in Britain and provide armed security services overseas. Its goal is to influence the political process of establishing a firm legal basis for the activities of British PSCs abroad. (The International Peace Operations Association (IPOA), a trade association in the United States where the private security industry is regulated through government legislation, has been in existence since 2001.) The BAPSC Charter commits the members of the association to transparency, implying that they have to disclose their corporate structures and their relations with their offshore bases, partners, and sub-contractors. Before being admitted as members companies have to undergo a thorough vetting process, performed by external reviewers, to ensure their transparency and integrity. The members of BAPSC commit themselves to follow all relevant rules of international, humanitarian and human rights law, as well as a number of standards of good behaviour that are formulated in a code of practice.

---

[11] This central argument about the significance of reputation as a factor in the acquisition of contracts cannot easily be applied to any other national private security market. Where companies operate more on the mercenary end of private security and offer offensive services, such as hitherto in South Africa and the countries of the former Soviet bloc, effectiveness and efficiency may be more important factors than companies' adherence to standards.

Furthermore, they pledge to avoid any armed exchange in their operations, except in self-defence; to take all reasonable precautions to protect staff in high-risk operations; as well as decline to accept contracts that might conflict with international human rights legislation or potentially involve criminal activity.

Although it should be natural for companies to behave in a legal and lawful way individual contractors are not always familiar with their legal status and obligations, in particular under IHL. Moreover, former members of the armed forces will know their rights and responsibilities as combatants, but may be unaware of their changed legal position as civilians. BAPSC members, therefore, commit themselves to the provision of appropriate and sufficient training, including in legal matters. In addition, BAPSC is aiming to introduce standards for legal training for its members' employees.

This is not to deny that the implementation of standards and the imposition of sanctions are challenging tasks for a trade association. If a member is accused of misconduct during an operation in countries such as Afghanistan or Iraq any investigation of the incident will be difficult to perform. Yet a trade association can exercise pressure on its members, impose financial sanctions, and suspend or withdraw membership rights. Moreover, it can lobby for the introduction of an effective complaint system by the government. This could, for instance, take the form of an independent ombudsman within a government department. The ombudsman, as an independent actor, would collect complaints against companies, investigate, and process them.

The institution of an ombudsman is an example of what the BAPSC terms 'aggressive self-regulation'. At its core lies a commitment to drive up standards in the industry. This not only implies compulsory training courses for the members of BAPSC, but also random inspections on the site of members' operations. If a company fails in an inspection, or even in a scheduled audit, the association will apply sanctions and impose fines on the company in question. The fines could then be used for additional training courses for staff to ensure future compliance with standards.

Because of these mechanisms companies who have signed up to self-regulation will ideally, in the long term, be perceived as offering reliable, professional, and high-quality services. In contrast to prevailing prejudices, self-regulation is considered here as a normative institution that may 'bring the behaviour of industry members within a normative ordering responsive to broader social values'.[12] It involves the companies themselves in the regulatory process. Through an industry-level organization the firms voluntarily surrender a degree of flexibility and potential business advantage by submitting to a range of rules and standards relating to their business dealings. Crucially, they will be considered as legitimate actors in the provision of security services on an international scale, and a firm's reputation

---

[12] Neil Gunningham and Joseph Rees, 'Industry Self-Regulation: An Institutional Perspective,' *Law & Policy*, vol 19, no 4 (1997) 370.

may increasingly become a decisive factor in the acquisition of contracts. Thus, the ultimate incentive for self-regulation lies in the increase of competitiveness in the race for lucrative contracts with major clients, such as Western governments.

A further mechanism that may help to convince most players in the industry to comply with a self-regulatory framework is the potential impact on insurance premiums. Once certain standards have become accepted, insurers may set their premiums significantly higher for companies that are not prepared to commit themselves to an acknowledged code of conduct or that have a record of bypassing it, not least because these companies may expose their own personnel to higher risks.

Establishing self-regulation as a preliminary mechanism until it is complemented by national or international regulatory schemes is in the interest of the industry, the government, and other stakeholders. In other words, voluntary self-regulation can function as a stepping stone to comprehensive regulation through legislation which all companies in the industry of the respective state will have to submit to. The companies that have actively shaped the standard-setting process in a self-regulatory scheme will therefore have a real market advantage in that they comply with standards earlier than their competitors.

In the meantime—that is, in the absence of any enforceable laws and regulations—self-regulation has the potential to be an efficient and effective means of social control. But this is not to say that the market is the answer to all problems. First of all, as Deborah Avant rightly argues in chapter ten of this volume, market forces are not least determined by the purchasing power—and hence the interests— of the major consumers. Norms of proper behaviour may well interfere with consumers' demands for effectiveness and efficiency in the delivery of a service. Critics further argue—to some extent legitimately—that self-regulation will ultimately favour the industry rather than the public interest. The public image of self-regulation is very much one of self-serving, profit-maximizing actors trying 'to give the appearance of regulation (thereby warding off more direct and effective government intervention) while serving private interest at the expense of the public'.[13] In other words, self-regulation is frequently perceived as 'an attempt to deceive the public into believing in the responsibility of an irresponsible industry. Sometimes it is a strategy to give the government an excuse for not doing its job.'[14]

These concerns cannot be ignored. In order for self-regulation to succeed, it is desirable that it be matched by complementary national action that allows the effective sanctioning of companies which are circumventing voluntary codes of conduct. In the case of Britain, this could take the form of an intervention by the abovementioned ombudsman or the refusal of the government to consider a company that is in breach of an existing code of conduct for a public tender. In

13 Ibid, 364.
14 John Braithwaite, 'Responsive Regulation in Australia,' in P Grabosky and J Braithwaite (eds), *Regulation and Australia's Future* (Canberra: Australian Institute of Criminology, 1993).

connection with such a built-in safeguard in the British regulatory framework, control of the industry will be enhanced significantly. Yet, ultimately, the only way of securing control of the private security industry consists of a matrix of international codes of conduct, national regulation, and industry self-regulation that complement each other in a meaningful way.

In other words, the broader trends in the transformation of the contemporary security landscape towards multi-national and multi-agency approaches need to be reflected by a multi-dimensional regulatory framework for the activities of PSCs and PMCs. In order to reach a stage where international, national, and private agencies can co-operate seamlessly in the enforcement of such a framework the political will to co-operate is fundamental. National governments remain key actors in this process, for the nation-state continues to be the sole actor capable of sanctioning violations of any regulatory framework by judicial means. Self-regulation may be a cornerstone of any regulatory framework, but it is no silver bullet.

At the end of the day, it is also up to consumers to favour companies that have established themselves as good corporate citizens. Codes of conduct can have a significant impact on the development of the industry if major consumers such as governments use their purchasing power to reward or sanction companies according to their compliance with standards of good behaviour. Thus, at least on a national level, self-regulation may be a first step towards the establishment of norms and standards in the industry. Yet the globalized market offers real chances for the emulation of standards by actors in other countries if good behaviour translates into business advantages.

14

Conclusion

From mercenaries to market

Simon Chesterman and Chia Lehnardt

The International Convention Against the Recruitment, Use, Financing, and Training of Mercenaries was opened for signature in December 1989 and eventually came into force after its twenty-second ratification in September 2001. The intervening period, however, saw a sea change in how soldiers for hire—reincarnated as private military companies (PMCs)—are viewed and used. In 1996 Kofi Annan, then UN Under-Secretary-General for Peacekeeping, contemplated hiring a PMC to secure a Rwandan refugee camp in Goma but decided against it as 'the world may not be ready to privatize peace'.[1] A decade later, PMCs have become a regular part of the military landscape and the International Convention is viewed as, at best, a curiosity.

Practice has led theory in this area, and governments have been unwilling or unable to develop a comprehensive regulatory framework covering the manner in which these private actors exercise traditionally public powers, most importantly the use of potentially lethal violence. As this book has demonstrated, however, it is a mistake to regard contemporary PMCs as operating in a normative vacuum, or to dismiss the possibility of market-based tools as merely self-serving industry propaganda. Nevertheless, much needs to be done if the existing patchwork of norms is to be strengthened, and if moves towards market consolidation following the Iraq 'bubble' are to be used as an opportunity to professionalize the industry. Both aspects are essential to meaningful accountability of PMCs.

Public powers, private actors

The failure of international efforts to abolish PMCs is not simply a collective action problem. On the contrary, states sometimes have a direct interest in retaining the

---

[1] Kofi Annan, Thirty-Fifth Ditchley Foundation Lecture, 26 June 1998, UN Press Release SG/SM/6613.

services of PMCs, whether to support themselves in times of weakness or to reduce the economic and political costs of pursuing a foreign policy. As Angela McIntyre and Taya Weiss' account of the African experience with 'soldiers for hire' in chapter four showed, this experience is very different from the picture David Isenberg paints in chapter five of US relations with PMCs. Weak states may be unable to exercise meaningful control over actors that are brought in to make up for a lack of government capacity; strong states may be unwilling to do so because PMCs are retained precisely to avoid the need for control and therefore responsibility. However, as Chia Lehnardt argued in chapter eight, the capacity or desire of a state to regulate its contractors does not determine whether that state is responsible for the conduct of PMCs. A central element of any normative regime for PMCs will thus depend on enforcing norms that presently exist and accepting that it is not possible to outsource accountability.

But what are those norms? The obligation of states to ensure that international humanitarian law is respected by certain private actors, including PMCs, is explicitly stipulated in the Geneva Conventions, discussed by Louise Doswald-Beck in chapter seven. This body of law holds out not merely the promise of punishment but also protection, in the form of prisoner-of-war status for PMC employees in some circumstances. At the domestic level, PMCs are in theory subject to the laws of the state in which they operate, but they tend to do so in states with dysfunctional or biased legal systems.[2] At times, as in Iraq, contractors may even be given specific immunity from local laws.[3]

For this reason, most attention tends to be focused on the domestic law of the home or sending state. Again, in theory, such states may have criminal jurisdiction over PMCs and their employees—England and Wales, for example, may try citizens for murder committed anywhere in the world[4]—but in the absence of an institutional capacity to investigate offences abroad this is a largely meaningless provision. Similarly, the Military Extraterritorial Jurisdiction Act (MEJA) provides the US military justice system extraterritorial jurisdiction over contractors in some instances, but prosecutors appear to be reluctant to pursue such cases.[5] Civil suits, such as those brought under the US Alien Tort Claims Act against CACI and Titan for conduct at Abu Ghraib in Iraq, can have a powerful demonstration effect and may compensate victims, but despite serious accusations both companies' contracts with the US government were renewed.[6]

---

[2] The conviction of Nick du Toit in Equatorial Guinea for his role in the 2004 coup attempt is a rare exception. See Michael Wines, 'Equatorial Guinea: Jail Terms in Coup Plot,' *New York Times*, 27 November 2004.

[3] Coalition Provisional Authority, Order Number 17 of 27 June 2004 (Revised): Status of the Coalition Provisional Authority, MNF—Iraq, Certain Missions and Personnel in Iraq, available at <http://www.cpa-iraq.org/regulations/20040627_CPAORD_17_Status_of_Coalition__Rev __with_Annex_A.pdf>.   [4] Offences Against the Person Act 1861, s 9.

[5] See chapter five by David Isenberg in this volume.

[6] Peter Beaumont, 'Abu Ghraib Abuse Firms are Rewarded,' *Observer*, 16 January 2005.

Selective prosecution or suit is, in any case, a narrow answer to a broader set of concerns. The purpose of regulation is not merely to punish or marginalize bad behaviour, but to put in place structures that will encourage good behaviour. A key lever here is determining the companies with whom governments can do business. Licensing systems applicable to both military goods and services exist in only few exporting states, however. As Marina Caparini described in chapter nine, even those states with elaborate regimes in place have had limited success in curtailing abuse. The United States establishes a tight net of government control in principle, but this is weakened by discretion and loopholes; the South African model is tighter still but lacks adequate enforcement capacity. While efforts have been made to strengthen the South African regime, there is still anecdotal evidence of companies either ignoring government edicts or simply relocating their operations abroad.

Wherever their home jurisdiction may be, such companies will continue to contract with governments. Laura Dickinson argued in chapter twelve that contracts themselves may be an important tool for shaping behaviour: agreements can be drafted to include relevant norms from public international law, to enhance oversight, or at least to require specific levels of training and accreditation. Greater substantive and procedural accountability would not provide the spectacle of criminal prosecutions but may be a more effective mechanism for improving day-to-day operations of PMCs.

Designing a regulatory framework out of this normative patchwork is difficult but not impossible. Key problems include clarity about the activities being regulated and consistency across jurisdictions, as Kevin O'Brien outlined in chapter two. Gaps exist not merely because of a lack of political will, but also because of structural limitations in the various legal regimes at play. International law traditionally addresses the rights and obligations of states; domestic controls on corporate activity tend to focus on the company. The abuses attributed to PMCs, however, are perpetrated by individuals. Indeed, a key distinction between the employees of PMCs and members of the standing army of a state are that a PMC is fungible: a PMC can be disbanded and reformed under a different name (as were the much-maligned Executive Outcomes and Sandline), and employees that have been disciplined in one company can move to another. Greater transparency and effective use of blacklists would reduce these problems, but the environments in which PMCs operate frequently demand swift staffing to remain competitive. For this and other reasons, increasing attention is therefore being paid to mechanisms to change the structure of incentives as a complement to the evolving norms.

Market forces

The interests and incentives of PMCs are frequently caricatured as being dominated by financial motives, epitomized by the International Convention's definition of a mercenary as someone who is 'motivated to take part in the hostilities essentially by the desire for private gain'.[7] The difficulty of proving such motivation led one writer to suggest that anyone convicted of an offence under the Convention should be shot—as should his lawyer.[8] As Sarah Percy showed in chapter one, the financial motive is an important part of the reason why private military activity requires control, but it does not answer the question of how that control should be exercised.

The liquidation of Executive Outcomes and Sandline International demonstrates both the effectiveness of the market and its limitations. The companies were dissolved in part because companies explicitly offering combat services had come to be seen as unacceptable, but the individuals involved in the various operations merely reconstituted themselves within different corporate frameworks. In addition to concerns about individuals avoiding accountability cited earlier, this aspect of the industry points to a second important difference from national armed forces: a state generally operates on the assumption that it will continue to exist over a long period of time; the professional and reputational accountability that goes with such expectations may not be shared by a start-up PMC that operates on a far shorter time horizon with a more flexible staffing table.

Markets can be a tool of regulation, but tend to work most effectively where there is competition, an expectation of repeat encounters, and a free flow of information. The PMC market can be challenged in all three areas. Frequently there is far greater demand than supply, creating monopoly-type problems and reducing the leverage of the state or entity contracting the PMC's services to impose strong oversight provisions; as James Cockayne suggested in chapter eleven, this may even lead to an agent capturing its nominal principal. Secondly, even where such leverage might exist in theory there may not be an incentive to exercise it in practice because the contracting party views the relationship as a singular event unlikely to be a precedent for future conduct, notably during a crisis in which a government seeks to stabilize itself against a threat. Thirdly, even where there might be established relationships—such as subcontracting through the US Departments of State or Defense—there is either minimal public scrutiny or active efforts to suppress the flow of information that might provide a form of oversight.

There is some evidence, however, that this market may be maturing. As Deborah Avant described in chapter ten, professionalization of the industry may exert a powerful influence on individual behaviour. The creation of industry associations such as the British Association of Private Security Companies (BAPSC) and the International Peace Operations Association (IPOA) is presented by their officials as demonstrating precisely the sophistication of the market. This may be partly true, but it also reflects the desire of some actors to establish themselves as 'legitimate'

---

[7] International Convention Against the Recruitment, Use, Financing, and Training of Mercenaries, art 1(1)(b).

[8] Geoffrey Best, quoted in David Shearer, *Private Armies and Military Intervention*, Adelphi Paper 316 (Oxford: Oxford University Press, 1998) 18.

and thereby to raise the costs of entry for competitors while enabling the charging of higher fees for similar services.

Such efforts to repackage the 'dogs of war' as the 'pussycats of peace'[9] are to be encouraged, but they are not enough. Industry calls for, among other possibilities, an ombudsman, discussed by Andrew Bearpark and Sabrina Schulz in chapter thirteen, would be a useful supplement to a regime that lacks adequate institutional capacities or political will. But in the absence of the underlying regime an ombudsman might in fact be worse than no regulation if it gives the appearance of oversight and thus removes pressure for change while not affecting behaviour.[10]

The appropriate analogy to be drawn here may not be with old-style mercenaries or the French Foreign Legion but with ExxonMobil, Total, and other multinational corporations that assume some functions of the state in which they operate. During negotiations that led to the International Criminal Court in 1998 there was discussion of including criminal liability for corporations, on the basis that this would make it easier for victims of crimes to sue for restitution and compensation. Differences in such forms of accountability across jurisdictions—where they existed at all—meant that consensus was impossible and the discussion was ultimately dropped. Six months after the Rome Statute was adopted, at the 1999 Davos World Economic Forum, UN Secretary General Kofi Annan proposed the Global Compact, challenging business leaders to abide by principles on human rights, labour, and the environment that are essentially voluntary.[11] This was an admission that efforts to regulate such companies through traditional legal means had failed, and continues to provoke debate about whether it amounts to a market-based tool to promote accountability or just a marketing tool.

It is possible that consolidation of the private military industry in the wake of the Iraq boom, demonstrated by a spate of mergers and acquisitions, will encourage competition, improve standards, and strengthen industry codes of conduct. Even so, it is likely that neither regulation nor the market can address all of the concerns raised by the privatization of force, such as the manner in which PMCs may shape discussion of security issues themselves outlined by Anna Leander in chapter three. And, in some cases, outsourcing security functions may underestimate the importance of involving the uniformed military directly, such as in the area of security sector reform discussed by Elke Krahmann in chapter six.

In the absence of international will to commit the resources necessary to stabilize fragile states, or domestic will to keep the use of armed force exclusively under government control, 'mercenaries' will continue to go to market. A pragmatic response

[9] 'Blood and Treasure,' *Economist*, 2 November 2006.

[10] A further tool of regulation may be insurance. It may be possible, for example, to require PMCs to have adequate insurance to operate and that insurance companies exclude from coverage inappropriate activities, such as the provision of combat services or participation in serious human rights violations including torture. Such a minimalist regime would influence the structure of incentives and, perhaps, shape behaviour.

[11] See United Nations, The Global Compact, available at <http://www.unglobalcompact.org>.

must focus on developing a governance regime that strikes a balance between commercial and public interests, between voluntary and imposed regulation; it must draw upon international law to establish baseline norms and domestic institutions to oversee the activities of companies and punish individuals for abuse. In the absence of such a regime, the marketplace of war will continue to be regulated only by bankruptcy and death.

Select Bibliography

James Cockayne

PRIMARY MATERIAL

International instruments

Convention Respecting the Rights and Duties of Neutral Powers and Persons in Case of War on Land (Hague Convention No V) (1907), entry into force 26 January 1910, Art 4.

Geneva Convention (I) for the Amelioration of the Condition of the Wounded and Sick in Armed Forces in the Field (1949), entry into force 21 October 1950, Art 13(4).

Geneva Convention (II) for the Amelioration of the Condition of Wounded, Sick and Shipwrecked Members of Armed Forces at Sea (1949), entry into force 21 October 1950, Art 13(4).

Geneva Convention (III) relative to the Treatment of Prisoners of War (1949), entry into force 21 October 1950.

International Convention against the Recruitment, Use, Financing and Training of Mercenaries (1989), entry into force 21 December 2001, GA Res 44/34, UN Doc A/44/49.

OAU Convention for the Elimination of Mercenaries in Africa (1977), entry into force 22 April 1985.

Protocol Additional to the Geneva Conventions of 12 August 1949, and Relating to the Protection of Victims of International Armed Conflicts (Protocol I), entry into force 7 December 1978, Art 47.

UN Commission on Human Rights, Commentary on the Norms on the Responsibilities of Transnational Corporations and Other Business Enterprises with Regard to Human Rights, UN Doc E/CN.4/Sub.2/2003/38/Rev.2 (2003).

UN Commission on Human Rights, Norms on the Responsibilities of Transnational Corporations and Other Business Enterprises with Regard to Human Rights, UN Doc E/CN.4/Sub.2/2003/12/Rev.2 (2003), approved by Resolution 2003/16, 13 August 2003, UN Doc E/CN.4/Sub.2/2003/L.11 at 52 (2003), available at <http://www1.umn.edu/humanrts/links/norms-Aug2003.htm>.

Other relevant UN Documents

Report of the Meeting of Experts on Traditional and New Forms of Mercenary Activities as a Means of Violating Human Rights and Impeding the Exercise of the Right of Peoples to Self-Determination, UN Doc E/CN.4/2001/18.

Report of the Second Meeting of Experts on Traditional and New Forms of Mercenary Activities as a Means of Violating Human Rights and Impeding the Exercise of the Right of Peoples to Self-Determination, UN Doc E/CN.4/2003/4.

Report of the Third Meeting of Experts on Traditional and New Forms of Mercenary Activities as a Means of Violating Human Rights and Impeding the Exercise of the Right of Peoples to Self-Determination, UN Doc E/CN.4/2005/23.

Report of the UN Special Rapporteur on the Use of Mercenaries as a Means of Violating Human Rights and Impeding the Exercise of the Right of Peoples to Self-Determination, UN Doc E/CN.4/2005/14.

Report of the Working Group on the Use of Mercenaries as a Means of Violating Human Rights and Impeding the Exercise of the Right of Peoples to Self-Determination, UN Doc E/CN.4/2006/11.

Report of the Working Group on the Use of Mercenaries as a Means of Violating Human Rights and Impeding the Exercise of the Right of Peoples to Self-Determination on the Resumed First Session—Addendum, UN Doc E/CN.4/2006/11/Add.1.

UN OCHA, OCHA Discussion Paper and Non-Binding Guidelines for the Use of Military or Armed Escorts for Humanitarian Convoys, 14 September 2001.

UN DSRSG of UNAMI, Guidelines for Humanitarian Organisations on Interacting with Military and Other Security Actors in Iraq, 20 October 2004.

National instruments and related materials

Britain

Foreign and Commonwealth Office, Private Military Companies: Options for Regulation, HC 577 (London: The Stationery Office, 2002), available at <http://www.fco.gov.uk/Files/kfile/mercenaries,0.pdf>.

Report of the Committee of Privy Counsellors Appointed to Inquire into the Recruitment of Mercenaries, Cmnd 6569 (Aug 1976) 10.

France

Assemblée Nationale, L'externalisation dans les armées, enjeux et limites, Paris, Assemblée Nationale 2002.

Assemblée Nationale, Rapport du Senat fait au nom de la commission des Affaires étrangères, de la défense et des forces armées sur le projet de loi relatif à la répression de l'activité de mercenaire, Rapport Nº 142 du 23 janvier 2003. Session ordinaire 2002–2003, available at <http://www.senat.fr/rap/l02-142/l02-1420.html>.

Joulaud, M Marc, Rapport sur le projet de loi relatif à la répression de l'activité de mercenaire, au nom de la Commission de la Défense nationale et des Forces armées de l'Assemblée nationale, rapport Nº 671, 7 Mars 2003, available at <http://www.assemblee-nationale.fr/12/rapports/r0671.asp>.

LOI nº 2003-340 du 14 avril 2003 relative à la répression de l'activité de mercenaire (1). JO Nº 89 du 15 Avril 2003, 6636, Texte nº 2 (NOR: DEFX0200004L).

Germany

Bundestag, Antrag der Fraktion der CDU/CSU vom 28. 9. 2004: Nichtstaatliche militärische Sicherheitsunternehmen kontrollieren, Drucksache 15/3808, available at <http://dip.bundestag.de/btd/15/038/1503808.pdf>.

Bundestag, Antwort der Bundesregierung vom 24.6. 2005 auf die Grosse Anfrage der FDP vom 20. 1. 2005 zur Auslagerung spezifischer Sicherheits- und Militäraufgaben an nichtstaatliche Stellen, Drucksache 15/5824, available at <http://dip.bundestag.de/btd/15/058/1505824.pdf>.

Bundestag, Antwort der Bundesregierung vom 26. 4. 2006 auf die Kleine Anfrage der Fraktion DER LINKE vom 6. 4. 2006: Umgang der Bundesregierung mit Söldnern, Söldnerfirmen, privaten Sicherheits- und Militärdienstleistungsunternehmen, Drucksache 16/1296, available at <http://dip.bundestag.de/btd/16/012/1601296.pdf>.

Bundestag, Beratung vom 21. Oktober 2004 des Antrags vom 28. 9. 2004 der CDU/CSU im Bundestag, Plenarprotokoll 15/132, p 12104, available at <http://dip.bundestag.de/btp/15/15132.pdf#P.12104>.

Bundestag, Grosse Anfrage der Fraktion der FDP vom 20. 1. 2005 zur Auslagerung spezifischer Sicherheits- und Militäraufgaben an nichtstaatliche Stellen im deutschen Bundestag, Drucksache 15/4720, available at <http://dip.bundestag.de/btd/15/047/1504720.pdf>.

Bundestag, Kleine Anfrage der Fraktion DIE LINKE vom 6. 4. 2006: Umgang der Bundesregierung mit Söldnern, Söldnerfirmen, privaten Sicherheits- und Militärdienstleistungsunternehmen, Drucksache 16/1196, available at <http://dip.bundestag.de/btd/16/011/1601196.pdf>.

Iraq

Coalition Provisional Authority, Memorandum Number 5 of 23 May 2003: Implementation of Weapons Control Order Number 3, available at <http://www.iraqcoalition.org/regulations/20030822_CPAMEMO_5_Implementation_of_Weapons_Control_with_Annex_A.pdf>.

Coalition Provisional Authority, Memorandum Number 17 of 26 June 2004: Registration Requirements for Private Security Companies (PSC), available at <http://www.cpa-iraq.org/regulations/20040626_CPAMEMO_17_Registration_Requirements_for_Private_Security_Companies_with_Annexes.pdf>.

Coalition Provisional Authority, Order Number 3 of 31 December 2003 (Revised) (Amended): Weapons Control, available at <http://www.iraqcoalition.org/regulations/20031231_CPAORD3_REV__AMD.pdf>.

Coalition Provisional Authority, Order Number 17 of 27 June 2004 (Revised): Status of the Coalition Provisional Authority, MNF—Iraq, Certain Missions and Personnel in Iraq, available at <http://www.cpa-iraq.org/regulations/20040627_CPAORD_17_Status_of_Coalition__Rev__with_Annex_A.pdf>.

New Zealand

Mercenary Activities (Prohibition) Act 2004, available at http://www.legislation.govt.nz/libraries/contents/om_isapidll?clientID=157563592&infobase-pal statutes.nfo&jump=a2004-069&softpage=DOC.

Philippines

Philippines Department of Labor Order No 61A-04: Suspension of all Recruitment Activities of Workers Bound for Iraq, 8 November 2004, available at <http://central.dole.gov.ph/uploaded/issuances/I0000214_do61A_04.pdf>.

Sierra Leone

National Security and Central Intelligence Act 2002, available at <http://www.sierra-leone.org/Laws/2002-10.pdf>.

South Africa

Prohibition of Mercenary Activities and Prohibition and Regulation of Certain Activities in Areas of Armed Conflict Bill 2005, available at <http://www.info.gov.za/gazette/bills/2005/b42-05.pdf>.

Prohibition of Mercenary Activities and Prohibition and Regulation of Certain Activities in Country of Armed Conflict Bill, version of August 2006, available at <http://www.pmg.org.za/docs/2006/060815mercenary.htm>.

Regulation of Foreign Military Assistance Act 1998, available at <http://www.info.gov.za/gazette/acts/1998/a15-98.pdf>.

United States of America

US Congress, Arms Export Control Act 2002, 22 USC § 2778 (AECA).

US Congress, International Traffic in Arms Regulation 1993, Pub L 90-629, 90 Stat 744 (22 USC§§ 2752, 2778, 2791 (ITAR)).

US Congress, Military Extraterritorial Jurisdiction Act, Pub L No 106-523, 18 USC § 3261, 114 Stat 2488 (22 November 2000).

US Congress, Ronald W Reagan National Defense Authorization Act for Fiscal Year 2005, 108th Congress, 2d Session, S 2400, 28 October 2004, sec 1088.

US Department of Defense, Directive Number 2311.01E, DoD Law of War Program, 9 May 2006, available at <http://www.fas.org/irp/doddir/dod/d2311_01e.pdf>.

US Department of Defense, Instruction Number 3020.41, Contractor Personnel Authorized to Accompany US Armed Forces, 3 October 2005, available at <http://www.fas.org/irp/doddir/dod/i3020_41.pdf>.

US Department of Defense, Instruction Number 1100.22, Guidance for Determining Workforce Mix (complementing DoD Instruction Nb 3020.41), 7 September 2006.

US Department of Defense Inspector General, Audit Report on Civilian Contractor Overseas Support During Hostilities, Report Number 91-105, June 1991.

US Department of Defense Inspector General, Audit Report, Retention of Emergency-Essential Civilians Overseas During Hostilities, Report Number 89-026, November 1988.

US Government Accountability Office, Contingency Operations: Army Should Do More to Control Contract Cost in the Balkans. GAO/NSIAD-00-225. Washington, DC: 29 September 2000.

——, Contingency Operations: Opportunities to Improve the Logistics Civil Augmentation Program. GAO/NSIAD-97-63 Washington, DC: 11 February 1997.

——, Defense Logistics: High-Level DOD Coordination is Needed to Further Improve the Management of the Army's LOGCAP Contract. GAO-05-328. Washington, DC: 21 March 2005.

——, Interagency Contracting: Problems with DOD's and Interior's Orders to Support Military Operations. GAO-05-201. Washington, DC: 29 April 2005.

——, Military Operations: Background Screenings of Contractor Employees Supporting Deployed Forces May Lack Critical Information but US Forces Take Steps to Mitigate the Risk Contractors May Pose. GAO-06-999R. Washington, DC: 22 September 2006.

——, Military Operations: Contractors Provide Vital Services to Deployed Forces but Are Not Adequately Addressed in DOD Plans. GAO-03-695. Washington, DC: 24 June 2003.

——, Military Operations: DOD's Extensive Use of Logistics Support Contracts Requires Strengthened Oversight. GAO-04-854. Washington, DC: July 19 2004.

——, Military Operations: High Level DOD Action Needed to Address Long-standing Problems with Management and Oversight of Contractors Supporting Deployed Forces. GAO-07-145. Washington, DC: 21 December 2006.

——, Rebuilding Iraq: Actions Needed to Improve Use of Private Security Providers. GAO-05-737. Washington, DC: 28 July 2005.

——, Rebuilding Iraq: Actions Still Needed to Improve the Use of Private Security Providers. GAO-06-865T. Washington, DC: 13 June 2006.

Voluntary codes of conduct and best practices initiatives

British Association of Private Security Companies, Charter, available at <http://www.bapsc.org.uk/key_documents-charter.asp>.

International Peace Operation Association Code of Conduct, available at <http://ipoaonline.org/>.

The Sarajevo Client Guidelines for the Procurement of Private Security Companies, available at <http://www.seesac.org/reports/Procurement%20guidelines1.pdf>.

The Sarajevo Code of Conduct for Private Security Companies, available at <http://www.seesac.org/reports/Code%20of%20conduct1.pdf>.

Swiss Government, Swiss Initiative in Cooperation with the International Committee of the Red Cross to Promote Respect for International Humanitarian Law and Human Rights Law with regard to Private Military and Security Companies Operating in Conflict Situations: Outline, 22 November 2005, available at <http://www.eda.admin.ch/eda/en/home/topics/intla/humlaw/pse.html>.

UN Global Compact, available at <http://www.globalcompact.org>.

Voluntary Principles on Security and Human Rights, available at <http://www.state.gov/www/global/human_rights/001220_fsdrl_principles.html>.

Case law

Al Rawi v Titan Corporation, 05-CV-1165, United States District Court, District of Colombia.

Costello-Roberts v UK, Series A No 247C (1993) (European Court of Human Rights).

Ibrahim v Titan Corporation, Civil Action No 04-1248-JR and *Saleh v Titan Corporation*, Civil Action No 05-CV-01165-JR, class action complaint filed in the US District Court for the District of Columbia.

Saleh v Titan 361 F Supp. 2d 1152 (SD Cal 2005).

Sandline International Inc v Papua New Guinea, International Law Reports, vol 117 (1999), 552–65, 565–93 (1999) (Queensland Supreme Court).

SECONDARY MATERIAL

'The Fog and Dogs of War: An Alleged Coup Plot and its Murky Aftermath,' *Economist*, 18 March 2004.

'Hired Guns Are Doing Well for Themselves,' *Economist*, 2 November 2006.

Abrahamsen, Rita and Michael C Williams, 'Security Sector Reform—Bringing the Private in,' *Conflict, Security & Development*, vol 6(1) (2006) 1.

——, 'Country Report: Sierra Leone, Country Report: Kenya, Country Report: Nigeria,' in the project on *The Globalisation of Private Security*, Department of International Relations, University of Aberystwyth, July 2005.

Adams, Thomas, 'The New Mercenaries and the Privatization of Conflict,' *Parameters*, vol 29(2) (summer 1999) 103.

Addo, Prosper, 'Mercenarism in West Africa: A Threat to Ghana's Democracy,' Kofi Annan Peacekeeping Training Centre, Accra, Paper No 2, November 2004.

Alston, Philip, 'The Myopia of the Handmaidens: International Lawyers and Globalization,' European Journal of International Law, vol 8 (1997) 435.

Amnesty International, 'The UN Human Rights Norms for Business: Towards Legal Accountability,' AI Index: IOR 42/001/2004, available at <http://web.amnesty.org/aidoc/aidoc-pdf.nsf/Index/IOR420022004ENGLISH/$File/IOR4200204.pdf>.

Australian Strategic Policy Institute, *War and Profit: Doing Business on the Battlefield*, 30 March 2005.

Avant, Deborah, *The Market for Force: The Consequences of Privatizing Security* (Cambridge: Cambridge University Press, 2005).

——, 'Mercenaries,' *Foreign Policy*, vol 143 (2004) 20.

Bailes, Alyson JK and Isabel Frommelt (eds), *Business and Security: Public-Private Sector Relationships in a New Security Environment* (Oxford: Oxford University Press, 2004).

—— and Caroline Holmqvist, 'EU Must Regulate Private Security Firms,' *European Voice*, 22 September 2005.

Barnett, Antony and Patrick Smith, 'US Accused of Covert Operations in Somalia,' *The Observer*, 10 September 2006.

Bianco, Anthony and Stephanie Anderson Forest, 'Outsourcing War,' *Business Week Online*, 15 September 2003.

Bigo, Didier, 'Les Enterprises Para-Privées de Coercition: de Nouveaux Mercenaries?', *Cultures et Conflits*, vol 52, no 4 (2003) 5.

Bishop, Joseph W Jr, 'Court-Martial Jurisdiction over Military-Civilian Hybrids: Retired Regulars, Reservists, and Discharged Prisoners,' University of Pennsylvania Law Review, vol 112, no 3 (1964) 317.

Bjork, Kjell and Richard Jones, 'Overcoming Dilemmas Created by the 21st Century Mercenaries: conceptualising the use of private security companies in Iraq,' *Third World Quarterly*, vol 26 (2005) 777.

Black, Crispin, 'The Security of Business: A View from the Security Industry,' in Alyson JK Bailes and Isabel Frommelt (eds), *Business and Security: Public-Private Sector Relationships in a New Security Environment*, (Oxford: Oxford University Press, 2004) 173.

Boldt, Nicki, 'Outsourcing War—Private Military Companies and International Humanitarian Law,' in *German Yearbook of International Law*, vol 47 (2004) 502.

Boot, Max, 'Darfur Solution: Send in the Mercenaries,' *Los Angeles Times*, 31 May 2006.

Borrowman, Scott J, 'Comment, *Sosa v Alvarez-Machain* and Abu Ghraib—Civil Remedies for Victims of Extraterritorial Torts by US Military Personnel and Civilian Contractors,' Brigham Young University Law Review (2005) 371.

Brooks, Doug, 'Messiahs or Mercenaries? The Future of International Private Military Services,' *International Peacekeeping*, vol 7(4) (winter 2000) 129.

—— and Jim Shevlin, 'Reconsidering Battlefield Contractors,' *Georgetown Journal of International Affairs*, vol 6 (summer/fall 2005) 103.

Bryden, Alan and Marina Caparini (eds), *Private Actors and Security Governance* (Münster: Lit Verlag 2006).

Buhler, Carl A, 'When Contractors Deploy: A Guide for the Operational Commander,' Naval War College, Rhode Island, 8 February 2000.

Bures, Oldrich 'Private Military Companies: A Second Best Peacekeeping Option?', *International Peacekeeping*, vol 12, no 4 (2005) 546.

Burmester, Henry, 'The Recruitment and Use of Mercenaries in Armed Conflict,' American Journal of International Law, vol 72 (1978) 37.

Burton-Rose, Daniel and Wayne Madsen, 'Corporate Soldiers: The US Government Privatizes the Use of Force,' *Multinational Monitor*, vol 20 (3) (1999).

Caferro, W, 'Italy and the Companies of Adventure in the Fourteenth Century,' *The Historian*, vol 58 (summer 1996) 794.

Campbell, Duncan, 'Marketing the Dog of War,' Center for Public Integrity, October 2002.

Carbonnier, Gilles, 'Corporate responsibility and humanitarian action,' *International Review of the Red Cross*, vol 83 (2001) 947.

——, 'Privatisations, sous-traitance et partenariats public-privé: charity.com ou business .org?', *International Review of the Red Cross*, no 856 (2004) 725.

Cassese, Antonio, 'Mercenaries: Lawful Combatants or War Criminals,' *Zeitschrift fuer auslaendisches und oeffentliches Recht*, vol 40, no 1 (1980) 1.

Casto, William R, 'Regulating the New Privateers of the Twenty-First Century,' Rutgers Law Journal, vol 37, no 3 (2006).

Chrirwa, Danwood Mzikenge, 'The Doctrine of State Responsibility as a Potential Means of Holding Private Actors Accountable for Human Rights,' Melbourne Journal of International Law, vol 5 (2004) 1.

Christensen, Gordon A, 'Attributing Acts of Omission to the State,' Michigan Journal of International Law, vol 12, (1990–1991) 312.

Cilliers, Jakkie and Peggy Mason (eds), *Peace, Profit or Plunder? The Privatisation of Security in War-Torn African Societies* (Pretoria: Institute for Security Studies, 1999).

Clapham, Andrew, *Human Rights Obligations of Non-State Actors* (Oxford: Oxford University Press, 2006).

Cleaver, Gerry, 'Subcontracting Military Power: The Privatisation of Security in Contemporary Sub-Saharan Africa,' *Crime, Law and Social Change*, vol 33, nos 1 and 2 (2000) 131.

Cockayne, James, 'Commercial Security in Humanitarian and Post-Conflict Settings: An Exploratory Study,' International Peace Academy, New York, March 2006.

Coker, Christopher, 'Outsourcing War,' *Cambridge Review of International Affairs*, vol 13, no 1 (1998) 95.

Coliver, Sandra, Jennie Green, and Paul Hoffman, 'Holding Human Rights Violators Accountable by Using International Law in US Courts: Advocacy Efforts and Complementary Strategies,' Emory International Law Review, vol 19 (2005) 169.

Cullen, Patrick, 'Keeping the New Dog of War on a Tight Leash: Assessing the Accountability for Private Military,' *Conflict Trends*, vol 1 (2000) 36.

Cushman, Jr, John H, 'Private Company Finds No Evidence Its Interrogators Took Part in Prison Abuse,' *New York Times*, 13 August 2004. See also <http://www.caci.com/iraq_faqs.shtml>.

David, James R, *Fortune's Warriors: Private Armies and the New World Order* (Toronto: Douglas & McIntyre, 2002).

Desai, Deven, 'Have Your Cake and Eat It Too: A Proposal for a Layered Approach to Regulating Private Military Companies,' University of Southern Florida Law Review, vol 39 (2005).

Dinnen, Sinclair, 'Militaristic Solutions in a Weak State: Internal Security, Private Contractors, and Political Leadership in Papua New Guinea,' *Contemporary Pacific*, vol 11, no 2 (fall 1999) 286.

——, R May, and A Regan (eds), *Challenging the State: The Sandline Affair in Papua New Guinea* (Canberra: RSPAS, Australian National University, 1997).

Dokubo, CQ, 'Private military corporations and the sovereignty of African states,' *African Journal of International Affairs and Development*, vol 6, no 2 (2001) 57.

Drohan, Madeleine, *Making a Killing: How and Why Corporations Use Armed Force to Do Business* (New York: The Lyons Press, 2004).

Duffield, Mark, 'Post-modern Conflict: Warlords, Post-adjustment States and Private Protection,' *Civil Wars*, vol 1, no 11 (Spring 1998) 98.

——, *Global Governance and the New Wars: The Merging of Development and Security* (London/New York: Zed Books, 2001).

Ehrenhaft, Peter D, 'Policing Civilians Accompanying the United States Armed Forces Overseas: Can United States Commissioners Fill the Jurisdictional Gap?', George Washington Law Review, vol 36 (1967).

Epiney, Astrid, *Die Völkerrechtliche Verantwortlichkeit von Staaten für Rechtswidriges Verhalten im Zusammenhang mit Aktionen Privater* (Baden-Baden: Nomos-Verlag, 1992).

FAFO, 'Commerce, Crime and Conflict: Legal Remedies for Private Sector Liability for Grave Breaches of International Law,' 6 September 2006.

—— and International Peace Academy, 'Business and International Crimes: Assessing the Liability of Business Entities for Grave Violations of International Law,' FAFO Report 467, 2004.

Faite, Alexandre, 'Involvement of Private Contractors in Armed Conflict: Implications under International Humanitarian Law,' *Defence Studies*, vol 4 (2004) 166.

Fidler, Stephen and Thomas Catán, 'Colombia: Private Companies on the Frontline,' *Financial Times*, 12 August 2003.

Forcese, Craig, 'Deterring "Militarized Commerce": The Prospect of Liability for "Privatized" Human Rights Abuses,' Ottawa Law Review, vol 31 (1999/2000) 171.

Fountain, Frank, 'A Call for "Mercy-naries": Private Forces for International Policing,' Michigan State Journal of International Law, vol 13 (2005) 227.

Francis, David J, 'Mercenary Intervention in Sierra Leone: Providing National Security or International Exploitation?', *Third World Quarterly*, vol 21, no 2 (1999) 319.

Fredland, Eric J, 'Outsourcing Military Force: A Transactions Cost Perspective on the Role of Military Companies,' *Defence & Peace Economics*, vol 15, no 3 (2004) 205.

—— and Adrian Kendry, 'The Privatisation of Military Force: Economic Virtues, Vice and Government Responsibility,' *Cambridge Review of International Affairs*, vol 13, no 1 (1998) 147.

Garcia-Perez, Isolde, 'Contractors on the Battlefield in the 21st Century,' *Army Logistician*, vol 31, no 6 (1999) 40.

Garmon, Tina, 'Domesticating International Corporate Responsibility: Holding Private Military Firms Accountable under the Alien Tort Claims Act,' Tulane Journal of International & Comparative Law, vol 11 (2003) 325.

Gerson, Allan and Nat J Colletta, *War, Poverty, and Privatization: Privatizing Peace: From Conflict to Security* (Ardsley, NY: Transnational Publisher 2002).

Goddard, Major S, 'The Private Military Company: A Legitimate International Entity Within Modern Conflict,' thesis, Master of Military Art and Science, Fort Leavenworth, Kansas, 2001.

Hampson, Françoise, 'Mercenaries: Diagnosis before Prescription,' *Netherlands Yearbook of International Law*, vol 3 (1991) 1.

Hartley, Keith, 'The Economics of Military Outsourcing,' *Defence Studies*, vol 4 (2004) 199.

Heil, Jennifer L, 'African Private Security Companies and the Alien Tort Claims Act: Could Multinational Oil and Mining Companies be Liable?', Northwestern Journal of International Law & Business, vol 22 (2002) 291.

Hessbruegge, Jan Arno, 'The Historical Development of the Doctrines of Attribution and Due Diligence in International Law,' New York University Journal of International Law and Politics, vol 36 (2003–2004) 265.

Hillemanns, Carolin, 'UN Norms on the Responsibilities of Transnational Corporations and Other Business Enterprises with regard to Human Rights,' German Law Journal.

Hoffman, Michael H, 'Emerging Combatants, War Crimes and the Future of International Humanitarian Law,' *Crime, Law & Social Change*, vol 34 (2000) 99.

Holmqvist, Caroline, 'Private Security Companies: The Case for Regulation,' SIPRI Policy Paper No 9, January 2005.

Hooper, Jim, *Bloodsong! First Hand Accounts of a Modern Private Army in Action. An Account of Executive Outcomes in Angola* (London, HarperCollins 2002).

Hoover, Mike S, 'The Laws of War and the Angolan Trial of Mercenaries: Death to the Dogs of War,' Case Western Reserve Journal of International Law, vol 9, no 2 (1977) 323.

Howe, Herbert, 'Private Security Forces and African Stability: the Case of Executive Outcomes,' *Journal of Modern African Studies*, vol 36, no 2 (1998) 307.

——, 'Global Order and the Privatization of Security,' *Fletcher Forum of World Affairs*, vol 22 (1998) 1.

Hubac, Olivier, *Mercenaires et polices privées: La priviatisation de la violence armée* (Encyclopaedia Universalis, 2005).

Hulse, Carl, 'Senate Rejects Harder Penalties on Companies, and Ban on Private Interrogators,' *New York Times*, 17 June 2004.

International Alert, 'The Privatization of Security: Framing a Conflict Prevention and Peace building Policy Agenda,' Wilton Park Conference, November 1999.

——, 'The Mercenary Issue at the UN Commission on Human Rights: The Need for a New Approach,' January 2001.

Isenberg, David, 'A Fistful of Contractors: The Case for a Pragmatic Assessment of Private Military Companies in Iraq,' British American Security Information Council (BASIC), Research Report, September 2004.

Jäger, Thomas and Gerhard Kümmel (eds), *Private Military and Security Companies. Chances, Problems, Pitfalls and Prospects* (Wiesbaden: VS Verlag für Sozialwissenschaften, forthcoming 2007).

Jinks, Derek, 'State Responsibility for the Acts of Private Armed Groups,' Chicago Journal of International Law, vol 83 (2003) 88.

Jones, Clive, *Britain and the Yemen Civil War, 1962–1965: Ministers, Mercenaries and Mandarins: Foreign Policy and the Limits of Action* (Sussex: Sussex Academic Press, 2004).

Jung, Stéphanie, *Les Nouveaux Entrepreneurs de Guerre. Défis juridiques et implications politiques du recours aux sociétés militaires privées*, Université Robert Schuman—Institut d'Etudes Politiques, June 2006.

Kahn, Mafruza, 'Business on the Battlefield: The Role of Private Military Companies,' Corporate Research E-Letter No 30, December 2002, available at <http://www.corp-research.org/dec02.htm>.

Kaldor, Mary, *New and Old Wars. Organized Violence in a Global Era* (Cambridge: Polity Press, 1999).

Kassebaum, David, 'A Question of Facts: The Legal Use of Private Security Companies in Bosnia,' Columbia Journal of Transnational Law, vol 30 (1999–2000) 581.

Kinsey, Christopher, 'Le Droit International et le Contrôle des Mercenaires et des Companies Militaires Privée,' *Cultures et Conflits*, vol 52 (2003) 91.

——, *Corporate Soldiers and International Security: The Rise of Private Military Companies* (London: Routledge, 2006).

Kontos, Alexis, 'Private security guards: Privatized force and State responsibility under international human rights law,' *Non-State Actors and International Law*, vol 3 (2005) 199.

Krahmann, Elke, 'Regulating Private Military Companies: What Role for the EU?', *Contemporary Security Policy*, vol 26, no 1 (2005) 1.

——, 'Controlling Private Military Companies in Europe: Between Partnership and Regulation,' *European Security*, vol 13, no 2 (2005) 277.

Kwakwa, Edward, 'The Current Status of Mercenaries in the Law of Armed Conflict,' Hastings International & Comparative Law Review, vol 14 (1990–1991) 67.

Lawyer, Jared F, 'Military Effectiveness and Economic Efficiency in Peacekeeping: Public Versus Private,' *Oxford Development Studies*, vol 33, no 1 (2005) 99.

Leander, Anna 'The Market for Force and Public Security: The Destabilizing Consequences of Private Military Companies,' *Journal of Peace Research* vol 42, no 5 (2005) 605.

——, 'The Power to Construct International Security: On the Significance of Private Military Companies,' *Millenium: Journal of International Studies*, vol 33 (2005) 803.

—— and Rens van Munster, 'Private Security Contractors in Darfur: Reflecting and Reinforcing Neo-Liberal Governmentality,' Copenhagen Business School, Institute of Intercultural Communication and Management Working Paper no 82, available at <http://ir.lib.cbs.dk/paper/ISBN/x656517874>.

Lehnardt, Chia, Regulating the Private Commercial Military Sector, Institute for International Law and Justice, Workshop Report, March 2006, available at <http://iilj.org/documents/12-05WorkshopReport_000.pdf>.

Lilly, Damian, 'The Privatization of Security and Peacebuilding. A Framework for Action,' International Alert, 2000.

——, 'The Privatization of Peacekeeping: Prospects and Realities,' in *Disarmament Forum*, United Nations Institute for Disarmament Research, No 3, 2000.

Liss, Carolin, 'Private Security Companies in the Fight against Piracy in Asia,' Asian Research Centre, Working Paper No 120, June 2005.

Lock, Peter, 'Sicherheit à la Carte? Enstaatlichung, Gewaltmaerkte und die Privatisierung des staatlichen Gewaltmonopols,' in Tanja Bruehl, Tobias Debiel, Brigitte Hamm, Hartwig Hummel, and Jens Martens (eds), *Die Privatisierung der Weltpolitik. Entstaatlichung und Kommerzialisierung im Globalisierungsprozess* (Bonn: Dietz Verlag, 2001) 200.

Macchiavelli, Nicollò, *The Prince* (trans Georg Bull, 1999), ch XII (London: Penguin Books Ltd, 2001).

Mair, Stefan, 'Die Rolle von Private Military Companies in Gewaltkonflikten,' in Sabine Kurtenbach und Peter Lock (eds), *Kriege als (Ueber)Lebenswelten* (Bonn: Dietz Verlag, 2004).

Malan, Mark and Jakkie Cilliers 'Mercenaries and Mischief: The Regulation of Foreign Military Assistance Bill,' South African Institute for Security Studies, Occasional Paper No 25, September 1997.

Mancini, Francesco, 'In Good Company? The Role of Business in Security Sector Reform,' International Peace Academy and Demos, 2005.

Mandel, Robert, 'The Privatisation of Security,' *Armed Forces and Society*, vol 28, no 1 (2001) 129.

——, *Armies without States: The Privatization of Security* (Boulder: Lynne Rienner Publications, 2002).

Michaels, Jon, 'Beyond Accountability: The Constitutional, Democratic, and Strategic Problems with Privatizing War,' Washington University Law Quarterly, vol 82 (2004) 1001.

Milliard, Todd, 'Overcoming Post-Colonial Myopia: A Call to Recognize and Regulate Private Military Companies,' Military Law Review, vol 176 (2003), 1.

Mourning, PW, 'Leashing the Dogs of War: Outlawing the Recruitment and Use of Mercenaries,' Virginia Journal of International Law, vol 22 (1992) 589.

Muenkler, Herfried, *New Wars* (Cambridge: Polity Press, 2004).

Musah, Abdel-Fatah and Kayode J Fayemi (eds), *Mercenaries: An African Security Dilemma* (London: Pluto Press, 2000).

Nossal, Kim, 'Global Governance and National Interests: Regulating Transnational Security Corporations in the Post Cold-War Era,' Melbourne Journal of International Law, vol 2 (2001) 459.

O'Brien, Kevin, 'Military-Advisory Groups and African Security: Privatized Peacekeeping?,' *International Peacekeeping*, vol 5, no 3 (autumn 1998) 78.

——, 'PMCs, Myths and Mercenaries: The Debate on Private Military Companies,' *RUSI Journal* (February 2000) 59.

O'Hanlon, Michael and Peter W Singer, 'The Humanitarian Transformation: Expanding Global Intervention Capacity,' *Survival*, vol 46, no 1 (spring 2004) 77.

Olsson, Christian, 'Vrai Process et Faux Débats: Perspectives Critiques sur les Argumentaires de Legitimation des Enterprises de Coercition Para-Privées,' *Cultures et Conflits*, vol 52 (2003) 11.

Orsini, Eric A and Gary T Bublitz, 'Contractors on the Battlefield: Risks on the Road Ahead?', *Army Logistician*, vol 31, no 1, (1999) 130.

Ortiz, Carlos, 'Regulating Private Military Companies: States and the Expanding Business of Commercial Security Provision,' in L Assassi, D Wigan, and K van der Pijl (eds), *Global Regulation. Managing Crises after the Imperial Turn* (Basingstoke: Palgrave Macmillan, 2004) 205.

Pelton, Robert Young, *Licensed to Kill: Hired Guns in the War on Terror* (New York: Crown Publishing House, 2006).

Percy, Sarah, *Mercenaries* (Oxford: Oxford University Press, 2007).

Perlak, Major Joseph R, 'The Military Extraterritorial Jurisdiction Act of 2000: Implications for Contractor Personnel,' *Military Law Review*, vol 169 (2001) 91.

Peterson, Laura, 'Privatizing Combat, the New World Order,' Center for Public Integrity, October 2002.

Potter, David, 'The international mercenary market in the sixteenth century: Anglo-French competition in Germany,' *English Historical Review*, vol 111 (1996) 24.

Rathmell, Andrew, 'The Privatisation of Intelligence: A Way Forward for European Intelligence Cooperation,' *Cambridge Review of International Affairs*, vol 11, no 2 (1998).

Renou, Xavier, *La privatization de la violence: Mercenaires et sociétés militaires privées au service du marché* (Marseille: Agone, 2006).

——, 'Private Military Companies Against Development,' *Oxford Development Studies*, vol 33, no 1 (2005) 107.

Roberts, Adam, *The Wonga Coup: A Tale of Guns, Germs and Mayhem in an Oil-rich Corner of Africa* (New York: PublicAffairs, 2006).

Rosemann, Nils 'The Privatization of Human Rights Violations—Business' Impunity or Corporate Responsibility? The Case of Human Rights Abuses and Torture in Iraq,' *Non-State Actors and International Law*, vol 5 (2005) 77.

Sandoz, Yves, Christophe Swinarski, and Bruno Zimmermann (eds), *Commentary on the Additional Protocols of 8 June 1977 to the Geneva Conventions of 12 August 1949* (Geneva: Nijhoff 1987).

Sapone, Montgomery, 'Have Rifle With Scope, Will Travel: The Global Economy of Mercenary Violence,' Californian Western International Law Journal, vol 30, no 1(fall 1999), 1.

Scahill, Jeremy, 'Blackhawk Down,' *The Nation*, 10 October 2005.

Schaller, Christian, 'Private Sicherheits- und Militärfirmen in bewaffneten Konflikten. Völkerrechtliche Einsatzbedingungen und Kontrollmöglichkeiten,' SWP-Studie 2005/ S24, September 2005, available at <http://www.swp-berlin.org/de/produkte/swp_studie.php?id=4976>.

——, 'Operieren Private Sicherheits- und Militaerfirmen in einer humanitaer-rechtlichen Grauzone?', *Humanitaeres Voelkerrecht—Informationsschriften*, vol 19, no 1 (2006) 51.

Schmitt, Glenn R, 'Closing the Gap in Criminal Jurisdiction Over Civilians Accompanying the Armed Forces Abroad—A First Person Account of the Creation of the Military Extraterritorial Jurisdiction Act of 2000,' Catholic University Law Review, vol 51 (fall 2001) 55.

Schmitt, Michael, 'Humanitarian Law and Direct Participation in Hostilities by Private Contractors or Civilian Employees,' Chicago Journal of International Law, vol 5 (2005) 511.

Schooner, Steven L, 'Contractor Atrocities in Abu Ghraib: Comprised Accountability in a Streamlined, Outsourced Government,' Stanford Law & Policy Review, vol 16 (2005) 549.

Schreier, Fred and Marina Caparini, 'Privatising Security: Law, Practice and Governance of Private Military and Security Companies,' Geneva Centre for the Democratic Control of Armed Forces (DCAF), Occasional Paper No 6, March 2005.

Schumacher, Gerry, *A Bloody Business: America's War Zone Contractors and the Occupation of Iraq* (Osceola: Zenith Press, 2006).

Schwartz, Juli, '*Saleh v Titan Corporation*: The Alien Tort Claims Act: More Bark Than Bite? Procedural Limitations and the Future of ATCA Litigation Against Corporate Contractors,' Rutgers Law Journal, vol 37, no 3 (2006) 867.

SEESAC, 'SALW and Private Security Companies in South Eastern Europe: A Cause or Effect of Insecurity?,' August 2005.

Serewicz, Lawrence W, 'Globalization, Sovereignty and the Military Revolution: From Mercenaries to Private International Security Companies,' *International Politics*, vol 39 (2002) 75.

Shearer, David, *Private Armies and Military Intervention*, The International Institute for Strategic Studies, Adelphi Paper 316 (Oxford: Oxford University Press, 1998).

——, 'Privatising Protection,' *The World Today* (RIIA), Chatham House, August/September 2001.

Silverstein, Ken, *Private Warriors* (London: Verso, 2000).

Singer, Peter W, *Corporate Warriors. The Rise of the Privatized Military Industry* (Ithaca: Cornell University Press, 2003).

——, 'Corporate Warriors: The Rise of the Privatized Military Industry and Its Ramifications for International Security,' *International Security*, vol 26, no 3 (winter 2001/2002) 186.

——, 'The Private Military Industry and Iraq: What Have We Learned and Where to Next?', Geneva Centre for the Democratic Control of the Armed Forces Policy Paper, November 2004.

——, 'Should Humanitarians Use Private Military Services?', *Humanitarian Affairs Review* (March 2005).

——, 'War, Profits and the Vacuum of Law: Privatized Military Firms and International Law,' Columbia Journal of Transnational Law, vol 42 (2004) 521.

Smith, Eugene B, 'The New Condottieri and US Policy: The Privatization of Conflict and Its Implications,' *Parameters*, vol 32, no 4 (winter 2002–2003) 104.

Spearin, Christopher, 'Private Security Companies: A Corporate Solution to Securing Humanitarian Spaces,' *International Peacekeeping*, vol 8, no 1 (spring 2001) 20.

——, 'Humanitarians and Mercenaries: Partners in Security Governance?', in Elke Krahmann (ed), *New Threats and New Actors in International Security* (New York: Palgrave Macmillan, 2005) 45.

Spicer, Tim, *An Unorthodox Soldier: Peace and War and the Sandline Affair* (Edinburgh: Mainstream Publishing House, 1999).

Spruyt, Hendrik, *The Sovereign State and its Competitors. An Analysis of Systems Change* (New Jersey: Princeton University Press, 1994).

Stinnett, Nathaniel, 'Regulating the Privatization of War: How to Stop Private Military Firms from Committing Human Rights Abuses,' Boston College International & Comparative Law Review, vol 28 (2005) 211.

Sturzaker, Damian, 'The Sandline Affair: Illegality and International Law,' International Arbitration Law Review, vol 3 (2000) 164.

Taljaard, Raenette, 'The Danger of Latter-Day-Mercenaries Private Military Companies,' *International Herald Tribune*, 17 January 2004.

Thomas, Gerry S, *Mercenary Troops in Modern Africa* (Boulder: Westview Press, 1984).

Thomson, Janice E, *Mercenaries, Pirates, and Sovereigns: State-Building and Extraterritorial Violence in Early Modern Europe* (New Jersey: Princeton University Press, 1994).

Tilly, Charles, *Coercion, Capital, and European States, AD 990–1990* (Cambridge, MA: Blackwell Publishing, 1993).

——, 'War Making and State Making as Organized Crime,' in Peter B Evans, Dietrich Rueschemeyer, and Theda Skocpol (eds), *Bringing the State back in* (Cambridge: Cambridge University Press, 1985) 169.

Townsend, Gregory, 'State Responsibility for Acts of de facto Agents,' Arizona Journal of International and Comparative Law, vol 14 (1997) 635.

Turner, Lisa and Lynn Norton, 'Civilians at the Tip of the Spear,' *The Air Force Law Review*, vol 51 (2001) 30.

Urquhart, Brian, 'For a UN Volunteer Military Force,' *New York Review of Books*, vol 40, no 11, 10 June 1993.

US Congressional Research Service, 'Private Security Contractors in Iraq: Background, Legal Status, and Other Issues,' Report for Congress, May 2004.

Uttley, Matthew, 'Private Contractors on Deployed Operations: The United Kingdom Experience,' *Defence Studies*, vol 4 (2004) 145.

Vaux, Tony, 'European Aid Agencies and their Use of Private Security Companies,' in *Humanitarian action and private security companies: opening the debate* (International Alert: London, 2001) 12.

Venter, AJ, 'Market Forces: How Hired Guns Succeeded Where the United Nations Failed,' *Jane's International Defence Review*, vol 3 (1998).

——, *War Dog: Fighting Other People's Wars—The Modern Mercenary in Combat* (Casemate, 2006).

Voillat, Claude, ICRC, 'Private Military Companies: A Word of Caution,' *Humanitarian Exchange*, vol 28 (2005) 33.

Volkov, Vadim, *Violent Entrepreneurs: The Use of Force in the Making of Russian Capitalism* (Ithaca: Cornell University Press, 2002).

Walker, Clive and Dave Whyte, 'Contracting Out War?: Private Military Companies, Law and Regulation in the United Kingdom,' International & Comparative Law Quarterly, vol 54 (2005) 651.

Werve, Jonathan, 'Contractors Write the Rules: Army Policy Governing Use of Contractors Omits Intelligence Restrictions,' Center for Public Integrity, June 2004.

Wilson, Peter H, 'The German "Soldier Trade" of the Seventeenth and Eighteenth centuries: a Reassessment,' *International History Review*, vol 8 (1996) 758.

Wulf, Herbert, *Internationalizing and Privatizing War and Peace* (Basingstoke: Palgrave Macmillan, 2005).

Yost, Mark J and Douglas S Anderson 'The Military Extraterritorial Jurisdiction Act of 2000: Closing the Gap,' American Journal of International Law, vol 95 (2001) 446.

Zamparelli, Stephen, 'Contractors on the Battlefield: What Have We Signed Up For?,' Air War College Research Report, March 1999.

Zarate, Juan-Carlos, 'The Emergence of a New Dog of War: Private International Security Companies and the New World Disorder,' Stanford Journal of International Law, vol 34, no 1 (1998) 93.

Index

PMCs = private military companies (PMCs)